LIFTING SHADOWS

The Authorized Biography of Dream Theater

RICH WILSON

This book is respectfully dedicated to the memory
of my father, David Wilson (1938–2012).

First published in hardback edition in the United Kingdom
in 2009 by Essential Works Limited

This updated paperback edition first published in the United Kingdom
in 2013 by Rocket 88, an imprint of Essential Works Limited

ISBN: 9781906615581

10 9 8 7 6 5 4 3 2 1

rocket88books.com

CONTENTS

INTRODUCTION

For once, I actually got in at the start. Back in the late Eighties, the UK was blessed with a national radio station that dedicated vast chunks of Friday and Saturday evenings to blasting the airwaves with flawless rock shows. Tommy Vance and Alan Freeman were the respective DJs, and although I can't actually remember which one of them first played a Dream Theater track – or which song it was – I was instantly blown away, and have been appreciating their music ever since.

The Dream Theater story may not be as gory as that of Mötley Crüe, or as littered with casualties as Def Leppard's, but it's no less intriguing. When you discover the inner turmoil the band have endured, the seemingly relentless industry battles and the "unfashionable" music they've created, it's amazing that they have survived for so long. Throw into the mix five talented musicians with diverse personalities and their own idiosyncrasies, along with the fact that their popularity is continually rising, their story becomes even more remarkable.

In collating together the material for this book, I've endeavoured to track down and interview as many as possible of the characters that have been involved in the Dream Theater story so far. Where possible, I've also let those people tell their story without too much pontificating or over-analysis, taking the view that the people who were actually there are best placed to interpret events. The fact that they were all keen, and readily donated their time, speaks volumes about the regard in which the band are held in the industry. The members of Dream Theater have also approved of this project and, in an effort to ensure factual correctness, they read the book prior to release. No changes to the content were suggested or made, which ensured that the book remained authorized but not sanitized. Of course, there were some who didn't want to be interviewed, which is regrettable but I respect their decision.

Huge thanks, then, in no particular order, to Chris Collins, Larry Freemantle, David Prater, Stephan Erickson, Charlie Dominici [www.dominici.com], Amy Guip, Derek Oliver, Dante Bonutto, Jim Pitulski, John Arch, Lucy Jordache, Pete Trewavas, Derek Simon, Derek Sherinian, Chris Cintron [www.cintronbrothers.com], Rob Shore, Bill Barclay, Ben Huggins, Kevin Shirley, Terry Date, Janna Glasser, Jens Johansson, Chris Jericho, Sebastian Bach, Jon Collins, Doug Oberkircher, Dung Hoang, Sir Richard Pumpaloaf, David "5-1" Norman, Erik Neldner, Bruce Dickinson, Eric Gandras, Hugh Syme, Storm Thorgerson, Jamshied Sharifi, Paul Northfield, Dave McKean, Derek Shulman, Eddie Trunk, Gail Flug, Andrew Ross, John

Hendricks, Steve Sinclair, Robert Mason, Jim Matheos, Neal Morse, Roine Stolt and Tony Levin. I would also like to publicly thank Rikk Feulner for his untiring helpfulness and consummate efficiency in arranging interview slots and backstage access over the last few years. In addition, I'm grateful to all the various fan clubs around the world who have also been extremely supportive and supplied mounds of archival material. My thanks to Kerry & Richard Parker, Steve & Jen Jarvis and Greg Annandale at Voices UK, Michael Bitter of *The Mirror*, Simone Fabbri and Marco Petrini of The Italian Dreamers, Denis Schoen, John Van Empel, Al Muirden, Caroline Hindriks, Su Butler, Anthony Guzzardo, Mark Bredius, Erik Hulsegge, Iris Hulsegge and Bertil Visser, John Sievers, plus Joe Carona and *Used Bin* magazine, and all at the MP.com forum. I'd also like to single out Neil Elliott for providing a vast array of vintage interviews and photos, as well as my loyal "gig buddy" Andy Mills for supplying me with his astonishing collection of magazine back-issues. Additionally, I am indebted to the incredibly talented (and far too modest) Darko Böhringer for providing me with some truly outstanding photographs, Bob Sackter for the killer mastering of the CD in the first edition, the ever helpful webmaster at dreamtheaterbook.com, Rai "Weymolith" Beardsley and the support and assistance provided by Frank Solomon. Thank you all.

There are also those who have helped me personally in this business over the last few years, and I am truly grateful to Paul Rigby for the "big break", and the kindness of Dave Ling, Ian Fortnam, Sian Llewellyn and all at *Classic Rock*, Tim Jones, Andy Davies, Essi Berelian, Jon Hotten and Joel McIver. I'd also like to single out and thank Jerry Ewing at *Classic Rock Presents Prog* magazine for involving me in that wonderful and long-overdue project.

There's an extensive list of friends who have all played their part, and a big shout goes out to, John Boler, Jeeva Sethu, Pat Keene, Andy Mathews, Jane Perkins, Mike Lucas and Richard Milner. A huge thank you to Gareth Mellor for his support and proof-reading ability.

A special mention must be given to the extraordinary knowledge of "Setlist" Scotty Hansen for the crucial level of assistance he has provided to this project, always having precise answers to all my obscure questions and tirelessly proofreading the many drafts. Please buy him a beer from me when you bump into him at Dream Theater gigs around the globe.

Additionally, the fact that you are holding in your hands this book is due to the vision and enthusiasm of John Conway at Essential Works. Thanks John. I'm glad you believed me!

From a personal perspective, I am also truly indebted to the unwavering support of my Mum and Dad. Thank you. I would also like to give a heartfelt thanks to my wife Jo for all the love and endless support, and for showing me that anything is possible if you believe. I love you!

Enormous thanks to Mike Portnoy, James LaBrie, John Petrucci, Jordan Rudess, John Myung and Mike Mangini for their invaluable help and honesty. Put simply, without their input, this book wouldn't exist.

RICH WILSON
Manchester, England, March 2013

ONE

LONG ISLAND CENTURIONS

Situated on the north shore of Long Island, around fifty miles from downtown Manhattan, Kings Park is the relatively sleepy commuter town where many of the members of Dream Theater have their family roots. Dating back to the early 1900s, its population swelled as many Irish, German and Italian immigrants were employed at the newly constructed psychiatric institution. Indeed, that imposing presence of the "Loony Bin", as the locals liked to refer to it, provided employment for a majority of the town's inhabitants until the final patient was discharged in 1996.

A mix of working and middle class areas, the blend of nationalities residing in the town ensured that sport and music were central to the society's consciousness, and Dream Theater guitarist John Peter Petrucci was born into those surroundings on July 12, 1967. Much like the other members of Dream Theater, he's courteous, amiable and entirely without any of the edgy arrogance that blights the personalities of many a rock star. Along with Mike Portnoy, he's one of the band's certified co-leaders, and although he may not be as vociferous as the drummer, his relatively contemplative style carries an equal and substantial amount of influence within the band. Oh, and if that's not enough, he's also one of the most technically gifted guitarists of his generation. It's perhaps surprising, then, that John failed to display an insatiable desire to become involved in music until a bout of sibling rivalry first motivated him to pick up a guitar at the age of eight.

"I grew up in a house where my older sister played the organ," smiles John at the memory. "I remember as a kid that was what made me want to play guitar. When you're a kid you are really competitive, and God forbid that *anyone* actually got to stay up late. She had an organ lesson at night when I was sleeping, and I would hear her playing and think 'Man. How come I can't stay up late and play an instrument?' So of course, I decided I wanted to take up the guitar. But my plan didn't quite work out as my lesson was during the day. I had a teacher who was an older guy and we were working through those traditional Mel Bay books. Plus I had an acoustic guitar that was really hard to play, so I didn't stick with it and didn't like it at all. I don't even know how long it lasted – probably only a few weeks."

Apart from his sister's tinkering on the family organ, the rest of the Petrucci household did not have a particularly strong musical background, as John explains.

"If you're talking about my parents, uncles, or someone else back in the family history then no, not really," he says. "My Dad liked to sing and my younger brother ended up playing bass guitar, but that was about it. Nobody really played anything. My father was a computer programmer and really was a pioneer in that whole business. I remember him bringing home one of the first modems, and it was as big as two typewriters. It had a huge thing you had to plug into the phone. So he was really in there from the ground up, and I remember he would even show me the first internet message boards. He was a businessman and was into computers, engineering and mathematics, and my Mom was a homemaker."

A few years later, John's passion for music was reignited by the numerous local musicians who'd put on free shows or perform in "Battle of the Bands" competitions. As unlikely as it may sound, the relatively sleepy middle class suburb of Kings Park was a vibrant hotbed of rock musicians – all craving a place on the rather limited local gig circuit.

"For some reason, in my neighbourhood *everybody* played an instrument," explains John. "It was really bizarre. You would just go over and hang out at somebody's house but instead of playing softball, you'd be sitting by the piano or maybe jamming. There were so many bands that it was unbelievable. You would just walk through the neighbourhood and you'd hear guitars in all the garages. So it was when I was about 12 that I really wanted to play the guitar again. I'd see all these bands and even though they were just kids, to me they were like *real* bands. I mean, they were nobodies but they had production, long hair, and their own p.a. systems. They would play in the gyms and dances and stuff. So we were like the little kids looking up to these bands. Music was always around me, so I really wanted to do that. After a few years I would just practise all the time. I was so into playing the guitar and just wanted to be the best guitar player ever! Then those guys turned me on to all these great players like Steve Vai or Al Di Meola."

Indeed, as John has regularly joked, all his early guitar heroes were named either Al or Steve. Apart from the aforementioned Vai and Di Meola, the likes of Steve Howe (Yes), Steve Morse (Dixie Dregs), Alex Lifeson (Rush) and the innovative jazz-rocker Allan Holdsworth were all pivotal influences. But there were other musicians, such as Roger Waters, Peter Gabriel and heavier artists like Judas Priest or Iron Maiden who were also key inspirations. Picking up the guitar once again, dedicating himself to the instrument and practising for hours on end, John became competent enough to want to jam with like-minded friends, and soon a band called Centurion was formed.

"Centurion was just when we were in high school," he recalls. "The bass player's name was Bob Santos, the drummer was Brendan Kelly and we had a singer called Eric Gandras. We would play cover versions of Rush, Zeppelin and Black Sabbath. We'd even do Mötley Crüe and Zebra songs. Then Kevin Moore came into the band and we played a lot of songs by The Doors as Kev was *really* into them. We would play church halls and dances. Kids would have backyard parties at their parent's houses and we would always be the band who played. Kev lived right around the corner from me and we were really close. In our neighbourhood, a lot of the families knew each other and the parents were friends, and they would go to parties together. There would be neighbourhood outings and picnics and things like that. So we saw each other all the time and we were best friends from when we were little kids."

That firm friendship with Moore would later become central to Dream Theater's formation, with the keyboardist sharing many of Petrucci's musical tastes and aspirations. Born on May 26, 1967, Kevin Francis Moore's musical education began at the age of five, when he was encouraged by his parents to take piano lessons – even though he apparently hated the rigidity of those sessions. But the formal hours he spent gradually developing his keyboard skills proved useful when he went to high school and found himself joining a succession of bands. Indeed, he had already been a part of two short-lived units – Crystalbeast and Sidewinder – before he linked up with Petrucci in Centurion. Moore's musical influences were also pretty wide-ranging and, apart from a love of The Doors, he has also cited the likes of Rick Wakeman, Keith Emerson, Chick Corea and Jens Johannsen as being keyboardists he admired. Tall, intense, with a sharp, dry sense of humour, Moore's desire to create fresh and pioneering music was a core motivator – something that has remained with him throughout his career. But back in the early Eighties, Moore was a lynchpin in Centurion and content just to play sketchy cover versions in front of as many willing audiences as the band could find.

"I remember our first gig was at the St Joseph Church in Kings Park," recalls Centurion singer/guitarist Eric Gandras. "In fact, I can distinctly remember that we played versions of 'Roadhouse Blues' and 'I Want To Hold Your Hand'. At the time, we were fiddling around as to who would do what with the two guitars, as John and I were both kind of trading vocal and guitar duties. But soon it was *very* apparent that John was a lot more passionate and talented than I was with respect to the guitar, so I kind of fell into the role of lead singer. We were covering stuff like Iron Maiden, Led Zeppelin, Van Halen, Black Sabbath and a lot of Rush because my vocal range was at the higher end. We started to play out at local gigs for free, or for beer. When we started to play more hard rock, Kevin left as the need for keyboards diminished – we were playing much heavier stuff. I remember John used to sit in his room and memorize the solos for the songs we'd be covering by playing his albums at half speed for hours. He really was a perfectionist. John was the creative driving force of the band and would pick the songs, practise continually, learn all the parts and arrange them for the rest of us. He had extremely high standards. I remember one summer, John calculated that he was going to practise 10 or 12 hours a day over 12 weeks, and he did it. He did that with all the sacrifice it entailed at the time. He just locked himself away."

"We started to play in a local bar called The Third Rail when we were underage – around 14 – and we warmed up for some good local bands, including one called The Good Rats," continues Gandras. "The song list continued to expand and become more complex, and John just got better and better. I guess in 1984 John and the band wanted more of a commitment from me in terms of taking singing lessons, as they were getting more serious. But I knew at that time I wanted to pursue a medical career and go into college, so I left the band. I figured it would allow them to find a replacement when they were still in school, but it was still a difficult decision for me. The last gig I played with the band was supporting a band called Lazer at the York Hall, which was actually on the psychiatric centre grounds. I had left the band, and they called me up six months later as there was a gig where their singer didn't show up. So I filled in for one last time, and that was a memorable experience, and at that point Kevin Moore had come back into the band. So we were playing some Boston numbers and other stuff with keyboards."

But despite Eric's expectation that the band would continue and thrive without him, Centurion gradually ground to a halt following that gig – a disbanding that was due in part to the amount of other tempting opportunities that were on offer. With the sheer concentration of budding musicians who resided in Kings Park, there were an ever-changing number of bands with a revolving door policy towards members. Consequently, the opportunity to play with a wide variety of musicians frequently arose, and exposed Moore and Petrucci to a wonderful and heady mix of diverse styles.

"After a while, we just started interchanging and jamming," explains John Petrucci. "There were these two guys who were really into the Grateful Dead. I'd just go over there, we'd go down to the basement and jam. We wouldn't actually play any songs and that was how I got all my improvisation chops. I remember we'd do blues jams and they were all into Hendrix. Then there were other guys who were into heavy metal and guys just into the technical stuff. So it became more of a community rather than just this band or that band. It was an interchangeable community of musicians."

"We would all just hang out and explore music together," recalls school friend and bassist Erik Neldner. "We all played together in different groups. A teacher, Phil Stentz, ran a jazz workshop that John Petrucci and I were in for a while, too. So we had that jazz ensemble, but more of the musical drive came from us. We just wanted to learn all the songs we were hearing, whether it was AC/DC, Def Leppard or whoever. Music was always in the air and there was nothing else to do really. It was either that or get in trouble, and the getting in trouble part got old. So music was what we turned to. But even then, it was sort of obvious that John Petrucci stood out as far as his raw talent went and his determination to practise a lot. He just excelled a little faster than the rest of us."

For John Petrucci, his musical taste was to be widened further when he became friendly with a long-haired bassist from the other, slightly rougher, side of town – one John Myung.

"John lived in the same town but lived across a main road," says Petrucci. "So I didn't know him as closely as I did Kevin until junior high school and then we ended up becoming really good friends. It was a separate neighbourhood in the same town but there was a whole other music scene going on there, and John had long hair back then so I was almost scared of him! I mean, they were like the *cool* kids who would hang out and were into Led Zeppelin and Rush. But we ended up not only being really good friends but playing together all the time."

Of all the members of Dream Theater, the enigmatic John Myung is possibly the most difficult to fathom – and he probably wouldn't have it any other way. Born John Ro Myung in Chicago, Illinois, on January 24, 1967, he possesses an almost Zen-like composure and his inherent shyness is legendary. More of a thinker than a speaker, his unwillingness to chat for hours might be construed by the uninitiated as a sign of aloofness, but that couldn't be further from the truth. Extremely polite and kind, he simply prefers his own company to that of strangers – and often even to that of his bandmates. This desire for solitude has even seen him on recent Dream Theater tours establishing his own "Myung World" at his side of the stage where he'll relax in restful seclusion prior to a gig. While the rest of the band are psyching themselves up in the dressing room, John is already seated on his leather sofa on stage right, waiting to join his bandmates once the house lights dim. To the outsider, that superficial lack of camaraderie may seem strange, but like many people, John just needs his own space – and it's a formula that has worked within Dream Theater for many years. And make no mistake, when he does speak out, his opinion always carries an enormous amount of authority within the band.

Musically speaking, his first encounter with an instrument came at the age of five, when his mother decided that he should take up the violin. Those lessons lasted for over ten years, but did he actually relish playing that instrument?

"Well, I think you kind of accept things when you are a child," he explains. "And now, looking back, I am glad of that experience but at the time I didn't really question it. It was a case of 'John, you're going to be doing this' and I just accepted it. I am actually thankful that she did, because I am sure that played a big part in helping me to be who I am today."

By that time, his family had moved from their Chicago home to the east coast, first settling in New York City before they headed out to Kings Park when John was seven. Although not part of an especially musical family, he does recall that there was always music resonating around the Myung household.

"My Mom was always listening to classical music, so I was always hearing records from her collection," Myung explains. "It was really the classics such as Beethoven, Bach, and Tchaikovsky. So when I was five she turned me on to that whole classical movement. My Mom was actually a nurse and my Dad was a corporate financial person."

As a teenager, John's musical taste naturally gravitated to that of his peers, and soon he was fervently snapping up albums by the likes of Rush, Yes, Genesis and Iron Maiden.

"Yeah, it turned out to be that way at least in our little collection of neighbourhoods," he says. "It was just something that happened. All my friends had older brothers and sisters who were into Rush and Yes, and it always seemed that we were turned on to music through them. At the time they had a certain influence over us, so after school we would listen to Sabbath and get turned on to all these great bands. Rock music just gave us direction. The kids that I was hanging out with began to play drums, and then someone would play bass, and they were forming bands."

Undoubtedly, listening to such prominent and innovative bass players as Rush's Geddy Lee, Iron Maiden's Steve Harris, and Chris Squire of Yes played a fundamental role in John first thinking about switching the violin for the bass. And when the opportunity arose for him to actually join a band as a bassist – even though he'd never even picked up the instrument – he didn't need asking twice.

"My neighbour needed a bass player and said to me 'Well, you know how to play the violin. Basically it's just four strings so you should play be able to pick it up really quickly. You probably know how musicians it already!' My friends were really supportive and were playing. I got playing in bands. So I picked up the bass and starbass players like really obsessed with the instrument and withRoth] and Jeff Berlin Billy Sheehan [Talas, Mr Big and Davght I heard something that [respected session man]. Just when I well of bass players who were so was really good, I would find a wh things. That's when I said to myself amazing and doing such incre ole

'This should tide me over for a while'. Then I was really obsessed by the music that was coming out by bands like Rush and thought 'God, people actually can do this for a living?' And that was it. That's what I set out to do."

Totally dedicating himself to the instrument – much like he had with the violin – John's devotion led to him spending around six to eight hours each day just practising. Indeed, that remarkable regime has continued, and such unrelenting rehearsing would in time become a form of meditation. But back in the early Eighties, Myung would sharpen his fretwork by playing along to classic Iron Maiden LPs, mimicking and matching their bassist Steve Harris. Just to increase the challenge, though, he had a habit of flicking the speed on his turntable up from 33rpm to a breakneck 45rpm.

"Yeah, that was something that I did just for fun," he laughs. "But it wasn't like I played through the whole record that way. At the time it was all turntables and I'd be playing along to all the records. And you would be staring at the turntable and I just started experimenting with different speeds and realized it raised the bar in terms of a musical challenge."

John Petrucci spent hours with Myung covering such Maiden albums as *Killers* and *The Number Of The Beast*, and it was those shared experiences that helped establish a musical and personal understanding between the pair that's still in place to this day.

"We've literally been playing together since junior high school," explains Petrucci. "We've played every single Iron Maiden song ever written. There are so many memories and such a great, unspoken chemistry. He doesn't have an outgoing personality but that's not to say that he isn't close to people. He is one of the most consistent people I have ever met, and really has stayed the same for the longest period of time."

With rock music dominating every facet of both John Myung and John Petrucci's school lives, it was apparent that it simply had to become their sole career focus. Petrucci does, however, recall that he enjoyed other artistically orientated subjects, noting "I did take a music theory class as well but other than that I really liked creative writing. I think that was when I opened up some doors and got some skills that would help turn into my love for writing lyrics and songwriting. So that really

Yet, such art as well, but every musician is into art, right?" compared to titing and artistic aspirations were insignificant when two Johns would dare to become full-time musicians. Quite how the career was, however, far it transforming their devout passion into a many of their guitar-slinging obvious – until the pairing realized that tional career paths via the same coll had all followed identical educa- in Massachusetts.

"I started to find out that all these great players, like Steve Vai and Al Di Meola, had been to Berklee College in Boston," says Petrucci. "So John and I started talking about doing that, and we actually ended up applying together. Initially, my parents weren't keen on sending me to a music school and they were very sceptical. I was also a good student and had good grades, so they probably wanted me to do something more like business or what my Dad was doing. I guess that was really just for me to have something to fall back on. But during my lunch breaks at school, I would practise my guitar and I always used to use the room of the band teacher, Phil Stentz. Somehow, he kind of picked up on me and I do remember that when I'd decided I wanted to go to Berklee out of high school, he was the guy who stepped up to the plate at one school meeting and said to my parents 'He needs to go there'. And that was without me being in any of his classes."

"So I just applied. There were people there that had sent a tape in and managed to get a scholarship – which I didn't even know about – so I missed the boat on that one! It was just based on academics and there was no audition until after I had been accepted, and that was a placement audition once you were actually there."

Perhaps realizing the nature of John Myung's passion for music, his parents took less persuading that Berklee was an appropriate destination for their son. "Yeah, they were very supportive of it, as I really wanted to do music," says Myung. "So I guess it was the obvious choice."

Kevin Moore was of a similar mind, although he made the decision to head to the State University of New York (s.u.n.y) in Fredonia, upstate New York, to enhance his keyboard skills. Around two weeks into their first semester at Berklee in September 1985, the two Johns had been struck by the ability of a drummer they had noticed in one of the college's many rehearsal rooms. Later bumping into that long-haired drummer from Long Island in a cafeteria one lunchtime, they struck up a conversation. His name was Mike Portnoy.

Ask Mike to reveal his character and the first words he'll utter are "obsessive" and "compulsive". In fact, he'll even go so far as to suggest that he suffers from the classic obsessive-compulsive personality disorder – a syndrome that cites such traits as an extreme devotion to work, a preoccupation with detail, reluctance to delegate tasks and a stubborn streak. It seems that based on these criteria alone, he may well have a point. A self-confessed control freak and workaholic, he insists that every aspect of his life is as structured, ordered and fault-less as the drum patterns he rattles out on his ever-expanding kit. Running in tandem with this persona is an addictive disposition that has at varying times turned his attention to drink, drugs and an excessive and ongoing quest to amass as many CDs, DVDs and music magazines as space in his home will allow. Yet, although some may view these patterns as character flaws, it's accurate to say that without Portnoy's meticulous drive and direct leadership qualities, Dream Theater would be an extremely different band. Protector of the band's name, their number one fan, and curator of memorabilia, he breathes Dream Theater from the moment he awakes until he retires to bed in the early hours.

Born on April 20, 1967, in Long Beach, Long Island, New York, Michael Stephen Portnoy's childhood revolved around music. Although neither of his parents were musicians, he claims that it was his father, Howard Portnoy, who initiated his love of rock at a surprisingly young age.

"My Dad and my Mom split when I was about 18 months old but he turned me on to music from day one," says Mike. "He was a *huge* music fan and I was immediately turned on to The Beatles, The Who and The Rolling Stones. Even when I was one or two years old I had my own record collection. I was collecting Beatles records and remember listening to these records with the green apples on them. Then I was turned on to The Who, and *Tommy* was one of my favourite albums. When I was around five or six, my Dad moved out to Carmel in California and became a disc jockey on the radio out there – which was directly inspired by the Clint Eastwood movie called *Play Misty For Me*. In that movie Clint Eastwood was a disc jockey for KRML radio in Carmel, and my Dad did exactly that. He moved out there and became a rock DJ on KRML radio.

"I'd go and visit him in Carmel over the holidays in summertime," he continues. "He would let me go on the radio with him and pick out the records because even by age five or six, I was already exploring different bands such as Led Zeppelin, The Doors, Jimi Hendrix and Cream. He had a morning show and I kind of became his sidekick. In fact, my first taste of fame was calling up to make a collect phone call when I was out there in California, and the operator recognized my voice and said 'Is this Mike Portnoy?' and I was like a little five-year-old kid! But nobody in my family is actually a musician. I grew up with my Mom. Once she had separated from my Dad, she remarried and that was when my brother Rennie and sister Samantha were born. I grew up with my Mom until she passed away in 1984. She basically brought me up and was always very supportive of my love for music, and later on when I started playing."

Once Mike's parents had comprehended the extent of his musical infatuation, they encouraged him to channel his enthusiasm into actually playing an instrument. Perhaps surprisingly, given his admiration for drummers such as John Bonham, his first instrument was the piano and it was around the age of seven that he began to take formal lessons with a local teacher.

"I had a little taste of fame with that, too," he smiles. "When I was in second grade, I wrote a song called 'Oh Yeah', and it was just two chords, E to C, E to C, back and forth. But I was one of the few kids who could sit behind a piano and play. They had a talent show and I played 'The Entertainer' from the film *The Sting* and of course my *famous* hit single 'Oh Yeah'! So I would go up in the talent shows or school assemblies, and play that. But after a year or two of playing piano I grew bored as it wasn't rock 'n' roll enough for me. I needed to play something more aggressive. I was always very hyper as a child – always tapping at the table – and in fact I'm still like that. So I think it was inevitable that I would end up on the drum set. I was visiting my cousins in Miami, Florida, around 1976, and they had an old beat-up drum set in their garage, and I just started playing on it. I think when I was a really young kid, I also got like little toy drum sets I would bang away on. But my cousin's beat-up set was a *real* drum set, we set it up and I just fell in love with it. After that it became obvious that I was destined to become a drummer rather than a piano player."

"For my eleventh birthday, my grandparents bought me my first drum kit. It was a little three-piece, blue Royce drum kit, but by sheer coincidence that very day my grandfather had a heart attack and he died about a week later. So it was kind of like a legacy that he left me. He bought me this drum set and practically died upon giving it to me. At that period in my life, I was going through a very big Kiss phase, so I started off just playing along to Kiss songs as well as The Who, The Beatles and Zeppelin. I've often said this, but my four biggest drum influences when I started were Peter Criss, Ringo Starr, Keith Moon and John Bonham. Shortly after that, The Who movie *The Kids Are Alright* came out. I saw that and it completely changed me. Suddenly, I went from being a casual Keith Moon and Who fan to being an obsessive one. It was the first time I saw Keith in all his glory, as well as seeing a drummer playing a lead role in a band. It really inspired me and he became my drummer hero."

Despite Mike's obvious keenness, his talents weren't initially identified at school, and after he was thrown out of a school band for horsing around with a friend around the age of ten, it wasn't until he reached high school that Mike returned to a school band. By this stage, he was already playing in his first rock band, Intruder, and had started to develop his technique. But it seemed that displaying his talent invariably led to his music teacher singling him out for criticism.

"At that point I was already this 'hot shot' drummer playing in a band and my music teacher Mr Kennedy really loved making an example out of me," Portnoy recalls. "He'd point me out in front of the whole class, try and cut me down and was always making an example out of me because I was this cocky little rock drummer. He wanted me to be more schooled and regimented, and he even kicked me out of bands a couple of times because I wasn't playing the correct game. I think it was like one of those classic examples you see in movies, where the teacher is constantly pointing out a specific student and trying to make an example of them, but at the end of the day you get their respect. And ultimately on graduation in twelfth grade, I ended up getting the big music scholarship of my entire class. It was the biggest scholarship that they offered, and I think that was his way of tipping the cap at me and giving me a wink that all along he believed in me, but was really trying to push my buttons and trying to motivate me to learn. And that's what I did."

"All through high school, I started to get obsessed with music and not just the drums. I started to take a music theory class with a guy called Mr Kaplin, who was a big influence on me. He was very supportive in a different way as he really saw my love for music and really encouraged it. That's why I was learning about scales, time signatures, key signatures, modes and how to read music. I became obsessed with all that and I wanted to become more than just a drummer. I wanted to really just immerse myself in as much information as I could. My music theory teacher saw that and embraced it. I came through that class with flying colours and would get full marks on my tests and really excelled in that department."

As a result, other school subjects were forced into the background by this burgeoning love for music, and by 1982 Mike had begun to discover and work his way through albums by such diverse acts as The Pretenders, Sex Pistols, Van Halen and Iron Maiden. Yet, it wasn't until he stumbled across the back-catalogue of Canadian prog rockers Rush that this fascination with performing music transformed itself into an obsession.

"Rush *really* changed me," he states. "And my discovery of them came at a point when I was really immersing myself in those music theory classes. Rush were deep musically with odd time signatures and things like that, and I was able to learn a lot about these by listening to them. After I got into Rush, I discovered other progressive rock bands like Yes, Genesis and Frank Zappa. In fact Zappa was, and is to this day, probably my biggest musical hero. So it was during that period of my late high school years that I really started to discover progressive music."

By the April of 1982, Mike had also formed a band called Intruder who played together for around two years. Along with guitarist Mike Bauer, bassist Eric Barbasso, and Mike Thomas on keyboards, Intruder concentrated on performing cover versions of Maiden, Motley Crüe, Judas Priest and Van Halen songs at church halls and "Battle of the Bands" contests.

"I remember I immediately caught Mike Bauer's ear because I could play 'Sweet Leaf' by Black Sabbath," says Portnoy. "He was playing with a drummer who didn't know how to play the off-beat in that drum pattern, so as soon as I sat down and knew how to play it, he was suddenly like 'This is the drummer I've got to play with – this guy is good!' So we formed Intruder and it was basically all cover tunes, but we wrote a couple of original songs. I remember we had a song called 'The End Of Our Life' which was a lyric written by Mike and myself. But we ended up breaking up in 1984 when I was a senior in high school, and that was when I started playing with a guy who lived down the block from me called Peter Best – no relation to the original drummer of The Beatles!"

"He was a much older guy. I was like a 16- or 17-year-old kid, and Peter was 35 years old. But he lived down the block, and he was a guitar player who kind of never really did anything. He and I started jamming, and we put together a band called Rising Power which was my first band that played original music. I brought a bass player along named Angus Whittaker who had also played with Intruder towards the final days of that band. Throughout my senior year in 1984–85, Rising Power wrote a whole lot of material which gave me the chance to have some creative input into the writing of music. We would play local shows, including at this club called February's in Elmont, Long Island. We would play every month or so and we did some demos, too, which was my first time in a recording studio."

Although Rising Power never managed to amass a fan base outside of their close circle of friends and acquaintances, the recording of songs such as "Adrenalized", "Goddess Of Pain And Pleasure" and "Master Of Illusion" gave Mike invaluable experience of creating original material and working in a studio environment. Even today, bootleg CDs of these songs regularly emerge on internet auction sites and are snapped up by eager collectors. It was also during this period that the young Portnoy had his only serious brush with the law.

"It was on July 4, 1984. I was out with friends and we were drunk," he explains. "One of the guys I was with broke a store glass window and all of a sudden the cops came after us. I didn't run because I thought, 'Well, what the fuck? They must have seen who broke it.' As I hadn't thrown the rock, I didn't think there was any point in running. So, sure enough, they grabbed *me*. I was put in jail for the night, and eventually the charges were dropped when my friend that had broken the window actually confessed to it."

With Rising Power splitting after only a few months ("Pete wanted to start playing with people his own age," laughs Mike), Portnoy hooked up with another local band, Inner Sanctum. Led by Adam Barbasso (older brother of Eric from Intruder), they were widely perceived as the local heroes and always had a ready supply of clubs wanting to book them. After the band had suffered a few drummer problems, Mike was asked to fill in for a couple of shows in the summer of 1985.

"After I played some live shows with them, Adam asked me to lay down drum tracks for some recordings which were basically done in my garage," Mike recalls. "Years later, he ended up taking those tapes, completing them and putting out a 12-inch vinyl record called *12AM*. If you look you can find bootlegs of that, too. But I was never really a full-time member of that band."

A few months prior to his last show with Rising Power, Mike had decided that – with music governing every aspect of his life – in order to progress and turn professional, the next logical step would be to attend a music college. Like John Petrucci and John Myung, he was intrigued by the potential of studying at Berklee, and following a visit to the Boston college, he was sufficiently dazzled to successfully apply for a place.

"Really, by the end of high school, I knew that I really had to go to Berklee and it was obvious that that was my destiny," he affirms. "It's very prestigious and so many great musicians went there before we did, so it already had this reputation. You know, Steve Vai, Steve Smith along with Vinnie Colaiuta and a lot of other drum heroes of mine. I knew I needed to check it out and once I had, I was sold and I *had* to go there. The place was filled with great musicians. You'd walk down the hallways and everyone was playing guitar or drums, and each one of them is better than the next. So it really motivates and drives you to be the best you can be. But to be honest, my Mom really wanted me to go to a more traditional school and just major in music. She wanted me to have something to fall back on, you know? Of course it's understandable that she would want that from me as a Mom, but she ended up dying in a plane crash on November 16, 1984, which was when I was in my senior year. She was my only obstacle to going to Berklee and once she passed away, I made up my mind that I wanted to go there. I didn't want to have something to fall back on. I believed in myself and wanted to just pursue the music and didn't want that safety net."

With his domestic life becoming far from idyllic following the death of his mother, Portnoy says that he couldn't wait to bundle together his possessions and drums, and head off to Boston to begin a new life.

"Moving from Long Island to Boston was easy as I was ready," he explains. "My Mom had just passed away and it was hell at home. It was a real hard thing to deal with, so I was ready to pack up and go to Berklee to begin my new life. I met John Petrucci and John Myung really quickly. The two of them had gone up together and were room-mates. I'd gone to Berklee to connect with other musicians and find a band. Within two or three weeks those guys saw me practising with my roommate Bryan. The two of us had set up our drum sets and were just practising together and they saw me, and approached me one day in the lunch room. I guess when they saw that I was wearing a Talas shirt they somehow connected with that and sensed that I was a similar type of person. So we decided to get together and jam, and we've been jamming ever since. We never even officially said 'Hey, let's get together and form a band.' We just started jamming one night and then it was like 'OK we'll see you tomorrow' and we showed up the next night and it just happened. It just somehow became understood that we would stay together. It is incredible. I mean, Berklee is filled with musicians from all over the world, from Germany, Japan, England and all over America. What are the chances of three kids, loving the exact type of music and coming from the same place, Long Island? It was almost like fate that the three of us connected."

Of course, they had no inkling at the time that this musical relationship would last to this day, and John Petrucci even recalls that on his arrival at Berklee, he had no intention of even forming a band.

"As far as I was concerned, we had a band before we went there," says Petrucci. "It was me, John and Kevin and we had different drummers we were playing with. When we went there, in a way it was like breaking up the band because Kevin didn't go there. So I don't think in my mind I was thinking about going there to form a band. It was like going to college, the first time away from home and we could immerse ourselves in music. I just remember that great feeling of freedom and being on my own and enjoying the whole dorm life. But Berklee is a different scene and isn't your typical college, as it's all musicians. It's not as though there were any sports teams or anything like that. But Boston was just great, as it is such a big college town. So there were so many events and concerts to go to. Plus it was a great experience meeting new people and getting turned on to all this different music."

"We all lived in the dorms at Berklee. I was in Room 608 and John and John were in Room 817," adds Mike. "So we were just two floors apart. But I remember that there were rehearsal rooms that you could rent out at night but you had to sign up for them in advance. You could get them in three blocks – from six to eight in the evening, eight to ten and ten to twelve. In order to sign up for a two-hour block, you had to go down first thing in the morning and wait in this line to sign up. Of course, we would want to rehearse every night from six until midnight. So in order for us to get a six-hour block, each of the three of us would have to go down every morning and each would sign up for each of the three blocks. So the three of us would wake up every single morning, Monday to Friday, sign up for the practice rooms and then from six to midnight every single night we would move our gear into this little room. And it was always the exact same practice room – E19. We started off playing Rush tunes like 'The Spirit Of Radio', 'YYZ' and

Iron Maiden songs, and then we eventually started writing our own songs together."

Back in the early Eighties, Berklee had a reputation as being the haunt of serious jazz aficionados, and was to some degree acting as a production line for jazz musicians. That status has somewhat changed, but back then, the two Johns and Mike were cast as rebels, as Mike recalls.

"Berklee was *very* jazz oriented," he says. "In fact, you'd walk up and down the hallways and see all these conservative jazz combos in rooms, then you'd walk by our room and we would be playing Iron Maiden's 'The Trooper'. I think now Berklee is a lot more metal and rock oriented. As crazy as it may sound, I think a lot of that has to do with people like myself, John and John kind of coming from Berklee. A whole new generation go to Berklee because they hear of Dream Theater stemming from there and they're into progressive and metal music. But back then, we were really the outcasts. There were only a few of us who were into jazz as well as heavy metal music. We went there listening to Rush, Iron Maiden and Metallica but at the same time we had a real appreciation for jazz, and especially electric jazz fusion such as the Mahavishnu Orchestra, Return To Forever and The Dixie Dregs that were spawning such great players as John McLaughlin, Chick Corea and Steve Morse. So we had a real appreciation for that side as well."

Despite Mike's assertion that they were almost treated as outsiders within the college, John Petrucci doesn't remember being on the sharp end of any jazz snobbery, saying "There was a lot of talk of that but I never experienced it. I would hear that all the time. Yes, there were either the jazzers or the rockers, but I didn't feel anything weird. I think you got to a point where you were playing with people who are serious about music, and who were good players, the style didn't really matter. I never experienced that kind of attitude of there being a rivalry. I felt we were welcomed in very quickly into the whole guitar community, which was huge. There were 2,000 guitarists in the school, and John Myung and I got to play on one of their performance centre nights. That was something you'd get if you'd been there for a certain amount of time, and you had to have all these credits. But we were invited up to play without all of that, so I felt they were very welcoming."

In the meantime, the fledgling trio had started the process of recording those frantic sessions in E19. Using a basic four-track recorder that had been bought for Mike by his ever-supportive grandmother as a high school graduation present, they had soon amassed a wealth of material – most of which has been released over the years on many an official and unofficial bootleg. For the record, the first material ever recorded was a ninety-second experimental piece called "Particle E. Motion" which merely comprised a brief Petrucci guitar motif overlaid on some mellow bass. Primarily written to aid their working knowledge of the four-track, other similarly succinct tracks such as "The Saurus", covers of Rush's "YYZ" and s.o.d.'s "Anti-Procrastination Song" were knocked out, before they concentrated their efforts on writing and recording more significant material.

Their first substantial piece was "Another Won", with "Cry For Freedom" and "The School Song" being recorded shortly afterwards. At this stage, all the material was instrumental but it certainly displayed a considerable amount of promise. There were the natural and almost obligatory nods to their early rock heroes Iron Maiden, Rush and Queensrÿche, but even at this stage in their career they were showcasing their knack for creating technically challenging and memorable tracks.

Within a matter of a few months, the unit had developed an unspoken understanding that they had formed the nucleus of a band – but one which still needed a name. As self-confessed Rush zealots, all three members of the band were determined to ensure that they bagged the best seats when the Canadian prog rockers rolled into Massachusetts during their *Power Windows* Tour. Waiting in the long line outside the ticket booth (after a night on the pavement before the tickets went on sale), the strains of the Rush classic "Bastille Day" were blaring from an adjacent fan's ghetto blaster. As the song reached its conclusion, someone noted that the guitar melody sounded majestic. Thinking that would be a fitting name to describe their sound, Majesty were born.

But a name hadn't been the only element missing from the band. They had already determined that in order for them to develop the sound they had envisaged, they needed to recruit both a vocalist and a keyboard player.

"We were playing every night and just wanted to complete the line-up," says Mike. "Not many people know this, but we actually auditioned a few keyboard players and singers at Berklee. But none of them were what we were looking for. So John and John told me about this keyboardist, Kev, that they had been playing with before they left for Berklee. So we always knew that if we couldn't find anyone at Berklee, we could always fall back on Kev. And eventually by November, after we hadn't found anyone, we decided to send Kev some tapes of what we'd been doing. Kev was away at Fredonia, so we agreed that over the Christmas break we'd get together and play with him and see how that went."

"I can remember that when I first met Kev, he reminded me of myself, John and John," continues Mike. "He was *exactly* the same type of person and into the same music. So he was obviously a perfect fit and the four of us just fell right in with each other. It was automatic after we'd played with him that he was set to be in the line-up. Over that break we wrote a song called 'Two Far', which was the first song the four of us had put together. Then come January he went back to Fredonia and we went back to Berklee but we decided that Kev was going to be part of the band."

Returning back to Boston in early 1986, Majesty minus Kevin committed themselves to begin working on a demo tape that could, in time, be hawked around record labels in order to try and secure a contract. Aiding them in this process were two fellow students, James Hull and Paul Falcone, who both possessed four-track recorders. Linking the two together, they were able to put down basic tracks, with the intention of adding keyboards and vocals later at the conclusion of the college year. But it was around this time that they began to question whether they were wasting their time at Berklee. Despite enjoying their time there, Mike recalls that they lacked the ability to focus on both the band and their studies. Clearly, something was about to give.

"We just decided that we had to pursue the band full-time," he says. "Berklee is so demanding. You really had to put a hundred per cent into it for it to work, and being a band is also extremely demanding. We felt we couldn't split ourselves between the band and school, so we had to make a choice. At that point we really felt a chemistry and connection between us, and decided when we went home in May we'd complete the line-up and stay in Long Island and not continue at Berklee. But I still gained a lot from Berklee in terms of the overall musical education. All day I was taking music theory, arranging, harmony, sight singing, ear training, and classes like that. I really gained a lot from that. But to be honest with you, I don't think I gained much in the drumming department. I was only taking one or two drumming classes, and that was the least of my focus at that point. I think I was already pretty developed as a drummer by the time I got to Berklee, and it was all just from self-schooling and playing along to records throughout my high school years and playing in bands. I had already developed a lot of my style at that point, so once I got to Berklee I was really immersed in the other stuff. And I would really get off at night playing with other musicians, which was always my biggest outlet."

The decision for the Berklee boys to quit their studies – and for Kevin Moore to similarly leave Fredonia – was incredibly bold. Effectively giving themselves nothing to fall back on, they simply had to transform Majesty into a successful unit. John Petrucci recalls that the band had become convinced their drive and self-belief was enough to steer them to the next level. "I was always so confident," he says. "There was just one point when it all clicked and I knew I was going to do it. It was tunnel vision."

God only knows what the respective parents thought about their sons becoming college drop-outs – especially given the hard talking that had been required to convince some of their relatives to let them go to a music college in the first place.

"Yeah, that really was hard for them to take," admits John Petrucci. "We all had to sit down and do a lot of talking. I mean, at first we even had to convince Kevin and then convince his parents. Of course, all our parents were friends so they would talk to each other. It was like, 'Now they want to drop out of college!'"

The support of their parents would be crucial to their prospects. Effectively jobless while they went through the rigours of paying their dues with Majesty, they needed somewhere to live. But with their parents relenting, supporting their actions and providing roofs over their heads, there was only one minor problem that needed a rapid solution – that of tracking down a singer. As with the keyboard position, the two Johns had a ready-made solution in a singer they had jammed with in Kings Park called Chris Collins.

John Myung: "We were friends with him at school, and I do remember that he was always singing along to Judas Priest or Queensrÿche songs. He was really into that style of operatic singing."

"Yeah, he just lived in the neighbourhood," adds Petrucci. "It was funny, because initially when we used to hang out he didn't even sing. Then I remember coming home from Berklee for that winter break and all of a sudden he was like 'Check me out!' and he could sing! He was singing 'Queen Of The Reich' [by Queensrÿche] and I was like 'Whoahh! Where did that come from?'"

On hearing Collins singing, Mike Portnoy didn't need to be persuaded that they had found the vocalist that suited their approach: "They played me some tapes of Chris singing Queensrÿche songs. He sounded exactly like Geoff Tate or Bruce Dickinson and we thought he was great. We decided that when we got home from school in May he would join the band and we would *finally* be complete..."

MAJESTIC BEGINNINGS

Born in Brooklyn on August 10, 1967, Chris Collins is a self-confessed and likeable rogue, and any conversation with him is always guaranteed to be compelling thanks to his extensive repertoire of lurid tales. But despite his affable persona, the tough years he spent as a child in

Brooklyn were responsible for shaping a robust exterior that he still retains today. Certainly, his streetwise demeanour made him unique when, as a child, his family moved out from the city to the somewhat plusher and greener surroundings of the Long Island suburbs. As a consequence, the activities that might have appeared in the "Hobbies and Interests" section of his curriculum vitae were distinctly at odds with some of the more mundane pastimes of his school friends and future bandmates.

"John Petrucci and I used to go BMX-riding at that time, but generally John was mellow and didn't hang around with me and my crazy friends," he laughs. "Once in a while, though, he'd come down with his bike as there were a few of us who were into doing stunt-riding and stuff. I also loved blowing things up in those woods. I used to build pipe bombs using Magnum gunpowder, sulphur and magnesium fuses, and used to blow the trees up. So yeah, you might say that I came from the other side of the tracks!"

For many vocalists, the desire to sing and front a band would burn from an early age. But although Collins always had a passionate love of music and delighted in immersing himself in radio singalongs when being driven in his mother's car, it wasn't until much later that he took the idea of actually becoming a singer seriously. For him, just discovering bands like Queensrÿche, Fates Warning and Iron Maiden, and then investigating in depth their back-catalogues was, during his adolescent years, more than enough.

"I used to jam around back then but never really got into a band. I did projects where I would jump on stage in 'Battle of the Bands' competitions," he says. "But a few of us would get together and both John Petrucci and his brother Chris would play. Later on, a drummer, Tony Metasa, whom I still work with today, joined us. But after John Petrucci and John Myung had gone to Berklee, I was forced to move away from Long Island. I got in trouble with the law actually and my mother couldn't control me, so she threw me out of the house. I went to live with my father in Queens and it was there that I formed my first band, Phantasma, with a guy called Tommy Jordan. He later became the guitarist with a band called Scarecrow in the Eighties."

The type of metal Phantasma created was decent enough and showed a certain amount of potential, but the band were faced with competing against a plentiful supply of other New York rockers who were all crafting a similar brand of melodic metal and vying to fill the restricted number of local headlining gig spots. Consequently, the realization that the riches of recording contracts, homes in Malibu, and platinum-selling records were never going to be offered to the fledgling Phantasma hit Collins hard, and once again he found himself searching for a meaningful and appealing day job that might be suited to his persona.

"I was a confused kid and was tampering around with drugs and stuff," Collins confesses. "I kind of needed direction. I remember thinking 'I love to blow shit up, I love to use guns – I really should use that talent.' So I joined the Marines! I signed some papers and was one step away from joining. Well, in the week before I was supposed to go for my physical and sign the rest of the papers, John Petrucci called me up. Isn't it funny the way fate can change on the drop of a dime? He was like 'Chris, how you doing? We need you Chris, we've got an album we want to cut and want you to come on out and sing!' So I thought 'Fuck the Marines' and I moved back out to Kings Park and joined Majesty."

Although Collins had last seen his former schoolmates a mere eight months earlier, the naked ambition that had been in abundance prior to them departing for Berklee had been augmented by a professional attitude and determination that had been drilled into them in their college classes. After seeing the plentiful supply of musicians the college was churning out, the Berklee bunch had also realized that to even stand the slimmest chance of converting their aspirations into the reality of actually earning a living from Majesty, they had to be totally committed. This transformation was something that was noticeable to Collins upon their return to Kings Park in May 1986.

"They had all really grown up, and I could see the change when they returned from Berklee," he says. "They'd literally left as enthusiastic kids and come back very organized and full of energy. They even had an album all planned out, and knew exactly what they wanted to do. To tell you the truth, I took that organization for granted. It really isn't easy to find a group of people as dedicated to one aim as they were. You can't stop that. The four guys were driven by one goal, knew their weaknesses and strong points, and were able to communicate with one another at such a high level. It's very hard to find and was incredible. And to me, that was how they derived their long-term success."

Musical plans aside, the band still had to face the harsher reality of finding jobs to supplement their ambitions. With most of the band living back with their parents, they were hardly going to starve or become homeless, but they still needed to buy equipment.

"I was working for a music store called Focus 2 in Long Island," recalls John Myung. "So I was doing a lot of driving and picking up equipment. It was just a case of going out to different dealers, picking up all the equipment and then bringing it back to the store."

Myung later supplemented his earnings by giving bass lessons, and was soon joined by John Petrucci who was an equally adept teacher. Petrucci had also spent a number of months working in a grocery store. But things weren't quite so pleasant for Mike, who found himself returning to a complicated family situation.

"I went back home to my family, to my stepfather, and moved back in with him and my brother and sister," says Mike. "He had remarried so there were some other brothers and sisters in the house but that fell apart really quick. I got into this big fight with him and got kicked out of the house. So I ended getting my own house and living on my own. I was the first of all my friends to get my own place and John Myung originally moved in with me. But let's just say that mine and John's very different lifestyles became apparent pretty quick, and he moved back home! It was in Long Beach and it became the band's headquarters. We would also rehearse there in those early years. After we left Berklee I ended up going to a music college on Long Island called Five Towns as I wanted to continue school and my music education. But I delivered Chinese food for many years during that period, and I also had another job at a record store, but I never collected pay cheques. I would use all the money I made as store credit and would buy all my records through whatever I'd make at that job."

Any spare time that the band had, however, was filled by their incessant desire to develop their material. As John Myung recalls, Majesty were determined to ensure that their music was as tight as possible before they even considered venturing out onto the live circuit.

"We really didn't do much playing out at first," he says. "We just stayed in the basement to practise, and every night we'd always meet at about six and play together until about midnight. We knew we had to be dedicated, and it was during that period of time that we managed to put a collection of songs together."

"They were very professional at band rehearsal," adds Chris Collins. "They weren't like your typical band where everyone brings the beers and sluts down, and everyone parties. I mean, there was never any hint of alcohol or drugs at band rehearsal. They were *so* dedicated."

There was also the matter of completing the so-called "Majesty Demo" tape that the two Johns and Mike had started working on when at Berklee. Eventually containing six tracks – "Another Won", "Your Majesty", "A Vision", "Two Far", "Vital Star" and "March Of The Tyrant" – it was merely a case of adding Moore's keyboard passages and Collins' vocals into the mix. The lyrics had been largely penned by John Petrucci, with Collins being given sheets of lines and guidance on cues but forming many of the melodies himself to suit his operatic style. With those tracks in the can, there was just the hurdle of finding a way of paying for the thousand copies that Majesty felt they needed in order to properly launch a promotional campaign. As she had with finding the funds for Mike's four-track recorder, his grandmother once again stepped forward to help him out.

"When I came back to Long Island after leaving Berklee, my grandmother *really* took me under her wing because my Mom was gone and I no longer had my stepfather to be supportive," expands Mike. "She was, God bless her, the best. The band needed a place to rehearse and she helped me find a place and helped soundproof it so we could play there, and she'd bought that four-track we recorded demos on. The band needed money to press our first demo and she paid for it. Later on, she even started helping with the fan mail and stuff like that. As I mentioned earlier, she and my grandfather bought me my first drum set. So really, as much as my Dad is responsible for the musical influence throughout my life, my grandmother was responsible for helping to support my career."

Those cassettes were duly mailed around the globe to any music magazine that Mike thought might be interested in hearing them. Accordingly, magazines such as *Rock Hard* in Germany gave Majesty dazzling reviews, and readers intrigued to hear more were soon writing to the band requesting copies.

"This was around the time when there was an underground metal movement and bands like Fates Warning and Watchtower were getting some recognition," adds Mike. "We ended up getting written about in a lot of these magazines. As a result of those reviews, they would always print an address where people could write to us to order up the tape. So we ended up pushing several hundred copies all around the world through that type of exposure. It was a real kind of underground scene that I had my finger on the pulse of, which really benefited the band in those early days. You know, we'd heard the stories of Lars Ulrich doing that with Metallica, and I was very much following that kind of promotional strategy."

Listening to these tracks now provides an intriguing insight into the mindset and intended direction of Majesty. Naturally, given the band's age and relative inexperience, the demos lack a certain songwriting panache and quality control, but despite those flaws there are glimmers of the raw and adventurous melodies that would come to prominence in their later years. With a voice that combined some of the characteristics of Queensrÿche's Geoff Tate, Maiden's Bruce Dickinson and Geddy Lee, even the regularly lampooned singing of Collins is pretty deft and far from the calamity that many would have you believe. Perhaps it's a little wavering in places, but for a 19-year-old untrained singer, Collins certainly had the capability to deliver with his unique voice.

Musically, the band once again came across like an agitated version of Rush – packing frantic and intense melodies throughout many of the tracks – but still managing to add their own idiosyncratic touches to ensure that they could never be accused of plagiarism. Of all the tracks, the relatively commercial "Your Majesty" is probably the highlight and hints at some of the attributes of *Power Windows*-era Rush. "March Of The Tyrant" is also imaginative and possesses a heavy progressive edge that endears it to the voice of Collins, who was always far more convincing when avoiding ballads. Consequently, the slower numbers such as "Vital Star" and "A Vision" suffer, although as Mike Portnoy rightly points out, the latter "has some really beautiful moments, not to mention an amazing guitar solo." And although they were pretty unsophisticated by the band's later standards, the mix of the material somehow captured the essence of Majesty and augured well for the future.

"Yeah, I think they were primitive for us, but they were good for their time," points out Mike. "Certainly a song like 'Another Won' or 'March Of The Tyrant' have some cool musical passages. They were obviously just done on a four-track, and I think Chris's vocals sometimes make some of the stuff hard to listen to and sound very dated. But I think that was the blueprint of where we would go. Even then we were fiddling with more melodic songs such as 'Vital Star' and 'A Vision', as well as the more accessible straight-ahead formula with a song like 'Your Majesty'. So it's a very primitive version of what Dream Theater would become stylistically. You had the progressive, the metal, the melodic and the more straight-ahead."

By early summer 1986, Majesty felt that the now completed lineup were sufficiently honed for them to consider venturing into the live arena. Not that venues as cramped as the Right Track Inn in Freeport or The Stage Door in Deer Park could be classed as arenas, but every rock band has to pay their live dues, and there were plenty of clubs on Long Island willing to let Majesty grace their stages. History shows that their first ever gig was at the Sundance in Bay Shore on May 28, 1986. Running through just five tracks ("Another Won", "Your Majesty", "Vital Star" plus cover versions of "Queen Of The Reich" and s.o.d.'s "Anti-Procrastination Song"), the gig might not have been as tight as they would have wanted it, but the thrill of just playing live more than compensated for any deficiencies. Even to this day, Chris Collins can recall, and sympathize with, the reaction of the sparse audience.

"I remember playing for a confused crowd," laughs Collins. "Majesty were just so progressive that people really didn't know how to take them. People were used to seeing bands where the music had hooks and stuff that they could bang their heads to. And you can't really bang your head to Majesty! I mean, I was a metal head, too, and I wasn't really into some of the music. I'm not saying that Majesty or Dream Theater isn't impressive, but for me, metal was never meant to be intellectual. Of course I could appreciate bands like Rush and Yes but I was never really into it."

"I don't remember much from that gig to be honest with you," says Mike. "That whole period is just a group of gigs to me. There was a couple of dozen that we did and they all kind of blur together. I remember it wasn't a full gig and was just a few songs, but that whole period was fun to play out. We didn't have a following at that point and just had friends coming to see us. But I just loved playing onstage, and it was one of the highlights for me back then."

Other gigs were soon booked at a variety of venues with L'Amours becoming a regular haunt. A sweaty, shadowy, grimy, sticky-floored cellar located in an industrial part of Brooklyn, L'Amours was a product of the same school of thinking that gave the world CBGBs and the original Marquee in London – an unwritten motto of "pack 'em in, serve 'em beer, fling together a stage at one end and you've got a rock venue." The kind of place that every rock fan will have been to, and, despite the obvious flaws, will have adored because of the intimacy. And Majesty were in illustrious company. Metallica, Guns 'N' Roses, Kiss, Megadeth, Judas Priest and Motorhead had all trod the barren boards at L'Amours at some point during their careers, and the venue remained active until early 2004 when it was finally forced to close its doors. One gig in particular, though, is carved into the memory of Chris Collins.

"I remember we were playing L'Amours, and of course this was a time when everyone was wearing Spandex pants," he explains. "So I figured I'd wear some, too. But halfway through the set, they ripped open right in my crotch. So there I was, on stage, trying to sing with my balls hanging out of my pants! But all kinds of things used to happen during those gigs. We were playing a gig at the Right Track Inn, and we had taped four tables together to make a stage for me. Right in the middle of the show my right leg fell through a hole in these tables. And I was stuck, trapped there, trying to sing with one foot through the stage, and the other one on it. I couldn't move!"

Yet, not all of those early appearances were lighthearted adventures, and not for the first time, the sledgehammer wit often adopted by Collins caused a great deal of internal band friction during one of their early gigs.

"We were playing one night and I was introducing the band. When I introduced John Myung I said something like [adopts booming announcer-style voice] 'and off to my left side, straight from the jungles of Korea... John Myung,' he laughs. "He got really bent and after the show he grabbed me and shouted 'Don't you *ever* mock me or my family again Chris! You understand?' He was so pissed off, so I never said that again! But Mike was totally cool about it. He was cracking up, and couldn't believe that it came out live in front of an audience like that."

But Chris also remembers other more bizarre and lighthearted moments he shared with John Myung.

"John was the kind of guy who would just hang out in the corner of a room and not say a word and then all of a sudden come out with something," says Chris. "I remember one time we were sitting in a studio and he had his hair down long in front of his face. It covered his face and his bass in front of him. And he just came out with 'Guys check this out – I can have a penguin ask for a peanut and jelly sandwich please.' And then he would play these notes on the bass that would sound just like someone saying, 'I am a penguin can I have a peanut butter and jelly sandwich please.' And you'd look at him like, 'What the fuck was that?'"

Throughout that summer of 1986, Majesty continued to make live appearances in the vicinity of Long Island and New York, and the positive reaction that their demo was achieving provided no end of encouragement. During this period, one of Mike's high-school friends, Andrew Ross, was acting as the band's manager.

"I remember I was paying attention to the band Inner Sanctum, the band Mike played drums with a little bit," explains Andrew. "There was one concert of theirs which was like an hour away from where they lived. They went out there and the bar was closed when they got there and was actually boarded up. It made me think about whether I wanted to do stuff like this myself, and I thought that I would like to get a chance to be a manager and see if I could do better. From those experiences, Mike knew that I wanted to do it and he called me when I was in college. That was towards the end of his first year at college and my second year, and he explained all about these guys he had met, how good they were and how they were quitting school and starting this band. He invited me to get involved as their manager, so I left college and just started from scratch really. I got a job working for a beer distributor and I used to use their van when we went out to do the Thursday night shows at L'Amours. I remember one time we had friends who wanted to come to the gig, but Mike didn't want them sitting on his equipment in the van. So they took a train and subway out from Long Island to Brooklyn, and I wouldn't have even known how to do that. They were at the show and I remember saying 'Sorry Mike, they are sitting on your drums on the way home – we're giving them a ride!'"

With Majesty receiving a decent reception from the regulars at the likes of L'Amours, Sundance and The Stage Door, Andrew was conscious that in order for Majesty to make the step up to the next level, the band would need to start headlining those clubs in order to hopefully attract the attention of record labels.

"We were trying to do that but it was hard. They had just got to the point when they were big enough to start thinking about that. They had gone from playing the Thursday night show to being on the bill on a Saturday night and they were the opening band for Talas. So that was a really big show in front of a lot of people and, after that show, they were offered a Saturday night as headliners. But that was when they threw Chris out of the band, and went from almost being at that next level back to having to start all over again."

Chris Collins recalls that from his perspective; he was struggling with the harsh reality of trying to balance a challenging day job with the musical demands of four psyched musicians, which began to put a tremendous burden on him.

"I was definitely unprepared for their professionalism and organization, as I'd never had guidance," he sighs. "There were other issues, as my family weren't in a position to let me get a job in a Deli where I had to wake up and be there at two in the afternoon to cut salami. I used to work 13 hours a day digging ditches, and then I'd come home and Majesty would be at my door, pissed that I was not ready. I had no time to shower, or eat, and it was one thing after another. After a certain point I was like, 'Wow, I'm like tired man. I need a shower, I need to eat and I have no energy to be artistic or inspired at all.' I didn't even want to be at band rehearsal. Plus, I don't think my parents recognized my talent or encouraged it. That caused problems with them that still have not healed to this day. I really had something, and that was the window of opportunity back in the Eighties, and if I had had a little bit more backing I believe that I could have pulled it off. I can still remember the point when the issue came up about my schedule and why I worked such a hard job. The band thought that I should get a lesser job so I could focus on them more. You know, my family would have thrown me out of the house! John Petrucci's family, for example, were very supportive of him. They bought him guitars, cars, and lessons because they recognized that he had the talent and drive to pull it off. And he did it. I didn't have that and you have to recognize that. It really was stacked against me."

Digging ditches aside, the other members of the band also felt detached from Collins because of his lack of a formal musical education. He had also come into the band once all the material had been written and, consequently, there had been no opportunity for him to gel with the band. There was also a fair-sized gulf in terms of their family backgrounds and, although by no means Chris's fault, the differences in attitude soon began to manifest themselves.

"He didn't play an instrument, there wasn't a musical connection with him," explains Mike. "And the same way his vocals were put on the demo as an afterthought, he almost kind of felt like that in the band. Of course we were really into Queensrÿche and Iron Maiden, so we were excited to have a vocalist who could actually hit those high notes. But we found out soon enough that there's more to a singer than just hitting high notes. By the time fall of 1986 came around, it became obvious that Chris was a whole different type of person than we were. You know, the four of us all came from responsible families, and normal Long Island suburban middle-class homes. Chris came from more of a reckless background. He was more of a rowdy kid and I think there was a little disconnect there as well. He wasn't always responsible and didn't have a car. The four of us had cars and would drive to and from rehearsals, but he would always need to get picked up, and never had money to contribute towards paying for studio time. And that's not to put him down. I'm just saying that he didn't really connect with the four of us the way we connected with each other."

John Petrucci: "John, Mike, Kevin and I had all been studying music and we were really serious about the whole language of it. And he was kind of out of the loop on that, which made it difficult. There were a lot of things that made it hard for him which really had to do with just how he'd grown up. I do remember that he had to work really hard, him being totally shot and trying to make it all work. Even though we all hung out together, and we were friends as kids, our backgrounds were so much different."

By the late summer, the rumbling within the band about the suitability of Chris had reached such a level that it was clear something would inevitably have to give. His stint in Majesty had only extended to 15 live performances, and he played his last gig on October 25, 1986, at the Stage Door in Deer Park, where the band had supported Talas. Time, and a certain degree of pride, has blurred the memories as to whether Chris resigned from his position or if he was fired, but the general consensus seems to be that their singer was sacked at the beginning of November.

"I really don't want to sound like I'm bad-mouthing him, but he was disconnected and didn't feel like one of us," says Mike. "In fairness, when we were doing cover songs as well as the Majesty demo songs live, such as 'Queen Of The Reich' and 'Take Hold Of The Flame' by Queensrÿche, 'I'll See The Light Tonight' by Yngwie, a Dio song 'We Rock' and 'The Gates Of Babylon' by Rainbow, he was great. We were all just very impressed with his range that he could sing like Geoff Tate, Ronnie James Dio or Bruce Dickinson. But he wasn't much of a frontman, and at that point it felt like four and one to us, and I think it came across that way to the audience. Plus, we had made big sacrifices at that point. The four of us had dropped out of college to really pursue the band and we were dedicated. Whereas I don't think Chris felt that commitment. To him, it was just a band to jam with, you know? It wasn't a specific incident in the end, it just didn't feel right. We wanted someone that felt, looked, acted and thought the way the four of us did, so we just decided we had to make the change. We broke the news to him and I'm sure he was hurt as nobody likes being fired. It's always a tough thing to do, especially when you have a connection with them on a personal level."

Chris recalls things a little differently, claiming, "I left the band after that gig with Talas. I got sick of working too many hours and having them on my ass all the time about band rehearsal. I remember telling John that I couldn't do it any more. I have a lot of respect for Dream Theater, so I don't want this to be misunderstood. They definitely forged their own road. They did it on their terms, and they succeeded at it. When I was in the band, I was looking to be a little bit heavier than what they wanted. They wanted to be progressive metal, and I never wanted to be in a progressive metal band. That's what caused the breaking up between me and the rest of the band."

"At first I was shocked when they told me," recalls Andrew Ross. "Then I began to understand his limitations and started to agree with the band. I remember saying that we should do a few big shows first and then think about making the change. But they had made up their minds and that was it. I think musically he did the Geoff Tate impersonation but they thought it was just too much of that one high note and not enough versatility."

The task of telling Chris that his services were no longer required fell to Ross, as he explains.

"It was really bad because it was their idea, he was a friend of theirs and they decided that it was part of my job," he laughs. "I mean, I wasn't getting paid to do the job and I wasn't really ready for that. But it was OK and he didn't turn on me or anything. I handled myself pretty well and told him the best way I could. I guess he was upset and I don't really know if he saw it coming or anything."

In reality, Chris's position within the band was always going to be unsafe. Any musical quibbling aside, Chris had a typical, hedonistic rock star approach, attracted by all the excesses and trappings that role would bring. The rest of the band were purely motivated by the music, and ultimately Collins was about as suited to Majesty as Axl Rose would be fronting Rush. But now, facing a future without a singer, Majesty had the trauma of trying to find a replacement who lived up to their self-imposed high standards. The impending holiday season gave them a welcome break to compose their thoughts and intentions before they even contemplated placing adverts and beginning the auditioning process. With their progress hindered and going anything but to plan, they must have wondered why they'd gambled their futures by leaving college for a band that had already partially disintegrated. They simply had to hope they could quickly find a new vocalist in order to kick-start their stuttering fortunes.

FEARLESS FAITH IN DESTINY

Locating a suitable singer with a distinctive voice and an ambition to match their own was an immense challenge, and the band placed adverts in the "Vocalist Wanted" section of numerous local music magazines hoping to find Collins' successor. But their search was proving fruitless, and even some of the vocalists whom they had earmarked as appropriate candidates rejected the overtures made towards them, as Mike recalls.

"There was a guy named Mike Tirelli and I think he sings with Virgin Steel or Jack Starr," he discloses. "He was our target, as he had this Ronnie James Dio voice, but he passed on us and just wasn't interested. But we were young and could have easily just been some garage band that would've never gone anywhere. Anyone who was going to work with us at that point had to have faith in us and in the music, as we had nothing else going for us. But we went through dozens and dozens of auditions during that period, and we were very picky."

"Mike Tirelli was a really good singer," adds Andrew Ross. "I felt that if we had got the band to that slightly higher level, and Tirelli had seen them play in front of five or six hundred people, we would have been able to talk to him. Instead we were nobodies and couldn't talk to him. But we talked to a lot of people. I remember speaking to a guy who had just made an album and was in Yngwie Malmsteen's band. He was living in California. I sent him a tape, and he said 'It all sounds good. Send me a plane ticket and get me a hotel room in New York and I'll come out and see you.' I mean, if the guy had come over, I could have bought him a beer but at 19 years old, I wasn't going to be sending anybody plane tickets!"

The band auditioned a female vocalist, Barbara Chiovelli, who impressed them sufficiently to ensure that she returned on a number of occasions, working on an early version of a song that would become "The Ones Who Help To Set The Sun" before they ultimately passed on her.

"You know what, I wish I had kept that tape as she was fantastic and had a lot of stuff that she had written herself and sang," says Ross. "But they really didn't want any part of it and said that they didn't want to be a band fronted by a woman. And they really didn't mean that in a sexist way, but marketing-wise they didn't think that could be successful."

The singer search wasn't the only challenge that faced the band. Although Andrew Ross had been doing a decent job managing Majesty, the band felt that they needed someone with more experience as well as those all-important record industry contacts to propel them to the next level. As fortune would have it, the solution wasn't too far away.

"My grandfather owned a movie theatre, so I used to work there at the weekend," Mike explains. "The general manager there was a guy called Derek Simon. He was only working there part-time as he was in the music industry working for a firm called Concrete Marketing, as well as managing a band called Fifth Angel. Derek and I became friends, I turned him on to our music, and we became very close. So it was around this time that he began helping us out wherever he could, and began to make some connections for us within the industry."

"Even though I was on the very bottom rung of the music business, I was still above anybody else the band knew," confirms Derek Simon. "I suspect Mike passed me the band's original demo as we were both into the same type of music. I had no idea what to expect. Sound quality-wise they sounded very embryonic, but there was definitely something there and it appealed as it was just so different to what everybody else was doing at the time. Those demos were all instrumental, and it was only later that I realized they'd had a vocalist previously. But it was slow going, and it was a whole new process for me at that point as well."

With Derek Simon being lined up as a replacement, the band then had the traumatic task of telling Ross that he was being sacked.

"They said that they wanted to have a meeting and they came to my house and told me," discloses Ross. "They purposely came to my house rather than make me drive an hour to where they lived, which I thought was nice of them. I was surprised and you could tell that they felt bad and cared, but they had been convinced that they were better off with someone else. My impression is that Derek told them that they were going to need someone more professional. My opinion was that I could have kept going forward if we had got Mike Tirelli in the band and I could have managed them. I also think that if we had then got a big record deal and needed a management company, I could have still been a personal manager or something. I think I had proved that I was good enough with people and professional enough that I could have done that. But the timing was relatively good for me, as I only needed one more year of college and they told me in the June. So I ran to the local community college and took a couple of classes to catch up and then I went back to college."

Apart from understanding the drive and determination that Mike Portnoy possessed, Derek Simon also recalls that, once he began attending the occasional band meeting, he discovered the other members of the band were equally focused.

"Obviously Mike was the most outgoing and gregarious, but it was plain that John Petrucci was also a force. Kevin Moore had a dry sense of humour and was incredibly funny and bright, but he was also quiet and introverted at the same time. John Myung would seldom say anything but was polite and smart. That's not to say he wasn't conversational or friendly, but it just wasn't small talk, so when he did it always struck me as carrying a great deal of impact."

John Petrucci also remembers being able to easily trust Simon with the band's affairs. The guitarist was particularly struck by the fact that the manager was one of their peers with a similar outlook on life, and a shared passion for their music, as well as possessing the required business acumen.

"Derek was the first guy to really come along who had an industry sense and connection," he reasons. "But at the same time, he was a friend and was on our level. So he was somebody we would look up to, and was the first person like that in our lives. He was really helpful, professional, and facilitated a lot of the initial contacts."

Ironically, the one problem that Simon couldn't solve was also the most pressing. Since sacking Collins, the band had auditioned around a hundred potential replacements without success, and throughout the spring and summer of 1987 they were gradually becoming despondent. They had filled the time by developing and recording vocal-free versions of the songs that would eventually appear on their debut album many months later. Indeed, with the audition process dragging, they even considered permanently remaining an instrumental act.

"There seemed so little prospect of finding the right sort of vocalist that we did talk about staying as an instrumental group. But we always knew that Majesty needed a vocalist to complete the sound," revealed John Petrucci in an interview in RAW magazine back in 1989.

"Yeah, we thought about remaining an instrumental band because we had a love for a lot of electric fusion and instrumental music like the Dixie Dreggs and the Mahavishnu Orchestra," adds Mike Portnoy. "So we were wondering if that was our destiny, and if we could maybe go down that route. I think we were capable of it with the music we were writing, as so much of it was instrumentally based. We kicked it around, but ultimately we decided against it because we wanted to be like an Iron Maiden, a Metallica or a Rush where it was really a band, and there was a singer with songs. We wanted to have a career and be a band with longevity, and really that would have been very difficult as an instrumental band."

In wanting to keep their options open, the former manager Ross had even penned an astonishing letter to Ozzy Osbourne's management team in early 1987, offering their services as a backing band. Receiving no response, they continued to search for a singer and, fortunately, their quest ended when a local singer appeared at Mike's house one September morning in 1987 to audition. Born in Brooklyn on June 16,

1951, Charlie Dominici is your stereotypical fast-talking, sharp-witted New Yorker. Amiable, generous and humorous with a singer's self-assurance, his childhood oddly mirrored that of Chris Collins, with his parents having moved away from Brooklyn to the safer surrounds of Long Island when he was a young boy.

"It was east New York actually, which is a part of Brooklyn now that you cannot drive through as they'll steal the hubcaps off your car while it's rolling," laughs Charlie. "Or you'll get shot before you drive away from the stop light. It's a very bad, bad, neighbourhood now, but back then it was mainly Italian and Jewish. So most of my childhood was spent in Long Island."

Although making his reputation years later as a vocalist, his first instrument of choice was the guitar after being influenced as a child by the likes of the Everly Brothers and Chuck Berry. Another huge inspiration were the Rolling Stones: "I don't care what the Dream Theater fans might say. If they have an open mind at all, they've got to admit that for a band to go forty years is something," he says. "And to this day, if the Rolling Stones are playing, I'll drop everything and go and see the show."

His parents were also keen to encourage and nurture the love of music that their son was demonstrating, with his father buying the budding guitarist a Sears Silvertone with a tiny amp for him to practise. Soon he had joined a three-piece band called The Rogues.

"Their keyboard player was classically trained and he turned me on to Dave Brubeck and music like that. That made a big change in my musical development, as before that I was pretty much into the Rolling Stones type of rock 'n' roll, and this guy showed me something a bit more progressive. I was about 13 when we played for my elder brother's kid's baptism. We also used to play in a hall, and hardly made any money. My Dad passed the hat around and *made* everybody cough up the bucks, and we ended up walking away with a couple of hundred dollars. We were thrilled to death, and that made me see music as a possible lucrative endeavour."

Charlie was also encouraged by his teachers to follow his passion for music, but not in the usual way of joining a school band or heading to college for further study. Instead they suggested that by remaining there he was only delaying the inevitable, and that it would be easier for all parties if he quit the school as soon as possible.

"They told me it was definitely better for me to get the hell out of there and just play my guitar," he jokes. "They actually called my Dad into the psychology office because of my behaviour at school, and said 'There's nothing with him. The only time that he's alright is when he's cranking it to ten – he was born to rock.' And it was true. It was all about making music because I had to. It came out of me like the way some people move their bowel – it had to come out and that was the way my music always was."

By the late Sixties, a seventeen-year-old Charlie had managed to obtain a record deal as part of a duo called Billy And Charles. An album was recorded and released, although Dominici admits that he was far from happy with the finished article, with the record label releasing a far more commercial version than he had intended. Deciding the pairing wouldn't last, he headed out to California where he "lived on the coast in a vw bus with a little stove and bed in it, played my guitar and watched the sunset for a year." After leaving those idyllic surroundings, he headed for Woodstock, where even in the mid-Seventies there was an annual festival and a spirited music scene.

"Anyone who was anybody would hang out at Joyous Lake there and play," he recalls. "I remember playing my acoustic guitar there for just a bowl of rice. So if I got hungry I would hassle the owner to let me play a set and give me some food. At the time I'd rather play for a bowl of rice than play for money as it was all about getting fed. One day I was playing up there and this big black guy comes in, jumps up on stage with me and starts playing the piano. It turned out it was Taj Mahal, and we had a great time. It was always like that at Woodstock. There were nights when you had people like Paul Butterfield, Chick Corea, the guys from Steely Dan, Howard Johnson and all these amazing jazz cats playing."

Eventually Dominici moved away from Woodstock and joined a succession of bands that included Otis And The Elevators, before becoming part of a bar band called Livewire. They were renowned for performing in all-night bars, and had an habitual stint in one insalubrious venue that only began at 3am and didn't finish until seven in the morning. "We'd come out of the bar saying 'Where's my coffin?'" smiles Charlie. Realizing that playing such red-eye gigs wouldn't aid either his health or career, he moved to Poughkeepsie in upstate New York where he joined a covers band called The Easy Streets, and later numerous other acts including Gunner and Thick As Thieves.

"I had been developing my singing by then, and I started to become a pretty good vocalist," he says. "I could sound like Sting, Steve Perry or even Stevie Wonder if I had to, which is great if you're playing in a covers band. But I was then approached by Franke Previte and Billy Elworthy, who were in another band called Franke & The Knockouts."

Charlie added guitars and backing vocals to the band's first, self-titled, album but the band's leader, Previte, decided to pass on inviting him to join The Knockouts on the tour. It was a move that Previte apparently soon regretted.

"I guess they had a little bit of a tough time hitting the high notes I'd been hitting, and recreating the double guitar parts that were on the record in a live setting. And when they did the second album [*Below The Belt*], although I didn't record with them, they asked me to go on tour. By then my anger had diminished and I thought there was no point in cutting off my own nose to spite my face. So I figured, what the hell."

By that time, the band also included in their line-up drummer Tico Torres who later went on to join Bon Jovi. But Franke and the rest of the band were seemingly unprepared for Dominici's hell-raising antics whilst on tour.

"I was like Keith Moon on the road," laughs Charlie. "I was the guy who would walk into a room where nothing was happening, make everybody go nuts, then leave the room and shut off the lights. There was one time when we were in Saratoga, and after the gig we were in a motel. I just started this whole scene and had everybody running through the halls naked, destroying the rooms, TVs being thrown out of the window, breaking into the coin machine in the vibrator bed and all this crazy stuff. As soon as I got all this going, I left and went down into the bus and went to sleep. The next morning, the tour manager comes in to the bus, sees me sleeping and says 'Were you in here all night' and I was like 'Yeah, I've been here all night. Why? What happened?' And that was the way it was. Everyone had to pay like a couple of thousand dollars on their credit cards apart from me. Finally they couldn't take me, and I couldn't take them any more, so I got sent home from California."

"I then moved back to Long Island as I was losing touch with my family," he continues. "My Dad had got real sick and passed away. When I came back I wasn't really doing music, and in order for me to keep playing I didn't know what to do. I didn't want to go out playing in bars as the bar scene in Long Island was really rough. It was like bikers and out-of-control drunks, and was far worse than it was in upstate New York. So I decided to do some club gigs, where you put on a tuxedo and play for someone's party or wedding. It served its purpose and made the money to sustain me. The main thing I did for most of those years, from the age of 13 to about 30, was to play in bands and play out in bars and clubs to the point where I was making a living. It also kept me playing and kept my guitar and vocal chops up. Of course I was successful at it, as I have always been a good salesman, businessman, musician and singer. So the combination was ideal, and I actually made some pretty good bucks. While I was doing that, I met this girl and she was pretty wild and was into bands like Queensrÿche, and as soon as I heard it, it struck a chord. I thought it was what I should be doing and really should stop the 'Oooh baby, baby' crap that I was playing. So I decided to go and find a band that were doing that."

Within a few months of scouring music store windows and local newspapers, Charlie stumbled across the advert placed by a local band,

Majesty. Making a call to the band, he made arrangements to meet with their manager to collect a demo tape and the usual biographical blurb.

"I looked at the paper and I remember seeing this advert and thinking 'These guys are either totally full of shit or they're frigging amazing'," he explains with a smile. "So I thought I'd better check them out. Their manager met me at a gas station one rainy day and gave me a cassette which was the Majesty demo tape. I took it home, and as everyone can tell you, you listen to that tape and it's a little sloppy. It was the band trying to do then what they later learned to do so well. They were all really young guys, but what they were doing was amazing. I remember when I first heard it, I couldn't decide whether they were accidentally playing this great stuff or they were so bad that it was like genius bordering on retardation. You know, like an idiot savant who would come out with an amazing equation that would baffle science, but can't tie his shoes! And even though I thought it was kind of in its early stages, I was interested."

As intrigued as Charlie was, his workload of club dates ensured that he was unable to make arrangements to audition for a number of weeks, and when he finally spoke to Mike Portnoy, he was dissuaded by the drummer's request for the potential vocalist to bring his own p.a. system to the audition.

"I told him that I'd get back to him," he says. "I wasn't about to start lugging a p.a. system down to somebody else's house. So I didn't go. Another couple of weeks went by and then I ran into John Myung at a music store, Focus Music in Long Island, where he was teaching. I had recognized him from the photo that I'd been given. I walked up to him and started singing to him – '*Do you need the walls to fall apart*' – that were some of the lyrics to 'Your Majesty' which was one of the songs on the demo. He gave me this typical John Myung look that was like 'This guy is from outer space'. Anyway, I called Mike again and he persuaded me to go down to his house for the audition."

Seemingly, Charlie's persistence in attempting to secure an audition with the band had also been directed at John Myung, who recalled being somewhat perturbed at discovering the man who'd been inundating him with phone calls had been offered an audition.

"Pestered was the understatement of the year," he joked. "That man started a real telephone terror campaign and got on my nerves so much with his 'Hey, I'm Charlie' that I wanted to strangle him. But one day I came to rehearsals and there he was standing there. The other guys in the band told me he'd come to audition and that was basically fine by me. But then they told me who he was and I freaked. I went crazy and said 'Oh no! Not that guy! I don't want him near me, get rid of him immediately!'"

Charlie had managed to lay his hands on a suitable p.a. system which he had transported to Mike's basement, but even though he had a wealth of experience to draw on, the audition was almost a complete disaster.

"We were auditioning everyone using all the 1986 Chris Collins Majesty songs," says Mike. "So all of the people we auditioned were trying to come and sing this Chris Collins style and that's obviously not suited for everybody, so most of them failed miserably. Charlie came in and was singing songs like 'Another Won' and 'Your Majesty' and all the songs from that era. Obviously that stuff was just way out of his range, and as soon as he walked in we all saw there was a big age difference. We were around 20 or 21 and Charlie at that time was around 35, so between the age difference and him not having that Geoff Tate or Chris Collins range, we didn't think it was going well."

"Of course, I had short hair and a bit of a belly because I'd been eating well and getting older, and those guys were all long hair and pretty skinny," agrees Charlie. "So I felt like I was back where I was ten years earlier. They played me 'Ytse Jam' and I tripped over my tongue. They gave me a couple of songs to sing, and they were just about to say 'Don't call us, we'll call you', as in all honesty I sounded just like an average vocalist trying to sound like the guy they'd got rid of. So I asked them to give me a lyric sheet before I went as I was always better when I had no direction. John Petrucci handed me the lyrics to 'The Killing Hand' and I just started singing it and they were looking at each other smiling."

Once the band had heard Charlie singing in his natural range and adding his own original vocal flourishes to fresh material – rather than simply trying to impersonate the operatic style of Chris Collins – they were stunned.

"We really were just about to end the audition when suddenly the real Charlie came out," says Mike. "Charlie's natural range, when he's being himself, is amazing. At his audition, we were able to hear that side of him and we thought we could utilize his great voice to give our progressive music a little bit more of a pop edge. He was also a great musician, and he did play the piano and guitar which we knew we could use in live shows. So that is the only time in the band's history that we actually had a singer who was a musician as well. At that point, we decided that he was going to work and we took the chance to go with him."

But the offer wasn't made to Charlie immediately. Always cautious about making any hasty decisions, Mike took the opportunity to watch their possible new singer in the live setting. Charlie was still performing regularly at functions and remembers the drummer appearing one night in the audience.

"He used to come to those weddings just to get another view, look into things a bit more, see what I looked like, how I sounded and how I acted," says Charlie. "Really it was to get to know me as he'd only just met me. Mike is a very detail oriented person – he likes to call himself anal but I think that's his humble side. It's the side of him that would rather admit to being anal than to being a genius. A genius is always going to be what the average person calls anal. They have a habit of paying attention to detail and don't like things to happen that they are not aware of, and Mike is that kind of person. But anyway, about a week later they called me up and offered me the job for a probationary period. Soon enough that expired and I was in the band."

Justifiably, Majesty were jubilant to have finally vanquished their vocalist woes and they could at last continue their quest for a record deal. But notwithstanding their delight, Derek Simon recalls being slightly uneasy about Charlie's recruitment.

"He'd kicked around in bands for years and had a bit of an attitude of 'Well let me tell you something about the music business'," he says. "I mean, he's a super nice guy but when you find something that you are so musically proud of and want to be so perfect, I thought that maybe we were selling ourselves a little short. But I felt we had to get on with it and he was the best thing that we had heard, and if the band had decided on him, then it was OK with me."

Indeed, to the outsider, the selection of Charlie may have seemed a tad peculiar. The age difference was immediately noticeable, and no matter how young Charlie looked, there could be no disguising the fact that, image-wise at least, he was somewhat incongruous. Unquestionably, he did have a superb voice but his natural technique was also far removed from the operatic approach that would seem to fit the band's music. The experience he had acquired over lengthy stints on the road would, however, prove invaluable to the band as they set about making the transition from prog metal wannabes into an act that would attract a long-term record deal. But there were still public misgivings. Writing at the time in RAW magazine, journalist Malcolm Dome had already spotted the potential flaws in their new frontman.

"My only concern is Charlie," he wrote. "His voice is magnificent, but his persona is too enclosed. Not the tallest of persons, Dominici actually accentuates his lack of height through his moves. This is their Achilles heel. And while it should be the music that matters, nonetheless image can make or break a band in the late Eighties. This band have the capacity and – in four cases at least – the look, to break big. But Dominici is there upfront, and I hope his own image problem doesn't turn the dream into a nightmare."

Despite such disquiet, the band pressed ahead and by early November Charlie had accepted the offer to join Majesty on a permanent basis. Vocals were added to demos for the songs "A Fortune In Lies", "Afterlife" and "The Ones Who Help To Set The Sun", and soon the band had another deft demo to hawk around magazines and record labels. At this point, Majesty were still rehearsing in Mike's basement in Long Beach, but with the two Johns and Kevin facing a two-hour round trip from their Kings Park homes, a new band head-quarters was needed. The solution was to rent a basement under a hair salon, Giordan's, in the Long Island town of Huntington, which dou-bled as both rehearsal space and centre of operations, and eased their commute.

One peculiar curio is a video bootleg from the era known as the *Majesty Basement Tape*. Recorded in the winter of 1987 in that salon's cellar, the fifty-minute recording features a fresh-faced Majesty tearing through their material and hamming it up for the solitary camera. With hefty posters proclaiming their influences behind them – such as Marillion's "Sugar Mice", Beatles' *Sgt Pepper*, Yes's *Yesshows* and a Neil Peart – the band run through a number of instrumental tracks as well as an unexpected cover of Cream's "Crossroads". Somewhat amusingly, the camera is manned by a pixie boot-wearing Charlie Dominici who hurriedly prances back into shot whenever his vocals are required.

"Had we ever known that stuff was going to be shown to the public 15 years later we surely wouldn't have acted the way we did," cringes Mike. "It's pretty embarrassing and was just some rehearsals that Charlie filmed shortly after he joined the band."

As with any band, the process of posting bulk copies of their demo tape and biography to radio stations and record labels was scantly rewarded. If the labels bothered to reply at all, it was in the form of those notoriously impersonal, pre-printed "thanks but no thanks" let-ters. But their luck changed when they received a call from a fresh-ly-founded New York label, Mechanic Records.

ONLY A MATTER OF TIME

In attracting the attention of Mechanic Records, Majesty had inad-vertently turned against the traditional, tried and trusted route of obtaining a deal. They had distributed numerous demos – along with the obligatory biography and glossy photo – to every record label they thought might offer them a contract. But Mechanic's initial interest was generated through chance rather than the result of the band's concerted attempts at self-marketing. Mike's close friend, Chuck Lenihan, was the guitarist with New York hardcore band The Crumbsuckers, who had already released an album on the Combat Records label. The head of that label was Steve Sinclair who soon left Combat to form Mechanic – which in turn was a subsidiary of the much larger MCA label. Lenihan had been openly enthusing about the material Majesty had been forging, and with his curiosity duly nudged, Sinclair requested that Mike send him a demo. Despite Mike now describing the quality of the demo he forwarded as being "pretty crappy", the label boss was still stimulated by what he heard.

"I discovered Majesty when the band sent me a tape in the mail. I listened to it and was very impressed with it," recalls Steve Sinclair. "I would always listen to every tape I received. Holly Lane and Jim Pitulski, who also worked with me at Mechanic, became aware of the band at about the same time. We all wanted to see if they could reproduce this live, so I decided to attend a live rehearsal. I drove out by myself to Huntington one night and listened to the band's entire set and was so completely blown away that I insisted that Holly, Jim, and my partner in Mechanic, Jules Kurz, drive out separately and hear what I had heard. It seemed absolutely amazing to me that musicians of this calibre could find each other and make this incredible music. It was incredible talent in its purest form. So about a week later, Holly, Jim and Jules drove out to Huntington and they were equally impressed. With that corroboration, I found the courage to sign the band."

In spite of the keenness shown by Sinclair, Majesty had already been courting another potential suitor in the shape of the well-regarded label Metal Blade, as Derek Simon recalls.

"Through my work at Concrete Marketing I got to know the guys at Metal Blade very well," he says. "I went to them with a proposal – let us make a record for you, and then we'll give you an override on the next couple of records once we secure another deal. We were ninety per cent there in terms of their head, Brian Slagel, agreeing to it in principle. Musically, it wasn't really his cup of tea, but he had heard enough good things about them and was completely open to it. Anyway, at that point the demos found their way to Mechanic. There were a lot of new labels popping up at that point, and majors like MCA were funding independent labels like Mechanic. They were run by three people – Steve Sinclair, Holly Lane and Jim Pitulski. None of us had much of a clue as to what we were doing at that point, apart from knowing we had to get the band recorded and get a record out."

"So just when I was talking about making one record for Metal Blade and then giving them a percentage of wherever we put out our next record, here comes Mechanic Records with a seven-record deal, which to the average Joe on the street was 'My God they want us for seven records, they really like us!' And, as we know now, that has nothing to do with reality. Mechanic had started to have a little bit of success with the label and they were making a name for themselves. I think they had released an album by a band called Bang Tango, and there was a little bit of a buzz. And the opportunity to be with a young, upstart label that wanted the band for seven records was just something that the band really wanted to do. But not having negotiated a record deal before and not being in a position to bargain very much, we left there with a pretty unfavourable deal. Obviously that's all in retrospect, as at the time we were just happy to have $30,000 to go and make a record."

Mike Portnoy: "At the time we were looking for something a little more committed than a one-record deal from Metal Blade. That felt like it was not really a commitment but more of an experiment. Ultimately, we went with Mechanic as they were pitching the angle to us that we would have the attention of a new label with a small staff, but we would have the backing of MCA who was the distributor. So that was the sales pitch they gave us, and we fell for it hook, line and sinker. But of course why wouldn't we? It was a record deal and was everything we had been striving for, and it seemed on paper that it was our big break."

Jim Pitulski, a self-confessed lover of the prog rock greats, still has vivid memories of the first time that he and his fellow Mechanic head-honchos heard the band's demo.

"I have always been a big fan of the likes of ELP, Genesis, Yes, King Crimson and Pink Floyd," explains Jim. "I was really blown away that there was this young, new band that was playing this kind of music again. I hadn't heard anything like that in quite some time, so it was really refreshing. The band had a bit of a buzz on them, so we started investigating them a little bit. We went to see them at their rehearsal studio and they just smoked us. We were completely blown away by their musicianship and the dexterity that was on display. It was just incredible. Steve signed them and then we kind of took it from there."

Buoyed by the willingness of the label to agree to a long-term deal, Majesty duly signed in June 1988, with their signatures being placed on the contract in a brief ceremony at the band's attorney's office in New York City.

"It's funny as in the pictures of us signing the contract, Kev actually has fingers crossed behind his back – though that didn't hold up in court," laughs Mike. "But it was an exciting day for us. I remember we signed the contract and then went out to one of my favourite restaurants, Goldberg's Pizzeria in New York, to celebrate. Then we went back to Charlie's apartment that night and celebrated with some champagne. It was what we had been dreaming about. Little did we know that it was the beginning of the nightmare."

The advance provided by the label totalled a meagre $7,500, which had to be shared between the five members. But despite the lack of an extravagant upfront payment, Mike recalls still being overjoyed at finally seeing some financial payback for the years of toil, and wasted no time in spending his portion of the pot.

"Of course, at the time we thought it was decent," he smiles. "But by today's standards it was a joke. I remember I bought three new Zildjian cymbals to use on the album, and a DAT player. I thought I was really hi-tech to be the only person in the band that owned a DAT player!"

Within the short space of a month, recording time had been booked at Kajem Victory Studios in Philadelphia, and Terry Date was selected to fill the producer's chair. Date was being managed by Derek Simon's employers Concrete Marketing and had previously created sharp-sounding records with Fifth Angel and Metal Church. In spite of his track record, it was Date's bargain-basement fee rather than his past album work that, as Derek Simon remembers, played a pivotal role in him being chosen. "He was just the guy who stepped up and said, 'Yep, I can make a record for $30,000!'" says Simon. "At that point in time everybody was recording albums for $150,000–$200,000."

Steve Sinclair: "As far as the advance was concerned, I thought it was fair. As I recall, the band had little interest from other labels. I think that Metal Blade were mildly interested but not enough to make a serious offer, although they may have made them one of their usual $10,000 offers. I had just recorded Megadeth's *Peace Sells… But Who's Buying?* album for a budget of about $25,000 about two years earlier. That was a great album, so I thought that I could make an even better album for $30,000. You have to remember that I was coming from an independent background where I'd recorded albums for much less, sometimes five and ten thousand dollars, so this seemed like a lot to me at the time. None of the stuff I was recording at Combat Records, such as Exodus, Satriani, Agnostic Front or Megadeth cost nearly that much. The additional cash advance was very small by major label standards but cash advances were unheard of in independent label circles, so I felt that it was quite fair and something I was unaccustomed to doing at the time."

For producer Terry Date, the approach taken by Majesty was far more elaborate than the more straight-ahead metal of the bands he had worked with earlier in his career. Consequently, he found himself initially bamboozled by the density and variance of their music, but any reservations he may have held as to whether he should agree to the project were quickly dismissed once he had actually met the band.

"The first thing I did was say to them, 'We really have to write this down because I can't hang with you guys musically with this stuff'," laughs Date now. "It was a little too complicated for me, so we spent an entire afternoon writing down the time signatures for every section. That was about the time that I realized I had my hands full. Typically, I don't get too involved in that kind of stuff unless it's something that sounds funny, but with those guys it was *so* complex. I mean, I knew it was complicated, but didn't realize quite how complex until we actually sat down and charted it out."

"But I actually always pick projects by personalities, sometimes more than music, as we are going to be sitting together for quite a while. I remember going to their rehearsal place below a shop that you entered through a trapdoor, which made it a little more mysterious and funny at the same time. I think I actually stayed with Mike Portnoy during rehearsals and slept out on his porch or something. Then we did the record in Philadelphia. But I was really comfortable right off the bat."

The sessions at Kajem Studios began on the evening of July 18, 1988, and the band's first foray into a professional studio was made even more daunting given that they had the ludicrously narrow time frame of three weeks studio time to record and mix the entire album. That pressure was also amplified by the fact that, in order to alleviate pressure on their already tight budget, the band would have to become nocturnal.

"The studio we were at ran itself in a funny way," explains Date. "They would put two bands in one room every day, and would have one recording 12 hours at night, and the other band during the day. So we had the night shift and would go in at six or eight and work until six in the morning, and then someone else would come in during the day. We all stayed in a two-bedroom condo together in Gladwyne. There were two bedrooms and a sleeper bed out in the living room. All six of us stayed there, so of course when things got a little testy there was no place to get away. But it was fun. I think we had three weeks, including the mix, but I just thought 'OK, let's go and do it.' Looking back on it now, doing that record in that amount of time makes me wish we could do that again."

John Petrucci recalls that although recording during the hours of darkness was an unquestionable hindrance, the band were too wide-eyed and enthusiastic about recording their debut to let it overly bother them.

"We were young musicians and for all of us it was a really exciting moment," he reflects. "Just to be in a studio that we had locked out for a few weeks – we really couldn't believe we were doing it. It was amazing just to see how the whole studio worked, and even finding out basic things like what an engineer did. We were just so inexperienced, I was even borrowing amps at the time."

Prior to Majesty's arrival in Pennsylvania, the last occupants of both the studio and their temporary digs had been Queensrÿche – a band that all the members of Majesty admired – who had just completed the recording of the seminal prog metal album *Operation: Mindcrime*.

"We stayed in the same house, and I remember telling them I wanted to stay in the same bedroom as Geoff Tate so that some of his vocal talent could rub off on me!" laughs Charlie Dominici. "But the main memory of that time is that we had like three weeks to record such an amazing amount of music and vocals. When I did my parts it was a case of sing, sing, sing. I did two eight-hour sessions and I was done. So I pretty much did a live performance. There were a couple of things that were hard to sing and I was pushing my voice to sing stuff that was out of my range to begin with. I'm not really a high tenor, and I was never trained by an opera coach like Geoff Tate. I was trained by bikers in the bars telling me to sing a song I'd never sung before or they were going to break my legs!"

The debut, *When Dream And Day Unite*, was duly completed within the allotted timescale with the final touches being added on August 12. Yet, whatever feelings of triumph the band had about completing the album must have been tempered by the knowledge that, given a more realistic budget and a few more weeks, it could have sounded so much better. The band had created a musically worthy album that was intolerably blighted by the production that shackles the music at every turn. Devoid of width and clarity, the sound staggers through each track, limping along and only just managing to elevate itself above that of a rough demo. John Petrucci suggests that a significant part of the problem may have been linked to the band's greenness in a studio environment and their lack of top-of-the-range equipment – something that can hardly have aided the producer who had such a limited time frame within which to work.

"It didn't sound that good," sighs John. "I really don't know why, but maybe it was just our inexperience. We all played the music to the best of our ability. There were a lot of notes, orchestration, and instrumentation going on, and we were an inexperienced band. The keyboards were inexpensive, and it's not like we had state-of-the-art stuff. We just had to work with what we had."

"Terry is an amazing producer and mixer and he has an incredible track record," argues Mike. "But that was probably the worst produced album he has ever made. Everything else he has done – like the albums he later made with Pantera, Soundgarden or White Zombie – sounds great. I think it was the limited budget and perhaps because we had keyboards in our band which was something he wasn't used to. Maybe that compromised the mix as he was working with an unfamiliar instrument. I don't know. Obviously the production and the mix sound low budget and didn't do the album justice."

Charlie Dominici: "That album reminds me of a powerful animal that's stuck in a cage. Mainly because of the production, but also the time restrictions of getting it all done in three weeks, and the limitations of the producer himself. My opinion is that Terry Date had a tin ear. The highs are a little trashy and the lows aren't very fat, and the way he buried my voice? He made it sound like I was two-inches tall. Other than that, I really feel the playing and writing, though not necessarily the vocals, was the real essence of the band."

David Prater, who would produce two of the band's later albums, was also scathing of the album's sound. "I didn't hear their first record until long after I met them. But when I finally did I was gob-smacked by how bad it sounded," he says. "I mean it's several degrees out of phase in the stereo soundstage. Terry Date was a very fashionable producer at the time, but this record didn't bolster his pedigree. I think he just became indifferent and stopped caring. It sounds like they were mixing by committee: 'Turn my bass up!', 'No, you're too loud!', 'No I'm not!'. Wasn't it Churchill who once said, 'A dromedary is a camel designed by committee?'"

In hindsight, Terry Date is in open agreement that the record suffered as a result of the time and financial constraints imposed on the band by their record label, but maintains he is still proud of the album and what it ultimately achieved.

"You can't really work that fast and be particular about the sounds," he says. "At the time, I was all wide-eyed and innocent anyway, and just happy to go and rip the record without worrying about the consequences. It's all about the music in the long run anyway, and the sound is a bonus. So performances were everything, and with the shorter time you suffer as you have to cut corners somewhere. These days, I would have budgeted and begged for more time. But it was what it was, and if that band from 1988 came to me right now and asked me to do the record, I would ask for probably five weeks minimum just to record it. I'm never completely happy with everything I do and there is always something that can be done better. But considering the parameters we had to work within, yeah I'm really happy with it. It did its job and it launched the band. The purpose was really just to expose the band to a larger audience."

"Terry Date was the band's idea since he had produced Metal Church's *Blessing In Disguise* that Dream Theater really liked," remembers Steve Sinclair. "Other producers were considered, the usual cast of characters, but I had a strict policy of giving artists complete freedom in the studio, with no pressure at all to alter their sound to fit any format whatsoever. So I never objected to any producer choices made by any of my bands. Nor did I try to influence them other than helping out when asked. Mechanic meant complete artistic freedom for artists. Terry did a good job of capturing the essence of Dream Theater.

Of course the recording quality could have been better, but the album accomplished what I wanted to accomplish and showcased their musicianship very clearly. So I think we got a lot of bang for our buck. The sonic clarity was enough to garner incredible critical reviews and hint at the tremendous potential the band had. My goal was not to break them with one album. I was prepared to wait it out over three or four albums."

John Myung is also sympathetic to the producer's work, but is realistic in his assessment of the album when measured against some of their later efforts. "When I compare it to other albums, I see it for what it was," he says. "It was just young kids making a serious attempt at our first recording. In terms of a sonic experience, it pales in comparison to our later albums that I love. I guess, in a way it is hard to compare things because the situations were totally different, but the sincerity is there. Even listening to the demo stuff, it gives you a sense of where we came from and now it's actually kind of difficult to play because it's so busy."

With promotional cassettes being printed and pressed, Majesty's debut was all set to be hyped and released when they encountered a major setback. A Nevada-based band had already registered the name Majesty, as Kevin Moore recalled in an interview at the time.

"Well, we discovered that there's a band in Las Vegas called Majesty who had been going for about 11 years. They'd never had any product out or anything, but had trademarked the name. And even though we offered to buy the trademark, they refused."

Consequently, they faced the horrendous but unavoidable scenario of being forced to alter their moniker just weeks before the scheduled release of their debut. With radio stations already airing advance tracks and informing their listeners the band were called Majesty, and with a large fan base already built around that identity, the situation was a nightmare.

"We were heartbroken as we'd spent a couple of years building the band's name only to have it taken from underneath us," grimaces Mike. "All the advance promotion that Mechanic were doing was going to be shot to hell as we were changing the name. We went through a whole period when we were kicking around various names and trying to find a new name. We had even come up with a symbol based around the letter 'M' for Majesty and that was on the cover artwork. So we started going through all these names and wanted to come up with a name that began with the letter 'M'. The two most popular ones that we kicked around were M-1 and Magus. But they never worked out and then we considered Camera, which wasn't a bad name, and then we thought we had found the name of Glasser. Our lawyer at the time was called Janna Glasser, and I don't know why the hell we thought that would make a good band name, but we did."

"We actually did a show in the fall of 1988 in New York which was the CMJ Music Showcase [on October 27, 1988]," he continues. "We did the show and at the end Charlie announced that the new name for the band was going to be Glasser. And there was just this dead silence in the room, with absolutely no applause. So our hearts sank, and a couple of days later we were in rehearsal and looked at each other and were like 'Are we kidding? Is this our name? This can't be for real.'"

With no resolution in sight, Mike had informed his father, Howard Portnoy, of their fruitless search for a suitable new name. As he wrote in the *Images And Words* fanzine, Howard explained that some of his more humorous initial suggestions were mocked by the band.

"Some of my early submissions were Rancid Nipples, Foley Catheter, The Silver Beetles, Armpit Sweat and my personal favourite Asparagus Piss," he wrote. "Michael read these to the band one night to a chorus of silly guffaws and boos."

Not dissuaded by their mocking retorts, Howard continued to wrack his brains for an appropriate name, and the solution came to him one evening in November 1988 while watching *The Last Temptation Of Christ* at a local movie house. Located at 701 Lighthouse Avenue, in the picturesque coastal town of Monterey, California, The Dream Theater was a beautifully decorated, art deco cinema which he and Mike had regularly visited. Despite thinking that Dream Theater was just another name that would be rejected, he still called his son on the off-chance it might be acceptable, leaving the idea on Mike's answer-machine.

"I remember I mentioned it to the rest of the band that my Dad had left a message a couple of days earlier suggesting the name Dream Theater," says Mike. "To be honest, I kind of ignored it and never brought it up with the band. I thought we had settled on Glasser and didn't want to open up another can of worms as we'd been struggling for weeks trying to come up with a name. Then once we all realized that Glasser was ridiculous, I suggested it and they all thought it was pretty cool. It really fitted what we were doing and sounded like a classic name – like Iron Maiden, Black Sabbath, Judas Priest and Dream Theater. Those two-word names just sound classic."

Apart from the band's relief that they had found an internal consensus for their new name, Janna Glasser remembers being particularly thankful that they had decided against using her surname: "I don't think I encouraged that, and in fact I probably felt somewhat flustered and uncomfortable with the idea," says Janna now. "I was relieved that they came up with Dream Theater – and I'm sure they're relieved now that they did, too. Glasser isn't nearly as catchy as Dream Theater!"

Steve Sinclair: "The name change was indeed a nightmare. We all brainstormed and came up with hundreds of names. I forget who came up with Dream Theater, but there was quite a discussion regarding the spelling of 'Theater'. Should it be the English 'Theatre' or the American 'Theater'? 'Theater' obviously won out and I'm glad because 'Theatre' seemed pretentious to me. And with a band already in danger of being called pomp rock I didn't want to encourage that point of view."

John Petrucci was, in hindsight at least, also content with the name change away from Majesty, revealing in an interview in *Metal Hammer* magazine that "I guess it was a blessing in disguise because some people say that the name Majesty was too obviously pompous. You can't really categorize the name Dream Theater. You say 'What kind of band is this?'" It's not like the band is called 'Faces Of Death'!"

With the name Dream Theater now firmly in place, the obligatory alterations were made to the album's cover artwork, and *When Dream And Day Unite* was finally set for release. The cover artwork was striking with its distinctly old-school prog rock-style illustration, depicting a young man about to be branded by the band's old Majesty logo. The logo itself had been stumbled upon by Charlie who found the design in a book of seals (the symbol is based upon one used by Mary Queen of Scots). The sleeve was created by New York artist Amy Guip, who had previously designed the covers for *Smashes, Thrashes And Greatest Hits* by Kiss, as well as two covers for another metal band, Fifth Angel. The suitably dreamy effect that the cover portrayed was created by utilizing a technique whereby Guip's original photograph was retouched and painted over.

"I had done a piece of artwork in college that symbolized where I felt A.I.D.S was going at that time," recalls Guip. "This had a scarlet letter 'A' which was being branded onto the chest of a photo of one of my college mates. That I believe was the inspiration for the piece. They thought it would be great to do the same again but using the letter 'M'. The model was the same college friend, Steve Burman, who was on the original image that I'd created in college. The one thing I can remember about that sleeve is that the film with the photos on was left in a cab after the shoot – which made Steve *very* mad. But we eventually found it. It took about four days for it to come back and thankfully the taxi driver returned the film but not the camera!"

Released on March 6, 1989, and dedicated to Mike Portnoy's late mother Andrea Held Leone and Charlie Dominici's late father Ralph R. Dominici Sr., Dream Theater's debut was a fearless statement of intent. Certainly, leaving aside the muddy production, Dream Theater would never sound quite this way again. Perhaps the most noticeable attribute this album possesses is the driving "widdlywiddly" that Kevin Moore adorns onto the tracks. Those prominent keyboards would continue to play a pivotal role in defining the sound on their later albums, but the ebullient, classic prog rock solos would never quite be as prevalent or fresh as on this debut.

The opening track "A Fortune In Lies" – a tale written by John Petrucci about an acquaintance who was arrested for theft and his subsequent experiences – is uncompromising and purposeful.

Crammed with infectious melodies and cutting guitar solos, it combines all the elements, influences and principles that Dream Theater stood for. With the odd nod to their musical heroes – a middle section having more than a passing resemblance to Marillion's "Forgotten Sons" – the track still showed enough originality to grasp any prog rock or metal lover's attention. It also showcased Petrucci's flair for penning a killer lyric.

"I've always been really interested in writing lyrics," he explains. "Even in school, we had touched on it a bit and I'd taken some courses that helped with that. I kind of found that I had a knack for it and I was just drawn to it, you know? I'd sit there and really study all the album sleeves and carefully read the Rush lyrics. I'd even write quotes down in my books and on my desk. So it was something that hit me from the beginning."

"Status Seeker" was the last of the album's tracks to be completed and the song was speedily composed over a two-day period. It was also the shortest song and was a deliberate attempt to create a single, as John Petrucci explained at the time.

"It was an example of us trying to get our style into a more accessible format and just a shorter version of what we normally do," he said. "So the record company at one point said 'Can you guys take your writing style and maybe gear it towards radio?' And without sacrificing too much, we just kind of shortened the normal format instead of going on for twenty minutes, and it was our first single."

Although never released commercially "Status Seeker", along with the hefty "Afterlife", had been distributed to radio stations as a promotional single, and after accepting that they were far from perfectly produced, the band had enlisted the help of Rush producer Terry Brown to re-mix them.

"As far as the basic recording is concerned Terry Date was fine, but when it came to the mix-down he was burnt out and consequently the final mix is lacking in places," said Petrucci. "Terry Brown, who because of his work with Rush is a hero to us, was brought in to mix them. We'd have loved him to mix the entire record, but I guess budgetary considerations precluded that."

Unlike many producers, who can be somewhat precious about another producer meddling with their work, Terry Date claims not to have been too upset by the band's decision to re-mix his original recordings – especially given that they were to be re-worked a matter of weeks after he'd completed them.

"That kind of stuff never upsets me, especially considering what they were trying to do," he says. "By the time they were ready to do some other mixes, I was doing other things and really what they wanted was that sound that he was known for. So I've had my stuff mixed by other people and I've mixed other people's stuff, and that's never an offence to me."

Those singles aside, the debut benefited from all those months honing the material before a record deal was signed. "The Ytse Jam" was an imaginative instrumental (its name being a reference to their past – Majesty spelt backwards) and the likes of both "The Killing Hand" – another Petrucci-penned sci-fi lyric – and the bombastic "Only A Matter Of Time" would also prove to be crowd-pleasing classics for years to come. Elsewhere, "Light Fuse And Get Away" and "The Ones Who Help To Set The Sun" were also filled with progressive melodies that cemented the album's impact.

"The first album was good and heavy," says Charlie. "There was lot of chunk happening. What really made me excited about singing it was that it was really us. It was who we were and we weren't following anyone. Sure, we were into Queensrÿche, Metallica and Rush but I didn't feel like their influences were really predominant. At that time, the band was a sum total of all those parts. The synergy was there, and we were really original. My only complaint about the albums after that was that I thought the band became subdued, commercial and a little more conforming."

Staggeringly, despite the all too evident audio imperfections, the album was to receive virtually unanimous praise from the rock critics. But then, the band's approach was a refreshing alternative to the likes of the unfeasibly popular Ratt or White Lion whose slant on rock was far from innovative, yet still sold vast quantities at the time. In a review for *Kerrang!* Derek Oliver enthused: "Here is musical dexterity I have not heard since the glory of the jazz rock days or the Dixie Dregs. . . Keyboards run wild in all directions, conjuring up sounds from the common Hammond organ to the more select poly-Moog. Meanwhile, the guitar playing is of such an awesome technical standard I was immediately reminded of a sensational hybrid of Jeff Beck and Phil Manzanera. Then there is the drumming to consider. We must all sit down now and breathe deeply because in Mike Portnoy I see someone who is clearly better than Neil Peart or Billy Cobham. Dream Theater stick out of the current scene like a sore thumb. . ."

Metal Hammer reviewer Valerie Potter was similarly gushing, describing it as "The most original and inventive record I've heard in many a long and weary month. These ex-music college students have gathered together a rich time bandit's hoard of musical booty plundered from the last twenty years of rock music, mixing it with their own inventive ideas, and moulded the whole into a veritable treasure trove of an album. . . An astonishingly ingenious opus from a new band." Hell, Potter even praised Date's no-frills production declaring that "Terry Date has done the decent thing and kept the gimmicks down to a minimum, letting the songs speak for themselves."

Malcolm Dome, in an article for *RAW*, declared the album: "A magnificent exposition of individual bravura. If Metallica had grown up on Styx or Kansas, this is what they might have sounded like. It's a gathering of influences to create a genre. They will carve their own niche, open up the way for others, but Dream Theater are special and unique." Writing for *Metal Forces*, Dave Shack was also awed, claiming that he was "hard pushed to criticize this album at all as there's not a weak track on it. An essential purchase for anyone whose tastes run from Rush to Queensrÿche, Kansas to Crimson Glory and stopping at all stations in between. Exquisite."

Seemingly in 1989, reviewers were queuing up to pour praise and goodwill on to this debut, even with its unquestionable limitations. Ironically, some of their more sonically lush later recordings wouldn't receive the same type of almost universal adulation. Yet the passion displayed by the likes of Derek Oliver didn't pass unnoticed.

"The most exciting review and the one that had biggest impact on our career was the review in *Kerrang!* and the subsequent articles that were written by Derek," recalls Mike. "He took notice and supported the band. That review was the highlight of our career for me at that time, as *Kerrang!* was my bible. All through the mid- and late-Eighties, I subscribed to that magazine and loved the whole metal world. And the article had a picture of me and the caption said 'Heir to the Neil Peart throne' under my photo. I was just ready to end my career right there and then. In the back of my high school year book, when I graduated in 1985, it said 'Mike Portnoy's future plans?' And I'd written 'To become the next Neil Peart.' So four years later, to be written up in *Kerrang!* magazine with that caption was everything I'd ever hoped to achieve in that part of my life."

Inevitably, there was also the odd negative reviewer who took pleasure from panning the band. The most memorable was written by one S. L. Duff for *RIP* magazine who berated both Charlie's vocals and also a perceived reliance on the past for their inspiration.

"Dream Theater aren't a true progressive band," he griped. "Rather they just replicate the progressive bands of 17 years ago – mainly Kansas, a little Yes and a whole bunch of Rush. Vocalist Charlie Dominici may be spending the next several years trying to shed the inevitable Geddy Lee comparisons and it's going to be a full-time job. . . These guys are top flight musicians. 'Tis a shame they've put their abilities to use on such backward looking music. I'm sure that they won't see it that way, and that everyone at Mechanic will think I'm a dick (it's OK, I'm used to it) but I still know that I'll never, ever listen to this record for my own enjoyment."

In an interview in the same magazine months later, Charlie was however quick to defend himself against the insinuation that he was merely a Geddy Lee sound-alike – a bizarre accusation in itself given that Dominici's voice is far less squeaky than Lee's.

"It's an inaccurate comparison," he said. "The first line of our song 'Status Seeker' may sound like Geddy singing 'New World Man' but I'm not like him on the rest of the album. Our music more than anything else makes people think my vocals are like Geddy's. Dream Theater has a progressive edge and lots of time-changes like Rush."

But there was another looming issue facing the band. Their type of highly technical music was hardly the height of fashion, with their music relating more to the progressive acts rather than the vast array of mainstream hair metal bands who were infesting the charts at the time – a fact that was noted by Kevin Moore.

"We did get concerned with what was happening," he revealed in an interview with *Kerrang!* "Classic Eighties bands like Metallica were happening while most of our influences on that first album seemed to come from the Seventies. We weren't expecting any miracles at that point and we knew the band had to develop."

Yet, for all the eulogies bestowed on the band by a majority of the specialist rock press, the album was a commercial flop and failed to chart in either the US or Europe. At the root of this failure was the lack of any significant support from Mechanic Records. Once the record was released, the label appeared to lose all interest in launching any sizeable marketing campaign, and a promised video for a single release, a domestic tour and a mooted slot supporting Crimson Glory in Europe failed to materialize. An early indication of the problems that were to face the band occurred when they played a showcase gig at SIR Studios for Mechanic (and the label's MCA bosses) a month after the album's release.

"There were only about forty or fifty of them, and it was one of the best shows that we did," explains Charlie. "But they still didn't get it. They didn't give us the tour or MTV video, and that was the beginning of the downfall for me, and I felt that we weren't going to be going anywhere."

The source of the label's sudden lack of passion has never quite been established, but both MCA and Mechanic boss Steve Sinclair bore the brunt of the criticism from the band and their manager Derek Simon.

"Steve Sinclair had to get marketing budgets from them for everything that he did, and MCA were never a rock powerhouse in this country," he says. "They didn't seem to understand rock music and certainly not something this far off the beaten path. It was just like 'No, we're not supporting it.' So we did this bit of a roll out, went through the name change and the artwork issues, and then all of a sudden the record comes out, and there really isn't tour support. We had some money to get Terry Brown to remix the record to get it out to radio, and I just remember being incensed that the MCA promo staff couldn't get anyone to play the record. I was still talking to the programme directors at radio stations and the guys who were doing the rock shows, and they were all saying they really liked it. So I'd feed this information to the MCA promotion staff with memos just to try and follow up on all these opportunities. I just remember hearing back from Steve Sinclair that 'Boy, you've really pissed them off now!' And I'm like 'Why, because I suggested there might be a chance of airplay for us at such and such a station?'"

"There was a period of time when we had conversations with Steve Sinclair and he didn't really think we had a single," he continues. "There was some talk of maybe doing some new stuff and adding it to the record, and maybe working a single. I know for a fact the band demoed a song called 'A Vision' and I think that was the track that we took back to Mechanic and said 'Well here, have this one,' but again we were met with flat rejection.

"I never really knew at that point if Steve Sinclair really liked what Dream Theater did, or whether he just thought it was an opportunity to sell some records. In truth it didn't matter. But I think his lack of enthusiasm eventually just came from getting turned down by MCA all the time he went to them for dollars. I think he was honourable, and didn't make the band promises that he didn't want to or intend to keep. But here was a guy who was managing a label and had other records and relationships to think about apart from Dream Theater. I think he finally stopped trying to push buttons because he was risking his relationships and Mechanic's future."

Steve Sinclair also recalls that, despite his best efforts to secure funding for Dream Theater, he was fighting the blatant indifference demonstrated by the men in suits at MCA.

"It's very important to differentiate between Mechanic's motivations and interests versus MCA's," argues Steve. "For the record, contrary to the usual version of this story, Mechanic did not break one financial promise made to Dream Theater. I wanted to make a video. I would have risked every penny on this band to break them but MCA, particularly Geoff Bywater and his bosses, Richard Palmese and Al Teller, listened to the album and they had a different attitude. They complained that there were no songs less than eight minutes, that the songs were complex and that there were no traditional verses and choruses. They complained that they couldn't possibly take that to MTV, where the pop song was king. So they refused to make a video. That left touring, press, album radio and college radio as possible marketing avenues. We serviced a single to album radio but they were not biting because the single didn't fit the format. We hired independent radio promotion people, too. MCA were also complaining to me that Dream Theater's manager, Derek Simon, was pestering them too much and he apparently ended up alienating some of the radio promotion staff. That's something I do not fault him for because he was just doing his job. He was a good man and better manager."

"With MTV and album radio knocked out, MCA became pessimistic about the possibilities of breaking the band," he continues. "On a positive note, the press and college radio were both embracing the band with open arms, but those outlets did not create the sales necessary to justify expensive marketing efforts. Sales were at about 30,000 when the band asked for tour support which MCA rejected. Derek Simon's fighting attitude was contagious. I was fighting with Bywater and Palmese daily to get them to realize Dream Theater's potential, but to no avail. They wanted Guns 'N' Roses and I think they thought of Dream Theater as some eccentric prog rock oddball band that was far away from being formattable. In fact, I now realize that they thought of me and Mechanic Records in the same way."

Jim Pitulski claims, though, that he was never convinced about Sinclair's desire to break the band and claims that Mechanic were seeking to move the label into a more commercial area.

"Unfortunately, just prior to the record's release, I left Mechanic to join Columbia Records," says Jim. "I guess the label had a shift and I don't think that the release was ever really supported properly. Things were changing in the world of music and Steve was looking for an LA, Glam, Guns 'N' Roses type of spin-off band, and the album just kind of fell through the cracks."

Steve Sinclair: "Jim Pitulski is wrong about the lack of support for Dream Theater being motivated by music changing and me wanting to find the next Guns 'N' Roses. I truly loved Dream Theater and I was from an extreme music background. I wanted to stick it to the man and change the world but I didn't know how. I knew that in their own way, Dream Theater were musical anarchists who wanted to obliterate the pop song and change everything, and I dug that. Dream Theater fell through the cracks because MCA did not have the creativity and imagination to innovate in the musical world. They could only imitate."

The fickleness of MCA/Mechanic proved exasperating for the band who had released the album with expectations of appearances on MTV, lengthy tours and healthy hopes of fame and fortune. But without the financial backing, the release was inevitably going to fall somewhat pitifully by the wayside.

"All the legitimate bands were making videos back then," says Mike.

"So that was probably the biggest disappointment of all and made us feel so illegitimate. We were the only band in existence without a video in 1989, and they didn't do much promotion. There were some magazine interviews and some press here and there, but the album pretty much went by unnoticed. But we were also very young and naïve. We were dealing with people like Steve Sinclair, and as a person he seemed like he genuinely liked the band, and really can probably get the credit for discovering us. But he can only take so much credit if he had actually done something for us – which he didn't. Granted he did give us our first deal, but he pretty much dropped the ball in terms of doing anything with us."

"I just remember the album coming out and then nothing happening," agrees John Petrucci. "It was all exciting up until that point. There was talk of a tour and that was dropped. So there was no support. In the beginning they were always there and we were constantly going into New York City and having meetings, hanging out with these people. Then there was no tour and you couldn't get these guys on the phone."

The lack of a tour was especially damaging to Dream Theater's aspirations. With the absence of a single and any lasting radio airplay, only a prolonged set of concerts could introduce the band to a greater audience. But following the release of the album in March, the band played the sum total of four gigs – all of which were within a short distance of their Long Island base – and one of those was the aforementioned industry showcase gig. Depressingly, the band began to realize that they needed to make a change of record label if they were ever going to progress. Yet a replacement label wasn't the only alteration four members of Dream Theater felt was required. Following the album's release, nagging doubts that they had quietly harboured over whether Charlie was their perfect singer grew to a point where they could no longer be overlooked.

"You've got to put yourself back in 1989 and look at the bands that were around," says Mike. "They had these really great frontmen who looked cool, were young and had these soaring voices. Charlie was 37 years old, kind of short and stocky with short curly hair, just didn't look like one of us, and it was hard for him to carry himself that way. I think it became obvious really quickly that as much as he had a great voice, he was just not right for the band. We kept trying to make it work but it never really mixed. We'd see bands like Iron Maiden and Queensrÿche and they all had young vocalists with great ranges and we kept wanting that. He would constantly be singing Elton John, Billy Joel or Beatles songs in rehearsals, and would sit down behind the piano or pick up a guitar and sing that pop sort of stuff. That was when he was really at home, and his voice was amazing when he was singing pop. I think he was just in the wrong band. I've always said this, but it was always like trying to have Billy Joel sing with Queensrÿche or Iron Maiden. It just didn't work."

"Eventually, we came to a point in the middle of 1989 when it was obvious we weren't going to be going out on tour and Mechanic had done promoting the record," he continues. "It came and went with a whimper. The biggest thing we had done at that point was two shows opening up for Winger in February 1989. So by the summer, we were disappointed with the label and we started to reassess and thought that maybe Charlie was a bit of a problem, too. We'd started to discuss it by that period, and by the fall of 1989 we had done one local show at the Sundance on October 14. That was pretty much the last show we were going to do for *When Dream And Day Unite* before thinking about a next record. It was after we'd done that show we decided that we wanted to make a change."

"It's never easy to let someone go," adds John Petrucci. "But the decision was an obvious one to all of us. We just knew we needed someone else. Of course we had a really great time with Charlie, but we just knew the pieces weren't all there yet. Ultimately he didn't quite fit in."

Derek Simon recalls that the band had backed out of informing the singer that his services were no longer required, and had instead determined that such a problematic task fell within the remit of their manager. This assignment for Simon had been made even more awkward given that Charlie had recently decided on a very visible and permanent declaration of his love for the band which shone out from the top of his left arm.

"We knew a fair amount of time before we actually did it that it was going to happen," says Simon. "But there never seemed to be the right time to do it. And then one day Charlie shows up with the Majesty logo tattooed on his arm. And it was like 'Oh fuck!' But I have a very strong recollection of the rest of the band saying to me 'We think you should do it.' I mean, even in my relative inexperience at that point I thought 'Guys, yes I'm the manager but you're his bandmates.' But the band had reached a consensus, so it was up to me to do it. It finally happened in the rehearsal space under the beauty shop where we would periodically have band meetings after rehearsals. There was a meeting and we were all sitting around and I broke the news to Charlie. And I think the first words out of his mouth were 'OK'. In retrospect, it was probably just a nervous reaction to the situation. But I don't think it was a complete surprise to him, and it was obvious that it was four guys versus Charlie."

Simon's perception that Charlie was expecting to be forced out of the band is confirmed by the singer, who maintains that by that point he had also grown weary and despondent. At the root of Charlie's dejection was what he perceived to be Dream Theater's failure to create more accessible material and their label's apparent abandonment of their cause.

"They told me that it wasn't working and I just basically said, 'Well, you know what? It isn't working out for me either,'" reveals Charlie. "I was feeling discouraged, we weren't getting what we had been promised, I was starting to feel the rift between the band and myself with the age difference. I was bringing up suggestions that the band didn't agree with, about trying to maybe write tunes that would be a little more appealing to the general public so we could at least get noticed. But they didn't agree with that, and felt we should be who we are and write our 18-minute songs, and if people like us then great, and if they don't, they don't. That sounds great when you're 20 or 21 years old, but when you are a little older than that, you've been there, done that and you don't want to starve for another ten years."

"But I have to be honest, they came to me first and said they weren't happy with what was going on. The band were feeling that I wasn't doing what they needed, onstage or vocally. I suppose that there may have been an opportunity there for me to stay on with the band. I could have said 'Look, let's work it out, talk about what's wrong, try and fix it, have another probationary period and see if we can work it out.' I know they are all good people and they would probably have gone along with that. But I basically felt it was like a marriage that had got to the point where we could argue some more, but there are things that aren't going to change through talking. So I thought it was a good opportunity to bow out gracefully, and that's what I did."

For all Charlie's endearing features, it can't rationally be denied that he often struggled to deliver the songs live. Footage from the era shows him straining to hit the high notes on the likes of "The Killing Hand" and "Afterlife", and although he readily agrees that his natural singing voice lends itself more to a pop style of music, he believes that a combination of his excessive partying and an emerging reliance on illicit substances ultimately sealed his fate.

"I started to have a few personal problems in my life at the time," Charlie reveals. "I was doing a little too much of the wrong things in my leisure time. You know what I mean? I got a little out of control, and things multiply, and it got to a point where the relationship with my girlfriend of the time fell apart, and that fuelled my situation to get a little more out of control, which fuelled my situation with Dream Theater to get a little less under control. It snowballed in the wrong direction. I kind of got a little rambunctious and the rock 'n' roll nut came out in me and just got crazy, which made things even worse. I was into substance abuse, drinking and hanging out all night."

"The thing is, they are a little bit wimpy when it comes to partying," he giggles. "I remember a couple of New Years Eves where they got a little out of control, but they are amateurs! In Franke & The Knockouts we were animals on the road. That is the school that I am from, and I grew up with the Rolling Stones, destroying rooms, having scores of girls in the rooms, drinking everything in sight and anything else that was available. I toned it down quite a bit by the time I got to Dream Theater, but the toned-down version of the wild animal was still too much for them. Mike and I shared some living space for a while. He witnessed a couple of my crazy parties and couldn't believe that I went into the studio the following day and still sang like I'd had 12 hours sleep. He was like 'I don't understand how you do that!' And I said, 'Well, you probably never will!'"

Despite Charlie's assertion, the band deny that his extra-curricular activities were even considered when they made the decision to replace him. With the music always being the central focus for the band, if there had even been a hint that his drinking and drugging were affecting his performance, it's likely he'd have been sacked far earlier. Indeed, the other band members and Derek Simon weren't even aware of any substance abuse during Charlie's tenure with the band.

"I wasn't aware of that," admits Derek. "But then, he wasn't part of the 'band of brothers' and didn't hang out with the band in the same way that the other guys did. I do recall hearing a rumour later on that he had been using drugs of some kind, but it wasn't on our radar and had absolutely no bearing on our decision. Remember, we weren't really a touring band at that point. The band were just playing locally and I don't recall any overnight trips where somebody's behaviour might become more apparent."

John Petrucci: "I didn't think like he was overdoing it, and he certainly didn't seem like that kind of guy to me. Maybe he was doing it secretly. I really don't know."

Charlie's claim is even more astonishing given that he lived with Mike for a period of time. The drummer was a notoriously heavy drinker and, in his prime, could have represented his country in beer consumption if such an Olympic event had existed.

"Contrary to what he remembers about him being a party animal and that we were all clean-cut and straight, he was living with me for many of those months and I was a full-blown drinker," says Mike. "Me and my friends would party and drink every single night, but it never got in the way of the band. So maybe that was the difference. It was never a problem, and I think I probably drank more than him back then. Maybe he was doing substances quietly in the closet without our knowing, I don't know. But if he thinks that factored into anything then he is absolutely wrong. That must be some sort of paranoia that was maybe built in later on, when he was reflecting on what went wrong, because that had no part in our decision."

"That is a shock," replies Charlie. "I think that is more of Mike's perception, and he probably isn't aware of how much that craziness did interfere. I think if I had been a little bit more clear-headed I would have taken some lessons and coaching, and some theatrical coaching. He doesn't realize the extent of the misdirection and misguidance of the path I was on. People tend to see what is happening on the surface and don't know how much of it is basic inability and how much of it is an effect from the way you're handling yourself. The band may have been looking at me and going 'Is this the best the guy can do?' The fact is that it was probably the *worst* that I could do. If I had got my shit together and given myself the chance to do the best I could, I would probably still be in the band today."

Within a couple of weeks of that fateful meeting, there appeared to be a glimmer of hope that he could make a permanent return to the fold. The band had been contacted by British prog rockers Marillion, who wanted them to open for them at a gig at the New York Ritz on November 14. The gig was critical for the headliners who were unveiling their new singer Steve Hogarth – who had replaced Fish earlier in the year – for his US debut.

"At that point we were Marillion fanatics," recalls Mike. "Albums of theirs such as *Misplaced Childhood* and *Clutching At Straws* were two of my favourites back then. So suddenly we had this big opportunity to support one of our favourite bands in November 1989, and we'd just kicked Charlie out. So we called him up and asked if he wanted to do one last show with us, and he was great and agreed to do it."

The fact that Charlie was open to a final fleeting appearance fronting the band indicates the lack of bitterness he might have understandably held. But he does confess he was silently praying that with a decent performance he might win over the band once again.

"I just wanted to do that last gig," says Charlie. "It was partly me wanting to redeem myself, and realizing that I had let myself get out of control. In fact, I'll confess that during the two weeks before doing that gig at the Ritz, I stopped my craziness, substance abuse and partying, and I did my vocal exercises. I also took a couple of lessons from vocal coaches, and when I did the gig at the Ritz, I was probably thirty per cent better than I had been. So I felt that I did a pretty good job that night."

The gig proved to be successful for both bands, with Marillion bassist Pete Trewavas recalling that Dream Theater's approach and attitude was a vast improvement on some of the support bands they had suffered in the past.

"Those tours were quite a slog for Marillion," explains Pete. "We would be treated like stars in Europe, and then we'd be driving across America in a mini-bus without any means of sleep or support. We were always a bit wary of support bands in America because they were usually *really* awful heavy metal bands. They were put on by the local promoter, and the bands were always someone's mates or the local hero band. A lot of them walked in with a bit of an attitude, so we would shy away from them as much as possible. But I do remember Dream Theater being nice guys, and having a chat with Mike about things. They were coming up and saying how much they liked our albums. Plus they were – and still are – amazing players. I can understand why they have the audience they've got. You've got to admire them for what they do, and I really respect them."

A stunning live performance by Charlie was not, however, enough for him to re-establish his place in the band. The reasons for Dream Theater wanting to replace him had been carefully thought through, and the band were firmly entrenched in their position. As Charlie admits, it had been "too little too late". Their next daunting task was to track down someone of the right calibre to take his place.

FIVE

THE CANUCK COMETH

The turn of the decade was a wearisome time for Dream Theater. Finding themselves once again lacking a singer, signed to an obstreperous label but still realizing that their debut had created enough of a splash to warrant continuing, their thoughts naturally turned to trying to find a replacement for Charlie. It was a process that would last for an agonizing 14 months before they located a vocalist they were comfortable with and, more importantly, one who was at ease with their idiosyncratic method of working.

Perhaps predictably, given the band's problems with Charlie, they were determined to ensure that his eventual replacement was vocally versatile but also possessed a personality that had no desire to change the band or exert too much influence on what they saw as their territory – the songwriting. With most of their contemporaries allowing singers total control when it came to vocal melodies, Dream Theater's somewhat unusual approach of directing potential front-men to sing in a specific way wasn't welcomed by all who attended their rehearsal room for an audition. But then, at least the band were being candid about their intention to avoid employing any vocalist who suffered from the well-known malaise of "Lead-Singer Syndrome". As a band where music was always the priority, the mere idea of having a frontman consumed with concerns over his image or believing himself to be the only onstage focus would have been plainly ludicrous.

One of the first singers to be seriously considered for the role was John Arch. Arch had found himself at a loose end after his departure from Fates Warning following the release of their 1986 album, *Awaken The Guardian*. "John was actually the first person that we approached," recalls Mike Portnoy. "We were all Fates Warning fans and as far as I was concerned, he was the best singer out there and totally unique. To me it all made perfect sense. He was one of my favourite singers, he wasn't in a band and we were looking for a singer! John was already a friend of ours and was a fan of the music, so he decided to give it a shot."

Ironically, Arch reveals somewhat ruefully that his fleeting, backstage discussions with the band a few months earlier may have played a part in their decision to dismiss Charlie. Of course, he was hardly the first person to suggest that Dominici's live performances occasionally hampered Dream Theater, but when doubts were raised by someone as influential as Arch, the band were bound to take his observations seriously.

"The first time that I met Mike Portnoy was when Fates Warning were playing a gig down in Long Island around 1986," says Arch. "Jim Matheos [Fates Warning's guitarist] introduced me to him at that show. I hadn't actually heard of Majesty at that point, but Mike gave me a tape of the band and I was really impressed. I spoke with the band a few times after that and some of the members did approach me when they were playing here in Connecticut [February 13, 1989, Toad's Place, New Haven]. I remember we sat down and talked, and they asked me what my opinion was as to whether they should keep Charlie in the band. The thing is, I thought their musicianship was astounding but if there was a weak link in the band it was the vocals. Charlie was a very good vocalist, but I saw them live many times and he would have a hard time with live performance. His voice wasn't really that strong and wasn't really suited for Dream Theater's style of music. So I said that with all due respect to him – and I didn't want to take anything away from Charlie – but I just felt that for the future of the band it needed to be said."

Although harbouring doubts as to whether he wanted to return to the full-time rigour of recording and touring, but not immediately dissuaded by the three-hour commute to Long Island from his Connecticut home, Arch agreed to a provisional meeting one weekend to tentatively establish whether the two parties could work together. Certainly, in theory at least, the two looked to be perfectly matched. Arch's operatic vocal style, and his progressive metal background with his previous band, were characteristics that were high on Dream Theater's list of required attributes for their next singer.

"We just talked about things and took things really slow," he says. "Those guys are really smart and they were concerned as to whether I was ready to commit full-time to a band again. I was married, had a mortgage and responsibilities, and didn't know at that point if I was ready to go. But I did have that yearning to get back into it, and what better opportunity than to hook up with Dream Theater? So I was working with them for a couple of weekends. I remember the first weekend I went down and we hung around, kind of talked logistics as to how it could work, and whether I would have to move to Long Island. The second weekend was getting in the practice room with the band and belting out some old songs."

Those crude four-track demos included the likes of "The Killing Hand", "Only A Matter Of Time", and even a rattling version of Fates Warning's "The Apparition", and these imperfect recordings would later surface on many an unofficial bootleg. Although a seasoned professional, Arch confesses to being somewhat uncomfortable with the band's rigid ideas of how they wanted the vocals to sound.

"The band were like, 'This is what we want you to sing'," he explains. "That's not how most bands do it but that's how Dream Theater work. It puts a lot more pressure on the band members to write the music, to write the lyrics and then write the melody lines too. That was what differentiated working with Dream Theater from Fates Warning, where I wrote all the lyrics and melody lines to music that was pretty much really written. So there were two compositions that were being put together. That, combined with always being on the spot and having everything recorded, made it a little uneasy for me. I was so used to having a closed practice session and working on material until you feel confident that you're going to be proud of it when other people hear it. So I am a little nervous about having everything recorded, because not every night is a good night you know? That's just the way I feel. Mike is fanatical about recording everything that's done, which is very useful as a tool as far as the writing process goes. But I don't like other people hearing *everything* because there are some embarrassing moments. When I did go down to rehearse with them, they wanted to record it and listen to it after and see if I was fit for the band. But of course some of the songs were released on some bootlegs and they aren't my proudest moments."

"I mean, it's intimidating just being in the same room with the guys as they are such technical and creative musicians," he continues. "I remember Kevin Moore being very intense. We were going over the music and he was playing some very different things in a dissonant key and wanted to know what I would put over that vocally. That was like one heck of a test. They would also play some difficult sections to me from their new songs, and would say 'What do you think you would put to that?' which kind of puts you on the spot. That's not my most creative moment, sitting in front of people under pressure. My most creative times are sitting alone with the headphones on and being able to explore in my head melody lines, and to work on things that way. I would have thought that they were confident in my ability by my resumé and what I had done in the past but that's all fine and good. They gave me a great opportunity but in the end the timing was everything."

The prospect of prolonged periods away from his home and his wife – who was expecting their first child – wasn't a desirable proposition for Arch, and by the second weekend of working with the band he was already feeling homesick. Waking up at Mike Portnoy's house early one Sunday morning, waiting for the band – who are notorious night owls – to surface from their beds, Arch made the decision that he couldn't give Dream Theater the devotion that they expected.

"Dream Theater gave me an awesome opportunity," he explains. "But at the last minute I did get cold feet knowing that I had a child on the way, and didn't think I was able to make that kind of commitment. But even back then I think I realized the talent and dedication that these guys had, and if you can't do something one hundred per cent then you shouldn't give anything at all. I didn't want to be misleading them. So I remember waking up one morning at Mike's house after rehearsal and I told the guys how I felt and they totally respected that and I went on my way. I missed a golden opportunity but it was a trip to be able to sit down with the guys from Dream Theater and just listen to them play."

Mike Portnoy was particularly affected by the decision, later describing himself as "heartbroken" on Arch's return to Connecticut. The pair would, however, finally work together many years later on Arch's 2003 solo EP *A Twist Of Fate*.

With their first choice of singer declining the option of joining them, Dream Theater placed numerous adverts in the "Musicians Wanted" sections of the local and national music press. Fortunately, the band's debut had created a presence and the Mechanic deal – however superficial and shaky – was still in place, so there was no shortage of rock wannabes willing to mail the band their rough 'n' ready demos. In all, around 200 cassettes were received, and although many were of such abysmal quality that they were immediately rejected, there were a handful that showed enough potential to warrant an audition.

John Hendricks, a well-groomed Floridian with the kind of blow-dried, bulbous hairstyle that gave him the appearance of a New Kid On The Block, had supplied just such a promising demo.

"I was a student at the University of Miami Music School, and I had auditioned as a singer in a blues class," recalls Hendricks. "One of the people in that class was a guy named Mike Bauer, who had been in a band with Mike Portnoy back in Junior High. Bauer told me that he liked my voice, that Dream Theater were looking for a new singer, and said that I should send something up to them. I knew of the band already, as one of their roadies was also at the school, so there was a bit of a buzz about the band. So Bauer made the connection, and I sent in the demo which was about an hours worth of prog stuff I had written. I then got a call from either Mike or Kevin who said they liked it and wanted me to go up to New York."

Hendricks arrived in New York in December 1989 and formally auditioned for the band, although as he remembers, the audition didn't go especially well.

"It was far from my best singing moment," he laughs at the memory. "There was one night that Derek Simon came by, and I sang through all the songs live and it just wasn't great. The next day they called me up and said 'Well, as long as you are in New York, why don't you come by and we can work on some stuff?' So I went to Kevin's house, and they had me record 'Metropolis' which they liked enough for them to take to Derek Simon. Then I did another day of live stuff, and again I didn't sing well."

With both Hendricks and the band realizing his auditions hadn't gone according to plan, Hendricks returned to Florida to continue his studies. But he maintained a friendship with the band, and kept in contact with Kevin Moore who kept him up to speed with developments.

"I remember I told Kevin that I could do better and he said 'Send us some more material that shows you can sing live, and I might be able to get you another audition.' So I sent them another tape, which had cover versions on it, and in late January 1990 they asked me to go back to New York. I remember we did two rehearsals and I hung out at Mike's place and it went a lot better."

Indeed, the band were sufficiently enamored with his style of delivery to book time at Garrett Studios in Lynbrook, New York, to record demo versions of "To Live Forever" (a U2-inspired track that had been floating around since the Dominici days) and a new song, "Don't Look Past Me".

"That session went well and they wanted to move forward with it. I was up there for about three weeks, and really that was to see if we meshed as personalities. So I'd stay at Kevin's for a few days, then the two John's and so on. It all really felt so right. I remember working on 'A Change Of Seasons' and it felt so exhilarating and felt like a dream situation. It felt like we were on the same page musically, we got along, they were great guys, their families were totally cool and it was so much fun. At that point they were sold on the idea of me and they told me they wanted me to 'Go back to Miami, quit school and we want you to have the gig. You're the guy.' So I went to Miami, quit school and packed everything up. Then two days before I was due to go back, Derek Simon called and said it wasn't going to work out."

Seemingly, despite the band's confidence in Hendricks' ability, both the record label and Derek Simon had remained unconvinced.

"There was a period when the band had told him that he was going to be the guy," says Derek Simon. "When the band first made the decision that he was going to replace Charlie I just thought 'I don't know about this one!' There were even discussions on how he was going to relocate himself permanently to the New York area. But I had reservations from the word go, as I felt he was too pop."

"He didn't have that Bruce Dickinson or Geoff Tate soaring voice that we were really looking for, and had more of a Peter Gabriel type of approach," adds Mike Portnoy. "Yet we thought that there might be something unique there and flew him out. But he looked nothing like us, and had very short hair and looked almost like a new wave type of guy. So the image factor was a big concern for us, but we really liked his voice."

John Petrucci: "We were taking a chance going with him in that direction. I remember us talking about maybe having to change the type of presentation we were trying to make. We were really into progressive metal and the whole image of having long hair, and he came along with his short hair and looked pretty quirky."

Hendricks also recalls having lengthy discussions about how he could change his appearance in order to become a more natural fit into the band's image.

"Yeah, at the time it was all about the long hair. We had discussions where they said to me 'Don't cut your hair. We're going to get extensions for you.' We never did that but it was a big concern of theirs. But the overall vibe I got was that the label just wanted a different voice. I think they were after the Geoff Tate approach, which wasn't really what I was about. But I have to say that at the time, not getting into the band was a really big blow. It really caused me a lot of problems in that I lost a year of school and had to take a year out. I wish they had said something to me like 'This might not work out. Take the risk but know that this might not happen.' Then one thing led to another and I stopped singing. Oddly enough, when *Images And Words* came out, I went to one of their shows and spent some time with John Myung. He really questioned me as to why I had stopped and because of that, I got back into it again. I did some studio singing, did a Neil Diamond record of all things and now I'm teaching choir at a Los Angeles prep school."

In what was rapidly becoming a farcical and protracted search for a singer, the band next began working with Seattle vocalist Steve Stone. Stone had previously fronted the likes of Dallas-based Texas Diamond, Joe City, Xanthus, and Matrix before he replaced Queensrÿche's Geoff Tate in Seattle rockers Myth. Born Stephan Eriksson, his name had been changed to Steven Michael Stone by a Dallas production company as they believed the moniker was more marketable than the "difficult" name he was born with. Myth had been courted by a number of record labels, but when a deal failed to materialize, journalist Paul Suter (who was acting as their publicist) sent out a number of demo tapes to publishers and managers.

"Paul introduced the tape to a number of bands, including Lynch Mob, Steve Stevens and Dream Theater," Stone recalls today. "I'd heard Dream Theater's first album and the first thing I thought was, 'Man these songs are long!' Luckily I'd always loved progressive music and odd time signatures. Paul got a hold of Derek Simon, their manager, and Mike Portnoy called me after hearing [the Myth tape] to arrange an audition."

"It was around the spring of 1990 when Stone caught our ear," says Mike Portnoy. "He really did fit that Geoff Tate mould as he looked and sounded like him but he also had a bit of a Steve Perry edge to him. So it seemed on paper as though he'd be perfect and we flew him out. He looked awesome, had a great voice and it seemed like he was the man."

Echoing the thoughts of John Arch on the audition process he'd undergone, Stone recalls that despite being staggered with the band's commitment and technical prowess, he immediately sensed that his creative role in the band would be somewhat restricted.

"It was a really *interesting* audition," he laughs. "It was a seven-day audition with the constant reminder that the return plane ticket was in my pocket. But I never really took it in a negative way and I just thought 'Wow, these guys are really on top of it'. The audition was in a place under a meat store that Mike Portnoy had hooked up."

It was very intense as they were watching everything I was doing. I mean, I'd be singing a line, and they would be interrupting saying 'No not like that, like this.' One of the things that they would constantly emphasize about my singing would be that they wanted it to be more like [Journey's] Steve Perry, but I really wanted my own way of doing it and that was where some of the problems began."

Stone's initial audition and recordings were deemed enough of a success for him to continue working with the band, and fledgling versions of tracks the band had been working on – "Metropolis – Part 1" and "To Live Forever" – were knocked out and recorded in order to try and subtly acquire a new record deal away from Mechanic. In the meantime, the band continued to tighten their sound and work on new material with Stone being accommodated in turn at the band's family homes.

"I couldn't afford to live in New York on the $200 a week they were paying me," recalls Stone. "So I was living on the couches of everyone in the band and being shuttled from place to place. I ended up living on Mike Portnoy's cousin Ira's couch, as they'd decided to stick me there because it was becoming a problem going from parent to parent. At that time they were all living at home and had no real pressure. I mean, John Myung's only pressure was to work at the company one day a week; he had the rest of the time to devote to music, which he did. He used to practise seven or eight hours a day *before* rehearsal. The guy was insane! But he was so dedicated, and you really had to respect that."

But soon, the unsettled lifestyle began to take its toll on Stone. Missing his children who had remained back in Seattle, and realizing that his potential influence on the band's direction would be at best minimal, divisions became apparent between the two parties.

"A lot of the things that Dream Theater don't know are the conversations that happened when Derek [Simon] used to pull me aside," Stone explains. "In a nutshell, I had two kids who were five and six years old. Dream Theater was a huge break for me but I wanted to go and see my children during this process as I hadn't seen them for months. I wanted thirty days to go back home. Derek said something like 'Hey, I like what you're doing, everything's fine, but I hear you want to leave?' I tried to explain to him what was going on and that I had more than a little responsibility, and he almost threatened me with being black-balled if I didn't follow what he said. So I shut up, didn't say a word and just did my job."

Derek Simon: "I must say that doesn't ring any bells. I do remember the band doing the demos and thinking this was the guy. There were photos taken of the guys in the studio, all with big smiles and thumbs up, and we thought we'd finally found our vocalist. The demos were markedly better than anything the band had ever had from a vocalist before. It was all systems go, though I seem to remember Kevin Moore being very vocal about his reservations about Steve."

As striking as those recordings were, Steve Stone's tenure with the band was to come to an abrupt end following a less-than-inspired live debut on June 9, 1990, at the Sundance in Bay Shore, Long Island, when the band were supporting Marillion. Dream Theater opened their set with three instrumental tracks before Stone was introduced to the crowd to perform "Metropolis – Part 1", and both "A Fortune In Lies" and "The Killing Hand" from their debut album.

"I remember we accepted Marillion's invitation and we were originally going to do the gig instrumentally, as we figured it would be fun and we could play a lot of the stuff that we'd been writing," recollects Mike. "It just so happened that when the time for the gig rolled around, we were working with Steve and we pretty much had made him a band member. We'd decided he was it, he was up for the gig and he wanted in. It seemed like it was going to fly. So for this gig with Marillion we decided to do the first half of the gig instrumentally and then introduce our singer: Steve would come out, and we'd do the rest of the show with the new Dream Theater line-up. We did the show and halfway through I came to the front of the stage, made this big announcement and introduced Steve as our new singer and did a few songs. But it was a *complete* disaster."

"The thing is, I remember showing him Iron Maiden's *Live After Death* video in the days leading up to the show, and telling him the type of stage presence we'd always wanted our singer to have. And he came out and did a complete Bruce Dickinson impersonation," laughs Mike. "I mean, he kept yelling 'Scream for me Long Beach', which is of course what Bruce was yelling in *Live After Death* because it was recorded in Long Beach, California. He must have thought that the Sundance was in Long Beach, New York, because that's where he was staying with me. So he kept shouting 'Scream for me Long Beach' and everyone was looking at each other thinking: 'What the fuck are you talking about? We're not in Long Beach!' He kept running around the stage, back and forth and was the complete over the top opposite of Charlie. Charlie had been too reserved for us, but Steve Stone was so completely over the top that it was embarrassing. And because he was so over the top, within two minutes he had thrown his voice out and couldn't even sing. So it was a disaster. We left this big unveiling concert totally embarrassed. I even remember getting a couple of letters from fans who'd been at the show and they were *begging* us to reconsider. So it became obvious after watching the tape of that show that the whole Steve Stone thing was a sham and he ended up being a complete bullshit artist. It even turned out that his name was fake."

"It was just vocal gymnastics from the word go," giggles Derek Simon. "Rock star moves but with 'how-high-can-you-go' vocals, and at that point the band panicked. I still thought that he was the guy and that he just needed to be worked with, but the band decided that they needed to nip it in the bud. Yet, before that gig, it had pretty much been decided that he was going to be in the band. It wasn't even a case of seeing how it worked out."

"That was an *interesting* show," laughs respected rock journalist Gail Flug who was also present at the gig. "It was very surreal with Dream Theater doing half their set instrumentally and the fact they were opening for Marillion, so it wasn't really their audience. Dream Theater are a very laid-back band and Stone came out and was very animated. And I just remember thinking 'What the *hell* is going on here?'"

In hindsight, Steve Stone now readily admits that the gig was far from the shining performance and demonstration of his talents that he had intended. Realizing that the shambolic display had permanently eradicated his chances of joining, and sensing a growing impatience from the rest of the band, he was already making plans to scamper back to Seattle before they could wield the inevitable axe.

"I had been kind of nervous about the show, had warmed up way too much during the day, and harshed my throat out," Stone sighs. "So I had a bit of a struggle. That was probably the straw that broke the back for Mike Portnoy. I mean, I've had bad shows and good shows in my life, so I didn't think too much of it and decided that I could just learn from it and move forward. But I guess they had a meeting amongst themselves about the future and where I would stand, but at that point I didn't like the situation. I'd actually kept my return flight ticket to Seattle the whole time and I was planning on leaving the project, but didn't know how to tell them. The situation had become really uncomfortable."

"I remember they were having a meeting and I was actually packing my cases that night," he continues. "Then they came over to give me the news, and when they told me they no longer wanted me in the band, I was actually relieved and said 'Good.' Mike was like 'What do you mean, you're not unhappy?' and I told them that I was leaving at 10:00am the next morning to fly back to Seattle. Mike said something like 'You were going to leave tomorrow without saying anything?' He was really pissed about it and couldn't believe it. In fact, the last thing that Mike and I ever said to each other was when I asked him if he could give me a ride to La Guardia Airport. Mike said 'You expect *me* to take you to the airport?' But anyway, he did drop me off and not another word was said between us. But it made me see what was possible because those guys were really good. When you play with people who have that level of technical prowess it becomes an enjoyable thing. I walked away with no negative feelings at all, but realizing that if I wanted to stay in music at that level, I needed to get better."

The lack of a singer wasn't Dream Theater's only concern in the autumn of 1990. They were also continually troubled by the maddening battles with their record label who had already demonstrated a blatant lack of commitment with the woeful support and promotion they had provided for their debut. Understandably, Mechanic were unwilling to give the go-ahead for a second album to be recorded until a suitable singer had been unearthed, but the band had already realized that in order to progress they had to find a way to switch to a more accommodating label. Tentative discussions were made with potential suitors, with lawyers scouring the contract with Mechanic to try and locate a plausible escape clause. But with no label initially being willing to commit to them until they had solved the vocalist issue, the band were gradually becoming dispirited.

"We'd gone from what we thought was our big break with a record deal to finding ourselves with nothing," reflects Mike Portnoy. "The only thing that kept us afloat during that period was the music we were writing. We kept rehearsing and writing every night and that was what kept us alive. We'd show up for rehearsals and start talking about business – looking for a singer, getting away from Mechanic, putting out ads – and we would just be so depressed halfway through rehearsals [we'd feel] like quitting. Then we'd be like, 'Fuck it, let's just play', and we'd pick up our instruments and, by the time we left rehearsals, we were rejuvenated and suddenly remembered why we were together to begin with. But it was tough, and the business was really trying to keep us down."

"That was like the only point where I was really questioning what was going on," agrees John Petrucci. "It was a long period in limbo where we were still with Mechanic but trying to get away, and we were without a singer. We were all back to holding down day jobs, but still rehearsing five nights a week and writing all this music. We were having no luck with singers or with the label, and we were wondering what we were going to do. We had felt like we were really professional musicians after the whole experience of recording the first album and we really wanted to make that our lives. I remember wondering if we were ever going to do it again."

The next singer to enter the seemingly never-ending vocalist revolving door was Chris Cintron. Born Christobal Cintron and of Spanish descent, he had previously sung with New York rock act Reckless (not to be confused with the early Eighties Canadian pop-metal band of the same name). Reckless released their solitary *No Frills* album in 1987. Cintron had also provided backing vocals for Twisted Sister's *Love Is For Suckers* album the same year. Speaking with a genuine and honest affection about the period, Cintron recalls that Dream Theater had initially rejected his tape before contacting him again a few months later, to request he attend an audition.

"I guess they found a singer but he didn't work out, so they went through tapes again and I think Mike Portnoy remembered me," says Cintron. "So they gave me a call back and I went down to the audition. Apparently they liked me, so we started working together. It was a very interesting experience as they were all phenomenal musicians, but I remember thinking that to be their frontman I was going to have to take magic lessons to learn how to do illusions and turn into a tiger or something! There are only so many times that you can swing a microphone and jump around when they're going through their instrumental sections. When I first started working with the band, I remember they had a gig scheduled and I was willing to do it with them. But apparently, they'd had a problem with Steve Stone and done a horrendous gig with him, so they didn't want to make the same mistake – which I respected. I remember asking them why they were even looking for a singer as they were so good instrumentally. John Petrucci replied 'Chris, someone in your position really shouldn't be bringing that up, because you won't have a job!'"

As a result of their understandable reticence to risk unveiling another singer in front of an audience following their public humiliation with Steve Stone, the band performed a rare, totally instrumental, set at the Sundance in Bay Shore, Long Island, on November 17, 1990. Airing early versions of material that would eventually be released a couple of years later on what would become the *Images And Words* album, and an encore comprised of cover versions such as "Close To The Edge" by Yes, and Queen's "Bohemian Rhapsody", the band were at least able to maintain their live chops even if they still couldn't unveil a new line-up. In all, the band worked with Cintron for around six months, and together they began honing the material for their proposed second album.

"Chris really caught our ear and his voice reminded me a lot of Steve Walsh from Kansas," explains Mike Portnoy. "He had a really kind of bluesy, poppy, melodic edge to him but looked a little like Charlie, which was something we were trying to get away from. But after the whole Steve Stone incident we were very careful, and scared of making another wrong decision, so we didn't rush anything with him. We really liked his voice. He was the first person to ever sing "A Change Of Seasons" which we had written a year before, and I worked on vocal melodies with him."

But true to form, it wasn't long before both the band and Cintron began to develop nagging doubts about their relationship. Although there was nothing glaringly wrong with Cintron's approach, John Petrucci recalls feeling that the singer wasn't quite the perfect match they'd anticipated.

"The thing was, although I felt that he fitted in and had a very soulful voice, there was just *something* about him that wasn't right," says Petrucci. "He was ninety per cent there and I think ultimately it might have had something to do with his image."

Chris Cintron: "The only problem was that I don't think I got along very well with Kevin Moore. He was very musical and wanted to do things his way. I mean we all got along, but I just noticed that maybe if I was to get any resistance from anyone in the band it would have been from him. They had told me that I wouldn't see any royalties for at least two albums and that I wouldn't be involved in the writing at all. Everything was written and I kind of understood that, but for me as a frontman who is also a musician, that left a bitter taste. Eventually of course you'd get paid and the experience would be good, but it was just the fact it was like 'No, we don't really want to hear any of your input'. So I began to think, 'Well what am I doing here?'"

"After that I kind of screwed up because I started missing meetings," continues Cintron. "I remember I missed one important meeting with Derek Simon and the band told me that it was not a good move. They probably thought 'This guy is going to be a problem.' When I finally did meet him, we had an extensive conversation about what the road was going to be like for Dream Theater, and how it wasn't going to involve radio but was going to be a lot of work, long tours and just playing and playing. I was up for that, but I mentioned that I also wanted these guys to loosen up a little bit and let me in a bit more as they hadn't even seen what I could do! And they all kind of laughed, and I think Derek was excited about hearing that. So I thought from that point we were all gung-ho to go forward."

Throughout 1990, the band and their management had been having informal discussions with a number of prospective record labels, but one in particular had been showing an eager interest in Dream Theater's development. Atco Records (a subsidiary of Atlantic Records) were looking to enhance and expand their roster of acts, and one of their prominent A&R (Artist & Repertoire) men, Derek Oliver, had already been sounding out the band about a potential contract. Oliver, a respected music writer who had reviewed the band's debut in glowing terms in *Kerrang!* magazine a year earlier, had been working for Atco in Europe before being transferred to the New York office. After hearing rumours of Dream Theater's discontent with Mechanic, he contacted Derek Simon to subtly suss out their position.

"Derek Simon came over in early 1990 to the office and played me some stuff," says Oliver. "It didn't have any vocals on it but sounded great even on a weak four-track recording. So it was enough to convince me that this was a really great band that was getting better all the time, and I made a play to try and sign them."

With Oliver working out a strategy to encourage his Atco bosses to trust his judgement and sign the band, he became increasingly involved in considering their future direction and watched their singer tribulations with a keen interest. Critically, Oliver shared the same misgivings about Chris Cintron.

"We were working with Chris Cintron and were doing these demos and Derek couldn't get his head around it," explains Mike Portnoy. "We even went into the city with Chris and met with Derek Oliver at Atco. But Derek just wasn't into his look and wasn't completely sold on his voice either. So as much as we wanted to move forward, Derek couldn't really give us the green light as long as Chris was the guy."

This lack of commitment effectively placed the band in a holding pattern, yet they continued to work with Cintron believing that, given time, he could be moulded to become a more tempting proposition for Oliver. It was during this period that a bulky package arrived from Toronto, Canada, that would finally offer them a ready-made and perfect solution to their frontman woes. Containing a glossy black and white photo, a lengthy biography and a tape from his current band Winter Rose, Dream Theater were instantly blown away by the image and voice of one Kevin James LaBrie. What differentiated LaBrie from the previous potential singers was the combination a voice reminiscent of Geoff Tate, Steve Perry and Bruce Dickinson which was able to effortlessly hit the notes at the top of his range, as well as a natural, photogenic rock star appearance. In short, he seemed to be exactly what Dream Theater had been searching for.

"I remember we opened this package and the guy looked good, sounded amazing and had that voice we were looking for," effuses Mike Portnoy. "He had the range, a kind of pretty boy frontman look, and we secretly passed the tape around amongst ourselves [unbeknownst to Chris]. One night after rehearsal with Chris Cintron, we all got in our cars and pretended to leave. As Chris drove away, we drove around the block before the four of us reconvened at the studio and had a meeting. That was when we decided that our career was too important to just settle on a singer because we didn't want to hurt his feelings."

"We were pretty much set on Chris, and all of a sudden this guy from Canada came along," says John Petrucci. "So we got this bio and this 8 × 10 photo, and he looked cool. We heard the tape, which was live, and we were like 'Holy shit, where did he come from?' So we had this meeting to decide whether we should contact him and we figured that we had nothing to lose in speaking to him, but we obviously had to do it on the quiet."

Chris Cintron remained unaware of the band's scheming or the furtive long-distance phone calls being made to Canada, and arrangements were made for LaBrie to be shuttled to New York for a few days to meet the band. Arriving in New York on January 19, 1991 – the day the first Gulf War broke out – LaBrie was met at the airport by Mike Portnoy and John Myung with the intention of rapidly hammering out a few rough demos to scrutinize the singer's ability in a live environment, and establish whether they had enough in common on a personal level to welcome him into the band.

"I can remember that I stayed at Mike's place and he was living with his brother at the time," says LaBrie. "That very night we jammed, went out for dinner and we were really trying just to feel each other out. The next day we jammed a bit more and, as I was only down there for five days, we started demoing songs."

Putting LaBrie through a typically intense audition process, the band were instantly impressed with his vocal range and persona as Mike Portnoy explains.

"The very first thing he sang with us was 'Lovin', Touchin', Squeezin'" by Journey," he smiles. "James nailed it and we knew immediately he was the guy. Plus he seemed really cool and normal, and didn't seem flaky like Steve Stone. So we then started playing all the *When Dream And Day Unite* songs, 'Don't Look Past Me' and 'To Live Forever'. We also did some four-track work, including him singing a very early version of 'A Change Of Seasons' [an epic track which would eventually be released in 1995]. So that was over a four-day period, and by the end we decided that was it and our search was over."

Vitally, LaBrie's appreciation that Dream Theater were already being efficiently steered by Portnoy and Petrucci and didn't need a third person pushing himself to the helm was a key attribute that the band embraced. LaBrie also understood that Dream Theater were an unusual proposition in that the singer was never going to be the sole focus of attention.

"Yeah, his respect for our history was also something that we admired and that was a positive," agrees Portnoy. "On one hand, we welcomed fresh input and a new voice and wanted him to have a personality in the band as well. But on the other we were a little territorial over the songwriting as we'd become very comfortable with our format of writing. There were other singers that we'd worked with who were a little more forceful in trying to take over, and wanted to be the focal point. But LaBrie had a real handle and respect for what had gone before him, and didn't want to step on the writing chemistry. Also, when it came to doing interviews, we're not the typical kind of band where the singer is always going to be the focus. He realized that with the musicianship, the four of us were going to be of equal importance to the fans and to the media. It takes a special type of personality to be able to swallow that compromise. We were not going to change for anybody. We were doing what we were doing, and were looking for a singer who was willing to come along for our ride as opposed to trying to get in the driver's seat and change the direction."

"LaBrie was always resigned to that when he met with John Petrucci and Mike," adds Derek Oliver. "Their personalities are such that it is *their* band, they call all the shots, and the dynamics in the band are very, very peculiar. But I think LaBrie is a very smart guy – he just does his stuff and gets on with his life."

Having made the decision that LaBrie was to be their next singer, there was still the minor issue of informing Chris Cintron that he was out of a job. The task was made even harder by the fact that the band and Cintron had become close friends over the number of months they had worked together, with John Petrucci commenting, "We didn't feel too good about that but it just fell into our laps." A band meeting was hastily arranged, and Cintron was given the unexpected news that he wasn't fated to become their permanent frontman.

"We had a meeting and they told me, so it wasn't done over the phone or anything like that," explains Cintron. "They explained that they'd received another tape from a guy in Canada, who was more what they were looking for, and that they'd all voted but it had gone the other way. It came as a bit of a shock but also as a bit of a relief. The thing is, I was already going into the thing with some question marks in my head, and I don't think that is a good way to go into any situation, you know? But it was great working with them."

With the band already having two Johns, the thought of having two Kevins would have made conversations nigh impossible, so the decision was made for LaBrie to be known by his middle name, James. As the focal point of Dream Theater today, James LaBrie is, for the most part, an ebullient, bouncy and friendly character. Born in the small town of Penetanguishene, Ontario, on May 5, 1963, he led an idyllic childhood in one of the most scenic areas of Canada.

"Penetanguishene is actually an Indian phrase and it means 'Land of the white sands,'" says LaBrie. "But although I was born in Penetang', literally three miles away is another town called Midland and that was where I was raised until I was 18. It is right around the Great Lakes and it's a beautiful area. You know, there are lots of beaches, great stretches of water with lots of boating. And of course we used to get a heck of a lot of snow, so we were always downhill skiing or riding on snowmobiles."

LaBrie's family, and especially his father, were lovers of legendary crooners such as Tony Bennett and Nat King Cole, and it was perhaps an unavoidable consequence that he began to soak up the music that was constantly floating through the house. Even by the tender age of five, he'd taken an active interest in listening to and absorbing the music of other legendary jazz greats, as he recalls.

"My mother came from a family where she and her sisters would all sing in a choir and they had this folk group, where they would get together with guitars and sing," he says. "So there was always a lot of singing in the house, whether that was to the radio or records. We also had a piano in the house, so it was a very musical background. My father turned me on to Nat King Cole, Tony Bennett, Frank Sinatra and even Perry Como. Plus he was into big band music, too. So I was listening to these guys, and even at such an early age, I was thinking

'This is OK, these guys sound cool', but it wasn't until later on that I really appreciated them. Especially what Nat King Cole could do. I just think he had such a naturally gorgeous voice. It really was just magic when he opened his mouth."

Inspired enough to add his vocals to singalongs around the family piano, LaBrie was soon impressing at his school with his vocal ability, and began to be encouraged by his teachers to enter local talent and singing competitions.

"I was very competitive, though," he laughs. "I remember my parents telling me that if I came in second place I'd be miserable for a week. But it really helped to push me because I always thought I could do better. And of course, it soon became something that I was really into and because of that any other school subjects took a secondary position. Later, I actually sang in a barbershop quartet with my father, my Uncle Henry and my brother Bruce. That really helped me listen to the different tones of the voice. I was singing with a bass, a baritone, a tenor, so I would sing lead. I was about ten or twelve and we were only doing it on and off, but I loved it because it was all about our voices, and really trying to create a great blend. When we had family get-togethers we'd do a couple of numbers with all the relatives sitting around. Then they would get up and sing, someone would pull out the guitar, and a few would join in to sing other songs. Then someone would play the piano. So music was always a part of our lives, and made for a really fun time."

Today, it's almost impossible to picture LaBrie as anything other than a singer, but his initial instrument of choice was in fact the drums. By his early teens he had even taken to both singing lead *and* playing the drums simultaneously in a succession of bands. But as he reveals, it seems Mike Portnoy doesn't have too much to fret about in terms of competition for the Dream Theater drum stool.

"I played drums until I was around seventeen, which was when I realized 'You know what? I'm not really that great!'", he smiles. "I mean, I was OK and I could cope being the vocalist and playing drums in bands where we would be doing Zeppelin, AC/DC and Deep Purple covers where I would be the lead vocalist *and* the drummer. My first band was called Exodus, and I was 15 with a really high voice, so could do the vocals for Heart songs such as 'Barracuda'. But we also did covers of songs by April Wine, Anvil and Judas Priest. We'd do a couple of Rush tunes too, although I'd always be extremely intimidated by that because of the complex drumming. We also had a few originals, but if I listen back to that now, I just think 'Oh my God!' We played house parties or the local town hall, and we'd be selling tickets at school and on the street. The tickets were only like two or three bucks, but it was just a way for people to get some entertainment, get out and party. I think most people were sneaking in bottles of whisky! But in the end, I just thought it was all too much and wanted just to be a frontman and concentrate on singing."

Realizing that his home town wasn't exactly the centre of the rock or heavy metal universe, LaBrie made the decision that, after leaving school, he would need to move away in order to find the break with a band that he was searching for. With Toronto having a vibrant rock scene and only being located a hundred miles away from Midland, it was the obvious choice for his relocation.

"I knew that I had to get into a metropolis-type setting to find musicians to put together a really cool band, and possibly make something out of it," he says. "The record labels were in the city and I knew that if I put a band together, you could get into the bars and get people out to look at you. I kept getting the *Toronto Star* and checking the adverts for bands looking for vocalists. So I'd call these guys on the phone and we'd talk about what bands we were into. At that time I loved Rush, Queen, Pink Floyd, Yes, Black Sabbath, Judas Priest and Deep Purple. So I'd try to get the vibe as to whether they were into the same thing. I went down there one weekend and I jammed with three different bands and hooked up with these guys who were really good. They were into Pat Travers and Johnny Winter and also bands like Deep Purple, Foreigner and Kansas. So a few weeks later I moved in with the guitar player, Mark Waddell, and his family in their basement. We started jamming, and put together a band we called Trance, and hit the bar circuit. We did a few originals and it was a really good band. There were two guitarists, a bass player, a drummer and myself. It really helped me to develop my live interaction, and I remember I was always really pumped on Friday and Saturday nights playing these clubs. That was where I really wanted to be."

However, LaBrie swiftly recognized that although Trance provided him with an entertainment-filled weekend and certainly helped him sharpen his ability to work an audience, they were never a band that had the potential to advance to the next level. But, the maxim that you should always give every gig one hundred per cent because you never know who may be watching, finally paid dividends for James three years later, in 1986.

"We were playing at a club called Twenty Grand West in northern Toronto, and unbeknown to me a couple of the guys from Coney Hatch [Canadian rockers] were in the crowd," relates LaBrie. "At that time we were doing a version of Deep Purple's 'Child In Time'. So I was singing that right to the tee, doing all the high screams and all that stuff. About a week later I got a call from a friend of mine, a great drummer called Paul Marangoni, and he asked me if I knew Steve Shelski and Andy Curran from Coney Hatch. He then told me that they wanted to know if I would join their band, as their singer Carl Dixon wasn't in the band anymore. So I took them up on it, went to an audition and sang some of their tunes. They also gave me a new song that they were working on and asked me to write the lyrics for it, which I did. I came back and they thought they were great, so I ended up in the band. I was with them for almost a year and we did some touring and made a demo. They were with the Anthem label along with Rush but nothing really came from it. So we just kept doing the bars, and it was great for me to be playing in front of 2,000 people a night. But I was only 22 at the time and I was getting restless as nothing was happening. I guess we started butting heads a little bit, and I started looking elsewhere for another band. So I left Coney Hatch and they got another singer in, and eventually I think they went back to Carl Dixon."

Not entirely sure of which direction his next musical step would be, following his departure from Coney Hatch, James returned to the familiar surroundings of the Toronto bar scene with a band called Shock Candy. An adept covers band, they would run through pounding live renditions of anything from U2 to Mötley Crüe, although James admits with a smile that he "wasn't really keen on the Crüe numbers." For a couple of years it provided him with an income, but as he explains, he was rapidly becoming weary of endlessly trotting around the same old haunts.

"I was still into it and it kept me involved, but I was really fried on the whole bar scene and tired of all the confrontational situations that you're in with the members" he says. "So with a guy called Mike Stitt I started to do studio work. He'd be playing the keyboards and guitars, and I'd come in and start singing these songs. The tunes were a complete departure from what I was really into as it was more like a Gino Vanelli approach to music. It also had elements of The Police in there which was cool. During that time I was also working at a company where we did the lighting and built stages for bands, but I was in kind of a rut. Even then I was still putting feelers out to see if there were any bands out there that might be into doing a Genesis or Yes approach to music, but unfortunately I just couldn't find a collection of people who wanted to do it. After that, I put together a Journey tribute band called Positive Touch, which was named after a song on their *Raised On Radio* album. So we started playing the Journey stuff live, and on the weekends we'd be concentrating on writing and recording some originals."

Indeed, it was these original tracks that James created with Positive Touch that would, through a highly improbable chain of events, lead him to meet up with another keen Toronto-based musician, Rich Chycki, who just happened to be looking for a singer.

"What happened was that the bass player in Positive Touch, Brian, was buying a TV from this guy, and when they were over at his house they found that he was a musician," explains James. "So Brian asked him to listen to a tune we'd written and played him this tune called 'In The Hall'. This guy was called Rich Chycki, and he asked Brian if he could talk to me. I guess Brian was getting all paranoid and was thinking he was going to steal me away, but anyway he gave him my number and Rich called me up. He told me that he had a band and that he was writing all these originals. His last singer had been Sebastian Bach who had just landed the Skid Row gig about five months earlier. Anyway, he said something like 'Hey man, I don't want to steal you from this band, but I'd really like you to hear some of my originals. If you like what you hear, I'd love to get you to sing some of them'. So we met up and he gave me the tape and I went away and listened to it. It was really cool, sounded very refined and was well written, even though it was more like Whitesnake-meets-Skid Row. So I got together with Rich, recorded some of the stuff and put together a really good band called Winter Rose," he continues. "All the guys in the band were exceptional, and we started hitting the bars and did that for three years."

The man LaBrie replaced in Winter Rose also remembers being impressed with their new singer.

"It was a crazy thing for me to leave Rich Chycki and that band," says Sebastian Bach. "But I got a gig with a band called Madam X before I joined Skid Row. I remember going back to Toronto about a year later, and Rich had hired James. I met up with Rich at Rock 'N' Roll Heaven, as we were going to a gig there, and I met James. We hit it off immediately as we were both from the same area in Northern Ontario. Then I heard his work and just thought he was one of the greatest singers."

LaBrie: "At one point we did a tour with Lee Aaron and she started to say to me that she couldn't believe that the band hadn't been signed, and also said that I should think about pursuing a solo career. But I was trying to get a record contract with this band, so I wasn't even thinking about a solo career. But she contacted this guy called Pierre Paradis who was with a label in Canada called Aquarius Records. He was manager of a band called Voivod. So one Saturday morning I wake up in my apartment in Toronto, the phone rings, and it's this guy Pierre who had been at a Winter Rose show the night before at Rock 'N' Roll Heaven, which was a really popular club in Toronto. He said that he had loved the show and was impressed with what we were doing, but that he was more taken with me. He wanted to offer me a record contract with Aquarius, and wanted to put me together with Aldo Nova [fret-widdler guitarist] to write some music. Of course I was surprised that he didn't think Winter Rose had anything to offer. But he just said that he could see me sitting down with another couple of writers to shape something. So I told him I'd think about it, as I felt very dedicated and obligated to

Winter Rose. But I did call him back and decided to pursue it, while still trying to continue working with Winter Rose."

But before the Aquarius Records manager was able to try and forge an improbable working partnership between Aldo Nova and LaBrie, a chance telephone conversation between Paradis and one of the executives of Mechanic Records, Holly Lane, would provide an alternative route for the singer. Lane had told Paradis during the course of their conversation that their act, Dream Theater, had been without a vocalist for a number of months. Remembering that LaBrie had expressed an open adoration for progressive rock, he immediately contacted him to discuss sending Mechanic a demo. Sold by the plaudits that Paradis was laying on the band, LaBrie had no hesitation in sending a tape along with a brief biography and photo down to the band's Long Island base. In return, James received a copy of the "Status Seeker" single from the band's debut, but as he explains, a minor technical problem meant there was a frustrating delay before he could listen to it.

"The band had sent me a CD copy of the 'Status Seeker' single, but my CD player in my apartment was on the fritz, and I was really psyched to hear this song," said James. "So I went to a place called Majestic's Audio, and went in pretending that I was looking at a stereo system that I wanted to buy. So I said 'Listen – I want to hear this stereo system here as it looks pretty cool', and it was a huge system. And the guy went to get a CD to play and I said 'No, it's OK. I've got one here!' So I cranked up the sound and really was getting into it, and he was getting freaked out. Finally he said 'What do you think?' and I said 'Yeah, it's pretty cool' and left. Needless to say, I got my CD player fixed within a couple of days."

With the four members of Dream Theater also being optimistic about LaBrie's resumé and voice, they called him to discuss the possibility of an audition.

"I got a call from Kevin Moore who told me that they liked what they had heard, and that he hoped we could work something out. But later, he called me back and told me 'Sorry, we've decided to stick with the singer that we have', which was Chris Cintron. So I just wished him the best of luck. Then I get *another* call, this time from Mike Portnoy. He just said 'Kev, are you still into this? We'd really like to fly you down as we've reconsidered, and really want to jam with you to see if it's right.' So they flew me down, we jammed that night, everybody felt great and over the next few days we started to record some demos. And after that, they told me they wanted me in the band."

LaBrie instantly accepted the invitation to join the band and, with their line-up completed and secure, demos were recorded in an effort to help them attain a new recording contract – away from the debilitating clutches of Mechanic Records.

SIX

FACE THE BITTER FIGHT

With the initial LaBrie demos being passed to Atco's Derek Oliver for his assessment, the band were still confronted with the task of successfully negotiating an exit from the multi-album deal that shackled them to the Mechanic label. Despite attempting every method of extraditing themselves from the contract, Mechanic stubbornly refused all of Derek Simon's endeavours to speed up any departure. It took a certain amount of truth-bending and manipulative spin to finally seal the end of their tenure with the band, as Simon explains.

"Finally, Mechanic claimed to be willing to let us out of the deal but we could never quite get a release agreement out of them," he says. "It was everything from 'Sure, we'll get that to you,' to 'It's on the attorney's desk,' or 'Oh, the attorney had a cigarette on his desk and it caught fire but we'll get it to you' blah, blah, blah! Finally, I had to appeal to Steve Sinclair by saying, 'Look Steve, the band don't have a singer. We have no prospects of getting a singer. I've told them we are going to be out of this deal. It has been nine months and they are going to fire me if I don't get this done!' The agreement didn't appear immediately but it did within thirty days. At that point, by the time I played that card, we knew we had a singer. It was all part of the ploy to escape from Mechanic."

Steve Sinclair: "By the time the band asked to be dropped from Mechanic, MCA had already dropped them. So Dream Theater were still signed to Mechanic and I had to find another label to release them through, which I fully intended to do. So I sat back and waited for them to find another singer, and waited, and waited. They then asked to be released from their contract with Mechanic. Since I intended to find a major label/distributor that would understand and support them this time, and since I loved them so much, I refused to let them go. I was looking for another distributor and they were looking for another vocalist. They were out of commission due to not having a vocalist, so I felt that keeping them signed to Mechanic was not hurting their progress in any way. I wanted to continue to work with them but they obviously had lost faith in me and Mechanic. After waiting a long time, I think almost two years, for them to find a new vocalist, I finally lost patience. I asked them to find another label to purchase their contract from me and I guess that Derek Shulman had the vision and the intelligence to make them an offer. I don't remember the details of the buyout, but I recall the price was quite low. I didn't want to hold the band up or delay the progress of their careers. I just wanted to recoup some of what I had spent on them trying to get them to the next level – a task which I believed I accomplished despite all the controversy. It seems that the band have unfairly blamed Mechanic for holding them up but I can assure you that that is not the case. If I had thought that we were delaying their development at all I would have released them immediately."

Behind the scenes, negotiations with Atco's Derek Oliver led to a tentative agreement that his employers would sign the band once they had recorded a professional demo. The label was headed at that time by Derek Shulman, who had previously signed such acts as Bon Jovi when working at Polygram, and AC/DC and Pantera whilst at Atco. He had also been part of the experimental, progressive and well-respected band, Gentle Giant, who during the Seventies were on a creative par with the likes of Yes or King Crimson. Shulman had been interested in Dream Theater after hearing both their debut and the instrumental tracks the band had been working on prior to settling on a singer. This led to a so-called development deal – which effectively meant that the label would fund recordings and decide at a later date whether to fully commit to financing an act.

"I loved the musicianship and, when I became aware through both Derek Simon and Derek Oliver that they were available, I was obviously very interested," recalls Derek Shulman. "But at the time I first became interested, they didn't have a singer. So there wasn't a group per se, although they had some great tracks. It was odd to be talking about signing an artist based on four songs without any vocals. But eventually we agreed a development deal – and a fairly good one by the way. It wasn't a stiff contract. It was one where they would find the right singer and go into the studio, and then we hoped to finish off the deal."

Derek Oliver had also already settled on a producer for these official Atco demos, with the intention of using him for the proposed full album later in the year – assuming the sessions proved fruitful. David Prater (a former drummer with both Nektar and Santana) had enjoyed success a few months earlier by producing albums for the bands Firehouse and Diving For Pearls, and the crisp sound he'd achieved on those recordings had encouraged Oliver to contact him. Even today, Derek Oliver speaks of Prater's abilities in glowing terms.

"Prater is literally a genius," he enthuses. "I mean he is brilliant and should be making records right now. In my career I have worked with two geniuses. I believe David was one of them, and the other was Tony Visconti who produced T-Rex and David Bowie. He has an incredible mind, and having a conversation with him in person is just a trip."

But the process of finalizing the deal was far from straightforward. For a number of weeks, Oliver had harboured silent doubts over whether James LaBrie's voice was the perfect match for the band. Seemingly, his qualms centred on the loose four-track recordings that the band had done with James, and Oliver finally shared his worries with Prater.

"Based on the original demo tapes that they did with James, I didn't think that he was up to snuff," Oliver recalls. "But as I'll explain, I agreed in the end. I was impressed with David Prater at this point because I was really amazed by that record he'd cut with Diving For Pearls. David seemed to be on the up and I had a couple of meetings with him. We went up together one day to rehearsals in Long Island , and he loved the stuff and thought the playing was fantastic, so I decided on using him as producer. David thought that James would pass muster. James has an amazing range but can also be a little flat at times, but David assured me that he was good enough to coach him through that. We agreed this would be fine and that we should go and cut some demos. We struck an arrangement where David would cut three tracks, and then we would try and push ahead to the next stage of signing the band properly."

"Prater came along with the territory with Derek Oliver," explains Mike Portnoy. "We'd decided to bring James into the band in January 1991. James then came back in March 1991 to do some four-track demos of 'Learning To Live' and 'Take The Time', and while he was in town with us, we met with Derek Oliver and he brought David Prater down to rehearsal. We did have our wish list of producers that we wanted to work with [which included Chris Kimsey (Rolling Stones/Marillion), Terry Brown (Rush) and Neil Kernon (Queensrÿche)], but we were just beginning this relationship with Derek Oliver and he really wanted Prater to work with us. So we kind of got strong-armed into that. But we were excited to just have the ball rolling again, so we were willing to do whatever it took to get the whole process up and running. Prater had just done the Firehouse album which was very successful, and had just gone gold or platinum, so he had a top album at the time and we were easily swayed by that success."

As we'll discover later, the working relationship between Prater and the band deteriorated during a number of recording sessions, and even to this day acrimony remains rife on both sides. Consequently, the producer is unrestrained when recalling that initial meeting with the band.

"Derek Oliver asked me to accompany him to Dream Theater's rehearsal room in Long Island," he reflects. "Upon arriving, I witnessed an unpleasant exchange between the group and him, whereupon they insisted that he address their desire to know why they weren't already signed. Derek tap danced around the question and then introduced me as a friend of his. Shortly thereafter he asked them to play a few songs for me and they first played 'Under A Glass Moon'. Initially I was impressed, but soon grew tired of their ponderous musical ramblings. LaBrie hadn't been in the group for more than a few days and Derek Oliver hated him as a singer. LaBrie was trying his best to give a good impression, but Derek wasn't having any of it. We sat down after a few songs and Derek talked to them about working with me. They made it clear that they weren't interested in working with anyone who might suggest any changes in their music. I turned to Derek and told him it was time to go. I had heard enough. I said to Derek on the way home that first day that these were typical, self-absorbed Long Island rock musicians. Most of the time, guys like these aren't worth shooting. I told him I wasn't interested, but a few months later he told me he had signed them and that I had to do the record. He was an up-and-coming A&R guy back then. I figured I'd better get with him and I caved."

The desire to record such high-quality studio demos may, on the surface, appear an unusual step. Dream Theater weren't exactly hapless novices who needed to prove themselves. They were a band who had already released a critically well-received debut, and their musical abilities were beyond reproach. But the so-called Atco demos, which were recorded in May 1991, seemed to have the dual purpose of persuading the label to take the plunge as well as attempting to allay Oliver's worries over LaBrie's voice.

"Those demos almost served as a test run for us," says Mike. "We hadn't yet signed with Atco, and they basically put us in the studio to do that three-song demo. We went to Bear Tracks Studios with Prater, along with [engineer] Doug Oberkircher to do the three tracks of 'Metropolis', 'Take The Time' and 'To Live Forever'. I think the main purpose of them was for Derek Oliver to have these proper demos, with James singing on, that he could take to all the head honchos at Atco in order to secure a signing for us. One of the main people who played into that was Derek Shulman, who had been the lead singer with the prog rock band Gentle Giant, but was also the head of Atco during that period. Derek Shulman had signed Bon Jovi and Cinderella, so in the late Eighties he had a lot of success as a major label executive. He totally understood the world of progressive rock, and how we could do what we do but possibly cross over into a more commercial world as well."

Ironically, Oliver believes that having Shulman at the helm of the label wasn't as helpful as Portnoy imagines, claiming "Derek Shulman doesn't like to talk about or be reminded of his past in Gentle Giant. So he was kind of wary of finding a progressive rock band at that point. His perception was that he didn't want people to think that he was trying to recreate his youth. So it wasn't easy to get Dream Theater signed, even with Derek in place, though we did in the end."

"No, I certainly wasn't wary," counters Derek Shulman. "If Dream

Theater had been a Gentle Giant, Yes, or King Crimson sound-alike then I really wouldn't have liked it. I didn't even consider Dream Theater to be a progressive rock band. I hate labels, and the idea that Gentle Giant had been tagged as a prog rock band was absurd. I just considered that Dream Theater were a really good band who played good music. Had they sounded like Emerson Lake and Palmer, I'd have been much more scared. But they didn't. They just played very good songs in a kind of arranged fashion that wasn't three minutes of verse-chorus-verse-B section-solo- verse-out. And what's wrong with that?"

Viewed in the context of the early Nineties, when grunge was beginning to take hold and popular taste had deemed most heavy rock acts as passé, it was perhaps a bold move for Atco to sign a band as progressive as Dream Theater – a fact that Derek Shulman no doubt considered but remained unfazed by.

"Yeah, it was just at the beginning of the grunge thing," he says. "But generally, my decisions aren't based on what other people are doing. I felt it had to be either marketable or really good. And speaking as someone who signs artists and runs companies, when you see a marketplace going in one direction, you try and run in the other. But this was a band that sounded fantastic and also sounded like they could be commercially viable. They had all the chops down and were willing to do all the work that was needed to be done – like touring – as obviously it was going to be difficult to get them on the radio. So no, I wasn't wary about it because it was something that I really liked, and thankfully I had other artists who were selling huge quantities. I was pleased to be signing something that I personally could relate to, and who related to me not only as a record geek but as a musician who had been in a band who had done a similar thing to what they did – just touring and playing very good music."

While the band were ensconced in the lush, leafy surroundings of Bear Tracks Studios in Suffern, New York, with Prater recording those demos, an informal approach had been made by Oliver to *another* singer, Robert Mason, in order to investigate the possibility of him replacing LaBrie. The claim is even more astonishing when you consider the band's constant desire to control every aspect of Dream Theater's development, yet the move was apparently made without their knowledge.

"Something I feel has never been acknowledged is that I fought very hard to have LaBrie remain in the group," insists Prater. "I told Derek Oliver that he wasn't the one to make the call – I was. I'd produced a band called Adrian Dodz as a development deal with Don Grierson at Epic Records. I finished it just weeks before I started Dream Theater. I played it for Derek Oliver and he said he wanted their singer, Robert

Mason, to replace LaBrie. Mason turned it down. He thought he had a brighter future with The Lynch Mob."

"Robert Mason came into the office and we had a chat," admits Oliver. "I remember, he was very anti-joining the band which was strange. He didn't really have anything else going on, and the other music he was involved in wasn't in the same position as we had with Dream Theater, who obviously had a record deal."

Perhaps what is even more surprising is that Dream Theater's manager, Derek Simon, was also fully aware of the overtures that Oliver had been making towards Mason, but he had concealed the information from the band. This was probably a shrewd move on his part given the likely resentment and open hostility such a suggestion would have received from Portnoy and Petrucci. The pair had been wary when previous singers, such as Steve Stone, had tried to influence the band's direction and would hardly have reacted with glee if they had discovered that plans were afoot to potentially substitute their carefully selected vocalist without their consent. That said, Simon does downplay the seriousness of the proposal, claiming "I would recall if it was that big an issue, and it never got to a point where it was suggested the record wasn't going to go ahead if we didn't make the change."

Robert Mason: "Honestly, my friend and then Columbia Executive Derek Simon had been introducing me around in an effort to find a band, guitarist, writers and labels for me to join as a vocalist. I'd been given a Dream Theater demo tape by Derek who told me they were looking for a singer. I loved that type of music, but at the time I was probably a bit young and impulsive and wanted to do something a little bluesier. That was something that I wanted to make a statement with and I knew that was something which wouldn't have been encouraged in that band after seeing where they wanted to go."

"If Mason and Derek Oliver did have that conversation it was never brought to our attention," insists Mike. "I mean, not only did we never meet the guy, we never even spoke to him. But during that whole period, when you had Oliver, Prater and Jim Pitulski involved, there were so many decisions being made and conversations going on behind our backs, with them having ulterior motives and directions. So there were these powers-that-be having side-conversations with little conspiracies taking place behind closed doors. There really was so much of that kind of crap, so it doesn't surprise me. I mean, shit like that would *never* happen in this band today. It's unfathomable to me that people were making decisions for a band without them even being involved. But that was the way it was with us for many years, and it's the type of shit that breaks up bands."

"I really didn't know about that. Who's Robert Mason?" laughs John Petrucci. "But who knows what the hell else went on. The stupid thing about it is that it's not like we would say to them 'OK that's cool.' We had just gone through a year and a half trying to find the perfect guy, so we were hardly going to agree to something like that."

Thankfully, such drastic changes weren't needed and following the completion of the basic tracks at Bear Tracks, the remaining overdubs were carried out in the basement of Prater's apartment in Verona, New Jersey. Much to the displeasure of the band, each member would be called in turn to perform and record their parts individually at the home studio, and although the results were impressive, there was an underlying feeling that this method of recording had destroyed the band's newly fostered camaraderie. But such gripes aside, the three-song demo sounded crisp and achieved the aim of finally securing that record deal with Atco.

"They really were sensational," enthuses Derek Oliver. "For demos, they were amazing and we only spent about two or three thousand dollars on them. Everyone was over the moon about them, so we pushed the button and signed the band properly. At the same point, though, Epic Records had heard the demos and made a last-minute bid to steal the band from us, but we already had them under contract anyway."

In addition to Atco's initial outlay and advance, the band's new label also had to pay Mechanic Records compensation for Dream Theater's reneging on the agreed multi-album deal, although Atco boss Derek Shulman recalls that this was a relatively small amount. "It was almost negligible, was a very easy deal to do and I don't think there was a long-time override," he explains. "It was a straight buyout and a few thousand dollars. I don't think it was more than that."

"Basically we had to buy ourselves out of that contract," adds Mike. "Mechanic weren't willing to let us go. As much as they were not willing to get behind us and support us, they had us bound by contract. At the time Atco began to sniff around and show interest, Mechanic started to tighten the chain around us and wanted to hold us back. So when Atco and Derek Oliver were ready to make a firm offer to us, it became apparent that the only way we were going to be able to get out of our contract would be via a buyout that was funded by Atco. The biggest loss for us was that we had to give up our rights to the first album, which meant that neither Atco nor we could re-release it down the line. That was a shame but we had no choice at that point."

The frustration following the loss of control over any future re-releases of their debut was quickly diminished by the constructive environment that Atco were keen on creating for the band. Both Shulman and Oliver made it plain that they didn't want the band to change their approach to writing in an attempt to gain radio airplay, and during the protracted legal wrangling, Dream Theater were encouraged to work on new material for their proposed next album. It was during this time that fledgling versions of "Another Day", "Surrounded" and an instrumental track with the odd working title of "Oliver's Twist" (named, according to Mike Portnoy, in honour of "Derek Oliver's request to write a few more songs"). The latter would, after the addition of lyrics and a couple of edits, be renamed "Pull Me Under". With both the band and the label being delighted with these three new tracks, the decision was made that they would replace both "To Live Forever" and "Don't Look Past Me" – songs that had been knocking around their repertoire for a number of years – on the album's final track listing. Derek Shulman recalls being especially vocal in ensuring that the band remained true to their musical roots.

"Absolutely, I had been through that experience personally in Gentle Giant," explains Shulman. "Our music was as far as you could get away from commercial. We had a period in our heyday, when groups like Rush and Kansas came along, we saw these groups going from nowhere to multi-platinum and we were still chugging along selling 100,000 and never breaking through. So on our last couple of records, we decided to try and do what they did, and that was the biggest mistake on a creative, business and fan[-appreciation] level that we made. I could recount from those days and say to this band – who played an interesting but not radio-friendly music – not to sell out. That was especially crucial when they first started out, as that was when they would build their real fan base. I already had bands at Atco, such as AC/DC and Bad Company, who were on the radio, as well as bands that weren't on the radio at all but were breaking in a huge way, such as Pantera. Dream Theater were a band I knew would fit for Atco in terms of the picture I wanted. They were a true artist-band, who were going to make it on their musical ability and by touring. I was aware of that, and didn't want them to change or try and write something that was not really them. To try and manipulate them at the beginning into something they weren't would have been a disaster for them. So I am very glad we didn't shove them or try and bully them. I mean, they probably wouldn't have taken kindly to being bullied anyway, but we didn't even try. I had signed Dream Theater, not to try and create some 'new and improved' Dream Theater."

But there was still the outstanding matter of coming to an agreement with Atco as to who would occupy the producer's chair for the upcoming full album sessions, as Derek Simon explains.

"My recollection was that it all went pear-shaped from the beginning, at least on the business side," he says. "I was pleased David Prater wanted to make the record, but then the band's attorney called me and said that they'd just got the deal from David's management. It was something like four percentage points and $70,000. I mean, maybe we would have given Terry Brown that money at that point, but it was clearly a case of having the right deal but wrong producer. You know, we'll pay someone four points and $70,000 dollars but just not to him. Derek Oliver is one of the nicest people you'd ever want to meet, but he and Prater were very much in cahoots on the record. Certainly more so than the band would have liked, and I certainly felt excluded from the process. I called Derek Oliver, I told him that we were not paying this guy what he wants to make this record, and that we should go back to the list. But it was made clear to me that Prater was the guy who was going to make the record, and that we were going to have to compromise in terms of the financial aspect."

The drawback to Simon's argument was that as a new signing to a label, with only their commercially unsuccessful debut behind them, Dream Theater were powerless to object. A refusal to use Prater could have led to a dismissal from their new home, and at the time the band were understandably eager to please their new employers. Inevitably, Prater was hired to produce the album which had by now been given the title of *Images And Words*. Prater travelled to the band's Long Island rehearsal rooms and made basic live recordings of the songs that had been earmarked for inclusion on the album, and on October 14, 1991, the band began moving their equipment back to Bear Tracks Studios to begin the sessions proper, with Doug Oberkircher again employed as the sound engineer. But there was to be an unpleasant surprise for them upon their arrival. It had been decided by the label that the band's epic track, "A Change Of Seasons", was to be ditched from the album. Mike Portnoy was particularly crestfallen, given that the lyrics he'd penned for the track were of an extremely personal nature and dealt with the death of his mother.

"It was literally the first day we were in the studio," sighs Mike. "We were all excited to show up and finally begin the album. We had even done pre-production demos for 'A Change Of Seasons', so they'd given us every indication that it was going to be on the album. We showed up at Bear Tracks and then there was a phone call from Derek Oliver who told us we weren't recording that track. I remember spending two hours on the phone going back and forth, arguing, bickering and fighting, and this was how we began the sessions. We were starting out totally on the wrong foot."

"For the album we were trying to make for Atco, I felt that we needed to have a degree of commerciality," explains Derek Oliver. "I thought 'A Change Of Seasons' would have been far too long and taken up too much of the album. They had some fantastic material which was shorter, but they also had some long tracks as well. So it wasn't as if it was compromising their artistic vision by not allowing that track. I always felt that we would record that track, and in fact I instigated that later, but for *Images And Words* I felt that it wouldn't be right. You've got to get out of the starting gate. Don't forget it's very difficult for any band to have a record deal after being dropped and then getting another deal. I mean that's pretty tough, and I thought that the balance of songs they came up with before we went in to cut the record was just about right."

David Prater remains unrepentant about the decision, and claims that he refused to start the recording session until the record company had informed the band that the track was to be omitted.

"At the time of the recording, manufacturers of CDs would only allow 74 minutes of music, period," he explains. "Well, Dream Theater wouldn't hear of it. They wanted to do upwards of eighty minutes. At the time, that meant that what was essentially their first record would have been literally twice as long as their competition. It also would take twice as long to record and twice as much money in resources. Who in their right mind would want to listen to eighty minutes of this anyway? I ordered a work stoppage for two days until all parties involved figured it out. Remember, back then that track was over thirty minutes long. It would have been *Images And Words* plus 'A Change of Seasons' and then some. I said if you opened for someone on tour you would only play 45 minutes tops and really, more like thirty minutes. So, you would play one song and say 'Good night! We're Dream Theater!' It was ridiculous."

Prater's assertions are dismissed by Portnoy who points out that, at the time, "A Change Of Seasons" was only 18 minutes long and, with the other tracks totalling around fifty minutes, it would have fitted easily on to a single CD. But in spite of the band's vociferous protests, the track was ultimately cut on the strict understanding that Oliver and the label would allow them to record and release it at a later date. However, the resolution of this problem didn't solve the underlying current of unease in the studio, with both Prater and the band (specifically Kevin Moore and Mike Portnoy) regularly disagreeing over the changes the producer wanted to make to the material, and conflict between the parties became commonplace. To this day, emotions still run high on both sides when the session is recalled.

"Kevin Moore was absolutely intolerable," argues David Prater. "He insisted on renting a nine-foot grand piano and an arsenal of keyboards. You're talking $15,000–$20,000 just for the equipment, and our entire budget was maybe $125,000. Then it took him over three weeks to record his parts. I tried recording him the first day but it was too humiliating. He would do his lines perfectly and I would say 'OK, let's move on' but he would refuse. He was very passive-aggressive and kind of like a vandal with a can of spray paint. This went on for about an hour before I said, 'That's it. Doug [Oberkircher] you record this idiot'. After three weeks, Doug came downstairs into my office and said, 'We're done. Come and listen.' I went upstairs and was horrified at what I heard. He had intentionally played the wrong chord inversions for ninety per cent of his parts."

"What he did was criminal," he continues. "At a unit cost per day of about $2,500, he had spent 18 days on his parts. His little stunt cost us at least $35,000–$40,000, not to mention the aggravation and the toll it took on my staff. I was as mad at him as I've ever been in my life. I literally wanted to assault him, to make him feel as bad as he had made me feel. He was a rotten bastard then, and may be one now for all I know. After our little conversation, I told him that he was going to do his keyboards all over again, with me present. We knocked it out in a couple of days. The band felt that I wasn't musically sophisticated enough to notice altered chord inversions. This was their little practical joke."

John Petrucci denies that Moore had intentionally sabotaged the recordings, and rationalizes the playing of any erroneous keyboard notes as a result of their relative inexperience in constructing arrangements and performing in a studio.

"I don't know why he would say stuff like that," says Petrucci. "Of course Kev wasn't deliberately playing the wrong chord inversions. That was only our second experience in a studio and we were still learning about orchestrating parts and about space, and about being produced and producing. This stuff was still all new to us, you know? So there were moments – and it happens now but we're on top of it – where when you are in a rehearsal working on songs, you might not exactly hear what the other guys are doing. It was an archaic system when we were younger, huddled in a basement cranking out a sound where it all sounded good. But we never got into analyzing the voicings and inversions, so inevitably there were some clashes or wrong notes. And now, after a lot of experience we've a process where we sit down and write all that out to make sure everybody is on the same page. But back then, it was still a matter of experience, and that stuff was getting ironed out as we went and Prater was involved in that. But obviously there was nothing intentional. We weren't trying to perform musical malice."

Mike Portnoy: "I have no recollection of that," he says. "I just know that Prater was difficult to work with everybody, no matter what instrument was recorded. Prater had a knack for making people feel incredibly uncomfortable and making the sessions incredibly negative. I know that Kevin and I fought a lot with him. I think we were always the most protective of our music, and John Petrucci and John Myung were a lot more open. I think that is why John Petrucci got along with Prater better than we did because, at least in those days, he was very willing to be flexible and change things around. As far as the specifics of Kevin doing his keyboard tracks, I don't remember. But Prater would never have been happy no matter what anybody played. He would always insult you and say that you were nothing, that you weren't doing it right and that he could do it better. It's so strange because that album was our big break and the album that really opened up the doors for us. So I have fond memories of the period and the excitement that we were back to work again, but it was combined with such frustration. I remember being locked out of the studio and not allowed in. I remember sitting on the stairs outside the control room door with that unwelcome feeling and that tension that if I walked in there, I would be ridiculed or I would have to fight with Prater."

But by far the most controversial component of the overall sound on *Images And Words* was the use of so-called electronic triggers on Portnoy's bass drum, and more noticeably on the snare. In layman's terms, a trigger registers the hit of stick on to drum and converts it into an electronic drum-sound equivalent. Effectively, the result is that the recorded track sounds like it had utilized a drum machine even though it was actually played by the drummer. The benefits of using such a system are that the drum sound is consistent throughout and is able to effectively cut through the mix. The downside is that it doesn't pick up on whether a drum was played soft or hard, which obviously makes a huge difference to the presentation, and it can also prematurely date an album. With Dream Theater in no position to argue with the producer's choice of technique, the triggers were utilized – much to the drummer's chagrin.

"Believe me, I didn't like *anything* that was going on in the studio but I went with it," says Mike forcefully. "We didn't have any leverage and in a certain respect we were just happy to be back at work. But those are Prater's stock drum sounds. If you listen to my drum sounds on that album, they're the same exact sounds as Prater used on the Firehouse album. A lot of his resentment towards me was because he thought I was a show-off. Granted maybe I was, but that is the style of the band. We loved Rush and bands like that and that was whom we modelled ourselves after. We didn't want to become a Firehouse or a Bon Jovi, and Prater produced with that kind of mentality in mind. I think that was just his way and it's a lazy way of producing. Basically he can just put a sound on a snare drum and a kick drum and it sounds that way consistently from start to finish. It may work for Firehouse but when you're creating music like Dream Theater's, with a lot of different parts, sounds and dynamics, you can't just have *one* drum sound for a song like 'Another Day' or 'Metropolis'."

In the years that have passed since the release, David Prater has remained relatively quiet on the subject, although he admits to being less than impressed to hear Mike Portnoy's claim that he considers the album "un-listenable" because of those drums. In a startling rebuke to the drummer's denigration of the album's sound, Prater's barely suppressed annoyance is all too evident as he addresses his response directly to Portnoy:

"Well Mike, I know exactly how you feel. I think everything you've done without my involvement sounds even more unlistenable, and you did those albums exactly how you wanted. It's a matter of opinion, right, Mike? You've had your shot and your track record has been a miserable failure. You even used the same studio, the same engineer and a world-class mixer on virtually every record, and it still sounds like a Chinese fire drill. Michael, you ungrateful little girly-man. If I can keep my mouth shut for 13 years why can't you? Did you know that your kick drums on *Images And Words* were one hundred per cent triggered as well? I've never heard you bellyache about them? Oh, and by the way did you know that the Atlantic demos were the exact samples used on *Images And Words*? Again, I haven't heard or read anything about your disgust for them."

"There were many reasons why I triggered your snare," he continues. "Firstly, your snare sounded like faeces. It was also virtually impossible to get your snare to maintain a consistent prominence without having to constantly ride the fader level. Even with a computer it would have been Byzantine to say the least. And your playing was so cluttered. Michael Portnoy plays whatever Michael Portnoy wants to play whenever Michael Portnoy wants to play it. You claim to have reasons why you do this, but I think the only reason is because you want to one-up Neil Peart and win every award and readers' poll conducted *ad infinitum*. That's not even taking into consideration your product endorsements. You constantly bumbled through every moment in every song without any consideration for what maybe should have been played. Remember Mike, just because you can doesn't mean you should. Since you couldn't criticize the record company for obvious reasons, it made much more sense to go after me. And you did."

It should of course be remembered that Portnoy has won the *Modern Drummer* Reader's Poll award for progressive rock on countless occasions and, in 2004, was inducted into that magazine's Hall Of Fame, alongside such drum luminaries as Keith Moon, Bill Bruford, John Bonham and Neil Peart. Consequently, Portnoy feels his credentials speak for themselves, adding somewhat diplomatically, "I've done probably twenty albums since then without him, and it hasn't stopped me from being able to get a good performance in a studio. But we were young, eager, and ready to make an album, and we thought that maybe this producer knew what he was doing and would help the band. And ultimately I think he did. He did feel passionately for what we were doing, and really wanted to make it the best that it could be. Apart from the drums, it sounded huge. It was a vast improvement on the sound of our debut, and we made the album in two months as opposed to three weeks. So it was the first time we were hearing ourselves properly recorded."

James LaBrie is less restrained when addressing Prater's comments. "The guy is just rude saying that shit about Mike," he protests. "I mean, give me a fucking break! He's probably just jealous because Mike can do circles around him as a drummer. And Prater used to say to me that I made him sick for holding on to a C♯ for as long as I did, because he couldn't sing a C♯ but he always thought of himself as a singer. It was almost like he's a wannabe musician and he's pissed off at us. You know, don't take it out on us just because we're actually *doing* it."

With the atmosphere in the studio having degenerated into open hostility, a certain amount of sympathy has to be felt for those caught up in the squabbles. John Petrucci remembers being unwillingly selected by Prater as a go-between and having to deal with the simmering emotions of both the producer and Kevin Moore, while manager Derek Simon managed to avoid too many visits to the Bear Tracks battlefield.

"To be honest, it was a time when I didn't feel particularly welcome," laughs Simon. "Not from the band's perspective but from Prater's. I mean, Prater's view was that I was the guy who said he was overpriced! So I was *persona non grata*. David just couldn't work in an environment where everybody wanted to be around for every guitar track, and Mike wanted to document everything on video tape. But he certainly did some great things on that record. Sitting here now, with all the professional knowledge that I have, I am sure there are things that Prater, the band and myself would have done differently. I was probably a bull in a china shop at that stage. In retrospect, there would have been a lot better ways of handling things if all of us had been a bit more seasoned. I was a pretty green manager, with a band who thought that they knew exactly how everything needs to get done, working with a producer who has got it all under control, recording for a brand new record label, with an A&R guy who is doing it for the first time. It was a recipe for disaster really, and it's amazing that the record came out as well as it did."

It can only be imagined what assessment Derek Oliver was making when the reports of the disharmony reached him at his New York office. Here were a band whom he had personally convinced his bosses to sign, encountering severe problems with a producer he had insisted on hiring, seemingly blowing it through a series of disputes. But being observed from a substantial distance, his was probably the most impartial view of the events of 1992.

"It was quite clear from the moment that they started recording that this wasn't going to be easy," says Oliver. "Psychologically, it was an amazing meeting of minds in that studio. For a start, David Prater is a virtuoso musician. So effectively what happened here was that you've got another group of virtuoso musicians from Berklee coming in to record a record, who already had a vision of what they were going to do. Prater had the whip hand with the band because, unlike most producers, he can really play very well. Prater knew everything. So every time they would try and slip something by him he would pick it up and pull them up by their lapels. He is so finely tuned, and they met their match."

"But it was very tortuous. I kept going up to the studio, which was an hour and a half's drive from New York City, to mediate all the time between the two warring factions. It got to the stage where at one point I thought we were going to have to close the session and rethink the situation. But through judicious negotiation on my [part], I managed to keep things on track. I guess the band kind of felt that they were in a position where they couldn't argue to the point where they said they weren't going to do it, because they needed to get a record out. They were in a catch-22 situation. I do feel that I ultimately had to be cruel to be kind, and in many respects I sided with David Prater on a lot of the issues. I think ultimately that proved to be the correct decision as David really made that record. If he hadn't been there, that record wouldn't have come out sounding the way it did. He really was instrumental, and that record still stands as their best album. If only people knew what goes on behind the scenes when dealing with bands, studios, producers, madness, rampant egos and record companies. It's a wonder that any records actually get made and released."

With *Images And Words* finally completed and in the can, the band began to relax and envisage the possible single releases, and plan the touring to support the album. But there was to be another trauma for them to handle, one that had been bubbling away during their time at Bear Tracks – with little warning: they needed to find another manager. Derek Simon had been managing their affairs for around four years, but was in a position where he had minimal income and needed to find another job. He had been managing Dream Theater in tandem with another metal band Fifth Angel, along with Gene Simmons and Paul Stanley of Kiss. Although Kiss were initially content with Simon splitting his time between bands, with Dream Theater taking up more of his time he had to make a choice. Opting for Dream Theater was a valiant move, and although he coped financially for a while, it was obvious that he could no longer make a living managing the band.

"The thing was, I really never took a dime from the band," Simon discloses. "The only time I took any commission was from the Atco record deal, based on what was left and I think it was about $12,000. And I really had no other income and had to make a change. It was a heartbreaking decision, but Sony Music came knocking and asked me to work in their marketing department. It came at a time when I had just run out of ways to pay the bills. At that time, Dream Theater weren't playing shows, selling merchandise or doing anything that might traditionally have given us an opportunity to find another pay day and keep my lights on. I remember living in a very modest studio flat in New York and thinking 'Alright, I've finally got a company that's going to give me health insurance and a paycheck every few weeks, I'm going to have to let Dream Theater go.' But everything happens for a reason and somehow I've turned this into a career. As difficult as it all was, from getting them into and out of a bad record deal, the stops and starts with singers and borrowing money to fly Steve Stone across the country, the experiences were the best character-building events that I could've ever had in a career."

Meetings were arranged with a number of prospective replacements, with Yngwie Malmsteens's manager Jim Lewis and Deep Purple's Bruce Payne featuring prominently on their wanted list. But by the time the album recording sessions were drawing to a close, the band had developed a close working relationship with Sanctuary Management boss Rod Smallwood, whose company managed Iron Maiden among others. Although no contracts were signed, the pairing soon began teaming up to plot their next move. The affiliation between Sanctuary and the band led to a coveted support slot with Iron Maiden and, in preparation for this showcase gig, Dream Theater swiftly arranged three low-key club dates to ease themselves back into the live routine. Importantly, although the band had total faith in James LaBrie's vocals, he had yet to be blooded in a live setting, and the gigs were an effective method of removing any possible flaws before the Maiden performance.

LaBrie's first gig with Dream Theater took place on June 2, 1992, at Hammerhedz in Elmont, Long Island. By pure chance, this was also the same venue that Mike Portnoy had played, back in the days when it was known as February's, with his high school band Rising Power. Adding to any anxiety that LaBrie may have been feeling prior to the gig, the arrival of Sanctuary's Rod Smallwood and Merck Mercuriadis, along with Derek Oliver, intensified the pressure. But he needn't have worried. Playing a shortened set that included songs from their forthcoming album to an audience of a couple of hundred fans, the gig was deemed to have been a huge success. The following night's gig at Sparks in Deer Park, Long Island, was witnessed by one far-from-impartial observer, Charlie Dominici, who was intrigued to watch his replacement running through his live paces.

"They were always a local band to me when I still lived in Long Island, and I'd always go and see them out of curiosity," smiles Dominici. "I remember there was some guy behind me who knew who I was and he said something like, 'Hey Charlie, his vocals sound a lot better than yours,' which was really great, you know? Thank you *very* much! I really don't mean it to sound like sour grapes, but when we were in the band in the beginning, we had nothing. The bottom line is that it's easy to sound great when you've got all kinds of equalization coming through the mains and outboard gear. James had monitors on stage, voice doublers and someone who knows how to equalize the vocal and bring it out in the mix. I used to sing and hear nothing, so I'd push it a little hard, the voice gets aggravated and you start to lose it. The more you lose it the more you push it, and it snowballs from there. But it could have been worse. I might have not seen the advertisement and missed the opportunity altogether."

"But I thought both James and his vocals were great," he continues. "To be honest, I've never been really crazy about that 'whoaooh-ooh' style of vocal. To me, it's a little cheesy. What used to drive me up the wall when I first saw them live with James was when he used to do some of the songs from the first album, like 'Fortune In Lies'. He'd do it his way and I would be thinking, 'Oh, come on!'"

The gig also proved to be painfully memorable for John Petrucci, who in a Spinal Tap moment of lost concentration, managed to humiliate himself by falling off the front of the stage during one of his extended solos.

"It's always fun doing that," laughs Petrucci. "I actually don't think that was the first time I'd done that either. But the stage was small and had been extended in the middle, so there was a walkway that went into the audience. It was probably just made up of some road cases or something. James was out there singing and I was on stage left. I saw him up there and further out on stage, and decided I would join him. But of course I didn't have an extension on my side. So I just stepped right off the stage – which was a shock. There was a really loud noise and it was very, very embarrassing. I also fell backwards over my monitor speakers once, which wasn't much fun. But once you do something like that, you never really do it again. You learn to look backwards as you're walking!"

"It was hilarious," smiles James LaBrie. "One minute he was there doing one of his leads and then all of a sudden, bang! He was gone! It was as if the world had just opened up and swallowed him. You could see him being raised and then slowly being put back to his feet. It was *very* funny."

With LaBrie successfully blooded in a live environment and any unintentional stage-diving moments out of their system, Dream Theater were free to concentrate on the impending Iron Maiden gig at New York's Ritz Club on June 8, 1992. Maiden were touring to promote their successful *Fear Of The Dark* album, and the sold-out Ritz was an ideal opportunity to unveil LaBrie to a packed, metal-loving audience. Firing through songs such as "Pull Me Under" and "Metropolis – Part 1" from their forthcoming album, they received a generous reception from the Maiden die-hards and rightly left the stage in a jubilant mood.

"I couldn't believe it," said John Petrucci after that gig. "We never expected a reaction like that. Those kids were stage-diving during the acoustic parts. But I don't know, maybe they were just so psyched to see Iron Maiden that they were just being nice to us."

"It was incredible. The place went crazy from the very first note," added Mike. "There was slam dancing, moshing and stuff like that!"

The triumph of their performance at The Ritz enhanced their stature, and it was imagined that a management deal with Sanctuary would have followed as a matter of course. But by the beginning of July 1992, Sanctuary had made it clear to the band that they were shying away from making any permanent commitment to manage them.

The decision proved even more irksome for Dream Theater when it became evident that the withdrawal of support wasn't due to any hesitancy over their musical ambitions, but a financial wrangle between Sanctuary and Atco Records. One of the key figures within Sanctuary's New York office was their in-house business manager Rob Shore.

"At the time that Sanctuary were going to manage them, they put me on the project as the business manager of Dream Theater," explains Shore. "The reason Sanctuary decided not to manage them was because they didn't feel the support from the record company. There was no question that Atco had a passion for the music and understood it. But it was all about tour support and whether Sanctuary wanted to take on the role of being a benefactor to a band. Their argument was that they didn't want to sponsor this band when the record company wasn't willing to. So it was one of those decisions that I'm sure they regretted later, because the album became huge so quickly."

Ironically, almost the same depiction of events is portrayed by Derek Oliver, who was negotiating on behalf of the label, though perhaps inevitably he claims that it was Sanctuary who weren't willing to be flexible to achieve a deal.

"It broke down because of their demands to the record company," Oliver recollects. "I don't need to go into details, but it seemed like a pretty extortionate kind of demand to me, and they obviously weren't committed enough to the act to say that they were still going to manage them. Then when it came down to it they pulled out at the last moment. But it wasn't very good as it left us up against the wall."

With *Images And Words* set for release within a couple of weeks, the band needed to locate a manager with the required experience to navigate them through this crucial stage of their career, and, crucially, he needed to be someone they could trust. Having wracked their brains to try and cobble together a suitable roll call of potential targets, Jim Pitulski appeared high on their most wanted list. The band had remained close to Pitulski following his departure from Mechanic Records. As fortune would have it, he was also at a loose end.

"After I left Mechanic, I went from Columbia Records and then to PolyGram," remembers Pitulski. "Oddly enough, when I left Columbia to take that job at PolyGram, Derek Simon, who was their manager at the time, got the job that I had vacated at Columbia Records. I had then left PolyGram, involuntarily, and when Sanctuary walked away from the table John Petrucci called me up and said 'Look, we need management, can you help us out?' As I had time on my hands I agreed to help them out until we could find another full-time manager. But that turned into a full-time role, and we took it from there for several years."

The band also had been suitably struck by the business acumen of Rob Shore in the period that they had been working with him, and asked him to co-manage them with Pitulski. Shore dealt with touring, royalties and other financial considerations, with Pitulski concentrating on more creative aspects. As a result, the new pairing made their partnership official in the form of a company, Roundtable Management. With both Dream Theater and Atco satisfied with the latest management arrangements, they could concentrate on the upcoming album release. Little did they know it was an album that would go on to achieve worldwide mass acclaim and permanently change their lives.

SEVEN

CHANGING HORIZONS

Finally hitting the stores on July 7, 1992, *Images And Words* would in time become the band's largest-selling album, and the well-honed balance of heavier and slower tracks has ensured its enduring popularity. Despite the acclaim that had been bestowed on their debut, *Images And Words* remains to this day a slab of near-perfect progressive music that delivers what its predecessor hinted at. "Pull Me Under", a captivating up-tempo song, opens the album and includes all the essential facets of a Dream Theater track. With Kevin Moore providing the lyrics that loosely follow the issues raised in Shakespeare's *Hamlet*, the song has remained in regular rotation in the band's live shows to this day. Ending abruptly – not as some believed due to a bad edit, but as a nod towards The Beatles who used the effect on their *Abbey Road* album – the song was also destined a few months later to become the album's lead-off single. "Another Day" is a tender song that deals with the issues facing John Petrucci as his father battled cancer, and is enhanced by the addition of a haunting soprano saxophone performed by Bear Tracks Studios-owner and Spyro Gyra-musician Jay Beckenstein.

The soaring "Take The Time" laments the band's period of record label and singer woes, and is filled with samples taken from the film *Cinema Paradiso* as well as spoken sections from Frank Zappa, The Beastie Boys and Public Enemy to give the song an additional dimension. Mike Portnoy commented at the time that it "Has all those elements of catchy chorus, very progressive parts, heavy sections, melodic sections. We always considered that to be our 'Roundabout' or 'Bohemian Rhapsody'."

John Myung's lyrical contribution "Learning To Live" was written about the AIDS epidemic, with arguably the album's showpiece track "Metropolis – Part 1" encompassing lengthy progressive instrumental sections and a sci-fi lyric written by John Petrucci in the finest vein of many a Rush track. "Surrounded" was a song that had been written away from the studio by Kevin Moore, before he allowed it to be amended and altered by the rest of the band. As he explained at the time, "'Surrounded' was just a song I arranged first as a keyboard riff. We've never done that before where the keyboard is doing the rhythm. It just happened to be poppy and Van Halen-ish. I really didn't think that we were going to use it when I wrote it."

Press reviews of the album were predictably mixed, with the more fickle elements of fashion-led press always unlikely to bestow plaudits on a band as musically complex as Dream Theater. Perhaps the harshest review was penned by Chris Welch of *Rock World* magazine who grumbled: "Intense, melodramatic, demanding, Dream Theater have obviously poured their hearts and souls into these carefully contrived performances. The result is music you couldn't claim to like or enjoy, rather more admire from a convenient distance. It's like watching nuclear scientists constructing the first atom bomb. You appreciate the expertise but deplore the end result."

Fortunately, not all the reviewers were quite so ruthless. Writing for *RAW* magazine, Maura Sutton enthused that *Images And Words* was "An album set to do for prog rock what Nirvana have done for smelly cardigans. . . Overall this is a stunning effort with enough musical twists and turns to appeal to a wide variety of music lovers." *Modern Drummer* also rated the album, claiming: "Some say that progressive rock died when bands like Yes and Genesis began catering to the mainstream. But with *Images And Words*, Dream Theater proves itself a true torchbearer."

Rock Power's Paul Suter was of a similar mind, claiming the album was "An utterly unique record blending the vicious edge of 90s metal – spot those Metallica-like riffs – with 70s style British pomp and prog rock… Dream Theater will find a place in the hearts of those who seek a little more from their music."

Press reviews aside, those closest to the band during that era still correctly rate the album as one of their most complete and captivating releases.

"The album was a stunning creation produced out of near chaos by a collection of people, including me, that had very dogmatic opinions," says Derek Oliver. "The combined intransigence of Portnoy, Petrucci, Oliver and Prater was an experience that I do not want to repeat in a hurry, but on reflection I feel that it produced one of the great rock albums of the Nineties."

"Every time 'Metropolis' comes on, I keep thinking it's going to break into a Christmas song because of the sleigh bells," smiles Derek Simon. "I loved the intro to that song and then all of a sudden the sleigh bells come in, and all I can think of is 'ok, where are the eight tiny reindeer?' But it is still one of the best things that the band have done, and that's not through familiarity or fondness. I just think it's a really, really good record. Especially if you think of the growth the band made, both professionally and personally, between the debut and *Images And Words*."

Unsurprisingly, producer David Prater also speaks highly of the album, saying "Yes only made one *Close To The Edge*. Dream Theater only made one, too. And I produced it."

Drawing on the ethereal artwork style that had adorned the sleeves of prog rock greats such as Yes and Genesis, the cover for *Images And Words* was also especially striking. Depicting a young girl standing at the base of an antique four-poster bed, it was filled with numerous references to the album's lyrics as well as a flaming heart wrapped with barbed wire.

"We were into all those Yes and Pink Floyd covers, and liked the idea of having artwork that was striking and that utilized different elements of the lyrics," explains Mike Portnoy. "We didn't really have that with our first album as we used art that was already created that we liked. So it was nice to create something from our own imagination and see it brought to life. Most of the artwork ideas were Kev Moore's. We were sitting around in his apartment during that time trying to come up with an album cover, and we started discussing different elements of the lyrics. So there was the sparrow from 'Pull Me Under', the little girl from 'Wait For Sleep', and most of those images came from Kev's lyrics on that album. He was also the one that suggested the sacred heart of Jesus with the heart, barbed wire and flames symbolizing strength and passion."

In an interview with a Korean radio station, Kevin Moore revealed that the track "Wait For Sleep" was about "a girl whose sister died and about how she copes with that. It's about the fact that she's not religious, so she can't use religion to help her cope with it. So she somehow has to find a way to deal with it. Basically, the cover is kind of based on the song. That's the little girl whose sister died, and she's holding a picture of her sister there. Her sister's spirit is the bird, and the heart with barbed wire wrapped around it is a symbol of compassion."

The art had been meticulously created by one of Atlantic's in-house designers, Larry Freemantle. Freemantle had already built a strong reputation as an innovative artist, and his previous work had included the recognizable Led Zeppelin *Remasters* box set that featured the shadow of an airship hovering over a crop circle. Freemantle had strong links with an art company called Access Images who were pioneers in computer-aided design long before the use of graphic manipulation software, such as Photoshop, became the norm.

"The band were very hands-on in the early days of creating the sleeve," recalls Freemantle. "John Myung was probably the key person I met along with John Petrucci, and of course Mike was very much involved, too. They were very specific about what should be where on the sleeve. It was just a matter of trying to piece that together. A lot of bands are like the deer in the headlights when it comes to ideas, so their attitude was quite unusual. They were always great when they came to the table as they always had ideas. So I tried to make it look compositionally like an old painting. It was a collage of engravings and illustrations. The girl I think was called Andrea, and was just somebody that the Access Images photographer Dan Muro cast. And as for the font for the band's name, I hired a calligrapher John Stevens to create it as I wanted it to be personalized. But the band and I were huge Hypgnosis [who designed numerous Pink Floyd sleeves, amongst many others, during the Seventies] fans and that is pretty obvious. To me the *Images* sleeve now looks a little dated, because you see how things are done today. I just look back and think I could have done it in a different way."

The record was released with little fanfare, with only hardcore fans or those with memories long enough to remember Dream Theater's debut immediately adding it to their collections. With a certain amount of encouragement, Atco were however persuaded to release a single. As one of the lengthier songs on the album clocking in at just over eight minutes, "Pull Me Under" was perhaps an unexpected choice, and it was only through a number of alarming edits that the track was condensed to a mere five minutes to suit radio airplay. The purpose of the single release was hopefully to gradually rebuild a fan-base and create awareness of the band throughout the US, as Mike Portnoy explains.

"Originally when the label wanted to service 'Pull Me Under' to radio, we just thought it would be a good introduction to the band on maybe college radio or heavy metal stations," he says. "We thought that it would test the waters for a song like 'Another Day', which we felt would be the big single. So 'Pull Me Under' was supposed to just be a little introduction. But suddenly it caught on like wildfire, and American mainstream radio just lapped it up. All the radio stations around the country were giving us the exact same story of how they would play the song once or twice, and then the phones would not stop ringing. Everybody was calling wanting to know who the band was and it became the most requested song at every single station. At that point, the label immediately got us on the road and we began touring."

The initial success of the single was encouraging, and the radio air-play was to prove invaluable in at least getting the name of the band into the minds of the mainstream listener. Derek Oliver felt particularly satisfied with the band's early progress, given that Atco had initially been sceptical about a single release or even encouraging the band to hit the bars and clubs in order to try and push the album out on the road.

"It was not only their vision being realized but also mine," says Oliver. "Here was a band who had been on the ropes, dropped from a record company, playing the kind of music that certainly wasn't fashionable, and there were no other contenders in that niche at that time. I mean the record company didn't understand what the band were all about, and they certainly didn't understand releasing 'Pull Me Under'. They were very resistant to releasing a track like that, but as soon as it got onto radio it reacted in a huge way. And it was like pulling teeth with the record company. They didn't even want to put them out on tour. I remember having a stand-up, almost knock-down, drag-out fight with the head of marketing, who was saying that nobody would come and see this band play. So it was difficult."

The *Images And Words* Tour officially began on September 27, 1992, at the Limelight club in New York, and the band couldn't have had any idea this would transform into a lengthy expedition that wouldn't conclude until November the following year. During the first three weeks of the tour, the airplay that "Pull Me Under" received convinced Atco that a video needed to be shot to accompany the release. With the decision being made somewhat on the hoof, there was little time to arrange a complicated shoot or involve the band in any discussions as to how they wanted the song to be presented. Instead, a camera crew was dispatched to catch up with the band on their tour to film enough live footage to blend with some peculiar, acted scenes that the producers envisaged somehow matched the song. Featuring what Mike Portnoy now refers to as "the wolfman" aimlessly wandering around a grubby bedroom and tying a hangman's noose, the acted portions of the video didn't relate to the lyrics, and seemed to be merely used as filler between the live footage. The onstage action was recorded on October 21, 1992, at the Avalon Club in Chicago, and the entire video cost a paltry $10,000 to produce, and frankly it shows.

"We just had a film company come out to a show to burn some film as they had some left over stock," admits Jim Pitulski. "They shot this live stuff, and we wound up syncing it up to the record and a small narrative bit."

Mike Portnoy: "I hate that video. Still to this day, if we are ever shown on a TV show, they will show that video. In retrospect it's a horrible video, and the most low-budget thing we ever did."

The video was released to the likes of MTV just prior to the band travelling to Japan for the first time. The Japanese audiences were renowned for swiftly catching on to the type of metal that Dream Theater were producing, and by the time the band arrived in Kanagawa for their first show on November 17, they were already receiving an adoring welcome everywhere they went. Given that they had been used to driving themselves around from gig to gig in a decrepit van, they found the reception startling.

"I remember there were even fans waiting at the airport," confirms John Petrucci. "We were driven around by people wearing white gloves, and there were dinners laid on for us and so on. It was very different to what we were used to. Even the way that the promoter, all the people on the team and the label, handled things was just very, very professional."

"The main difference was the fanaticism in Japan," agrees Mike. "They were waiting in hotel lobbies, and always giving us gifts. Now we have come to know this tradition and how the Japanese fans are, but the first time it happened to us we were totally taken by surprise, and it really felt like Beatlemania. We had never been treated like real rock stars before, and it was amazing. During the concert they are incredibly quiet. It's kind of strange because five minutes before show time you can be backstage, and it is *dead* silent. You'll wonder if the doors have even opened and when you look out, there are 2,000 people just sitting there in silence. They are even like that during the concert itself and unless you are playing really energetic songs they'll just sit there, really quiet and attentive. That's good when you're playing the quieter songs and you want that kind of attention. But sometimes, when you're playing the heavier songs, it's a little awkward because you're giving off all this energy on stage and you're getting a very respectful look back. Now of course we've grown accustomed to that."

They returned home after their Far East jaunt to be struck with the realization that "Pull Me Under" had become as huge a triumph on MTV as it had been on the radio. In spite of the obvious visual deficiencies, the video was being heavily rotated on the music channel and, supported by their ongoing tour, things quickly began to snowball with the album being snapped up at stores across the US.

"We were very surprised by that," admits Mike. "That song was all over the radio and MTV, and suddenly we were going all over America in a van. It was really super, low-budget, playing small clubs, but it didn't matter. You know, we were just so excited to be playing for the first time in Kansas, Chicago, Detroit and Milwaukee. There was just a whole world out there. 'Pull Me Under' was on the radio all that time, people were coming out to see us and we were starting to get a fan base all over the place. But in the band's entire career it was the only MTV coverage we ever had. As bad as the video was, MTV got totally behind it and it was in rotation for five or six times a day. We couldn't turn on the TV without seeing it during the fall of 1992."

John Petrucci: "I remember we continued the US tour after we came back from Japan, and every one of those shows were sold out. Suddenly this song was getting played on the radio. It was weird, and there was a definite point where you just knew that something was happening. We'd be going places and it'd be a case of 'Wow, we're sold out again tonight.' Then there was all this interest by the record label, and all these people you've never seen, or even heard of before, from Atco, were coming out to see us. The success was what I had always dreamed of. At that point we had been through a period where we'd left college to take this chance, we were already signed and had nothing really come of our first record. We had been through singers, and through a period where nothing was going on. So there was nothing better to have [than] that kind of success because you finally felt that it was working. You had not only proved it to yourself but to other people around you – people who may have believed in you or not."

John Myung cites fortuitous timing as being the central factor in the success of the single, believing that both the sound and the attitude of radio station managers were key.

"It was fate and was just meant to be," says the bassist. "It literally was one of those storybook tales, and was one of those perfect situations that you dream about. But it almost seemed like we needed so many different things going for us. The programme controllers at radio stations really took to the sound of the record and, stylistically, it was perfect timing. The soundscapes had that very Eighties style of production, and it seemed like the success of that record was the window of the Eighties metal sound closing before it began morphing into the

Seattle sound. It was actually great for something like that to happen to us, because it definitely helped us out. From the success of that one song we were able to start to play decent venues."

Images And Words would eventually go on to sell over half a million copies in the US alone, which far exceeded the best estimates of the record label and the band's management, as Rob Shore explains.

"The first time I saw Dream Theater was with Rod Smallwood and Derek Oliver before the album came out," he says. "I can remember Derek saying, before it came out, that he hoped the album would sell 15,000 units. It did a lot better than that! But that video was a fluke, and the song just took off, both on radio and TV. Everyone was very surprised but they exploited the MTV show *Headbanger's Ball* very well. I remember I was handling Iron Maiden's business management, and Dream Theater opened for them before *Images And Words* came out, and it was for a $500 fee. They needed every penny of it, and it was being distributed to the driver, for the gas. Within a year we had a $100,000 gig in Japan. So that was how fast it happened."

Watching with a mixture of disbelief and perhaps a certain amount of jealousy at the band's rapid ascent, were both Charlie Dominici and Steve Stone. During their tenures with the band they had both tried in vain to encourage the writing of shorter, more accessible songs. Seeing the band flashing before their eyes with a hit single every time they turned on the TV was proving to be unbearable.

"I always used to tell them that the songs could be three songs instead of one," sighs Steve Stone. "I was thinking that they could go down to six-minute songs instead of fifteen. Then this little song called 'Pull Me Under' came out and I couldn't believe it. I sat back and went, 'You bastards!' They broke it down to a three- or four-minute mentality and look what happened. It's great to have these epic numbers, but you've got to mix it up a bit."

Charlie Dominici agrees, but any jealousy was diminished by the pride he felt at seeing his friends and former bandmates finally revelling in the mainstream limelight.

"It was kind of gratifying but at the same frustrating to see the band finally doing a commercial-type song," he says. "I mean let's face it, 'Pull Me Under' is a song that must be one of the most acceptable for mainstream listeners of metal and rock. It was exactly what I was telling them I wanted us to do. I kept harping on about it and saying, 'Look at Rush, they were nothing until they recorded "New World Man". After that they were on the radio, and then people started listening to "Tom Sawyer" and stuff like that.' I remember I was in a bar somewhere and I saw them on *Headbanger's Ball* on MTV and couldn't believe it. For me, it was a bittersweet feeling as I felt like 'Why didn't they listen to me and do that when I was in the band?' But at the same time I was really happy for them, because through it all, Mike and all the rest of the guys in the band are like family to me. They're like my little brothers. So when I see them succeed, just like when you see your little brother succeed, there may be a little part of you that is jealous but the big part of you is proud and happy. And that's how I felt about that. I really couldn't have been happier for them."

Throughout the autumn and winter of 1992 to 1993 the band continued to tour relentlessly, gradually moving from club venues such as Harpo's in Detroit or Starz in Milwaukee to smaller theatres. Playing a gig virtually every night, with a day off being treated as a luxury, the conditions on the road were far from glamorous with the five band members and their road manager Dave Chieca crammed into the back of a van, and taking it in turns to drive the distances between cities.

"It was hard," says James LaBrie. "I remember being really sick with the 'flu, lying in the back of the van with the chills after a gig just hoping it was all over soon. There would be overnight drives where we didn't sleep and had to go straight to the soundcheck for the next gig. We'd be staying in all these cheap motels and it was bizarre. I couldn't believe we were doing it. But the funny thing about being in the back of a van was that I had to have a really big jug with me. As I drink tons of water on stage, I had to have this jug to piss into – otherwise I would have been asking the guys to pull over every ten minutes. We had a bed in the back of the van, and the rest of the guys in the band were really cool because they let me have dibs on it, so I could get to sleep. They knew it was important for me to get some sleep so that the voice would be happening. We even had a little TV in there and Mike always had movies and entertainment for us."

"We just had to be very dedicated," he continues. "Of course, I'd done the van thing before when I was in all those bar bands. But this just felt different as it was the best band I had ever been with. We really thought that we would keep going for it no matter what we had to sacrifice. So we were in the van, sharing rooms in not the best of hotels and then playing in nice clubs to die in, but we didn't care. It was quite a transition from being in the back of a van, and playing small clubs. I remember one club we played in Philadelphia, I think it was our second or third show, and there were literally thirty people in the crowd. But so what? We played every song from *Images And Words* and a few from *When Dream And Day Unite*, and we nailed it. All thirty people were pretty freaked out. Once 'Pull Me Under' really started to hit, all of a sudden we were in a proper tour bus and playing to sold-out clubs every single night. Every day, whatever city we pulled into, we had prime spots on radio, doing contests and giveaways, and being taken out to dinner by the label or radio station. It was amazing how it turned around."

Mike Portnoy: "We would be playing six shows a week. None of us had families back then, though our girlfriends at the time were the women who would become our wives. Only James was married so we just got in the van and went. The first three months were in a van, then come January 1993 we started to have some success and upped it to a bus. Then the bus became a bus and a truck, and it just kept evolving. The pace never let up. We must have played Dallas, Texas, four or five times throughout that tour. We just kept hitting every nook and cranny in America, and I think that was really crucial for the band. It really laid down the foundations for years to come."

Keen to capitalize on the wave of enthusiasm that "Pull Me Under" had created, the record label were understandably quick to advocate a second single release. This time, though, they were willing to offer a considerably larger budget for the accompanying video and selected the accessible "Take The Time". Recorded on February 14, 1993, in Los Angeles and directed by Chris Painter, the video was an infinite improvement on its predecessor. Focusing solely on the band performing and without any wolfman diversions, if anything it could be accused of being too slick with the band members a blur of garishly coloured silk shirts, chest hair and leather pants. Although severe editing was again needed to reduce the track to a more acceptable length, the single failed to equal the level of adulation or airplay achieved by "Pull Me Under" which, given the more straightforward nature of the song, was surprising. However, with the rock scene infiltrated by grunge at the time and the likes of Soundgarden controlling the airwaves, the timing of the release was far from perfect.

Despite such battles against passing trends, the band were receiving the accolades of their peers, with Sebastian Bach (then with Skid Row) turning up at their gig on March 5, 1993, at The Stone Pony club in Asbury Park, New Jersey. After downing an inhuman amount of beer, he headed down to the front when Dream Theater took the stage, and after a frantic bout of applause, cheering and extreme moshing, managed to split his head open on one of the spotlights before heading home.

"I really don't remember that," laughs Bach now. "But that doesn't surprise me as they were pretty crazy times. I know I loved their song 'Pull Me Under', so that was probably the song I did that to – if that in fact happened!"

But not all of their fellow bands were as openly supportive. One notorious incident occurred a few months earlier when an argument broke out between Dream Theater and members of Saigon Kick, prior to a gig at The Stone in San Francisco. The latter had demanded that they headline the show, and after strenuous negotiation worthy of an international arms treaty, it was agreed that both bands would play sets of an equal length with Dream Theater performing first. Amusingly, after they had finished their set, a vast majority of the audience departed leaving around thirty people in the auditorium. Too humiliated to even contemplate hitting the stage, Saigon Kick left the venue without even playing a note.

Also, there were always new international markets to hit, and in late March 1993, Dream Theater headed to Europe for a stint that included playing two London gigs at the legendary Marquee club. One of these appearances [April 23] was recorded for a live album which was released later in the year. Not known for his love of sightseeing, Mike Portnoy made a rare excursion from the band's hotel to the Abbey Road Studios in order to recreate Paul McCartney's famous barefoot stroll across a pelican crossing, fulfilling what he describes as a "lifelong ambition". This first European leg also featured stretches in Denmark, Sweden, Germany, Holland and Italy before they returned home to begin yet another US leg, entitled the Music In Progress Tour, in early May. Supporting the band were the Galactic Cowboys, who had just released their *Space In Your Face* album. The two bands became close friends, and developed a close working relationship that would see the Cowboys appearing on stage each night to sing backing vocals to "Take The Time".

"That was a lot of fun as there was no pressure on us," recalls Galactic Cowboys vocalist Ben Huggins. "Once we figured out our parts we would come on and be as crazy as we wanted to be onstage for that song. I remember them suggesting it to us, as back then Mike didn't sing backing vocals as I guess he didn't have the confidence. But there were days when we had a gig without them, and Mike would come on the bus with us for the gig. He'd always come out when we were doing our set during a song 'Pump Up The Spacesuit', and he would do a rap, march around the stage and jump on my back to try and knock me over."

The tour continued on track until the actions of a reckless truck driver nearly caused the bands to miss a gig in Detroit, as Huggins explains.

"We met this brand new truck driver as the old guy had to jump to go on another tour," he says. "This new younger guy comes in, and was kind of cocky. He was telling everyone where he had been and everything he'd done, and was bragging about how fast he was going to drive the truck to Detroit. So both bands get on our buses and take off and were heading for Detroit when the next thing we know, someone radios our bus driver, and he pulls over. The tour manager gets off and everyone was gathered around trying to figure out what was going on, and he said 'It looks like our new truck driver got his truck stuck under a bridge!' So we had to get both bands on one bus, and send all the crew back on the other bus to get the equipment. By that time, some dude had backed up a truck and started impounding the stuff. He didn't work for the city, county or state but was some freelance impounding guy. He was unloading stuff and taking it away. So the crew got there and told the guy to stop. But the truck was like a sardine can and had been opened on the top halfway back. So they rented a truck and got back the stuff. The next day, of course we all knew that this new truck driver was on his way out before he did, so we had to try and act normal around him. But he was still saying stuff like 'Hell, that was a once-in-a-lifetime thing huh?' Like who is going to keep a guy who drives a truck under a bridge and gets it stuck?"

Fortunately, despite the major inconvenience of a lengthened commute between the two cities, the gig went ahead as planned – minus one truck driver who was sent packing with a suitably reduced ego. But a more unfortunate incident happened on July 3, 1993, in a small town called Fergus Falls in Minnesota, as James LaBrie recalls.

"We were just hanging out in the bar of a hotel," he says. "We were having a great time, and there was a local band playing there who asked us to get up and jam with them. So we were jamming away, and a lot of the locals were there. Now you've got to remember that we were in a place where people kind of *look* at guys that have long hair. Let's just say that they didn't look too favourably on us. So we were doing our thing and Mike Portnoy had his video camera with him. He was getting footage because we liked to document where we were at, and it was a fun thing to do. I guess one of the girls there just freaked out and told him to get the camera out of her face. One of the boyfriends came in and told Mike to 'Fuck off' and Mike started to retaliate verbally. And the next thing I knew it was just one big brawl. We had a lighting director named Poop and he got a bottle over the head, and at that point all hell broke loose. I remember scrapping with this guy who must have been six foot seven or something. I was just enraged that these guys came at us, and it was pandemonium. The police showed up very quickly and they appeared to be on the side of the locals. There were two cops between me and this big guy and I jumped right through them. So the cops grabbed me and wanted to throw me in jail, but thankfully our tour manager defused the situation."

"It was mainly myself and James, a couple of the guys from Galactic Cowboys and a bunch of our crew guys," adds Mike. "I actually have the whole thing on videotape too, as the camera was on when I was swinging it at some guy's head. But in hindsight we were young, rowdy and stupid."

The police gave the band an ultimatum that they had to leave the town by early the following morning, or they were going to be chucked into the local jail. Predictably, they didn't need telling twice.

"We were like 'OK. I guess we'll never be back here again,'" laughs James. "I mean it really was no big deal. We were minding our own business and having a good time, and so what if Mike had his camera out? And one of these big girls freaked right out on him and everything went from there. It was just insanity."

Although for the vast majority of the time LaBrie is affable and relaxed, he readily admits that he was a bit of a "scrapper" in his youth, and up until a few years ago was, if pushed, prepared to use a certain amount of physical force to settle arguments.

"I guess I was just a sensitive person and it didn't take much to tick me off," he explains. "So I showed my disagreement with my fists. It started when I was in elementary school. If someone said something that I didn't appreciate, I'd say 'Meet you outside at recess and let's go for it.' Another part of me was that I couldn't stand bullies at school, so if I saw them picking on somebody I'd get into a fight even if it meant me getting done in. And then later on in life it was just me being silly. You know, somebody looking at me sideways and the next thing I know, I'm scrapping with the guy. I look back now and it was pretty crazy stuff. I do remember one time I was at a Max Webster concert with some friends of mine. I got into a scrap after the concert with a guy who probably weighed 95 pounds soaking wet, and he cleaned my clock in two minutes. And it was around that time I said to myself, 'You know what? Maybe I should start thinking differently!'"

"Obviously I had to learn how to control myself, and the last time I got into a scrap was probably about eight years ago," he continues. "I was in a bar with a group of friends, and this guy kept looking at me sideways. I was stood near the bar and he came by me and did the typical hitting-my-shoulder thing, but made a point of it. I just grabbed him right there, because I knew what was going to take place, and started giving him shots right in the head. I knew if I didn't do it, he was going to clock me in the back of the head when he walked by. It was just crazy. Fortunately I got the better of him, but I was thinking at the time that I should really stop this stuff as I've got a family. You've got to grow up at some point. But I don't know what it is. I still get it a bit sometimes if I go out with friends, and it seems to be certain people don't know how to take men with long hair. It's that whole, stereotyping thing which is silly. So now if I get any vibes like that, I just make sure I don't make eye contact and mind my own business. I mean, it's not like I have to watch it every time I go out, but there's still the odd time you sense that there's a guy there with the wrong attitude."

That tour with the Galactic Cowboys remains one that both bands look back on with fondness, with a light-hearted camaraderie developing between the two similarly minded parties. The Cowboys, though, were renowned for their pranks and for not taking themselves too seriously, which sometimes contrasted with Dream Theater's more career oriented goals.

"It sounds bad, but there were times on that tour where we would rib those guys about the fact that they would only want us to come out on stage because they wanted us to be their personality," laughs Ben Huggins. "They were so into the whole artist thing that they would suppress their comical edge. They really wanted to burst out and do it, but didn't know if the fans would like it. So they would have us come out instead. Then if anything went wrong they could just say 'Oh yeah, it was those Cowboys!' So there was a certain amount of pulling them out of their shells. Kevin Moore wrote these great limericks about the next city we were going to. I was cracking up laughing saying he should read them as they were hilarious. He said he couldn't but suggested that I did. So I would come out and read them during the instrumental 'Eve' which had a break in it. During the break I'd come out, do the limerick, take a bow and leave the stage. Then they'd kick back into the song."

"On the last night of a tour you always do some stupid pranks," he continues. "Mike and I had a fondness for Frank Zappa. So when we were playing on the last night, he'd sampled a line from Zappa's 'Broken Hearts Are For Assholes', and in between every song he'd play the line 'You were dazzled by the exciting costume of Ko-Ko'. So in every break he'd play it over the PA which took us all by surprise. I've no idea if anybody else got it though!"

In the summer of 1993, "Another Day" became the album's third single and, using the same director who created the lush feel on "Take The Time", would superficially at least appear to be a guaranteed hit. Yet despite the commercial undercurrent of the song and the opulence of the video, it was never even played on MTV and was overlooked by radio. Somewhat perplexed by the single's failure, the band returned to Japan for four dates in August, including a performance at Nakano Sun Plaza in Tokyo which was filmed for release as the home video *Live In Tokyo* later that year. After spending a solid year on the road, they returned to the USA to take a warranted month-long break, with John Petrucci finally having the time available to marry fiancée Rena Sands, whom he had met a number of years earlier when she was the guitarist in the band Meanstreak.

But despite the four-week hiatus, Atco released the *Live At The Marquee* EP, which had been recorded five months earlier in London. Incorporating such engaging songs as "Metropolis" and "A Fortune In Lies" and the killer instrumental "Bombay Vindaloo" (named after a particularly vicious curry), the EP neatly highlighted the progress they had made and was enthusiastically received by their fans who until that point had only had access to sonically flawed live bootlegs. The

EP was also lauded by the press, with RAW's Mark Greenway giving it a 5/5 review, claiming it was "An unparalleled collection of Prog diamonds. . . *Live At The Marquee* proves beyond all doubt that Dream Theater can pull off their Einstein rhythms onstage. Supergroup status awaits."

In the finest tradition of so-called "live" rock albums, it had been touched-up after the event with a few dabs of studio wizardry and a few overdubs.

"To be honest, James ended up re-doing his vocals for that," Mike confesses. "So I always wondered if we should have named it '*Dream Theater Live At The Marquee But With James LaBrie Live At Bear Tracks*'!"

With the rumpus over the use of the triggered drum sounds on the original *Images And Words* recording, it's staggering to learn that they were also slyly used, and without the band's knowledge, on the live EP too. Jim Pitulski claims: "The band used Doug Oberkircher who was the same engineer, and he insisted on using the triggers. I guess he didn't think there was a good enough live sound." This however was something that was wisely kept away from the band, with Mike Portnoy even to this day not having previously been aware of their use.

"I guess it's possible but I haven't listened to it recently," he says with surprise. "It was mixed by Doug, but we weren't present as we were still on the road when he mixed it. So we basically were handed the tapes when they were done and that was it. But it sounded good and we were happy with it."

The final leg of their incessant touring saw the band return to Europe and was in the main uneventful, with the exception of their UK gigs. During a performance at the London Astoria, the band's personal possessions were stolen from the dressing room, including James LaBrie's passport. After the following night's gig in Wolverhampton, LaBrie had to return by train to the capital to arrange a replacement, dashing back to Nottingham for the next show and arriving with twenty minutes to spare. Understandably in a sour mood, he was in no mood to deal pleasantly with the heckler who had made winding up the singer his evening's entertainment.

"We were doing the song 'Surrounded' which starts off very intimate as it's just piano and vocal," he recalls. "So this guy was there going 'Whoaaaahh' and singing *very* badly. At first I went with it and the rest of the crowd were looking over thinking 'What the hell is going on here, this guy's got to stop, he's ruining it!' So I stopped and said something like 'Looks like we got ourselves a wannabe singer here, but do me a favour and let *me* sing this.' So he stops, and we'd start in again and of course he'd do it again. This happened about three times and Kev [Moore] comes walking over to me on the stage and says, 'Let's try this one more time. If this guy does it again, you and I are going to jump into the crowd and pummel him!' So we begin the tune again, and sure enough the guy starts. So I just tossed the microphone down and jumped off the stage, and where was Kevin Moore? He was still there back behind his piano just watching me."

"So I grabbed the guy, walked him out and threw him out the front door," he continues. "I remember I said to the guy, 'Look, I asked you nicely, this isn't a circus.' I tried walking back to the stage, but couldn't get back there because the doors were locked. The tour manager had to walk me down the stairs, and all the way around to get back on stage. In the meantime, I'm hearing Mike in the background singing the tune. I eventually walked onstage and Mike was laughing. But it got kind of silly, as that guy was threatening and saying stuff like 'I'm going to come back, blow away the band and shoot everybody'. So they called the police and they kept an eye on him."

By the end of the tour in November 1993, the band had played an astonishing 194 gigs in 17 countries, and *Images And Words* had sold over 500,000 copies in the US alone. Dream Theater had been transformed from an underrated cult band into legitimate mainstream contenders.

"We went from releasing a nothing album and almost calling it quits in 1990 to sitting on top of the world a couple of years later with a gold record," says Mike Portnoy. "Suddenly, *everything* we had dreamt of was beginning to happen..."

EIGHT

UNTIL THE CIRCLE BREAKS

The sole drawback to the flourishing fortunes Dream Theater had been enjoying following *Images And Words* was that it had intensified the expectations for its successor. After all, the band were now familiar faces on MTV and in the rock press, and the fans who had bought the album and helped sell out their gigs night after night were frantically awaiting new material. The pressure was on the band to produce something worthy of their newfound fame and mushrooming reputation, and the record label moguls, with dollar signs in their eyes, were hoping for another bumper payday.

"It was the first time that we made a record knowing that there was an audience who would be listening to it," says Mike Portnoy. "With the first two albums, we were still nobodies and had no idea if *anybody* was going to listen to what we were making. Suddenly, we had half a million people there waiting to hear the follow-up to *Images And Words*. Somebody once said that you have your whole life to prepare for your first album and have about two months to prepare the follow-up, and that was very much the situation we faced in early 1994."

The writing sessions for what would eventually become the *Awake* album commenced in earnest in February, after the band had taken a month-long break. Setting themselves up at Prince Studios in New York City and working solidly on ideas for two months, they swiftly created numerous songs with such temporary and bizarre working titles as "Kittens On Crack", "Blowfish", "Beach House Reality" and "Squid". The intensity of those sessions managed to produce an immense amount of material, but the creative demands caused a certain amount of artistic tension within the group. In an interview of the time with *RAW* magazine, Kevin Moore revealed: "There's no bandleader. There are arguments that last forever because there's nobody to come in and draw the line." These disagreements would often be over such minute details as single chord changes, as Mike Portnoy admits.

"We would argue for days over shit like that," he laughs now. "But back then, the dynamics were different because Kevin was a very strong-minded artist. When it came to the music, you had John Petrucci and I playing the roles we still kind of play, and Kevin was also a forceful element. In those days, John Myung was a little bit more out of his shell, so the bass was a bit more predominant in the writing process. You had four very opinionated elements in the band. The fighting never came to blows, but there was a lot of bickering over every single element, like the fine details of what the third note on the 64th bar should be."

By this stage, the band had been moved from the Atco label to the East West imprint (both of which fell under the overall control of Atlantic Records). The label's assumption that the next album was bound to be another mainstream triumph had also amplified the burden already felt by the band. After seeing the success of "Pull Me Under", the label remained firmly entrenched in their belief that a repeat performance could be achieved with the right material. They were also attempting to sway the band into creating a heavier album which they pre-supposed would be easier to market. In the two years following the release of *Images And Words* the rock scene had changed drastically, with both grunge acts and the brutal approach taken by the likes of Pantera gaining widespread exposure.

"The label were anxious for Dream Theater to get a heavier sound," confirms Jim Pitulski. "They were pushing us in that direction, so there was a conscious effort made to move in a darker direction. The record was getting ready to drop, and East West needed their big hard rock record for the fourth quarter of the year. So they hurried us up and pressured us into that release."

Although the band and their management undoubtedly sensed that the label were seeking to manipulate their direction, this is denied by Derek Oliver – but he does admit that there was an overriding label preoccupation to encourage the band to write another hit single.

"It's wrong to say that we wanted the band to be heavier," says Oliver. "We wanted the band to move in the same direction as they had come out of the starting blocks with. People knew Dream Theater as the band that played 'Pull Me Under', which had that wonderful Iron Maiden-meets-Metallica sound. My thoughts were that we needed to essentially repeat that formula. So part of the problem, when we did the demos, was trying to get *the* song that we could take as the lead track and that people would latch on to. I remember they brought in a lot of demos, but there was no obvious 'Pull Me Under' on there. I kept asking John Petrucci if he could come up with another riff like that in terms of immediacy but it never quite came. I think he tried very hard to satisfy me, but ultimately they didn't really come up with a track that was a natural successor."

"The irony about that statement is that with the introduction of the seven-string guitar on the *Awake* album, the tone for a more riff-based style of writing was established," counters John Petrucci. "This style would further cement the fusion of metal and progressive music, which is what Dream Theater would ultimately be known for. I think it paved the way for many of our strongest and heaviest later songs like 'A Change of Seasons', 'The Glass Prison' and 'The Dark Eternal Night'."

In hindsight, it's ironic that "Pull Me Under" – which brought the band everything they had ever wanted in terms of critical acclaim and a solid fan base – would prove to be a millstone around their necks for many years to come. Dream Theater have never been a band who were naturally suited to writing with commercial interests in mind. They often had a compact, pop edge to their music, but it was never an intentional compromise aimed at giving them a Top Ten single. If radio played their songs it was merely a bonus, but predictably the record label and their accountants never quite saw it that way.

"'Pull Me Under' was an amazing thing but it was also in a way a bit disastrous," agrees Mike Portnoy. "Suddenly, and for many, many years throughout the Nineties, it gave the label these expectations of us being able to churn out more hit singles. 'Pull Me Under' was just a freak of nature. So when it became time to make *Awake*, suddenly they were looking for more hit singles."

Once the demo process had been concluded, the tracks were presented to the record label for their consideration. Derek Oliver admits to being dissatisfied with the results, but although it may appear simple to castigate him for exerting pressure on the band to somehow conjure another radio hit, he was also placed under a substantial amount of pressure by the suits residing in their ivory towers at East West HQ.

"*Awake* was flawed," claims Oliver. "The songs were good but not truly great, and standing alongside *Images And Words* it might well have complimented their former album but it certainly didn't exceed it. I pushed hard for better songs but internally in the record company I was fighting a losing battle. The president of the label was a woman called Sylvia Rhone who was calling me into her office incessantly, insisting that the band record the follow-up instantly. Her interest in the project was reduced to just one factor which was the billing for the company. The company's market share at the time was in the toilet, and one of the better prospects on the horizon for East West was a new album from Dream Theater. The band were a valuable commodity and advance orders on the *Awake* album could have been in the region of 300,000 or more That meant she could show instant billing of 300,000 at $7 each, which is about $2,000,000 plus. As she was in a constant panic to get the superstar acts on the label to record new albums, in the end the album's content was secondary to the main motive."

Despite Oliver's reticence about the marketability of the material on *Awake*, the band were given the go-ahead to begin the studio sessions once a suitable producer had been found. After the problems Dream Theater had encountered with David Prater on their previous album, they were unwilling to even contemplate working with him again. Once again, Derek Oliver was instrumental in attempting to locate a producer who could fit the band's tight specification.

"Getting a producer was another major headache," smiles Oliver now. "Obviously they wouldn't go back in with Prater, which I still believe was a major mistake. So we interviewed a lot of producers. We were talking about Ritchie Zito and Kevin Shirley but the band weren't keen. I also suggested John Cuniberti who had produced Joe Satriani's *Surfing With The Alien*, which was a sonically fantastic record, and I brought him in to meet with the band, but he was unimpressed. Then I suggested John Purdell and Duane Baron who had cut the Ozzy album *No More Tears* which was another great sounding record. I also thought they would understand that we needed the heaviness on the guitar and try and help Petrucci come through with that. It got to a point where the band were under pressure to use Duane and John and those sessions took place in LA."

The sessions began at One On One Studios in North Hollywood in May of 1994 and, compared to their previous studio experiences, the band were inspired by the working arrangements and fresh atmosphere created by the pair of producers.

"Those guys were great and so easygoing," recalls Mike Portnoy. "They were the perfect balance between what we'd had with Terry Date and David Prater. Terry had concentrated on the recording and engineering. With Prater, as much as it was a nightmare, he was the type of producer that was giving a lot of ideas. So with John and Duane, they were a good balance as they were spending a lot of time on the sound and recording process, but they would also have the occasional input and add an objective ear. Not as many ideas as Prater, but after that experience we were more than happy to have a set of producers that were going to take a step back and let us do our thing. The basic tracks were recorded at One On One Studios, which was where Metallica had done their *Black* album. Then we moved into Devonshire Studios, which was also in LA, for most of the overdub work."

"It was great working with them," adds John Petrucci. "I think everyone felt we were able to express ourselves a lot more genuinely. The experience from the road, learning more about our sound and what we like and don't like enabled us to be more prepared. The producers were totally into capturing that and being patient with us. So everybody walked away being completely satisfied with their performances and their sounds."

The album was to be mixed in New York, with both band and producers relocating to Unique Studios to finalize the album's sound. In typical Dream Theater fashion, though, the mixing didn't go too smoothly as Derek Oliver recalls.

"The first mixes of the record sounded dreadful, as if they had been recorded in a tin box," says Derek. "But that was because the band were in the mixing studio and everyone was having their input. So they were all pushing the faders up on their own particular instrument. Then John and Duane called me and said 'I don't know what you've been hearing, but we can't go on with this.' So it was kind of the same situation that they had with Prater as they were taking over and had stepped over the line again. So we had to ban the band from attending the mixing session. After Duane and John were left alone to do their jobs, they came back with some fantastic sounding tracks which Jim and I were very happy with. Of course the band disagreed, but they probably agree now that it's a good sounding record."

"Well yeah. We tried doing it one way and that didn't work," admitted James. "We were all in the studio when it first started and it was just unfair to the producers. Obviously each guy was focusing on his instrument, so it was like 'Wait, I want me up more!' So they were trying to please everyone and you just can't do that. You have to have some objectivity, so they were left alone. The one great thing – even though we were out of the studio – was that they were aware of what we wanted and didn't want. When David Prater mixed *Images*

And Words it was really unfortunate because he forgot to bring some sections out and he really didn't understand what we wanted for the final music. When Duane and John went in, they knew everything that needed to be there and how we wanted it to be represented."

But any complications over the precise sound of the final mix had already become entirely insignificant. Towards the end of the recording sessions in LA, Kevin Moore had announced to his astounded band-mates that he was to leave the band, citing the somewhat clichéd "musical differences" as a justification. Some of rock's nastiest feuds, such as David Lee Roth's departure from Van Halen and Fish's exit from Marillion, had used similar explanations to camouflage a mul-titude of sins that generally weren't musical in nature. But in Moore's case it did seem to hint at the truth. The keyboard player had cut a sullen and increasingly lonely figure in the studio during the process of both the writing and recording of *Awake*. With a couple of excep-tions, his input had been minimal, and he gave the distinct impression to his bandmates that he was merely a man going through the motions.

In a statement issued by the band's management a few months later, Moore declared: "Musically, I think my approach to writing has changed a lot in the past several years. It came to a point where my views were so different to the rest of the band that we were having trouble relating to each other's ideas. At the same time, I was finding a great deal of fulfilment writing and recording my own material. Eventually this became more important to me than anything else. Finally, I came to the decision that I needed to concentrate on my own creative identity, and that a split with the band would be the best thing for both the band and myself. I truly believe that Dream Theater have a lot more to offer the music world, and I have deep respect for each of them as musicians and as people. I wish them all the best."

Dream Theater's co-manager Jim Pitulski remembers the moment that he discovered Moore had decided to resign.

"I'll never forget it," he sighs. "Kevin called me up in my office and said, 'Is your office door closed?' And I said 'No', to which he replied 'Well, maybe you should close it.'"

"Now, we'd noticed that he had been getting a little distant, so when he said that to me I just said, 'Kevin, please tell me that you're not going to tell me what I think you're going to tell me?' But he said, 'Yeah, that's it. I'm leaving the band.' At that point, all our lives were hinging on Dream Theater's success, so it was a fairly dramatic day. We tried talking him out of it but he wouldn't hear of it. In retrospect though, he did do something cool. After the record was recorded in Los Angeles, he returned to New York, sold his belongings, packed everything into his station wagon and said, 'I'm moving away from Long Island.' So I asked him where he was moving to, and he said, 'I'll let you know when I get there.' He really had no idea what he was doing, and he just started driving cross country. I kind of admired that."

Although Dream Theater were stunned that Moore had decided to leave the band at the moment he did, they had been more than aware of the growing distance between them musically, and, critically, on a personal level too. Of all the friendships between the band members, the relationship between Moore and John Petrucci had always been tight, and the guitarist was particularly affected by the news.

"It was very hard for me and something I had never really envisaged happening," he shrugs. "Not only were we friends but we had been playing music together for so long that I almost couldn't conceive playing without him. So it was scary on a lot of levels. He was an integral part of the band, creatively, so how were we going to work without him? And the timing seemed bizarre. There we were, writing a follow-up to a successful record in Los Angeles, staying in these apartments, recording this record and nothing could have been better. And then he told me he was going to leave. It was like 'What? What are you talking about?'"

"I know while we were writing the material for *Awake*, and I guess even before that, he was starting to get into a lot of different music," he continues. "When we were growing up, we were all into the same things. We all liked Rush, Yes and Iron Maiden. Then all of a sudden he was listening to this other music that had nothing to do with that style of metal or progressive rock. Dream Theater were going in a certain musical direction, and maybe he didn't want to play that kind of music any more. Even now, I still really don't know what was going through his head, but that was kind of what I saw."

James LaBrie learnt of Moore's exit the day before he was to record his vocals. But even though he'd been absent from the writing process in the New York rehearsal studio, he recalls not being overly shocked to hear that Moore was leaving.

"The whole thing didn't come out of the blue," explained John Myung at the time. "He had felt that way for a while and it surfaced after *Awake* was recorded. It was more along the lines of peace of mind and what he wanted to do musically that he couldn't do in the band. He's a passionate person and he wasn't being fair to the band or himself. Out of all sincerity he didn't want to continue."

James LaBrie: "You could kind of see it coming as time went on. Even when we were finishing the *Images And Words* Tour, it was kind of weird and there already seemed to be a change in Kevin. He seemed to be more distant and wrapped up in himself. I didn't really know at the time whether I was reading it right but I do remember getting that vibe. It wasn't that he was rude or unpleasant with anyone you know? If you talked to him he would talk to you. But when Mike, John

Petrucci and John Myung were in the rehearsal studio putting together the music for *Awake*, he wasn't there as he had been in the past. And when he *was* there, the guys told me that he'd be sitting reading a magazine when they were trying to work out riffs. That didn't sound like a guy who was into it or cared about what they thought of it."

"I was in Los Angeles for a while before I started to record my vocals," he expands. "I remember a couple of times Kev and I went out in the evening to go to a bar, hang out and shoot shit. He was saying things like 'Sometimes in life you've got to figure out what's really important to you' and although he wouldn't come right out and say it, I was reading between the lines and thinking that if this isn't him telling me he's had enough, I don't know what he *is* trying to tell me. But the fact that it was confirmed really bummed me out. I just thought it was sad because there was so much more we could have done with Kevin if he'd been into it. I sometimes, although very rarely, sit back and wonder where the albums might have gone musically if Kevin had stayed in the band and had been passionate about it."

The "musical differences" explanation for Moore's departure is partly accurate. Since leaving the band, he has continued to compose and release music under a variety of guises (such as Chroma Key), and they have all been far removed from the kind of Rick Wakeman-style widdly-widdly sounds he created with the band. Instead, he has concentrated on writing atmospheric material more suited to film scores than progressive metal. But in hindsight, Mike Portnoy suggests there were other factors that perhaps added to Moore's dissatisfaction.

"I think another part is that for the first time in the band's career there were serious girlfriends in the equation," he says. "John and I had met our wives-to-be, and I think that probably played a little role in Kev's detachment. I don't know if it was jealousy or resentment. In the old days, on a weekend we would always get together and play, go to movies or concerts. Suddenly, we were with our girlfriends on a weekend and Kev was the only one who didn't really have a girlfriend throughout all of this. James was already married, and John Myung was kind of in his own world anyway. I may be reading too much into it, but I honestly feel that was a factor."

Another possible motivation for Moore was that he had never been too comfortable being in the spotlight. With an album as popular as *Images And Words*, hiding away from fans and the media became increasingly impossible.

"He was a very private person in the sense that he didn't like to share his feelings too much," explains Mike. "Suddenly he was doing interviews and constantly being questioned about what his lyrics meant and stuff like that. He's one of those types of artist that I think is more quiet and insular, as has been evident by everything he has done since leaving Dream Theater. He's very comfortable living a quiet, anonymous life and making art for art's sake. I don't think he really cares if he can make a living off music. The big success of Dream Theater throughout 1993 really shook him up a bit. We were doing interviews and had record company people showing up every day and wanting things, taking us to radio stations and record stores for in-store appearances. The whole machine of the music business just wasn't his cup of tea."

Rob Shore offers another angle on Moore's decision, suggesting that the prospect of prolonged touring proved a depressing thought for the keyboardist.

"I don't think it was personal," he says. "I can understand how a situation of going on the road can become intolerable with people that you just don't want to hang out with anymore. I think he still loved all the people in the band, but it was just the idea of being on tour with the same people. I just don't think he could take it any more."

The departure of the keyboard player had been kept under wraps and away from the record label until the last possible moment, hoping that they could quietly find a replacement and avoid unsettling their East West paymasters. It also gave the band a certain amount of breathing space, and allowed Mike time to concentrate on a vital engagement – his marriage to long-time girlfriend Marlene Apuzzo on July 30. In a peculiar twist of fate, Marlene had been the guitarist in New York metal band Meanstreak, along with Rena Sands (who had earlier married John Petrucci in September of 1993) and bassist Lisa Martens Pace, who many years later would marry John Myung.

"As soon as we finished recording we went home for the wedding," recalls Mike. "Even at my wedding we knew that Kev was leaving the band as he had already told us, but we hadn't told anybody else. The label and management were getting fired up for the new album, and we didn't want to take the wind from anyone's sails. We just wanted to deliver the record before anybody knew about it."

One of the wedding guests was former Fates Warning vocalist and one-time temporary Dream Theater vocalist, John Arch. Arch recalls that he was shocked to learn that Moore had left the band.

"Kevin actually didn't want to sit with the band and he sat over at our table," he says. "But what a disappointment that he was out of the band. I really felt that it was almost destiny that these guys had met each other. It was evident in the music how well they worked together, and he added a whole dimension to that band."

In a manner befitting such a rock 'n' roll couple, a wedding band was booked who were able to recite songs slightly heavier than the usual party band. What the assembled guests didn't know was that the frontman was none other than Charlie Dominici.

"After Dream Theater, I stayed in music and did some more of the club date type of gigs," explains Charlie. "Not just weddings, but private and corporate affairs. I'd play places like the Waldorf Astoria and the Ritz. At the time Mike called me and wanted someone who knew how to do a wedding and a little bit more rock 'n' roll than the average wedding band, and his natural choice was me. I was thrilled and gave him a real good wedding day."

Mike Portnoy: "Even when Charlie was in the band with us, he would do wedding gigs on the side. So when it came for me and Marlene to look for a wedding band, he was the first person I thought of. I called him to see if he would be interested, and see if he would be offended or insulted by the idea of it. But he thought it was a great idea and was up for it."

The fact that Dominici agreed to perform was quite unexpected. Not that there was bad blood between the two parties following his sacking back in 1989, but it certainly took an incredible strength of character for him to appear.

"I felt quite sad for him really," remembers Derek Oliver. "Obviously the band at that point had been riding high with *Images And Words*, and then there's poor old Charlie singing in a wedding band."

But despite such reservations that many of the guests may have had, by the time he had finished his set Charlie had the audience in raptures.

"Yes it was a wedding band, but I tell you what, I have a lot of respect for him," enthuses John Arch. "I always thought he was an excellent musician and he was actually very good. He was an awesome guitar player too."

Naturally, the band couldn't keep Moore's departure under wraps forever and the news had to be conveyed at some point to Derek Oliver. Oliver admits that he was stunned to hear of the resignation.

"It really was a bombshell," he confirms. "I always felt that Kevin's contribution to the band was pretty much immeasurable. This isn't meant as a slight on the band but they have intense personalities. There's Mike who is very hot-headed; John Petrucci who isn't quite as hot-headed but equally as recalcitrant; and John Myung who kind of goes with the flow, but in his own silent way has a huge influence over the others. So I felt Kevin was the under-rated member of the band and was a bit of a glue in that situation. When he left it was quite a shock for me, as I never saw it coming and they were on the edge of maybe having a huge second album. I said to him 'Are you sure you want to do this, as you can do your solo projects after this?' But he was adamant."

The necessity to find a swift replacement for Moore was even more pressing given that a headlining, showcase gig at the Concrete Foundations Forum in Burbank, California, had been scheduled for September 9. With the new album set to be unveiled in a live setting for the first time, Dream Theater had just a few short weeks to locate and bring into the fold a new member. With such an unyielding schedule, the band even tried asking Moore to play one last gig with them as a favour. But, as Rob Shore explains, he snubbed their pleas.

"I remember he was insistent on leaving on a certain date: we had this gig in Burbank and he just refused to go," he sighs. "We had a band meeting and I said that I'd talk to Kevin as I was convinced I could talk him into it. But he had made up his mind, and the more I tried to talk him into it, the less chance I had. If I had said nothing I would have made more progress than I did. But to this day Kevin Moore is one of my favourite people in the world. We had a great time working together, and I respect and admire him for doing what he did."

Dates were set for auditions in New York, and the band began putting out feelers within the industry to try and detect appropriate candidates. One of those who appeared suitable and attended a trial was Jens Johansson who had established his credentials through high-profile work with the likes of Yngwie Malmsteen's Rising Force. Indeed, it seems a tentative, informal offer had already been made to Johansson by the band's management to fill in the keyboard slot on a temporary basis – an offer which was later retracted – as Jens remembers.

"I think their management company at the time just told me I was to fill in on a couple of shows at first," says Johansson. "I think the band were a bit out of the loop since they were all out on some trip. Then shortly after that, some retard at their label announced that Kevin had left and in the same release, that I was a full member of the band already! Before that, nobody knew Kevin was even leaving, so because of the newsworthiness of that, and me 'being in Dream Theater' it got a lot of coverage – which was annoying. But that was retracted and I guess everyone was a bit anxious and confused."

"We never really clicked with him," says Mike. "Maybe it was because he was Swedish and we're American, and we had trouble picturing him really blending with us on a full-time basis. Also, as much as we admired his lead playing, we weren't sure as to how he would be in terms of a composer or as someone who can contribute parts in verses or choruses."

Derek Oliver and Jim Pitulski were however convinced that Johansson was the right choice, but despite their best efforts to persuade the band to at least let him join on a trial basis, they remained steadfast in their refusal.

"The band were always contrary to whatever the right decision should be, so they were like 'No we're not going to do that'," laughs Derek. "So Jim and I were trying to influence them by telling them that Jens was the guy, but they weren't having any of it."

Another keyboardist the band approached was Jordan Rudess. With

Mike Portnoy receiving an award for best up-and-coming drummer in a drum magazine and John Petrucci topping a similar category in *Guitar* magazine, they logically decided to establish who won the comparable award in *Keyboard* magazine. Rudess had received the accolade that year, so he seemed to be the natural choice.

"I didn't know who they were before they called me," laughs Jordan. "So I went out and bought the *Images And Words* album to listen to, and that was pretty much all I knew about them at the time. It was probably a good thing I didn't hear their debut album as I probably wouldn't have liked it! But I put *Images And Words* on and I thought they were so tight. It was the first time I had heard any kind of progressive metal, so I was excited and suitably impressed with their abilities."

"I remember I played my song 'Over The Edge' for them at my audition," he continues. "I'd also learned 'Take The Time' and 'Pull Me Under' which I'd written out in my little music manuscript page and brought along. I think the guys were blown away with the 'Over The Edge' piece, so I started to teach it to them and we had fun with that. The vibes were very good, it was all cool, and we all went away to think about it. Anyway, it turned out later that they really wanted me to do this gig and join the band."

Mike remembers that Jordan's audition had "blown his mind", claiming that he was the "best keyboard player we'd ever seen." After considering his options, Jordan agreed to play the Foundations Forum gig with the band, but turned down the opportunity to join them on a permanent basis. Around the same time as the Dream Theater offer, Jordan had been approached by guitarist Steve Morse who'd asked him to link up with the Dixie Dregs.

"It was a very interesting time in my life because my oldest child was only a year old at that point," explains Jordan. "She was a year old, I had a job with Kurzweil and the possibility of a job with the Dregs for shorter runs of shows. The offers literally came in the space of a week or two, so I had both things floating around my brain trying to figure out what to do. I had the choice of doing the Dregs shows and still keeping my job with Kurzweil or I could take a chance for less money and join Dream Theater. But that would've meant a lot more travelling and not seeing my little one, and at that point we didn't know if Dream Theater was just going to be a flash in the pan. So all in all I decided I would be better off going with the Dregs, continuing with Kurzweil and being around for my family as much as possible."

In the short term at least, the decision ironically meant that Jordan hardly saw his family while he spent a fortnight locked away transcribing music for both bands in preparation for the looming gigs.

"It was insane," he recalls. "I was in the studio non-stop for two weeks just learning all that stuff. I remember actually borrowing an

Eventide Harmonizer because it had this ability to slow some parts down, and with some of the Petrucci riffs I really needed it to hear what the *hell* he was playing!"

Naturally, everybody had high expectations for the Burbank gig. The industry showcase was an opportunity for Dream Theater to demonstrate that their new album had the potential to equal *Images And Words* as well as prove that the loss of Kevin Moore could easily be shrugged off. With Jordan up to speed, everything was set for the band to make a forceful return. But the band hadn't factored into the equation the antics of guitarist Yngwie Malmsteen, who was playing immediately before them. For reasons known only to himself, the Swede decided to ignite his guitar during his set. With the gig taking place in the unusual surroundings of a hotel, the building was hurriedly evacuated by the fire commissioner, and the ensuing pandemonium meant that Dream Theater's onstage time was pushed back to the early hours.

"At that point, with everybody evacuated from the room it kind of blew the excitement out of our showcase," reflects Mike Portnoy. "So by the time the fire commissioner let people back in, half the people were tired or drunk and others had gone back to their rooms. In hindsight, it was probably a good thing as we ended up not playing that well. It was scary for us playing for the first time without Kev, so the tempos were very fast and we weren't that tight. Plus we were out of shape from not having played live in so long. So maybe it was a blessing in disguise that our showcase was deflated a bit by Yngwie."

Adding further insult to injury, Malmsteen appeared in the Dream Theater dressing room to make a grovelling apology for his guitar-torching behaviour. Once the band had accepted his request for forgiveness, he proceeded to spill beer all over a couch and himself, as well as devouring the contents of their deli tray, ensuring that Dream Theater left the venue both dejected and hungry.

At the end of September, the album's lead single "Lie" was released in an effort to generate radio and TV interest akin to the surge of awareness that had accompanied "Pull Me Under" a couple of years earlier. The accompanying video showed the four-piece band running through their paces at assorted New York locations, such as the Brooklyn Bridge and the streets of Tribeca, with even a midtown Manhattan tunnel being temporarily closed to traffic to allow the band to complete the shoot. But despite the snappy video, the single failed to make any impact on the chart. The song itself was originally intended to be part of "The Mirror", as James recalled in an interview with *Album Network*.

"I remember one of the first tapes they sent me to start jamming with up in Canada was 'The Mirror'. We used to jam instrumentally to it on the last tour and then we built it into a song, with the lyrics and melodies but also within the song was 'Lie'. I heard this groove and I was going 'Oh my God, that's a song in itself!' So I called up the guys and said 'Man, I really feel strong[ly] about this song. Can't we take that groove and build a song?' So that was how that came about."

Released on October 4, 1994, *Awake* wasn't as instantly gratifying as its predecessor, and was an album that took abundant listens before the tracks seized hold of the listener. Yet the lack of immediacy has ensured that it remains one of the more notable and durable releases in Dream Theater's back-catalogue. It may not have been filled to the brim with potential hit singles but the stunning arrangements and sheer variety of the material proved *Images And Words* had been no fluke. *Awake* was a potent statement of their future objectives, and features James LaBrie's vocals at their earthiest. "People will think 'They've changed singer again!'" he joked at the time in an interview with *RAW* magazine. "My vocals on this album are more varied and a lot more aggressive."

The lyrics to the nimble opening track "6:00" were penned by Kevin Moore prior to his departure, and hinted at his growing feelings of detachment from the rest of the band. Certainly they insinuated that being a member of Dream Theater had merely become a job to him, with lines such as *"So many ways to drown a man / So many ways to drag him down"* possessing an undeniable poignancy and resonance. On the flipside, the album's most melodic track "Innocence Faded" had lyrics written by John Petrucci, and were inspired by the gradual deterioration of his friendship with Moore.

"The way that I write lyrics a lot of the time is that I'll take an initial spark of an idea," explains John. "And that certainly is in there. But then I'll kind of generalize and add in other situations. So I couldn't say it was solely about that, but it was definitely inspired by that. There was a feeling of it not being the same way it had been, and the realization that things were not always going to remain the same."

Elsewhere, the complex interplay on the compelling instrumental "Erotomania" once again demonstrated the band's continued love of creating technical, old-school progressive rock melodies. Mike asserts it was written as a "bit of a joke and parody", adding that it had been written pretty much "off the cuff" – a claim that, if true, makes the track even more remarkable. The seamless delicacy of the acoustic "The Silent Man" provided a rare laid-back moment, and according to James LaBrie in an interview at the time, the lyrics "deal with communication breakdown, for instance between a father and a son. We feel that we have to play certain roles when around one of our parents, and we never really get to know the real person. I'm lucky that I behave with my own father like I would with a friend. We can joke around and go for a beer."

"Lifting Shadows Off A Dream " is a mesmerizing and delicate track and was based on an idea that John Myung brought to the studio, as John Petrucci explained.

"That song has an interesting story. The way it starts with the two chords going back and forth. John Myung had these lyrics, which were really just a poem, and he wanted to make a song out of it. He had this idea and just two chords! We were like 'John, where are we going to go with just two chords?' We worked on it, wracked our brains, recorded the jam and by the end of the night were like 'Ahh fuck it. This sucks.' We came by the next day, listened to the recording and thought it could be really cool. All of a sudden it evolved into this song."

Another elegant track was "Voices" which neatly combined lilting melodies with a driving guitar riff. The lyrics were written by John Petrucci and dealt with the subject of mental illness, as he explains.

"It's about a psychotic disorder," he says. "The facts in that song are based on actual medical documents as I did some research on schizophrenia and stuff like that. So it is fictional but based on that factual information. The religious terms come into it to make things more vivid. When I was writing it, I saw these terms and medical things that were just brilliant. Like there was a guy who felt that his skin was inside out. I read that and was like 'Oh my God! That's unbelievable; I've got to write that.'"

The closing track on *Awake* is also the album's most peculiar. Written by Kevin Moore and brought into the studio as a completed piece, the mournful "Space-Dye Vest" sits awkwardly with the rest of the album. Bizarre both lyrically and musically, LaBrie revealed the meaning of the song in an interview with RAW shortly after the album's release.

"Kevin Moore saw this photograph in a fashion magazine of a beautiful model wearing a space-dye vest and he fell in love with her," he said. "He carried that magazine around with him for ages, but he realized that the only way the innocence could be kept, so that he could retain that love for her, was if she stayed on the page. If he'd met her, all that would have been lost. A strange song."

With the song being extremely personal to Moore, and the music he created to accompany the pretty bizarre lyrics not having any of the usual Dream Theater attributes, Mike Portnoy reveals that he now wishes that it hadn't been included on the album.

"When we first heard it we thought it was so very, very different we didn't think we even wanted to fuck with it," he explains. "At the time we decided to put 'Space Dye Vest' on the album because we thought Kev was staying in the band. In retrospect, if we had known earlier that he would be leaving I don't think we would even have put it on the album."

Tellingly, the band have never played the song live and have stated that it's their intention never to do so.

As for the album's title, James LaBrie revealed at the time that "Awake is the perfect word to describe the album's lyrics. What we're basically talking about is the awareness of your existence – becoming closer and more in touch with yourself and ultimately discovering what works best for you as an individual as you try to get through life."

The sleeve was another otherworldly creation of Larry Freemantle who had designed its predecessor's cover. A dark and mainly monochromatic design that somehow matched the music, Freemantle was once again directed by the band to integrate numerous lyrical references, such as a clock face showing a time of 6:00, a mirror and a spider encircled by a web.

"The band were very definite about what they wanted, and where they wanted it," recalls Freemantle. "The mirror was to be buried in the sand with a factory in the background so it was just a case of putting it together. But putting that together was a little problematic because the company we had used on *Images And Words*, Access Images, had broken up. So I ended up sorting that out and basically used Photoshop to get that together from stock imagery. It was done really quickly and I always felt frustrated with that sleeve as I lost too much time on it. I was always up against deadlines on certain things and it got away from me."

In spite of the plentiful redeeming features on *Awake*, press reviews were generally subdued. It must of course be remembered that it was released just as the shoe-gazing, miserable purveyors of the fad known as grunge were taking hold. The British press in particular seemed dazzled by the work of Kurt Cobain and his cohorts, and anything that wasn't based around three-chords or packed with lyrics championing depression as a lifestyle choice was in for a hard ride.

The usually sympathetic *Metal Hammer* harshly bemoaned: "Progressive rock is basically a very adolescent notion of what 'grown up' music might sound like – more notes, longer solos and, best/worst of all, convoluted concepts... Their propensity for pomposity extends to the ballad 'Silent Man', which would probably like to be Queensrÿche's 'Silent Lucidity' but in fact sounds like Stryper on a particularly pious day... Musical masturbation for sure, but that's adolescents for you."

Q magazine, whose hostility towards progressive rock is well known, were less cynical, writing: "Fans of Marillion may well love this, and even the sceptical listener can enjoy the crunching, radio-friendly choruses of 'Scarred' and 'Caught In A Web'."

Fortunately, reviews in the US were generally more positive, with *Guitar For The Practising Musician* describing *Awake* as "everything an art-rock album ought to be." *Guitar World* placed the album in their top ten releases of the year, summarizing it as, "Faster than a silver bullet, tighter than the jeans I bought six months ago, more powerful than a box of Ex Lax, this shred party left me punch-drunk and, for once in my life, fully *Awake*."

Yet, despite the impact of grunge, the album peaked at a respectable Number 32 in the US and 65 in the UK, although Mike Portnoy admits that the grunge genre had become an irritation.

"There might have been a little bit of resentment in the early days because suddenly these bands that were so anti-musicianship were becoming fashionable and hugely popular," he says. "So, as much as those types of bands took pot shots at us, it was also easy for us to shoot back at them. Maybe because we're serious musicians or because we played progressive music we were a little more open-minded. We were able to see the merits of some of those bands, such as Alice In Chains, Soundgarden and a few years earlier Jane's Addiction. A lot of these bands were doing it well, though there was a fair share of shit as well. But it was pretty much the end of the period for metal, and even MTV's *Headbanger's Ball* was finishing. So by the time *Awake* came out we were starting to feel as though the climate had started to change."

The more pressing dilemma confronting the band was the need to locate another keyboard player. With a world tour looming, they held another round of auditions, and were swayed by the prowess of Derek Sherinian. As John Petrucci explains, with one minor exception, they had no reservations about asking him to join them.

"Derek was great," he smiles. "One of the things that led us to make the decision to have him in the band was that he was very like Kevin. He really sounded like him when playing and was very easy to get along with. Just a really cool guy. The only thing was that at the time, we all had long hair and he had short hair. But I mean, big deal – look at us now!"

"Plus he was a very capable player and had a similar musical interest to us as he was very into Ozzy, Van Halen, Judas Priest and stuff like that," interjects Mike Portnoy. "He also had a jazz background and was at Berklee the year before we were there in 1984, so it just felt like he was one of us. He was a normal person who didn't come along with much baggage, and had experience from playing with Alice Cooper and Kiss. So all of those elements were the reason we took him. We were unsure as to whether we could make a full-time commitment to him, so initially we took him on as a hired gun just to do the tour and we would feel him out from there."

The ever vivacious and entertaining Derek George Sherinian was born in Laguna Beach, California, on August 25, 1966. Once described by Gene Simmons of Kiss as looking like "the love-child of Paul

Stanley and Cher", he possesses an appealing rock star attitude and flamboyance that attests he made the perfect career choice to match his personality.

While not a descendant of a particularly musical family – his parents and relatives were involved in various businesses and real estate – he developed a love of playing the keyboards at a young age, and by his late teens his talent had enabled him to take his place at Berklee College in Boston. A year ahead of Dream Theater's Mike and the two Johns (and consequently not an acquaintance of theirs), he also departed after three semesters to pursue a career in rock. Returning to California to set up home in Los Angeles, he linked up with former Band Of Gypsies drummer, Buddy Miles, touring with him for a couple of years before he was offered an opportunity to join Alice Cooper's band. During his time at Berklee, he had become friends with guitarist Al Pitrelli who was already a member of that band, and Pitrelli had suggested to the legendary rocker that Derek would be an ideal choice for a vacant keyboard position. Working with Cooper from 1989 until 1991 (and at sporadic shows until 1996), Derek performed on the *Trash* and *Hey Stoopid* tours – even making a fleeting appearance alongside Alice in the cult movie *Wayne's World* – before Kiss approached him to join them as their off-stage keyboardist. The position lasted for around a year, with Sherinian appearing on the live recording *Alive III*. It was following his tenure with Kiss that he was made aware by his friend (and Joe Satriani's then drummer) Jonathon Mover that Dream Theater were searching for a keyboardist, as he explains.

"Until that point I had heard people talking about the band and saying they were really technical players" he says. "But I hadn't heard any of their music and didn't know their sound at all. Al Pitrelli was also friends with John Petrucci as they were both from Long Island, and they used to teach at the same guitar store. So I had Al put in a call on my behalf to John. I think Al basically said to him 'Look, you've got to hire this keyboard player. He's my friend, he's great. You've got to check him out and at least give him an audition.' So John called me right away and that conversation went well. Then their management sent me some CDs to learn the songs for the audition."

Dream Theater had selected "Pull Me Under", "Take The Time" and "Caught In A Web" as the audition songs. Although he had over a week to comprehend the complexities of the music and rehearse for the tryout, Derek recalls being somewhat daunted by the prospect.

"I had the fear of God struck in me from listening to the material," he laughs. "I mean, I'd listened to fusion music before and old-school progressive rock, but I had never heard anything so heavy with that type of precision. So I looked at it as a challenge to better myself musically and really explore what these guys were doing. I remember going to New

York; we went through the tunes, there was a good vibe and I felt really comfortable with them. I just told them at the end of the audition that I'd never been in a progressive band before but that I thought what they were doing was great and that I thought I could contribute. They saw I had uniqueness to my playing and my solo style, and I remember Mike commented on that right away. I also said that I was willing to work extremely hard. I left feeling it was 50/50 but it could've gone either way. So I was very excited the following week when I got the call back asking me to step into the band."

With Derek being offered the position at the beginning of October – albeit on a trial basis – he was left with a mere fortnight to memorize all the keyboard parts in preparation for the tour. While Dream Theater's shows at the time weren't any longer than many other bands, their repertoire was far more complex and difficult to play. Understandably, this caused the new boy a certain amount of consternation, being far removed from his experience with previous bands.

"In the past, when I had been on tour with Alice Cooper and Kiss, they would rehearse in a room for two weeks," he explains. "Then they would go into the pre-production room, which was a big soundstage, to work out all of the lights and all the kinks to the show for a month. So in total they did six weeks of rehearsal for five days a week before the first show and that was for *simple* music. So when I came into Dream Theater there were no rehearsals booked and it was insane. It's one thing going in to play for an artist with hit songs that you've heard since you were a kid, and the songs are ingrained in your mind. It was another thing altogether going in with music you've never heard before that is totally off the charts as far as technical prowess. And to retain about two hours worth of material in that short a period of time was overwhelming. But it is amazing what one will do to ascend. I knew that if I could get over the obstacles and cut this gig, it would open up huge doors for me in the future. So when I was in New York at the rehearsals, I would play the songs at night over and over on a loop so that I would be subliminally programmed and it would ingrain it in my head. The only way I was going to have a shot was to totally immerse myself."

Although the thought of working with the band proved appealing, he was more than aware that his presence might not have been welcomed by all the fans, especially given that he was replacing Moore who had been elevated almost to the status of prog rock God by some of the more fanatical members of the audience.

"Yeah, well any time you replace an original member of a band there are going to be people who are immediately against it," he says. "I was against it when Sammy Hagar came in to replace David Lee Roth because I was a huge Van Halen fan, and the original members were sacred. I understand that and accepted that going in."

The first leg of the Waking Up The World Tour began on October 20, 1994, at The Strand in Providence, Rhode Island, and continued throughout the autumn, taking in cities across the US and Canada before ending in Hollywood on December 9. The tour had included a sentimental, college "homecoming" gig in Boston for the two Johns, Mike and Derek when they played at Berklee College's Performance Centre. The gig actually took place in the same auditorium that the band used to endure weekly "listening analysis" classes, which added to the sense of occasion.

The performances during this segment of the tour had been championed by many observers as being particularly incisive, but for James LaBrie a break in the Caribbean would prove to be catastrophic. His wife Karen had splashed out on a Christmas break to Varadero Beach in Cuba with the intention of helping to revitalize James for the impending legs of the tour. But the contents of his breakfast on the morning of December 30, 1994, would ultimately affect him for years to come.

"We woke up, and for breakfast I had rice, pork and eggs," says James, visibly shuddering at the memory. "I remember eating and saying to Karen 'Does this taste OK to you? I'm not sure if this is rare or is this the way things taste down here?' And she thought it was OK but it didn't taste right to me. Two hours later, I was back in my room and started sweating profusely. Then I started to get dizzy and throw up and I was extremely sick. If you've ever had food poisoning you'll know that you wish you are dead. I was at the point of dry heaves, where there's nothing left in your stomach but you're still nauseous. There's nothing you can do. I was delirious and felt like someone had drugged me. I remember being over the bowl and doing these dry heaves when this squeak flew out of my throat. I tried to speak to Karen but I couldn't talk, and it was three or four days before I had a voice back, and even then it was very weak and raspy."

With a tour of Japan beginning on January 14, 1995, James was terrified that he may have permanently impaired his voice, and on returning home headed straight to an ears, nose and throat specialist for them to gauge the damage.

"The specialist told me in layman's terms that it was like ruptured vocals cords," he explains. "I asked him if it was irreparable and he told me it wasn't, but that it would take time to heal. He said that the best thing would be to not sing for six months to a year. I told him it was impossible as we were in the middle of a world tour. I actually went to see three throat specialists and they all said that it was literally going to be years before I could sing or sound like I had done before. I was in total shock, and devastated. The thing is, on the US leg I had felt so on top of my game, and that my voice was getting stronger. I had been so psyched and couldn't wait to blow everyone away around the rest of the world. We weren't in a position for me to take a six-month break so I had to keep touring."

Concerned though he was about whether his voice would be able to endure another prolonged bout of touring, James was at least able to sing – although with limitations – and with an album to promote and concerts booked, there was no other realistic option but to head for Japan. Adding insult to injury, however, his journey to rendezvous with the rest of the band in Kanagawa turned into another nightmare.

"It took me 46 hours to get to Tokyo for that first show," recalls James. "Our flight from Toronto into New York was diverted to Pittsburgh as we couldn't land in La Guardia because of thick fog. So they had us on the tarmac in Pittsburgh for five hours. By the time the flight was re-scheduled to arrive in New York, we were missing our flight from JFK to Tokyo. So I had the manager scurrying around getting me on other flights. We eventually got to JFK and flew to London, England, where we had another six- or seven-hour wait before we then got a flight to Tokyo. It was insane. I literally landed in Tokyo two hours before the gig. The promoter's rep picked me up, drove me to the hotel, I took a shower, got back in the car for a drive to the venue and went straight onstage. It was cruelty."

Jetlagged and hoarse, LaBrie toiled through the gig and, although far from his finest performance, it partially dispelled his apprehension and proved that though uncomfortable, he could at least continue with the tour. After their next gig in Osaka, the band went to the local Hard Rock Café where they presented the venue with platinum award discs for *Images And Words* and a couple of autographed drum heads. Suitably refreshed after a heavy night celebrating, they retired to their hotel rooms in the early hours. But at 5:45am on the morning of January 17, 1995, they were violently woken from their sleep when an earthquake, centred on Kobe and measuring 7.2 on the Richter scale, struck.

"It was really terrifying," reflects Mike. "I had only been asleep a couple of hours and was probably still drunk when it happened. I didn't even think it was real and thought I was dreaming. It felt like we were being bombed and that it was World War III or Armageddon. It was like a nuclear bomb had gone off, and I really didn't know what to make of it. I remember looking out of the window and just seeing the entire building swaying back and forth, and I thought it was going to tip over. At the time I didn't know that they were built to sway like that. Everyone was gathered in the hallway going 'What the fuck was that? What's going on?' We were all terrified. I never ran down 27 flights of stairs so quickly in my life. There were like old Japanese people in the stairwell and I'm just like running right past them and jumping over them just to get the hell out of there."

Jim Pitulski recalls the band and himself staggering around the hotel corridors in a state of panic, with the notable exception of the unruffled Derek Sherinian.

"The whole building has motion sensors, so all the lights in the room were on and it threw me right off the bed," he says. "I immediately started calling the guys in their rooms to make sure everyone was OK. People were completely freaking out and tearing through the hallways yelling and screaming. I actually still have a chunk of the building that had fallen out of the roof that I keep on top of my entertainment centre. Everybody was freaked except Derek, as he lived in LA and had experienced earthquakes before. I remember him calmly walking out of his room, wearing sunglasses, eating an apple with a really scantily clad Japanese girl on his arm, and he just said 'Rock 'n' roll baby!'"

In the immediate aftermath, the band cancelled their scheduled second night in Osaka, but travelled to Fukuoka to continue the tour a couple of days later. Understandably, the band had seriously considered scrapping the tour, as Mike explains.

"We did a pay-per-view TV broadcast a few days later, and that was one of the reasons we had to stick it out," he says. "There was a serious feeling of sadness and loss throughout the entire country as it was a monumental earthquake in Japanese history. I guess that was another level of our history between us and the Japanese people as we kind of shared that experience and went through it with them, and that has bonded us with Japanese fans all these years."

Although continuing the tour, the band did hold a minute's silence at every gig in memory of the 4,000 people that had been killed. The true horror of the quake was also brought home to Jim Pitulski when he met with renowned Japanese tour promoter, Mr Udo, before a gig in Tokyo.

"I remember him telling a story about a friend of his whose house had collapsed in Kobe," he reflects. "His little girl was calling out to him but he was unable to save her and Mr Udo started crying. It really was shocking to see this immensely powerful man breaking down in front of us."

Dazed by the experience, Dream Theater headed back home for a couple of days before hitting Europe to begin another leg of the tour. The first stop was the BBC studios in London for an appearance on Bruce Dickinson's radio show. The band had met the singer back in 1992 when they supported Iron Maiden, and all of Dream Theater were self-confessed Maiden fanatics. As it turned out, Bruce was an admirer of theirs too, and after the band had run through live versions of "Lifting Shadows Off A Dream", "6:00" and "Caught In A Web", he joined them to sing the vocals on a cover version of Deep Purple's "Perfect Strangers". The rendition of that song proved to be a perfect rehearsal for the following night's gig at the celebrated London jazz venue, Ronnie Scott's Club. Mike Portnoy had been inspired to convince the band to perform a set consisting entirely of cover versions, as well as taking the opportunity to invite some special guests to perform alongside them in front of an invitation-only audience of around 300.

"That was the first time we had done something out of the ordinary in terms of a live show," explains Mike. "So it was a little bit of an adjustment to play a small club, come up with a set list of different music and get all these special guests. It was a lot of work. While we were in Japan, we were learning all the songs and working on them at soundcheck which was a lot of extra work. Jim Pitulski played a big part in putting that show together and gathering some of the special guests. It was, at that point, one of the coolest things we had ever done."

Selecting songs that had influenced Dream Theater throughout their career, the set was varied, ranging from instrumental versions of Elton John's "Funeral For A Friend" and "Love Lies Bleeding" to U2's "Red Hill Mining Town", with a generous sprinkling of material from rock greats such as Kansas, Genesis, Led Zeppelin, Rush and Journey. The first guest performer was Napalm Death's Barney Greenway who added his own distinctive guttural vocals to Metallica's "Damage Inc.". Indeed, so staggering was his technique that, in video footage of the event, both James LaBrie and John Myung can be seen laughing with looks of incredulity on their faces. Greenway was followed by Marillion's Steve Hogarth who added piano and vocals to a rough and ready rendition of The Beatles' "Happiness Is A Warm Gun" before that band's guitarist Steve Rothery appeared onstage for a tender version of Marillion's "Easter".

Arguably the highlight of the entire evening was the appearance of Yes guitarist Steve Howe, who put his idiosyncratic licks to a consummate and expansive instrumental medley that included sections from that band's "Machine Messiah", "Heart Of The Sunrise", "Close To The Edge" and "Siberian Khatru".

"The strangest thing was that he didn't seem to know the songs from the Yes medley that we had planned," laughed John Petrucci at the time, in an interview with journalist Dave Ling. "In rehearsal he was saying 'How does it go again?' But when we came to the show he was so psyched to be there."

Speaking in an interview in RAW magazine, Howe confirmed that he'd thoroughly enjoyed the experience and spoke in glowing terms about Dream Theater's performance.

"It's excellent that they're making this music, they have the electricity and dynamism to do it, although obviously they're heavier than Yes were," he said. "But they know what they want to do, and they have the expertise to do it. They're still young and seem to have the same dedication that Yes did all the way through the Seventies. There just isn't enough of that kind of progressive music around, but somehow Dream Theater's fan base seems to be growing all the time, so they must be doing something right. They've got the balance right between heaviness and precision, and they've got a good direction."

Barney Greenway also later declared: "Having been roped in for my unmusical assets, I felt like a square peg in a round hole as the dressing room debated notation progressions, and various melodious throats were exercised. Being a relatively unknown Brummie with no pomp credentials, I expected to be shot down in flames when slotted in alongside the Rothery/Hogarth finesse of 'Easter' and Howe's intricate twiddling on the Yes medley. However, the gig was undertaken with a wealth of good spirit and onstage it went like a breeze."

With the gig being held in such an intimate venue, the logistics of ensuring things went as intended proved to be a horrendous experience for those working behind the scenes. Although Jim Pitulski had efficiently made the crucial arrangements with the guest performers, it was left to Dante Bonutto who worked in the London office of the band's label to co-ordinate backstage events as well as arrange the recording of the gig for a later release.

"To be honest with you, it wasn't my idea to do the Ronnie Scott's thing," he says. "It was a great idea on paper, but it was a nightmare because Ronnie Scott's is not designed to deal with a band like Dream Theater. The logistics of the show were so hard. We had a big mobile outside recording it as well and a lot of people turned up for the show and there was trouble getting everybody in. Obviously there are tables at Ronnie Scott's so there were people standing at the back. But behind the scenes it was one of those where we were wondering why we had ever done it. It was like trying to put a pint and a half into a pint glass. I mean, Mike's drum kit alone *was* the stage, but it was one of those nights that you still talk about. I also remember the venue trying to pull the plug before the band had finished playing because they were slightly over-running. I just made the excuse that 'It's their last song' because they didn't know that a Dream Theater song is not a normal song, so we were quite a way off finishing the set. They let me get away with it but I got a lot of grief that night."

Jim Pitulski also recalls the management at the venue threatening to forcibly enforce a curfew by cutting the onstage power.

"I remember I was literally on my knees begging," Jim laughs. "The band went over and they really were going to pull the plug. There was this heavy-set woman who was running the place, and she was going to pull it because the set was running long. I was pleading, 'Look, we've got a mobile recording truck out there, MTV is here, please don't do this!' And finally they let us finish."

With the venue being booked for a jazz night after Dream Theater's set, Dante was asked at the end of the show to make an announcement requesting that the fans quickly leave the building. Thoroughly hacked off at the backstage troubles, he vented his frustration with some biting sarcasm, pronouncing: "Can everyone now make their way out as quickly as possible as I think there is some jazz going to happen – so it's worth leaving."

"They took offence at that because I'd used the word jazz in vain," laughs Dante. "But I was really pissed off by that point. We had a party afterwards in The Royal George pub, and the band had really enjoyed it. I was amazed at how many people turned up. We had issued a certain number of tickets but everyone came, and everybody on the guest list as well. I was also amazed at the guest musicians they pulled in – it was a very high-calibre performance."

Following the gig, the band headed for mainland Europe to continue the tour, and while on a rare day off in Germany on February 5, they filmed the video for the next single release, "The Silent Man". With Mike Portnoy having an obsessive passion for movies, he had always sought to become involved in directing and had submitted a treatment for the video (basically a rough synopsis) to the other members of the band using a fake name. The band were impressed by the proposed storyline and at that point Mike revealed he was the author. Yet, despite his best efforts at persuading the record label to allow him to direct the shoot, they stood firm and only offered him a co-directing credit. Pamela Birkhead was employed as the other director, but on the day of the shoot, Mike became violently ill and when not needed on the set to perform spent hours curled up in his tour bus bunk. The video featured the band as a four-piece with Derek still being regarded as a session player. But the band had decided that his tenure as a hired-gun was becoming increasingly untenable, given the contributions he had made during the few months he had been with them.

"After spending that time on the road we had got to know him musically and personally," says Mike. "He had a great sense of humour, was very professional and considerate to our history and didn't try to step on that. So there was no reason for us not to bring him on full-time."

Derek was officially asked to join the band as a *bona fide* member on February 21 during an overnight ferry journey to Helsinki. Mike's tour diary noted the incident.

"Today's ferry ride was a monumental event in Dream Theater history," he wrote. "Me, James, John P, John M, Derek Sherinian and our tour manager Bill had a nice dinner at the end of which we welcomed Derek Sherinian into the band as a full member of Dream Theater. He was pleasantly surprised and extremely psyched. Welcome aboard Derek. Me, the new boy and some of the crew spend the night in the casino playing blackjack. I win about $200 before losing it and eventually breaking even. Finally pack it in about 3am and head up to my cabin to crash."

Delighted though Derek was, he had already noticed a difference between the hedonistic rock 'n' roll lifestyle that he enjoyed to the maximum and the rather more reserved attitude of the rest of the band.

"It was a *whole* different scene," he smiles. "Before an Alice Cooper gig, he would hire strippers. Before we went onstage with Dream Theater, the guys would be practising to metronomes. That encapsulates it. So it was a band but it was devoid of any rock 'n' roll vibe – it was all about the precision. But that was cool and it really was a nice change as I'd been very frustrated in the past. As fun as it was to be on rock 'n' roll tours with all of the accoutrements that went with it, for myself as a keyboard player it was extremely frustrating to be restricted to playing pads and simple keyboard things."

Despite the fun Derek was having on tour, not all the members of the band were as content. The ruptured vocal cords were causing havoc with James LaBrie's singing on a nightly basis, and the uncertainty over whether his voice was going to break at any given moment meant he became conspicuously despondent throughout the tour.

"It was absolutely miserable, and it was an extremely dark and depressing period for me," James reveals. "Not wanting to be dramatic, but I remember being in my hotel room in tears thinking, 'What the hell is going on here? What am I going to do?' Literally every fucking night on the European leg, I wouldn't know if my voice would be there or if it would cooperate. And I'd lost some of my range at that point so I wasn't able to go up and hit a C# or a D or E in my higher register. I used to be able to hit those notes and hold them forever. Seriously, I didn't feel that my voice really started to come back until maybe the *Six Degrees Of Inner Turbulence* Tour in 2002. That's when I *started* to feel my range and strength coming back."

Croaking and creaking his way through some of those gigs, James became increasingly anxious that he was letting the rest of the band down. But his worries proved unfounded as the band closed ranks around their singer and tried to console and support him the best they could.

"There we were, with a great album, and they were used to me going out onstage and wailing every night," he recalls. "Obviously they could tell I was struggling and it had to be hard for those guys."

"So that is why I have the utmost respect for everyone in the band because they stuck by me, supported me and were very understanding. Even though I know they had to be frustrated at times, they still showed me that we were in it together and just told me to do the best I could."

"It must have been really scary for him," says Mike. "Back then we still didn't have total control as we were still a young band. So we were probably playing pretty heavy touring schedules in that period as well. It had to be a tough thing for him because his body is his instrument. If I have a bad cold or flu, I can still play drums. It may suck and may not be fun, but at least I can do it."

John Petrucci: "I can't imagine having to sing with physical limitations. If I had a similar thing happen with my hands it would have been incredibly frustrating. Obviously he always has had such a great powerful voice and the registers of the songs and pace was very demanding. But I never felt any real doubts, although I did think we might have had to take a break for him, which would have been fine. But we always maintained such a hectic pace so it never seemed like there was an opportunity to do that. But of course I felt concern for him because he was struggling. I felt bad for him."

Although managing to get through the rigorous schedule with his voice relatively intact, James admits that the crisis had also been psychologically damaging.

"It really changed me as a person," he elaborates with a sigh. "I used to always be sitting around with the guys, joking around, and then suddenly I wasn't a funny guy anymore. I was depressed and in a real low. I was miserable a lot of the time and the guys knew it. It changed the way I would get into conversations with the guys, it changed the way that I would have opinions on what we were going to do live or album-wise, and it took away a *lot* of my confidence. I'm not kidding you when I say it really did change me as a person. It was a very dramatic and taxing time for me, and I had to dig deep to find the strength to go on. It was just because I was very passionate about the music and my whole involvement in it that I kept going…"

SEIZE THE DAY

The remainder of 1995 would prove to be just as busy for the band. During a rare three-week break from the frantic Waking Up The World Tour in May, Dream Theater had even wedged in a studio session to enable them to record a track that was a long overdue release. "A Change Of Seasons" had been lurking around the band's consciousness in demo form for six years, and was originally to have been included on the *Images And Words* album before being jettisoned at the last minute by the record label. It had been tentatively agreed with Derek Oliver that at some point he would authorize its recording, but with it failing to make the cut for *Awake* there was an increasing trepidation that it might never see the light of day. But the band's loyal fans knew all about this semi-mythical marathon song, as a primitive version had been performed during two gigs – once at the Limelight in New York on March 4, 1993, and the other in Bonn, Germany, on April 13, 1993 – and like the band, they desperately wanted to hear a full studio recording. Enter the internet...

Coincidentally, Dream Theater fans were beginning to connect online via the Ytsejam mailing list, and soon someone had the astute idea of setting up a petition in order to try and convince their label to allow the band to record "A Change Of Seasons". The band had already utilized the internet in the days long before it was the norm, when thirty-second samples of the "Lie" single from *Awake* had been made available for download. But the planned manner in which the petition was organized was nonetheless impressive. Completing the pincer movement against East West Records were Mike Portnoy and Jim Pitulski, who constantly badgered Derek Oliver until he finally relented.

Clocking in at over 23 minutes of solid and delightfully pretentious prog rock, the track was deliberately fashioned to compete – in terms of both length and complexity – with the likes of "Supper's Ready" by Genesis, "Close To The Edge" by Yes, or even Rush's "2112".

The track had undergone a long gestation period but this delay had at least given the band the opportunity to refine it, as Mike explained at the time.

"It was originally written back in 1989, and I don't think a day has gone by when a fan hasn't asked me about it. We've changed it a lot musically. I've altered it lyrically and James changed a lot of it melodically. We decided when we got the green light to go ahead with it that we should rework the whole thing and put the 1995 touch on it. It was cool because it was our first recording with Derek and that gave us the chance to do some writing and arranging with him."

The lyrics were far more than the whimsical tales of surreal worlds that had been the tendency of their Seventies forebears, and were extremely personal to their author, Mike Portnoy. Essentially dealing with the circle of life, the lyrics centre on the anti-procrastination concept of *carpe diem* – seize the day – and the tragic events that affected Mike in late 1984.

"The whole story with *carpe diem* and how I wrote the lyrics is actually true," discloses Mike. "It was November 16, 1984. That afternoon at school, my health teacher Mr Lynch was giving a lesson in class about *carpe diem*, you know, seize the day. Basically about how precious life is, and how you never know when somebody you love or something in your life is going to change at any moment and when you least expect it. He gave this lesson and said, 'When you get home tonight, why don't you give your mom or dad a hug and kiss, and let them know how much you love them – because you never know what might happen, and to not take the people you love for granted.' It was a very moving lesson he taught that day."

"That night I went home and my Mom was getting ready to get on a private jet to go to Atlantic City for the weekend, and I was getting ready to go out with my friends. Right before I left to go out, I went up to my Mom and gave her a big hug and kiss, and told her that I loved her. She was taken aback as I wouldn't normally have done anything like that. She was like 'Wow, what was that for? Where did that come from?' And I said that I just wanted her to know that I loved her. I walked out the door and that was the last time that I ever saw her. She was killed that night in a plane crash. And that's what the whole *carpe diem* thing in 'A Change Of Seasons' is all about, and directly from that moment in my life. If that teacher hadn't given that lesson that day, I would probably have run out the door and I would never have had a final moment with my Mom, and never been able to tell her that I loved her. A week earlier, I'd gotten into a very big fight with her, and if I hadn't had that last moment with her I probably would have carried guilt around with me for the rest of my life. That was a gift from God for me. I don't think that it was a coincidence that lesson was given to me that day, and that I was able to use it that night. It was just one of those strange things. So that's why I wrote about it, and I even have the words '*carpe diem*' tattooed here on my arm. So I try to never forget that and try never to take my life and people that are in my life for granted. Because at any moment, you never know what might happen. 9/11 is an example of that, and what happened to Dimebag Darrell [ex-Pantera and Damageplan guitarist, murdered onstage in 2004] is another. You never know what's right around the corner and you have to love what you have while you have it."

The concept was also heavily influenced by Mike's movie infatuation, with the issues raised in the Robin Williams films *The World According To Garp* and *Dead Poets Society* filtering into the song. Indeed, snapshots of the latter have regularly been shown behind the band on stage during live renditions of the track, with spoken snippets lifted from the film also featuring in the studio version.

"The other movie which really had a big impact, in addition to those two, starred Jon Voight and was called *Table For Five*," adds Mike "And my God, if there is any movie that I can relate to in terms of dealing with my mother's death, that's the one. I actually did use some samples from that in 'A Change Of Seasons' during the whole 'Darkest Of Winters' section, where you can hear John Voight saying 'There was an accident and she was killed', or something like that. But that movie is dealing with a father and his children coping with the death of a mother. It was a movie that summed up for me all the feelings and emotions that I went through as a child during that period."

But there was a price for Dream Theater to pay in exchange for Derek Oliver yielding to fan and band pressure. In a barely credible decision – given the animosity that already existed between the two parties – Oliver boldly insisted that the track be produced by David Prater.

"I really wanted to convince the band because of the commercial failure of *Awake* that we should rekindle the relationship with Prater – even under duress," confirms Oliver. "Prater, for all his faults – and there aren't that many – was the only producer in my opinion who fully understood what Dream Theater were actually all about. He knew where the weaknesses were and because he would direct his energy on those pressure points, the band couldn't hack it. So I made those overtures, but the band were very adamant that they didn't want to do that. But I begged and begged, and eventually they agreed to try it out. So we tried to recreate that vibe from *Images And Words* with the band and Prater back at Bear Tracks Studios."

"It was only green-lighted under the condition that we work with Prater again," says Mike. "I think when *Awake* didn't deliver an immediate hit single, like 'Pull Me Under', Derek probably equated that to us not using David Prater. I think he was anxious to re-open that relationship. So he made us agree to work with Prater again, but he also made Prater agree to not put any samples on my drums as he knew that was my biggest issue with the production on *Images And Words*. So we reunited at Bear Tracks along with Doug Oberkircher after all those years."

It was of course hoped that the rekindling of that relationship with Prater would help create the necessary spark to produce an album that matched *Images And Words* in terms of album sales – although technicalities would ensure that *A Change Of Seasons* was ultimately released as an EP.

"In my opinion, what brought them back to Bear Tracks after working elsewhere on *Awake* was a desire to try to recapture some of the magic of *Images And Words*," adds engineer Doug Oberkircher. "They decided to return to Bear Tracks and to hire David Prater for the recording of 'A Change of Seasons' and they hoped to capture some of the essence of the *Images And Words* sessions after slightly disappointing sales of *Awake*. Bear Tracks was also a world class recording studio that was very affordable for them to use. They were able to negotiate great rates for extended bookings there."

Yet, for all the good intentions of such a reunion, even David Prater was astounded that he should have been considered for the project and remembers, in a typically forthright manner, the moment Derek Oliver contacted him with the proposal.

"Yes, I was surprised," he admits. "First of all when Derek Oliver called me to work on the record I said sure. But then he said, and I quote, 'Prater, if there's one sampler on in this room when I come out you're fired. End of story. If I hear that you've triggered anything you're done.' He was totally serious. Jim Pitulski told me that the fan club had gotten sick of the drivel Dream Theater was releasing and petitioned him to go to the record label and get them to do something about it."

The main issues with Prater that arose during the *Images And Words* sessions had been his use of triggered drum sounds. With those removed, the problems between Mike and the producer had at least been resolved. Prater's other main adversary back in 1991, Kevin Moore, was no longer in the band. So on the surface at least, there seemed to have been the prospect of a harmonious working relationship.

"I actually got along with Prater during those sessions," admits Mike. "I think I went in trying to be as diplomatic and open-minded as possible. But there was also a certain amount of satisfaction as I knew that we had leverage over him. When we made *Images And Words*, we hadn't had any success and he called the shots. When it came time to make 'A Change Of Seasons' we had a gold album, had toured the world many times over and we basically knew he was disposable. So I went into the sessions feeling more secure and I was able to deal with his bullshit and personality a little more light-heartedly."

Derek Sherinian also managed to forge a productive working relationship with Prater, and recalls: "I thought he was very efficient and felt he got some good sounds. I really found it to be a pleasure, and I'd like to work with him again."

Perhaps predictably, it didn't take long for some tensions to regenerate, but on this occasion it was James LaBrie who rapidly found himself at loggerheads with the producer. James recalled the atmosphere had already been prickly before he entered the vocal booth to sing his parts, and an argument soon ensued over the chosen method of recording his vocals.

"On the first day of recording 'A Change of Seasons' Petrucci pulled me aside and begged me to do something about James carrying on like Robert Plant," claims Prater. "He said the crew wanted to kill him. I said let's see what happens. Sure enough, when we started recording his lead vocals he started to get agitated because he wasn't getting his performance right, and started insulting Doug and me in the control room. He tried to blame us for his lack of preparedness. Basically, I do composite vocal tracking and James had been doing punch-in vocal tracking with whoever his last producer was. Punch-in vocal tracking is a terrible way to obtain a performance. James then told us that we had done *Images And Words* that way. Doug jumped in and said that we didn't. James was cornered at that point and became very angry. I had heard enough, and said for him to call the car service and get a ride back to the hotel and not to come back until he acted like an adult."

"His problem with me is that I usually don't say what he wants to hear," continues Prater. "When he's wrong, and he usually is, I can promise you he won't like what he hears. Also, I was very stern with regards to LaBrie's enunciation. He would often form improper vowel sounds simply because he didn't know any better. 'Foreverrrrr', would become 'forevahhhhhhh'. I could go on and on. LaBrie had a fantastic voice but he needed a lot of guidance. He's also a big strong man with a fiery temperament who can easily intimidate a person who doesn't know how to handle him. Kind of like a big horse. Once you gain their trust you can get a lot of work out of them. They can also kill you very easily."

Perhaps unsurprisingly, James recalls events slightly differently, but admits that the dispute came extremely close to a physical confrontation.

"The crazy thing is that I'd already done a full album with David Prater, and the way we recorded that album was that I would sing a verse of a song," he explains. "I'd then go back and listen to it and maybe sing it again if I felt it could be better. Then once I was happy with that, I'd go on to the next section. It was done section by section on that album, so I could concentrate on it and make sure I got the right character voice. That worked out beautifully and in fact Prater wasn't even there most of the time. He'd stick his head in, listen to it and go, 'Oh, great man. OK. Well you don't need me here for a bit, I'm going to go to the store.' So when we got to recording 'A Change Of Seasons' I was in the vocal booth taking the same approach. I said to him 'OK, let's start and get the first verse up and I'll start singing.' But he said he wanted me to sing the whole thing from beginning to end. And I was like 'What are you talking about? I'm not doing that David. I'm concentrating on sections like I always have. I'll save singing the twenty-minute tune from beginning to end for when we play live, thank you *very* much!' I think he said something like 'I don't think so – the label hired me to come in here to save you guys' butts!'"

"So I told him to stop throwing that shit in my face, especially when I was standing there getting ready to sing," he continues. "Talk about blowing my whole mood. I eventually said to him, 'Look, I'm the singer here and I'm telling you how I like to do things. I'm not trying to be difficult but we'll do it verse by verse as this is a huge song and I want it to sound amazing.'" "And he goes 'Fine. I don't even want to fucking look at you right now. Get the fuck out of here!' So I threw my headphones down and went into the engineer room and said, 'Are you fucking with me? Who do you think you are?' And then it was kind of defused from there. He left, I walked out and walked around the studios about fifty times to cool down. Now here's the funniest part of all this. I came back in and guess how I sang the tune? Section to section."

Although the mists of time may have obscured exactly what happened in the studio that day, for the record, David Prater insists that he had used the composite recording technique for both *Images And Words* and "A Change Of Seasons".

"No, I always had LaBrie sing four or five takes of the first verse, then take a short break, then sing the second verse, take a short break and so on. Perhaps then we'd take a few minutes to review the gist of the performances before moving on. LaBrie is saying that I did it completely the opposite of how I did. In other words, he is totally full of shit and hasn't a clue of what he's talking about."

James LaBrie: "Ultimately, it was all bullshit and unnecessary and it really did almost come to blows. Doug Oberkircher thought I was going to kill him that day because Prater was being totally disrespectful. And he was doing this with everyone in the band, and had this attitude towards everybody when we were recording that album. It was just really bizarre and I was like 'Why is this guy even here?'"

The vocals were eventually recorded, and although the feud was left to simmer for the remainder of the session, Mike Portnoy at least found the situation amusing: "There was a part of me that was really happy to see someone else really fighting with Prater because he had proved it wasn't just me or Kevin Moore who were having problems with him," he laughs.

With Derek Oliver having insisted on Prater working with the band again, he could hardly have been shocked to have both parties trying to call him to complain on an almost daily basis. One of the issues was that the original lyrics contained the words "mercy fuck". Prater was concerned that this phrase was to be included, and in an effort to lengthen the studio time to rectify the problem, he attempted to contact Oliver to warn him. Yet Prater claims that the A&R man began to deliberately avoid him and didn't return his calls.

"That's correct, I didn't," says Oliver firmly. "You've got to understand that we had a limited budget and an agreement with David to produce it for ten or twelve days. There was no more time. When you record a record you can't suddenly say that you need more time when you're halfway through because there's a budget you have to stick to. Someone's got to pay for that. If you've only been given a certain amount of money, and you're with a company that really doesn't give a fuck about Dream Theater, they're not going to give you an extension to that budget. So it's true. I never returned a lot of his calls because basically, if you start opening a dialogue with David you'll never resolve it. So one of the best ways to deal with it is to not return the call, as you know what it's about, it's about some complaint or someone fighting at the studio."

"But there was friction all the time," he expands. "I think at times there was shoving going on between Mike and Prater during the first record and during the second there was more of the same going on. It was tortuous trying to get through it. I mean all the time I was getting calls from each camp trying to tell tales about the other one. So trying to get this thing recorded was another nightmare. But it was clear that they were never going to work with each other again after that. Basically, Dream Theater are a hard band to work with. The bottom line is that they're not stupid. They're intelligent guys and they are very opinionated – which in a way is very good, as I would much rather have that than some bunch of lame-brains who have no clue as to what their vision is."

Ironically, it was the unease felt by James LaBrie that ensured the offending phrase was removed from the track, with the word "sympathy" recorded separately and replacing the contentious "mercy fuck". In an interview of the period with Neil Elliott in the *Images And Words* fanzine, James explained: "It's one thing if I speak with that word in my own personal life, and I don't want to sound pompous or hypocritical for that matter, but to me I really do not want to be associated with that type of language, with profanity, in the context of music. I think that there are many words within the English diction that can be just as powerful or just as emotional."

"Well, that's pretty ironic coming from somebody who constantly uses that word on stage when speaking to the audience," says Mike now. "But honestly, I think all of the hoopla over my lyrics initially having the phrase 'mercy fuck' was blown way out of proportion at the time. The fact is, many well respected lyricists throughout music history have used the word 'fuck' in their lyric, ranging from Roger Waters to Fish to John Lennon to Neal Morse. And of course, the same could be said for filmmakers, ranging from Stanley Kubrick to Martin Scorsese to Quentin Tarantino to David Lynch. It's not some taboo word that should cause a world-wide state of panic. I feel as a lyricist or artist that sometimes you need to use strong words to convey strong emotions. And Dream Theater history has shown that the 'A Change Of Seasons' censorship was all just Derek Oliver and David Prater flexing their muscles and making a mountain out of a molehill. So-called profanities showed up in some of my later lyrics, such as 'Burning My Soul', 'Honor Thy Father', 'This Dying Soul' and even the Petrucci-penned 'As I Am', and the world didn't collapse on its axis as a result!"

Bickering aside, the producer recalls one incident when he persuaded

John Petrucci to trust his judgement when it came to selecting a suitable guitar solo to enliven the middle of the track.

"Petrucci asked me to help him on his guitar solo and he was playing a relentless flurry of boring exercises," explains the producer. "I listened and started laughing hysterically. I turned off the machine and told him that the solo he played off the top of his head on the reference track was light years beyond this. I played it for him several times before I stopped the machine and told him that it was 'O.K. to just be yourself and this solo was absolutely you.' It was, and is, beautiful. I said 'You're *that* good. Who are you trying to impress, Steve Vai?' It took the better part of an hour before he realized that what he played off the top of his head was better than what he did after sitting for days trying to cleverly devise a solo. He said he was trying to justify his reputation as a guitar-slinger."

"Yeah, that was improvised," confirmed John Petrucci in an interview with *musicplayers.com*. "I didn't like it but David Prater came back and was like 'That's the solo. That's awesome!' And I was like 'That sucked, I just improvised it!' I remember trying to redo it and he was getting impatient with me. So we left it and to this day I'm not crazy about it."

For all the sparks in the studio, the finished EP – much like *Images And Words* – sounds undeniably crisp and polished. Whether or not the drum sound on the previous Prater production was to everyone's liking, both recordings remain beacons in Dream Theater's back-catalogue. The tension certainly seemed to help capture exceptional performances, and although Prater and Dream Theater would never be able to work together again, "A Change Of Seasons" genuinely rivals those epic tracks by the progressive rock greats that had inspired its creation.

That said, it was a track that had not been a deliberate attempt to imitate the past. When Dave Ling, then of *RAW* magazine, suggested that the song proved that the band "secretly wanted to be Yes", James was forthright in his denial, retorting: "When we sit down to write there's nothing to predetermine how long a song is going to be... We start the song and when the message is completed that's it – we don't add five minutes just to be like our idols."

For the uninitiated, the prospect of wading through a 23-minute track would – superficially at least – seem to be a daunting proposition. Yet the song is wisely split into seven distinct sections that maintain a constant flow of fresh melodies, so any hint of repetition is eliminated. The opening segment "The Crimson Sunrise" is a delicate instrumental piece that gradually builds to a keyboard-driven crescendo before launching into the "Innocence" and "Carpe Diem" suites that deal with the crux of the piece's subject matter. The final portion, "The Crimson

Sunset", is equally moving with the father passing on his knowledge to his son just before his death: *"Seize the day and don't you cry / Now it's time to say goodbye / Even though I'll be gone / I will live on."* Yet in spite of the track's topic, the most notable aspect is that it manages to avoid becoming maudlin or over-sentimental. It merely provokes thought rather than falling into the trap of clumsily forcing the concept down the listener's throat.

The danger of over-expanding the piece to the point of it becoming boring for the audience was also something that the band were extremely conscious of, as John Petrucci explained at the time in *Hit Parader*.

"Yeah, especially when we're playing in front of people and they're leaving," he laughed. "You definitely think about that. But it is hard to keep somebody's interest for an entire album side or for twenty minutes. I think one of the things that you develop hopefully as a musician and a songwriter is the ability to keep something interesting and to have a clear purpose so when somebody listens to it there's an immediacy that they can relate to. And that doesn't always happen, and the odds are sort of stacked against you when a song is twenty-minutes long."

The release was augmented by the addition of live tracks recorded at the Ronnie Scott's gig earlier in the year. Of these, the so-called "Big Medley" – that neatly mixes excerpts of such songs as Pink Floyd's "In The Flesh", Queen's "Bohemian Rhapsody" and "Turn It On Again" by Genesis – is undeniably the high point, and perfectly encapsulates that evening's mood. Falling under the description of EP rather than album due to the relatively succinct amount of original material, *A Change Of Seasons* was released on September 19, 1995, and peaked at Number 58 in the US chart.

In terms of artwork, the band once again used the services of Larry Freemantle, with the design drawing heavily on the lyrical concept of the title track. With a boy perched in the winter snow on the front cover, and an old man on an autumnal beach, it also contained a reference to the date of Mike's mother's death – November 16 – in the form of a calendar. The sleeve was put together quickly by Freemantle, who arranged for photographs to be taken of the models before digitally mixing together the final images.

"I really just dealt with Mike on this sleeve, and he was very specific with what he wanted and where," explains Freemantle. "It was just a case of piecing the things together. We hired a photographer to take the shots, and hired models for the kid and the old man, and then just composited them together."

Press evaluations of the recording were in the main positive, although most touched on the fact that the release was only ever going to be adored by those already converted to the Dream Theater approach. Steve Beebee in *Kerrang!* wrote "Fans will cop an earful of the 23-minute title track and find themselves escorted into mellow mists of ecstasy. Quite simply, if you're already a Dream Theater fan you'll adore this beyond words – and if not, you won't. The band are about as inaccessible and unfashionable as it's possible to get. Their songs are not so much tunes as monumental tapestries of sound. Like a master artist, Dream Theater add layer, after layer, after textures, with astonishing finesse. Awesome... if you like that sort of thing."

Lyn Guy, writing for *Metal Hammer*, described the title track as "A melting pot of time-changes and varying moods, 'Seasons' is by turns gentle, dramatic and even fearsome; an epic adventure that will delight devotees of the band... 'Seasons' is a must for Dream Theater fans but that really is the extent of its commercial appeal." *Guitar For The Practising Musician* similarly claimed: "The musicianship from Petrucci and his bandmates is stellar as usual (there's one stunning instrumental riff in the middle that delightfully blasts off into the chromatic ozone), though if you weren't a fan before, this probably won't convert you."

To promote the EP, the band had lined up a series of shows, visiting Japan for three gigs at the end of October, before playing four East Coast concerts as part of the "Home For The Holidays" mini-tour. Their next project was to return to the studio to write and record their next album, which they had hoped would be released in 1996. But with Dream Theater, things never *quite* seemed to go as intended.

TEN

LINES IN THE SAND

With a string of flourishing releases behind them, Dream Theater could have been forgiven for imagining that they would be left alone by their record label to plough their own inimitable – yet still profitable – furrow. After all, *A Change Of Seasons* had been snapped up by their fans without the perceived necessity for a single. Yet, the often erratic behaviour of their label was once again to prove testing, and when they hit the Dream Factory Studios in East Rutherford, New Jersey, in early 1996 to start creating material for their next studio album, there was no way of foretelling that it would be an agonizing process, full of excruciating battles that would eventually drag the band to the brink of self-destruction.

Previously, the label had allowed Dream Theater a reasonable degree of flexibility, but pressure was being exerted on their A&R man Derek Oliver to encourage them to write more concise, commercial tracks that could be sold to radio. Consequently, although they were creating songs at a frantic pace, they constantly had to endure the ignominy of having their carefully crafted demos repeatedly rejected by the record label moguls. It was a wearisome period of uncertainty that would last for almost a year, and leave the band questioning how they were going to escape from such a debilitating cycle.

"By now, East West Records had been folded into the Elektra label and instead of corporate pressure dissipating it became even more intense," explains Derek Oliver. "Sylvia Rhone had become the president of Elektra and was now overseeing a huge roster, and was faced with tremendous financial overheads. Her focus had switched from the hard rock mainstays of the Atco/East West roster to the urban, eclectic and alternative acts that came with Elektra. In my opinion, she would have dearly loved to have dropped Dream Theater, and we did in fact have discussions about transferring the contract to Warner International. But she was attracted to the band's overseas success in Japan and Europe, and that prompted her to keep them on the label. However, she was clear that this time around they should come up with some shorter, snappier tracks so that radio could get behind the band again."

From the label's perspective, the release of a punchy single could, given the right airplay, provide them with the perfect advert for the album and logically, it would have a positive effect on sales. But crucially, they were missing the point. Dream Theater have never been a band for whom the single format was a natural medium, and "Pull Me Under" was a result of fortunate timing and shrewd editing. And although that was something Derek Oliver doubtless understood, he was under the strictest of instructions to ensure that commerciality was at the forefront of the band's mind as they toiled away in the studio. The trick for the band was to write songs that were deemed to be acceptable to the mainstream but which didn't overly dilute their identity. But rejection of their work was not a reaction that Dream Theater had previously experienced, and when the likes of "Raise The Knife" and "Where Are You Now" were presented to Oliver in March of 1996, they received a somewhat muted response.

"That was weird," laughs John Petrucci. "I can just remember writing all this stuff, demoing it and being totally psyched. And I'd then go in and play it for Derek and he'd say 'Yeah. I really don't think there's anything there'. And I'd be like 'What are you talking about?' I'd never really had a response like that before. I remember going back to the studio, being all pissed, and then having to go back to start writing songs again."

"We would write a whole bunch of songs, like 'Lines In The Sand', 'Trial Of Tears' and 'Just Let Me Breathe' that felt like Dream Theater and we'd hand them in," adds Mike. "Derek would play it for a few people and there would just be *no* reaction. He was fighting all the other people at the label as well and it was tough for him. So they would ask for something more commercial, as they basically still had that 'Pull Me Under' mentality. Then we would go off and write something more accessible like 'Hollow Years' or 'You Or Me' and those were the ones that got them excited. They were just looking for singles. I mean, we started writing 'Metropolis Part II' during 1996 as we were finally going to write the sequel. It ended up being this 20-minute epic, and again that got no reaction from the label. We'd write two or three songs, demo them and then hand them in the new batch every couple of months."

"But it was always a case of back to the drawing board. That is a horrible way for a band to write music – just trying to please a suit-and-tie executive who is going to completely determine the fate of the band. It's absolutely ludicrous that one guy's ridiculous taste was going to either catapult or bury a band. It's everything that is wrong about the industry, and why the whole period was so frustrating. We were so terribly disappointed with Derek Oliver's inability to stand behind us and to get us where we wanted to go without being consumed by the machine. Derek was telling us to write and write, and wanted us to go in a more commercial direction. John Petrucci was more willing to accept that kind of change, whereas I was still fighting against us changing just for other people."

In an interview in *Metal Edge* magazine, John Myung noted that the process was "Very draining and sometimes you wonder what's going on. I think, as a band, when it comes to writing stuff we can pretty much try and block it out without thinking about it much. In a sense, getting together and playing is an escape for all of us."

Working under such strain was hardly a conducive environment for Derek Sherinian to try and make an impact during his first writing session as a member of the band. But despite the ongoing traumas, he recalls the period as both rewarding and enjoyable.

"I was excited because prior to that I had just been playing the material on *Awake*," says Sherinian. "So this was my first opportunity to make my mark with the band. I was very immersed in it. At that time I was living in Astoria, Queens, New York so I had a long commute of about ninety minutes just to get there. I used to take the subway to Times Square and then the bus to New Jersey where we rehearsed by the Meadowlands for five days a week. John Myung was always kind enough to drive me home on a night, so I didn't have to take the subways."

But given the undue pressures, there were signs of creative cracks forming within the band during that songwriting process. Although these minor skirmishes never got out of hand, they were still serious enough for James to make mention of them in an interview with *Burrn!* magazine, claiming "Sometimes it gets a little heated because someone might be very passionate about a certain thing that they see, or a vision they think is appropriate for a song. So obviously you're going to run into a bit of a clatter sometimes."

John Myung also noted the occasional tension in the same article, "It's not like we put the boxing gloves on and go at it. But there is a lot of extraneous communication, verbally, that goes on until we finally have something that works for us all."

Without the input of Kevin Moore, who had unquestionably played a pivotal role in Dream Theater's lyrical and musical development, it would have been reasonable to have expected them to struggle during the writing process. Yet Mike claims that his contributions had diminished to such a degree during *Awake* that they hardly noticed his absence.

"I think the only area that we missed Kev's input was probably lyrically," he says. "He really was a great lyricist and suddenly we had to make up for that. Up until that point, I'd only written one lyric on *Awake* and, of course, 'A Change Of Seasons'. It used to be that John Petrucci and Kev would split the lyrics. Now, with the absence of Kev, John would have to write a bit more, and James or I would have to step up to the plate to kind of cover it. I ended up with three or four lyrics and James did about three or four also. Musically we didn't miss Kev's input, as that didn't exist on the *Awake* album, or at least up to the level that we had been used to. Derek more than covered the musical contributions, as he was a player who enjoyed jamming and giving ideas. Kevin had become distant musically during those last few years. So the musical formula was probably better than it had been in years."

"So yeah, Derek fitted in easily. A lot of people mistakenly blame everything that was wrong with *Falling Into Infinity* on Derek. That's not the case at all. His input had *nothing* to do with the change in direction. He was willing to write a twenty-minute epic just as much as he was to write a four-minute commercial song. He just wanted to play and offer whatever he could musically – no matter what the direction – and was a great team player. Derek never imposed himself on us but was always willing to contribute wherever we wanted it. So he was able to contribute a lot to songs like 'Lines In The Sand' and 'Trial Of Tears', as well as the more ballad-esque songs such as 'Anna Lee'."

Sherinian also came out fighting at the time when cross-examined by the *Images And Words* fanzine as to his role in the band, retorting:

"Whenever an original member leaves a band, people get tripped out and it is understandable. The bottom line is I'm here, I'm going to lay down some shit for the next record and hopefully you'll like it. And if you don't, well, that's too bad."

In addition to the ongoing tussle with Elektra, Dream Theater were also having to deal with the deterioration of the relationship between their joint managers, Jim Pitulski and Rob Shore. The rapport between the pair had steadily declined to such a level that it was proving impractical for them to continue working together. But was there any one incident that sparked the feud?

"I think it was the assassination attempt," jokes Rob. "No, in all seriousness, it was just a culmination. I think there were just too many cooks in the kitchen. It became a personality clash, and a good way to put it is that we just weren't getting on. When we started it was clearly defined what each person did. We used the Sanctuary model [Iron Maiden's managers], where Andy Taylor was the financial guy and Rod Smallwood was the creative guy. But those roles got mixed a little. Not that it was anybody's fault as it just kind of happened. So we did step on each other's toes. Which was too bad in retrospect and now that I'm older maybe I would have handled it differently. At the time it went down the way it did."

With Pitulski and Shore's Roundtable Management company subsequently being dissolved, Dream Theater were faced with having to make a painful choice as to which of the pairing they wanted to take control of their affairs. Part of the problem that had sparked the disagreements between their managers was the fact that John Petrucci regularly found himself disagreeing with Jim Pitulski over decisions that affected the band.

"We just weren't seeing eye to eye as I had a different idea on how I wanted things run," explains John Petrucci. "Jim always had a genuine love for the band, an interest in our career and was passionate about the music and everything else. But I think there are a lot of relationships in the music business that become very personal. You are dealing with people on a day-to-day basis and making decisions about your career that have a direct impact on your personal life. So it can start to get to a point where there are certain things you'd not want to do a certain way, and it starts to snowball. You really have to have an understanding and chemistry with the person who is directly involved. So for whatever reason it wasn't happening any more."

Given those issues, it was understandable that Petrucci had made it plain that he wanted Rob Shore to take over the management role, adding: "Rob is a person in my life that I've always felt from the beginning was a person whom I genuinely liked. We also kind of think along the same wavelength, we understand each other and I trust him and his judgements. I seek his advice and we have a great friendship that has developed through the years."

Critically, although Mike Portnoy had no hostility towards Shore, the drummer was a close ally of Jim Pitulski. As a consequence, and for the first time in their history, Dream Theater's unofficial co-leaders were at loggerheads.

"It sucked that we even had to make a decision like that," says Mike. "It was kind of like if two parents get divorced, the child shouldn't have to decide who gets custody! But that was the situation that we were in, and we were like children trying to pick between their parents. It was a bit of a struggle within the band because some of us wanted Jim and others wanted Rob. So internally we were facing a bit of turmoil and opposition. I desperately wanted to stick with Jim, so I think the main struggle was between me and John Petrucci. I think in hindsight we should have opted for neither of them. But I guess if we were to walk away from the two of them entirely, they probably would have ended up re-connecting and ganging up against us because they would both have lost our business."

"The band were sort of split," adds Jim Pitulski. "Derek was of the opinion that they should be getting big time management. I think he was talking to Toby Mamis who was Alice Cooper's manager and worked for Shep Gordon. He was trying to pull the band in that direction. John Petrucci wasn't seeing eye-to-eye with me about things. Mike and James wanted to stay with me, but we had to make a decision."

With Derek Sherinian also expressing concerns that the band needed the assistance of more heavyweight management, the waters were muddied further – although he vigorously denies that he approached either Mamis or Gordon with a view to them taking over Dream Theater's affairs.

"Never in a million years would I have my worst enemy be managed by Toby Mamis," laughs Sherinian now. "I didn't know who in particular I wanted to manage the band, but I felt we needed someone with more influence than Rob Shore or Jim Pitulski. At that point, the band had the option to go to a bigger management company which was something I was always pressing for. With the cult following that it had, with proper direction and management that could assert more influence, I thought that the popularity of the band could quadruple."

But in spite of the reservations and perhaps an underlying resentment from some of the band, Rob Shore was eventually chosen as their manager. But that wasn't the end of the matter. With Jim Pitulski effectively left out in the cold, he took legal action against the band in an attempt to recoup some of his losses.

"We showed up to rehearsal one day in New Jersey and there was a county sheriff waiting for us to serve us papers," recalls Sherinian. "Let's just say that the mixture of creative and legal doesn't work very well and it was a very sickening feeling to see my name on that document."

"Suddenly it was starting to get ugly, and the business side was more important than the music," adds Mike. "You had lawyers getting involved and that kind of shit tears bands apart. It started to happen with us, as we were suddenly disagreeing on a lot of shit. John Petrucci and I didn't agree on the management choice, and that was something I eventually gave in to. But we did end up going with Rob throughout 1996 and 1997. He's a great business manager and still to this day we use him as a business manager. But as a band manager? It was a problematic period for us. That was the first of many battles that I gave in to throughout that entire process, and led to a lot of frustration on my part, and ultimately a year and a half later to almost breaking up the band."

Once Shore had taken over sole management duties, the band's differences were glossed over and they attempted to write material which met their own high standards and potentially appealed to Elektra. But the limited rapport they had with the label was dented further when a number of key figures who had previously aided their career were suddenly replaced in a drastic corporate shake-up.

"Everybody completely changed," says Mike. "All the way from the important people in our career, like Derek Oliver, down the line to the people you don't often see or hear like the radio promotion people, the publicity people and marketing guys. So we were suddenly handed this new staff of people that didn't necessarily get Dream Theater or even *want* to get Dream Theater. The industry is a tough business, where they just take the easiest route and easiest marketable band possible. They don't necessarily want to develop a ten-year career with a band. They just didn't want to deal with us."

Derek Oliver: "I always felt that my relationship with the band was quite strong. But things had got to the point with the label that there wasn't any going back in trying to get another hit record. Dream Theater might as well have continued doing what they do to the point where the label got fed up with them being on the label. Then I left, and the people there didn't have the ability, or indeed willpower, to work with the band."

The accusation that the label became increasingly disinterested is one shared by Dream Theater. In particular, they were alarmed by the apparent attitude of Oliver's replacement, Josh Deutsch, whom Mike describes as "Really knowing nothing about the history of the band, and he just wanted to hear something that radio would play."

Apparently exasperated, Deutsch finally gave the band the go-ahead to record the album that would become *Falling Into Infinity* in March 1997. Yet there was another unforeseen bombshell when the band were railroaded into using a producer they were concerned would commercialize their sound even further. During the months of writing, a number of producers had been cited by the band as being their perfect match. These included the likes of Peter Collins, Trevor Horn, Paul Northfield, Daniel Lanoire, Steve Lillywhite and even Trevor Rabin of Yes. Indeed, they had even considered working with Kevin Gilbert, but tragically the producer had died before he got a chance to even meet the band.

"I was in talks with Kevin as I was a fan of his solo stuff and his stuff in Toy Matinee," recalls Mike. "He was interested in the possibility of us working together and after speaking a few times, I'd sent him some of the demos we were doing at the time. A few days after receiving the package, and leaving an excited message on my answering machine, he was dead. It was a shocking loss of a great talent and always makes me wonder what could have been."

But Kevin Shirley, who had just finished working on Aerosmith's *Nine Lives* album, had been selected by Elektra as being the man they wanted behind the mixing desk. Mike recalls being less than besotted about the suggestion.

"Kevin was brought up by Derek Oliver just before he stopped working with us," he says. "None of us were terribly blown away by the idea of working with him because he had just done the Silverchair album. And really, the only thing that looked interesting to us was the fact that he had engineered the Rush *Counterparts* album. Other than that, we weren't blown away by his track record. But we still had a meeting with him. I actually think Kevin felt the same, and wasn't terribly blown away by working with us either."

Mike's inkling that Shirley was hesitant to even consider working with them is confirmed by the producer, who was unsure as to whether the band would be open to his desire to steer them in a slightly more commercial direction.

"Derek Oliver called me and asked me to come to his office and he played me some of the stuff from *Live At The Marquee*," recalls Shirley. "I thought it was pretty cool and I especially liked the sound of the organ and guitars, as I felt it had this Deep Purple approach which I was a big fan of. But I wasn't particularly keen on working with them if truth be told. I didn't think that they had the desire to break out of the niche they were in, and didn't think they would want to do a record which was on a bigger scale."

But following a fruitful meeting between the two parties, Shirley agreed to travel to Amsterdam to see the band perform live on April 14, 1997. The band had decided to play a number of gigs by way of escaping the studio blues. Originally, the "Fix For '96" shows constituted a number of US dates around Christmas, but in order to air the new material in Europe, too, a mini-tour of mainland Europe had been scheduled. And it was the rousing reception they received at that gig in Holland that finally persuaded the producer that he should work with them.

"I thought their fan base was amazing," effuses Shirley. "It was the first time I had seen people who knew all these complicated licks. There were air guitars, air drums and all sorts going on and I just thought they were amazing. The musicianship was obviously excellent, but really I became interested because I felt that I could bring something to the table."

In spite of the success in persuading Shirley to work with the band, recollections of that short series of European gigs are painful for Mike after he managed to dislocate his wrist mid-set at a gig in Munich on April 11.

"I just remember going to play a huge fill, and I guess I bit off more than I could chew because at the end of the fill, I felt my hand go numb," winces Mike at the memory. "I thought it was just a muscle cramp or whatever, and I looked over and my wrist was completely snapped backwards, with my hand facing the opposite way. At that point my stomach just sank, I turned blue and had to stop playing for a moment. My tech banged my hand back into position and I continued playing the rest of the song with my left hand, and had to put my right hand in a bucket of ice. But it wasn't the first time I'd done something like that. On the *Awake* tour Waking Up The World, in Toronto [October 25, 1994], I threw my back out right at the end of the drum solo. All of a sudden my back cramped up and froze. I was stuck and couldn't move. We had to stop the show and James had to ask if there was a chiropractor in the audience. Sure enough there was, and he worked on me for ten minutes in the dressing room while the other guys played a blues jam to kill the time. And then in more recent years I had tendonitis in my right elbow and forearm, and had to wear a brace for most of that tour. But since then I've been going to a chiropractor regularly and getting a massage at least once a week – even on tour."

Returning to the States following those dates, Shirley was looking forward to working with the band and felt that he would be able to sharpen and help mould Dream Theater to create a more mainstream sound. And although Dream Theater were aware of Shirley's reputation, it wasn't until pre-production work began on May 12 that the full ramifications of his input became clear. By this stage, the band had amassed enough material to comfortably record a double album, but with Elektra adamant that the budget would only extend to a single disc, their first challenge was to trim down the track-listing. Consequently, songs such as "Metropolis Part II", "Raise The Knife", "Where Are You Now" and "Speak To Me" were put aside, but the pruning of their material didn't stop there. Soon, the producer was chopping and reworking songs using the editing software Pro Tools to transform the sound and approach of many of the tracks. This only added to the immense irritation that Mike was already feeling due to the ongoing management issues.

"At first it was a big battle and I felt shades of David Prater all over again," says Mike. "I just really didn't have the energy or strength to go through another Prater thing where I was battling with a producer. It was the first time in the band's history when the songs were being re-written for us. Even with Prater, he never rewrote anything, he would just maybe change the instrumentation here and there, and make the recording process miserable."

"So there were a lot of feelings during this period. On the one hand, I was the control freak trying to maintain that last bit of integrity. But on the other, I was looking in the mirror and saying, 'Maybe I don't know what's best for the band,' and 'Maybe I need to loosen up and let some of this stuff go.' And I would talk to my wife and other people and they would say, 'Maybe you shouldn't try to be so controlling.' So I just rolled over and let Kevin do what he wanted to do and went in there with an open mind. Although I was hesitant, I was trying my best to have an open mind and realize that maybe I wasn't right or knew what was best for the band. The other guys had no problem with it and it was mainly me. Finally I gave in. Kevin made a lot of changes and completely re-arranged songs such as 'Lines In The Sand' and 'Burning My Soul'. I mean, he took the whole middle section out of 'Burning My Soul' and wanted to make it a whole instrumental on its own, and that's how 'Hell's Kitchen' came about."

But there were other Shirley-induced alterations that would cause more unease within the band. The first of these was a Petrucci-penned ballad, "Take Away My Pain", which was a tender track written about the emotions felt by the guitarist when watching his father pass away in hospital. The original demo was far slower, simpler and more emotive than the busy version that emerged on the album, which was embroidered with maracas and an assortment of overdubs that seemed a tad incongruous.

"Urghhh! Even to this day, I can't listen to it," spits Mike with obvious disdain. "It was the most heart-drenched, emotional statement that John Petrucci ever made. He wrote that right after his father died, and he actually read those lyrics at his father's funeral. There was so much emotion in that original version and Kevin just turned it into a Caribbean trip to Disneyworld on the final album. He added a Latin thing, and James is singing what should have been the most emotional lyrics ever like throwaway words."

Despite Mike's annoyance, John Petrucci is somewhat more

diplomatic when addressing the changes made to the original version of the song.

"Yeah, Mike never liked the treatment to it and always liked the original," he smiles. "But I was cool about it. I think the way that I originally wrote it and played it was more like a power ballad type of thing. I was into getting a fresh perspective on the song. It's funny, as there are some really cool things happening on the final version that's on the album. There's a guitar part that Kev had suggested, where he said 'I'm going to play the track and want you to just play anything.' I had a wah-wah pedal and just did this take throughout the track."

"It's just kind of running through it and it drifts in every so often. You can especially hear it at the end and during the chorus. It was an approach that was so different, was very cool and wouldn't have otherwise come out."

On the surface, given Elektra's stated optimism that the album would yield a crossover hit single, it appeared that they had openly directed Shirley to shape the material to ensure that they achieved their aims. But the producer denies that he was working under any orders to try and turn Dream Theater into a more commercial proposition.

"No I wasn't. It was just something I thought that I could do," says Shirley. "I mean there were some things that they did that I thought were fantastic. But sometimes in the course of a song, they would play something once, and I thought we could find and make hooks in these things. You know, maybe look again at a chorus and try to make a song a little more accessible to the general public. I had meetings with the guys, particularly with Petrucci and Portnoy, and they were both really open to it. All the demos had been cut and I went in and made some quite significant changes, and Mike was OK with them at that point. To be honest, I don't think the band were in the best shape at that time. They were struggling a lot with themselves about what to do, and I think that I was one of the things they reached for that they thought may fix it. I don't think Elektra really cared. Josh Deutsch was their A&R guy and they were selling enough records to make money for the company to make sure they weren't a liability, but nobody was putting any energy or resources into it as they would always sell records. Josh Deutsch took over from Derek Oliver, and he had no interest in the band whatsoever."

Shirley's most controversial decision was to involve an external writer to assist the reworking of "You Or Me" (later renamed "You Not Me"). You might imagine that this in itself wouldn't have posed too much of an obstacle, but the musician in question was none other than Desmond Child – who was well-known for penning soft rock, hit songs such as "Livin' On A Prayer" for Bon Jovi and Aerosmith's "Crazy". It seemed a highly unlikely partnership, and Mike in particular found the suggestion distinctly unpalatable.

"Once again we said 'OK, we're willing to try anything,'" he explains. "We were just desperate to make another album and move on with our career. Just as we signed on to work with Kevin, the Aerosmith *Nine Lives* album he'd produced was Number One in the charts. So we were thinking we were working with the number one producer and someone like Desmond Child who has written huge hit songs. We thought that maybe they did know best, and could turn this album into a fucking massive hit. And of course that never happened. But for me it was a really tough pill to swallow, and Desmond didn't even want to meet with the whole band. Basically, just John Petrucci went down to Florida and although they were John's lyrics, the music was written together. It really bothered me that Desmond was going to rewrite one of our songs with only one member. That's not the way we write. But it's not like we had any options, because if we fought it or said no, the whole machine would have been turned off anyway. So we didn't have a choice."

"So John was willing to go with all that shit and I was desperately fighting him for the sake of holding on to the band's integrity," continues Mike. "I was holding on to all those ideals with all my might. All that kind of stuff was beating us up internally as well, and it was making me nuts. Suddenly I felt the control of the band slipping through my fingers and that everything the band had stood and fought for over all the years was just being thrown out of the window. And it was just for the sake of the industry, the business, the lawyers and the record companies."

"I've always felt that it is important to pave your own way and to not be swayed creatively by the wrong people," explains John Petrucci. "Having said that, at that time I was absolutely interested in working closely with people who were established, respected professionals, in order to learn new things and to gain a fresh perspective on everything from songwriting to recording and producing. I think it's important to try to achieve a balance between staying open-minded and receptive to fresh ideas and protecting and furthering your own creative identity. I don't think that Dream Theater has ever lost sight of that or sacrificed any of our musical integrity over the years. The skills I developed during that period have been instrumental to my success as a songwriter, lyricist, guitarist and producer, and to my pursuit of bettering the band's musical identity and presentation."

John Petrucci was duly flown down to Florida to meet with the colourful Desmond Child, and fondly remembers the experience.

"That was wild, and he was highly hospitable," he laughs. "I remember he picked me up from the airport and we were driving to his place, and he said 'I gotta tell you that I have people coming to my place all the time. I get phone calls from Madonna and it is just business as usual.

But when the people at the studio heard you were coming they were like "Dream Theater? No fucking way!"' So sure enough, there were a few fans there who were so into the fact I was going there. But I was only there for a day, and the whole feeling was that we went for juice, had a barbecue, checked out his place and it was a really relaxed comfortable vibe. I remember thinking 'This guy *knows* how to live!' And then we eventually went into the studio and got to work! On a selfish front I'm really into song and lyric writing, so it was great to just be able to sit there, work with him, get his insight and just to have him show me things. And some of the things that he told me then still stand out, like to keep a story and a focus when you're writing lyrics. So it was really cool. Certain people have certain talents, and it was great to experience that."

The guitarist also openly admits that he was receptive to the guidance of Shirley, but in hindsight recognizes how working with an outside writer caused an immense degree of dissension within the band.

"I was pretty open to it and didn't mind it at the time," says Petrucci. "I like Kevin, and I was open-mined to trying a bunch of different things. That's not to say that it wasn't bizarre to have someone who hadn't written the music come in and start editing stuff. Mike wasn't into that kind of input and wanted more control of our situation. I think I relate to that more now than then. We certainly see eye-to-eye with that now and I don't want people telling me what to do. But at the time, I just thought 'Why not?' I just didn't see anything wrong with it and it was great for me creatively."

Derek Sherinian had already come across Child when the keyboardist was playing with Alice Cooper, and still remains amused at the thought of the two parties working together – especially given the potential clash of personalities. "Child is very colourful, flamboyant, and on fire and I would've loved to have seen that dinner with Petrucci and Desmond sitting there socializing," he laughs. "I would've paid money to have seen that."

For all the animosity that was aimed in his direction – both during and in the years following that decision – Kevin Shirley remains convinced that working with Child was the correct choice, and claims that despite Mike's later protestations, the drummer was amenable to the proposal at the time.

"I've seen all those interviews with Mike when he has said that, but I really do think he was receptive at that point," he says. "I think what made the difference was we went in, they spent a lot more money but their record sales didn't change at all. To be honest it was tough trying to get a single. I'd spoken to Desmond as he really does know how to write a hit song, and they came back with something really good. But if truth be told, James couldn't sing the song like the rewritten demo.

So we ended up struggling and trying to adjust the song to suit James's voice. The demo moved more in a Yes direction with lots of harmonies, which I thought was going to be very cool, but we just couldn't get that. We ended up with something that sounded like two separate songs, and it wasn't a very good version of it."

Ironically, given the band's condemnation of some of his editing decisions, Shirley recalls that he was also far from content with some of Dream Theater's preferences. One example was a guitar solo on "Hollow Years", with Petrucci changing his mind as to how he wanted it to sound on the final album.

"John had done *the* most exquisite nylon guitar solo," explains Shirley. "We mixed it on a Friday night and I actually sent out to get some Chianti as I thought the solo was perfect for it! It was just one of those solos that had kind of an Italian vibe, and had such a good feeling about it that I could almost hear the trees and imagine the wine. Of course, John took the mix home and called me on the Saturday morning and said that he didn't think he could live with the solo. I said 'You're kidding right?' But he wasn't. It was so full of feeling, power and was so tasteful, and I told him it was the nicest solo in the album, but he still said he couldn't live with it. The mix was still on the tapes and he came in to the studio."

"As we were recording on analogue tape, and didn't have another track, I had to erase the original. But he told me not to worry as he had in mind exactly what he wanted. Of course I erased the solo, he played it exactly as he wanted it and it kind of destroyed the whole song for me. The mood went straight away from being a feel-piece to being a precision-piece, and it didn't need to be at all. So those are the kind of things you ended up battling about. He was happy with the solo and I wasn't, but at the end of the day it was his record. Another thing I tried to bring to them was a sense of feel. I felt the sounds were sometimes impoverished by the need for perfection. So, in 'Hollow Years', 'Anna Lee' and 'Peruvian Skies', we tried to make it sound a little looser. I played John some Pink Floyd stuff and said 'Look at how sloppy Gilmour is, but it still works and has a good feel.'"

John Myung was quick to praise Shirley's work in an interview with *Bass Player* magazine.

"Kevin Shirley was able to inspire performances I didn't know I had in me. For example, the first half of 'Peruvian Skies' is very Pink Floyd-like. One night Kevin brought me into the control room and told me that the bass playing wasn't doing anything for him and he wanted me to take a different approach. I started recording and wasn't sure where I was going with it, so we took a break and Kevin put on Pink Floyd's 'The Wall' and told me, 'Go out there and play with a Roger Waters mindset'. So I immersed myself in what was happening on that track and did the best I could on several takes. The next day when I listened to it, I was amazed. It didn't even sound like me. I'm thankful that he didn't just say 'OK, play this song.'"

Derek Sherinian asserts that the process of working with Shirley was both fruitful and satisfying, adding, "I thought he was really open to all of my ideas, he had a good eye and there was a certain simplicity to the way he worked. I also liked some of his edits, but I felt others were incorrect and the songs should have remained in their original form."

Yet for all the distracting tribulations that had tarnished the writing and pre-production work, the band recall that the actual recording sessions were surprisingly trouble-free and enjoyable. With the band wanting to remain close to their New York homes and new families, Kevin Shirley chose the old Power Station Studios (that had recently been re-christened Avatar) as the location for the sessions, and the recording of *Falling Into Infinity* finally began on June 2, 1997.

"The irony, once we got past pre-production process, was that I and the rest of the band had an amazingly good time making that record," says Mike. "As much as I had a problem with Kevin Shirley's changes, he and I got along fabulously and to this day have a great relationship. So once I'd accepted those changes, making the record was incredibly pleasurable. We got very experimental making the album and kind of set up shop. I had two drum sets, John Petrucci had a dozen different amps and guitars to choose from, and Derek brought in all these keyboards and a Mellotron organ. It was also the first time that we had tracked an album song-by-song as opposed to instrument-by-instrument. That was something we decided with Kevin, as we wanted each song to have its own identity. So we would take a song like 'Hollow Years' and track it piece-by-piece until it was complete, and just focus on getting the right sounds for that song. And we would do that all down the line. So we were able to give each song its own personality."

John Petrucci: "Those recording sessions were awesome. I had every Mesa Boogie amplifier and cabinet you could possibly imagine, and the whole place looked like a huge music store. The recording process was so creative and each song was approached differently. It was a lot of fun and I certainly learned a lot in those sessions with Kev."

"The whole recording process was different," recalled John Myung in *Bass Player* magazine. "With our earlier albums, we'd record all of the drums at once, and then we'd do the rhythm guitar for all the songs at once, then all the bass lines and so on. When you do that, you don't really explore the nature of each song and you kind of get numb to everything. For this album, we decided to record one song at a time, and when we were done, Kevin would mix it and master it, and then we would move on to the next song. That was great because it allowed us to give each song the attention it needed and to explore all of our creative options. We also got a more diverse album, and the songs ended up with more dimension and character." *Falling Into Infinity* was duly completed on July 30, 1997, and released by the label on September 23. In truth, it is one of the patchier albums in the band's back-catalogue. Created in an atmosphere where commerciality had been unceremoniously stapled to the forefront of their minds, it sounds as confused as the band undoubtedly were during those elongated writing sessions. Perfectly demonstrating that conflict is the opener "New Millennium". Far too often during the track, once a decent riff is established the band veer off in an unexpected and superfluous new direction. It's not that the album's bad. It just sounds inconsistent with the songs wildly flitting between styles, giving it the aura of a "Greatest Hits" package.

Yet in spite of the album's awkwardness, it still contains some of Dream Theater's most abiding tracks. For all the arguments over the edits, re-writes and the search for a perfect radio-friendly song, "Hollow Years" and "Take Away My Pain" are beautifully crafted and lilting ballads that provide a balance to the album's darker moments. "Burning My Soul" and "Just Let Me Breathe" are also highlights, and contain some of the harshest lyrics Mike Portnoy has ever penned.

"My three lyrics on the album were all created by record company frustration," reveals Mike. "'Just Let Me Breathe' and 'New Millennium' were directly aimed at the industry and the label, and 'Burning My Soul' was almost written directly to Derek Oliver. You know – *'Using your words / Controlling my life / Can't you see it's my words / That give you your life'* – is all about a label trying to control a band. The line *'I say it's green, then you tell me it's red'* relates to us trying to get the green light to make a record and them just saying no and stopping us in our tracks. Plus there's *'Keep your thoughts and ideas inside your head / We've got someone who can think for you instead,'* which is all about using Desmond Child. So my lyrics were definitely all about that, and the only other lyric I wrote during that period was for 'Raise The Knife', which was the first song we wrote during the *Falling Into Infinity* process. Those lyrics are dealing with some of the early changes we went through and they were specifically about Jim Pitulski and Kevin Moore."

There was also a warranted dig at transient pop-rock band Blind Melon, who in an article in the *Guitar For The Practising Musician* magazine, had described *Images And Words* as "The kind of music you listen to right when you start to get pubic hairs." Referring to that band's late singer Shannon Hoon (who died from a drug overdose), the lyrics read – *"Shannon Hoon and Kurt Cobain / Make yourself a household name"*. And following with the line – *"Until you kill yourself / And then the sales got through the roof,"* there were no punches pulled.

"That was just as simple as one of the guitar players insulting us or

John Petrucci in a magazine," says Mike now. "But that's typical. We've kind of become used to other musicians in the industry taking stabs at us. A lot of the people don't really like progressive rock or musician oriented music, and that makes us an easy target for bands like Blind Melon to take a stab at. I got the last laugh by immortalizing their singer in the lyrics."

Another shady track is "Peruvian Skies", a song that contains all the facets of a great Pink Floyd and Metallica track, but which dealt with the uncomfortable subject of child abuse.

"It's about a fictional girl named Vanessa and how her father was abusing her," revealed John Petrucci. "With a perspective of listening to things going on, how she's trapped in that and how she'll take all of this into her own child's upbringing."

The album also contained the lone appearance of the mysterious Del Fuvio Monks on backing vocals. In reality, this was John Petrucci, Mike Portnoy and Derek Sherinian working under a comical pseudonym. "Under the surface, the Del Fuvios were a secret organization based on mockery, bitter diatribe, and sardonicism. We were so fucking brutal, it was unbelievable," joked Sherinian.

One of the album's more progressive moments was the mesmerizing "Lines In The Sand " which demonstrated the band's ability to seamlessly meld together a variety of genres and time signatures.

"The main riff came from something that Derek had written and we had started working on during some of the soundchecks on tour," revealed John Petrucci, in an interview with *Guitarist*. "The guitar solo sounded very Floydish to me, so I went for that Gilmour tone and more of a melodic approach."

That track also included a vocal contribution from Kings X frontman Doug Pinnick.

"Yeah, we heard this melody when we were writing the song, and we decided to give Doug a call as he's one of our favourite singers," explained John Myung. "He's been a friend of ours for quite a while. He was really happy that we had thought of him, so we flew him to New York to record it. It was amazing working with him as he's a true professional. He just came right in and banged it out."

John Myung's main contribution was to the similarly expansive "Trial Of Tears ". He had worked on a demo – which contained guitar, keyboard and bass parts – before presenting it as a semi-finished piece to the band.

"It was a song that went through many different stages," he explained in *Bass Frontiers* magazine. "The first demo that I made was a really raw version of that. We worked on it as a band and took it to a whole new level. It turned out to be this really incredible song that went from the version that I did, to something that incorporated the whole band.

Lyrically, it was a very therapeutic song for me. It deals with ego and my perception of it, and understanding how it can cage you and really alter your perspective, but then realizing that life is too short and you have to make a decision. You also need to learn how to deal with regret while still moving forward. There's one line that talks about how you're 'Not much better' than the man you hate.' That's pretty much a play on one of the ten commandments of love thy enemy. It's just a whole bunch of different things that I was going through just put into a song."

The album title itself was chosen with the eventual cover artwork in mind, with John Myung explaining in *Burrn!* magazine that "It just tied in nicely with what we wanted to do visually with the album artwork. Storm Thorgerson liked the title and brainstormed on it, and sent us a bunch of his sketches based on that theme and the results were amazing."

The artwork is indeed striking, and one of the more memorable in the band's back-catalogue. The relatively simplistic design showed two men perched on top of sea-based platforms, staring at each other through binoculars. The effect is enhanced to give the impression that they are also being viewed through binoculars. Rather than entirely mock up the cover image in the studio using a computer, Storm Thorgerson opted to actually build the platform, employ a pair of models, and stick them in the sea off Camber Sands on the south coast of England.

"Obviously we had to put the poles in the water as it was *sort* of done for real," says Storm. "We only actually used one platform, and we then took two shots before reversing them back in the studio. It would have been too difficult to do it any other way, as we wouldn't really know how far apart they should be anyway. But it is actually someone sitting on the top of the platform. I think they were two different guys, and they were probably friends in order for it to be cheap!"

Although there were plenty of links to the album's title – with the infinity sign appearing throughout the design – Storm reveals that part of the inspiration for the cover actually came from a Gary Larson *Far Side* cartoon.

"There was a cartoon he did of a birdwatcher looking through his binoculars at this bird that is about to attack him," he says. "It was that kind of weird stuff that Larson does. I mean, his picture wasn't about infinity but it was about binoculars. The binocular theme was derived in part from him. But the main idea was that you're looking at the person, who is looking at the other person, who is looking back. So in a sense it is endless as in infinity, though it's not a repeat. You are looking at the person on the right, who is looking at the person on the left, who might be about to look at you. So in effect it was a 'who is watching whom routine'."

The inside pages of the booklet were partly designed by Storm's colleague Peter Curzon who recalls: "I know we used a lot of black on the inside of the booklet, which was to do with the border and surround on the front cover. Plus we used a lot of rounded shapes in there to tie in with binoculars. And we also added a lot of hatchet markings like you get in those surveillance pictures, which again ties in with the binoculars theme and people looking at each other."

The album was released in October 1997 and peaked at Number 52 in the US chart, but failed to even hit the top 75 in the UK. Alarming as that might have been, it was the somewhat muted reaction from Dream Theater's fans that would be more disquieting for the band. For the first time in their history, they were berated by certain elements for what the latter perceived as selling out in an unashamed attempt to appeal to the mass market. Those accusations were also hinted at in the music press, and interviews of the period were often hostile affairs, with Dream Theater forced onto the back foot in order to defend themselves.

When quizzed about the accessible nature of the new material in *Burrn!*, James retorted: "Let's face it, we were at a point in our careers where we wanted to go to the next level and wanted to expand. So definitely with this album, we said that we should touch on a few angles with one being 'Let's try to get a few more listeners'. And the only way you can achieve that is to write something that's a little more radio-friendly, but not selling out."

In a typically forthright manner, Mike was also quick to add, "Well, people may say that, but realistically we have always had all kinds of songs on our albums. We've always had mellow songs or poppy songs. If a couple of them click this time around and we get a lot of radio play, then we'll probably be accused of selling out. But I'll be pretty frank here, at the risk of insulting other bands – I think a lot of the changes that we've made through the years are a lot more honest than some of the changes that Queensrÿche or Metallica have made. I mean when I listened to the last Metallica album [*Load*] or the last Queensrÿche album [*Hear In The New Frontier*], to me they sounded like blatant sell-outs."

John Myung was also quick to defend the album's direction, claiming that "It's really hard to try and build a career without radio. You need it now. There's only a certain amount of weight the band can pull through touring. So it's really important to let people know you are alive and that there's a band called Dream Theater that exists, that we do write songs and put out albums. It's very competitive out there with so many records coming out all the time. And that's where radio comes in. If you have a successful song, and it gets played, then people will hear you, and if they like what they hear, they'll go out and buy you. So that's one way to start the relationship with us and our fans."

Reviewing the album for *Metal Hammer* magazine, Jerry Ewing sprung to the band's defence, claiming "Dream Theater's refusal to conform to modern music's expected norm has repaid them with a large fan base on both sides of the Atlantic. Unlike peers Queensrÿche, they have not adapted their own sound to tackle modern themes. In other words, all credit to them for not 'going grunge'. Rush may still rule this particular roost, but on this showing, the young pups are catching up fast."

Another justification for the album's direction was provided by John Petrucci in *Guitar World*, when he claimed, "The record that comes to mind in exemplifying what we were trying to do is *Dark Side Of The Moon*. That's such a ridiculously intense cerebral experience. It's Pink Floyd – the ultimate in musicianship, writing and psychedelic experience. But how often do you hear those songs on the radio? If you can maintain your musical integrity, push the limits of your own creativity and at the same time create music that becomes a part of people's everyday lives, that's the ultimate. And that's what we are trying to do."

In hindsight, of course, the flaws of the album are readily admitted by the band, and Derek Sherinian neatly summarized the issues when he declared, "I think that *Falling Into Infinity* has some good moments, but there was a lot of negative reaction from the hard-core Dream Theater fans about this release. It was more commercial and designed to cross over, but the crossover songs were not strong enough to break through. So the result was a lot of unhappy fans and I was very unfairly blamed by a lot of fans for the result of this CD."

The battles with the press during this period came to a head when Germany's *Rock Hard* magazine printed a story claiming that James and Derek had been unceremoniously fired. Responding to the article, James was somewhat diplomatic, but vented his frustration at other dodgy stories about the band that had also been circulated.

"I think the guys in the band were more pissed off than I was about that," he said "It was started by a band in Los Angeles. To be honest, when I first heard it, I was amused. Then the other guys found out about it and they were screaming 'This is fucking bullshit!' I talked to my buddy at *Rock Hard* and they apologized profusely, but I had to question why they never checked the integrity of their source. It got way out of hand. I read all kinds of crap on the band. Someone's died, someone's been sacked, wars between Dream Theater and Queensrÿche. I know Geoff Tate, he loves Dream Theater and vice versa. I hear all kind of crap dragging Geoff or me down, and it's crazy. Geoff and I are totally different singers and both have something to offer. And if you don't like what either of us has to offer, then fuck off."

Just to add to the uncertainty around the band, prog rock legends Yes had cheekily approached Derek Sherinian with a view to him joining them on tour. Yes had been unable to find a suitable replacement for Rick Wakeman.

"There was an answering machine message that Rick Wakeman was not doing the tour and they were looking for someone to replace him," explained Derek. "No one from Yes had ever approached me. And that got somehow turned into this rumour."

In an interview with *Burrn!* magazine, Mike amusingly suggested that they should have looked in another direction: "It's a compliment for his playing but I'm glad he's staying with us. If they were smart, they should have actually called Kevin [Moore] because he's the one that needs a gig."

Mike had noted that the British press were also giving the band a tough time, with some of the more trend-obsessed metal magazines preferring to bestow plaudits on emerging bands such as Korn, Foo Fighters or pop-rockers such as The Stereophonics.

"The English press has always been terribly hard on us," reflects Mike. "We came around playing progressive music at a time when grunge and metal was hip and cool. We were anti that. I remember one show that might have been on the *Falling Into Infinity* Tour, where from the stage I publicly bashed *Kerrang!* magazine. It was also in the days when I was drinking, and by the time the end of the show came around, I was usually half out of the bag. But I remember, at the end of the night, going up to the front of the stage – it might have been The Astoria or The Forum – and just saying 'Did everybody here have a good time? And there are 2,000 pleased customers here this evening? So when *Kerrang!* comes out with a review next week, tears us apart and insults not only us but you guys, I expect 2,000 hate letters telling them to go fuck themselves!' They have always been like that with us and magazines like *Kerrang!* were taking stabs at us. It wasn't until *Classic Rock* came around [in 1998] that we had an outlet of press in the UK that understood what we are, and the background in terms of the style of music that we come from."

Indeed Mike probably has more than a valid point when you bear in mind that *Kerrang!* notoriously reviewed the band's gig on 15 March, 1995, at the London Forum during the *Awake* tour Waking Up The World as "Wank metal" adding: "These solo spots don't get standing ovations, but neither do they become targets for rotten fruit. Maybe this whole thing is just working with a different set of rules. Or maybe Dream Theater have a problem. Sure they play for a value-for-money two hours, but why bother if the last half-hour's like having teeth tugged?"

Staying consistent with their intention of trying to squeeze a hit out of the band, the label were also insistent on filming a video to accompany the album's lead single, "Hollow Years". Dream Theater themselves were somewhat hesitant about the idea, and when you consider that it cost in the region of $100,000 to produce – without any guarantees of airplay – it's easy to comprehend their concern. Shot in Toronto, the video is a lush affair but only features fleeting glimpses of the band being driven around the backstreets. The remainder is packed with extras wandering the streets or staring in a "deep and meaningful" manner out of windows, giving the feel of a healthcare insurance or vitamin pill advert. Inevitably, the video failed to ignite the imaginations of the all-important suits at MTV, and it received little airplay.

More disturbing was that despite its direction, the album itself failed to break any new ground, with no discernible increase in sales. The irony is that for all their pressure in demanding the band write to a certain formula, once they'd recorded an album in line with those stipulations, the label failed to throw any marketing muscle behind the release. But was Kevin Shirley surprised at the lack of success?

"Not when I saw how much input Josh Deutsch had," says Shirley. "He honestly didn't care about it at all, and it wasn't the fault of the band. The label just did not care at all. I don't even think it is a secret and they just put the album out there. So unless you were a Dream Theater fan you wouldn't know it was out, and nobody else was really hip to the fact that anything was going on."

"The record entered well in the charts, but didn't do anything in America in terms of breaking new ground as everybody had hoped with this kind of album," agrees Mike. "We figured if we couldn't crossover with an album like that, then we never would. We gave them an album with four or five strong singles, so we thought if this album never broke new ground commercially then we should just forget about it. We did everything we could do to try and give them that type of record, and if they failed to do anything with it, then as far I was concerned, we'd done our share."

With the band's most difficult album finally released, Dream Theater were free to concentrate on the forthcoming world tour, and hoped it would provide some relief from their troubles. In fact, things were about to get much worse.

ELEVEN

WALKING ON EGGSHELLS

The tour commenced on September 11, 1997, in São Paulo, Brazil, with Dream Theater returning to the US to complete a number of dates later in the year, before stints in both Europe and North America extended the tour well into 1998. Yet the optimism of the band as they headed out on the road was soon to be dissipated by internal frictions and ongoing business problems. With Rob Shore suddenly vacating the manager's position ("I just wasn't enjoying my life at that point as a result of all the conflict, though we ended on really good terms" says Shore), there was the significant matter of finding an appropriate replacement to look after their affairs.

"We had to rebuild the team at the start of the tour, and we ended up getting some new management, who I'm not even going to name as they don't deserve it," says Mike forcefully. "They had no idea how to handle us as we *seriously* needed direction. The people we talked to, and some of the people we took on, were reactive and not proactive, and that wasn't good for us. Ultimately we ended up parting ways with them and that created some more lawsuits on top of everything else. The business management we were working with had no idea how to manage our money, and were just spending shit left and right. We ended up getting sued by this person and that person, and it was real ugly."

James LaBrie: "As an organization and a band there was so much peripheral confusion and bullshit going on. Business management was changing as were label personnel. People we had established a relationship with since the beginning were gone. So we were wondering who these new people were and whether they would understand us. It was a ridiculous period and was *very* trying. The tour kept that whole feeling of darkness and we felt we weren't where we wanted to be and it wasn't happy."

Significantly, the relationship between Mike and John Petrucci had also deteriorated to breaking point. With Mike frustrated at what he saw as Petrucci's acquiescence in allowing the band to be steered by the likes of Kevin Shirley, and the disagreement the pair had in choosing between Pitulski and Shore as their manager, the rapport they had previously enjoyed was under serious strain. Derek Sherinian recalls one specific incident that caused a serious rift.

"It all turned over when Mike fired John Petrucci's guitar tech, Mark Snyder," divulges Sherinian. "We were playing a show, and my keyboard rig went down. My tech wasn't having any luck in fixing it. Mike was looking over at Mark Snyder – even though he was Petrucci's tech – and I guess Snyder wasn't moving fast enough for Mike's liking, so he threw a drumstick at him. Mark just turned a flashlight on to his hand, and flipped Mike the bird. At the end of that gig Mike fired him. A substitute tech came out but he wasn't up to snuff, and John was *very* pissed. So that just caused a lot of stress."

Tour manager Bill Barclay also recalls the incident, and suggests that Mike had become gradually irritated by the fact that Snyder was paid more than other members of the touring crew.

"Mark was a stupendously good guitar tech," he says. "He's a lovely bloke, but let's just say that he was getting paid more than any of the other crew. I don't think Mike liked the idea that he was getting a bit of special treatment. The thing about John Petrucci is that he is so anal about his guitar system that he's really nervous about it. He's the same with his equipment as he is with his playing, and he's absolutely obsessed and meticulous about that. So Mark would get away with a lot really, but it was to give John peace of mind, because if he doesn't have that, he becomes very nervous. His equipment has to be spot on. So there was a bit of a clash there and Mike was quite vocal about it."

The fallout from Snyder's dismissal was substantial. With John Petrucci and Mike already quarrelling, the sacking of John's treasured guitar tech only made matters worse and their relationship began to visibly fragment.

"It was insane at one point and the two of them weren't talking," claims Sherinian. "There were issues between John and Mike brewing up and it got to the point that the two of them did not speak at all. They would play the shows together but there was no other communication between the two. That happened for at least a month, and it was very uncomfortable for everyone else involved."

"I don't know about that," muses James cautiously. "There was definitely a period where they were butting heads, but I don't think they weren't talking to one another. It was tense but it wasn't at the point where there was a complete communication breakdown. That didn't occur. But there was just so much pressure and misunderstanding on that tour."

Mike Portnoy: "Yeah, we had a big falling-out during one period of that tour. We were playing a gig in London Forum or Astoria. Those were in the days I was still drinking and although I still have a bad temper, back then there were no holds barred. When you are an active alcoholic you end up saying a lot of stupid things that you end up regretting afterwards. That was a night something happened onstage. I have seen bootlegs of it, of me actually throwing the drum set around, and trashing my percussion table and throwing shit at Mark Snyder. He and I just had a big blow-out. I was the 'rock star' freaking out on him for not doing something the way he was supposed to, and Mark Snyder has a bit of an ego himself. He's the rock star crew guy who refuses to be talked down to, so he fought back. And God forbid that a crew guy talks back to a band member! So it blew up in a big drunken scene, with the aftermath lingering for weeks, and it put John Petrucci in an awkward position. The other disagreement with John was just personal and behind the scenes stuff, and was to do with the balance of family life and professional life. That is a struggle we all go through every day. Plus, I was probably holding a lot of tension towards John during that period because of the compromises we made. So it was something that got a little ugly for a few weeks."

"Mark Snyder is a dear friend of mine who has built every rack system for me from the beginning right on through to the *Systematic Chaos* world tour, including my G3 racks as well," adds John Petrucci. "Mark is a God and guru of all that is rack, gear and electronics related. Having him out on the road with me was not only a rarity, but also a privilege in my eyes, so Mike firing him without my approval just crossed the line. That situation could have been talked about and resolved much more diplomatically. I would have never done anything like that to another band member so that did cause a ton of tension between Mike and me."

Such awkward situations aside, the band continued their unrelenting global journey to perform in sold-out theatres. But one of the more visible changes on that tour was the outlandish appearance of Derek Sherinian and his luridly decorated keyboard riser. Prior to Sherinian becoming a full-time member, he cut a bashful figure on stage, preferring to dress plainly with little interaction with the crowd. But following his permanent appointment as Kevin Moore's replacement, a new Derek Sherinian began to manifest itself. Wearing flashy and unbefitting clothes, he festooned the keyboard area with lava-lamps and a rug and even admitted himself that his part of stage had the appearance of a "cross between an opium den and a bordello."

"I knew it would help elevate me and make me more famous," says Sherinian without a hint of irony. "It was a very calculated move. I knew during this transformation that a huge portion of the fans would resent the flamboyance but I knew that another portion would dig it. I wanted to step out from being the guy quietly playing keyboards in the corner and make a bit of a mark. The key to that was that I always had to make sure that the playing was there to back it up."

"I remember we were rehearsing at SIR Studios in New York for the tour," he continues. "I'd purchased these four lava lamps, and a television that only showed static, which I'd set up at the rehearsals before they got there. So I had this *huge* production set up on my keyboard riser. First thing Mike said was, 'That's fucking great – I love it!' Then

I think Petrucci didn't say anything. After we had started playing and started doing some shows, I added this Seventies, white shag pile carpet on the riser with it and I had incense going too. But it was a total anomaly onstage because nobody else had anything on there and I had this full production. I remember a couple of weeks later, Petrucci came up and said, 'Derek, you know, all this stuff up here looks a little bit out of place.' So I just suggested we put them all over the stage to add a bit of a vibe and some colour. So if you notice, towards the end of the tour, the lava lamps extended all the way back and across the stage. Portnoy even put the same white shag pile carpet under his riser. So it was spreading a little bit!"

Despite the obvious entertainment value, the transformation was hard to accept for some of the more pedantic, prog rock aficionados within the band's fan base. But if Sherinian's image was too much to take, then the appearance at a number of gigs of two surrogate bands – Nightmare Cinema and the outlandish Nicky Lemons And The Migraines – pushed them over the edge. In an attempt to bring some light-hearted moments to an otherwise downbeat tour, Dream Theater occasionally transformed themselves into alter-ego bands. Nightmare Cinema saw them switching instruments and comprised James on vocals, John Myung on keyboards, John Petrucci on drums, Mike Portnoy on bass and Derek playing a sparkly, silver guitar. Limiting themselves to performing one number – Deep Purple's "Perfect Strangers" – the results were surprisingly impressive. The more out-landish Nicky Lemons And The Migraines involved Derek Sherinian playing the part of "Nicky Lemons", sporting a bright yellow feather boa around his neck, with the rest of band belting out rapid, punk-in-fluenced numbers – often to a bemused audience. But Mike doesn't have any misgivings about incorporating such surreal renditions into their set.

"I personally don't regret it," he says. "But I think James and John Petrucci look back and cringe. Derek and I were kind of on the side that pushed that stuff because we enjoyed not taking ourselves too seriously. But you know, I think that maybe we lost a little bit of our professional edge when we would do silly stuff like that. I think most of the fans liked it, could smile and see the humour in it. But then there were also a handful of fans that were looking at it going 'What the fuck are these guys doing?' Something like Nightmare Cinema is obviously fun and tongue-in-cheek. But to some people, the Nicky Lemons thing was so completely out of left field that they didn't know what the fuck to make of it. Derek was like fronting the band with a yellow feather boa and kind of doing a David Lee Roth impersonation, while we were playing like Ramones songs behind him. To some people who had a sense of humour, it was awesome, but to some of the more typical, snobby prog purists, they argued that you'd never see a band like Rush or Yes go to that extreme on stage."

"If you're on the road and travelling, you need comic relief," laughs John Petrucci. "I guess you could take that too far but it was funny. I love the name The Migraines – it's classic, and I can't believe nobody has used that. I guess a lot of the times you base things on models in your career and think that Rush or Metallica would never do something like that. So you have these professional role models but it doesn't really matter. You can do whatever you want."

In an interview of the period, Derek Sherinian hammed up his part, claiming, "Nicky Lemons is my alter-ego and is larger than life. The times that Nicky Lemons appeared on stage, the crowd went ballistic. I honestly believe that Nicky is part of me and when he takes the microphone, Derek doesn't exist. Nicky has written two songs, 'I Don't Like You' and 'Monkey's Ass', and the name of the album will be *Ugly American*."

Ignoring these distractions, there were a number of other highlights, not least the onstage appearance with the band of Iron Maiden frontman, Bruce Dickinson, at the House Of Blues in Los Angeles on May 18, 1998. Running through "Perfect Strangers" and rough versions of three Maiden classics, the vocalist had some difficulty remembering all the lines, having enjoyed a solo career away from the British band for the best part of five years. But ignoring such memory lapses, Dickinson enjoyed the experience.

"The band's tour manager, Bill Barclay, used to be Adrian Smith's guitar technician in the early days of Maiden," explained Dickinson. "So after a few beers together, the keyboard player gave me a yell and asked if I wanted to go and do 'Perfect Strangers' with them, something we had already done together on a live radio session. So we did 'Perfect Strangers' at the end. And then, of course, the band wandered off into 'The Trooper', followed by a verse of 'Where Eagles Dare', and one of 'Killers'. So I obliged and an enormous amount of fun was had by all."

Fun it may have been, but a few short weeks later, the pressures and irritations that had been plaguing Mike for the previous 18 months finally came to a head. Following a festival appearance on June 19, in Nurmijärvi, Finland, the drummer had drowned his sorrows in a protracted drinking session with members of Pantera. The togetherness displayed by that band both on- and offstage provided a stark reminder of the failings Dream Theater were encountering, and the increasingly tortured drummer decided that he'd had enough. As is typical in such situations, the breaking point was over an insanely trivial matter. Bizarrely, in this instance, it was over a hamburger, as his alcohol-fuelled early-hours munchies finally thrust Mike over the edge.

"It was absolutely silly what went on," explains Bill Barclay. "We did the festival, which was out in the middle of nowhere, and it was a three-hour drive from the town where we were staying. It had been a long day, everyone was wrecked, and we'd all had a couple of drinks. We finally got back into town at about 3:30am and someone noticed there was a McDonalds that was still open. It was kind of off the track a little bit, but not much – probably a couple of streets away or something. Anyway, Mike wanted to get something from McDonalds. So I said to everyone, 'Who wants to go for a McDonalds?' and there was a dead silence. Everyone wanted to go back to the hotel. So I said we'd go back to the hotel, and I'd deal with it back there – meaning if he wanted a burger, I'd send someone up to get him one or I'd get him a lift. I went into the hotel, dropped my bag and went back down to the bar to have a beer with a couple of the crew guys and Mike just went off on one."

"He started screaming and shouting 'I pay your wages blah, blah, blah,' and I just lost it. I got up and walked straight towards him. I think he must have thought I was going to flatten him. But I walked right past him and said 'Mike, I'm not going to talk to you when you're like this', and went back to my room. The next thing, there was bang, bang, bang on the door. I said 'Mike, don't be doing this man.' But he just started ranting and raving, saying, 'I'm fed up with this band. You're all fucking boring. This is it. I've had enough, I'm out of here.' He told me to book him a flight out of there for the next day. I just said to him that maybe *I* wasn't the right man for the band, and that as far as I was concerned, *I* was out of there. I told him it was absolutely stupid the way he was acting. James must have heard all the commotion and came up, so then there was a bit of a thing between them. I'd never seen him like that before, and he was being outrageously out of order."

In hindsight, Mike agrees that his actions were far from reasonable but adds: "It was just the straw that broke the camel's back. I got really drunk that night. I wanted to stop to get something to eat on the way back from the gig, and the tour manager wouldn't pull the bus over. I just went over the edge."

"It all came to a head after we'd done that show with Slayer and Pantera," says James. "I remember watching these guys with Mike and these bands were so tight, together and bombastic. They were incredible live. And I remember that we went on stage and you could just feel the vibe and excitement wasn't there. I mean, we were *trying* to put on a great show, but there had just been too much peripheral damage. So I think that might have been the final straw. We were on the way back to the hotel when Mike just kind of blew up."

"Mike wasn't happy that whole tour," he expands. "It was just a whole quagmire of negative energy going on. I just think it was years of pent up frustration. You know, the musical direction that he saw the band going in, the ton of personnel changes at the label, new management which at that time was misdirected. We were all feeling this complete oppression and having people represent us who were in fact misrepresenting us. We just weren't a happy band. You had five guys who didn't like how the label had directed us and pushed us into what we had found ourselves in with that album. So at times we were going, 'What the hell? It's not worth continuing if this is going to be it.'"

The following day, the band flew from Finland to Amsterdam for their next scheduled gig in Rotterdam on June 22 (which was ironically recorded, for posterity, for the live album *Once In A LIVEtime*) with both the drummer and tour manager still in tow. Mike arranged a meeting on the bus transferring them from the airport to venue, and made it plain to his bandmates that he was leaving. But with a number of gigs remaining on the tour, he agreed to honour those European dates before quitting.

"Mike, for one 24-hour period, just lost the plot," says Barclay. "I could have punched him in the mouth but it's not my way. He insulted me and I was really pissed off. The fact that he actually came up to my room in Finland and pursued it, made me angrier. But in the bar in Rotterdam before the show, I was watching a soccer match with a few of the crew. Mike actually came into the bar and apologized to me in front of everybody, which I thought was big of him. It must have taken a lot for him to do that. And as soon as he said that, it was water under the bridge for me."

In addition to the issues cited by James as reasons behind the drummer's unhappiness, Mike reveals that the ongoing rancour between himself and John Petrucci also played a major part in his decision.

"I had given up," he asserts. "By the time we got to that fan club show in Holland I was basically quitting the band. The industry had chewed us up and spit us out. Once mid-1998 rolled around, *nothing* good had come from the changes, and there was only negative feedback. That was when it came to a head. I realized I couldn't be in a band that doesn't have control over its own artistic voice. Even the haircuts were horrible. It was like a midlife crisis for a band. We were going through so much bullshit and changes. Yet I probably could have handled that if internally the band was still strong. But even within the band there was a power struggle between me and John. I felt John was giving in to a lot of the industry stuff with just me fighting it, that those guys were being swayed and it was too much for me."

John Petrucci: "I think that Mike and I have always had strong visions as to the direction and sound of the band. As a main songwriter and given the nature and style of our guitar driven music, I'm just naturally going to be in a position not only to sway or steer us down a certain path, but also to want to be in control of the sonic landscape. Being a guitar player and lyricist puts me in that driver's seat. Mike's passion as well, also needing to maintain a sense of creative control, inevitably led to disagreements and conflicts. We are just not always going to agree on the same things conceptually or practically all the time. It's just impossible. It ultimately comes down to how those conflicts are discussed and handled in the end. Back then we were all learning."

With Mike being blatantly disenchanted throughout the tour, his announcement didn't come as too great a shock to Derek Sherinian, who notes: "It was obvious he was miserable and that something had to give at that point. I was bracing myself for it being the end of the band."

However, Mike recalls that despite the warning signs, the other members of the band were still somewhat stunned by his decision.

"I don't think they ever thought that any of us, and especially me, would go so far as doing something desperate," he stresses. "We had been through so much. We went through two singer changes, Kevin leaving the band and so many ups and downs. And you know what? I could deal with all that crap. When there's external shit being thrown at you it makes you that much stronger, but once you start having the internal shit and lose that control on the inside, there's no point in even fighting any more. When you're losing the battles within the band, it was no longer fun or unified. It was no longer us against them, it was us against us."

The uncertainty continued during the Paris show on June 25. With Mike fearing that this appearance may have been his last, his parting words to the crowd of "Au revoir mon ami" had a deliberate poignancy. But using all their powers of persuasion, the band managed to convince Mike to at least see out the remainder of the tour, which included a summer stint in the US playing with Deep Purple and Emerson Lake & Palmer. John Petrucci recalls that at the time, with or without the drummer, he was determined that the band would continue. But in hindsight he now accepts that if Mike had left at that time, Dream Theater would effectively have been finished.

"I think it would have been difficult to continue," he says. "Mike's such a huge part of Dream Theater and this was something that we had built together to that point. So it wouldn't have been the same thing. Obviously when it was all happening, you're like 'Fuck it. I'm going to do whatever I have to do and I'm not going to stop.' But realistically, could we have continued? No. I couldn't see that. At the time you don't want anything to collapse or want to think that anybody could take that all away. But it wouldn't have been the same."

The drummer hadn't planned or even considered his future intentions, saying "I never even thought that far. At that point I had really started to establish myself as an individual drummer, and had begun winning awards and had been on the cover of all these drum magazines. I had been doing clinics all around the world and doing side-projects and session work, so I think I felt confident enough that I could continue to have a successful career as a drummer just based on my reputation. But I never really thought about where exactly that would go."

Mike's resolve to at least see out the arranged tour commitments would in time prove to be fundamental to their survival, as it provided the band with the breathing space to try and find a solution to their troubles. It was during that time that the band again stumbled across Frank Solomon (who was managing Deep Purple's guitarist Steve Morse) and Bruce Payne (Deep Purple's manager). Both were already known to Dream Theater as they had at various times discussed the possibility of taking over the band's affairs. On those occasions, the band had turned down their offer due to a perceived lack of industry leverage. But it was during that summer tour that Payne and Solomon proposed jointly managing Dream Theater.

"I remember when Bruce and I met with them," explains Frank Solomon. "It was backstage in Los Angeles and we were in the dressing room. We were talking and Mike said, 'Listen guys, don't think this is going to be a long-term thing or anything like that, because if things don't change drastically, I can't see this band continuing'."

"Yeah, we made it clear to them that we didn't know if we were even going to continue past that tour," explains Mike. "At least John Petrucci made it clear to me that he wouldn't continue the band without me, and that if I left, it would be the end of the band. So we told them all of our problems and frustrations and laid it all out for them. They proposed giving them a chance, and for us to give them a shot at managing the band, which we did. The first step towards rectifying everything was to tell the label to get the fuck out of our business and stay out of our hair. We had to get green lights from them without playing them any music, and for them to just let us make the kind of records we wanted. Plus we wanted to be able to self-produce ourselves, with me and John calling the shots."

James LaBrie: "I guarantee you we would have broken up if they had continued to push us down that road and try to mould us into something other than what we were. There would have been no other option but to say 'Screw it. We've had fun. Bye.' The label had wanted us to be something different and we were like, 'Wait a second. The only reason we got to where we got is because of who we are, and us sticking to our guns and us doing the music we feel is sincerely us. And now you're trying to change us? Give us a break. Go get one of your puppets or your pretty new faces, but don't do that to us.' So it was quite obvious that that moment in our career was probably what every band faces, in that we were either going to transcend or fall."

Frank Solomon's first daunting assignment as the band's manager was consequently to try and win over Elektra into leaving the band alone, which given the label's previous form wasn't going to be an easy task. But as Frank recalls, Elektra's head Sylvia Rhone and A&R man Josh Deutsch were probably left with few other options.

"I just went to them and said, 'This is the situation. You've got a band that is selling a lot of records and we really want to do things our way. The band know their fans, and if we are not allowed to do that, it's just not going to happen and everybody loses,'" says Frank. "And that wouldn't have done anybody any good. We were happy for them to monitor our progress but that we didn't want any input into the songs, we want to produce ourselves, pick our own mixer, and do all that kind of stuff. They were worried that our record budget would get spent and that they'd have nothing for it. So I just told them that it wouldn't happen and that they had my word. At the same time we would keep them abreast of our progress so that they knew the payments they were making towards studios were all going to a justifiable end. But it had to be our way, and they basically said 'OK – We'll give it a go.'"

The band had also stated that they were considering making their next record a concept album – which in the late Nineties could be construed as career suicide. But Frank's argument was so strong that they allowed the band total freedom – much to his surprise.

"I don't know how I was able to convince them, but I did," he smiles. "I just told them to trust the band as they knew their fan base, and that we weren't out there to destroy our careers – that was the last thing we wanted to do."

Mike's other bugbear related to the internal management of the band. As a self-confessed control freak, the "fake democracy" that prevailed when Dream Theater were making decisions began to grate. In order for him to remain part of the band, he needed John Petrucci and himself to be openly recognized as the leaders.

"We just wanted to acknowledge that John and I would run the show," says Mike. "There would be no more of this fake democracy we had lived under, where we would pretend everything is decided upon equally. When it came to writing music and making decisions we still functioned as a democracy – or pretended to. That resulted in fights that would just go on and on and on. I would usually end up winning the argument anyway. So all we were doing was eliminating hours and hours of arguing and getting the same results. Now, maybe one out of 50 issues will become an issue with us, whereas back then 49 out of 50 were issues. That was important to me and I told the band that I felt underappreciated, with all the work and time, and I was still not recognized or acknowledged as the leader that I really was. It bothered me, and that was a big part of the healing process."

"It's funny because in the years since then, it's become very clear and definitive that John Petrucci and I run the band. A lot of fans on the outside may think that would be a cause for resentment from the other three guys, but to be honest the band runs so much smoother than it ever has because all we are doing is not bullshitting or lying to each other. I think everybody trusts our roles. They trust my role where general decisions and the direction of the band is concerned. And they trust John's role of maybe having more musical input than the other guys."

Perhaps the key to the acceptance by the other three to a relinquishing of internal control lies in their personalities. John Myung is hardly the forceful type who would relish driving the band forward. With James living in Canada, he was pretty disconnected from his bandmates anyway, and during the late-Nineties he often wouldn't even be present during their writing sessions. And Derek Sherinian was, despite being with the band for almost four years, still viewed as the new boy whose position was still far from secure.

"You know what, I think it was a natural process that happened whereas certain people are more proactive in situations," says Petrucci. "Some people are more able to be in charge, are strongly opinionated or outgoing. They just naturally lead situations and there's nothing wrong with that. It's really necessary. You can't have everyone just floating around. You have to have leaders – whether it's in a family, a business or a band. There are tons of things that Mike does that, thank God, he does. Someone needs to take control of this stuff and you can't sit there and have meetings about every little thing. Whether that's on a business or personal level, there's always going to be a person or two who rise to the occasion or have an interest. And some people really just aren't interested in that. When I'm in a studio, I think it's awesome and I'm interested in every little detail. Some people might not be into that. So if that doesn't interest them, it's a natural process for them to step back."

"I think everybody understands their role," interjects Mike. "I've always been very outgoing, obsessive, and controlling. And John Petrucci has always been very concerned over the music, the sound and the production. James has always been a little bit of the outsider because he's not with us all the time and John Myung has always been very quiet and doesn't offer many ideas. So the dynamics of the band are pretty obvious."

John Myung accepted the decision and reveals that he didn't notice too much of a change once Mike and John were dutifully manning the helm, saying, "I remember it was always that way. That was just the chemistry that we always had. Even at Berklee, when we were recording demos, it was Mike and John who were behind the four-track."

A similar attitude was adopted by James, who says "Every band has one or two guys who seem to be steering the ship. You can easily fall into a problem if there are five guys weighing in. So you need that line of command to be given to someone. Mike and John Petrucci have had those duties. Mike takes on a lot for the band and organizes a lot of shit, from the Ytsejam official bootleg releases, to writing the set lists and creating these shows that become DVD releases. He is thoroughly involved, and probably from the moment he gets up to when he goes to bed, he's thinking Dream Theater. And John is the same way. He's got a clear vision as to what he wants to happen musically."

That clear vision and yearning for absolute control would extend to John and Mike insisting on them adopting the role of producers on all future albums, as well as directing the shape of Dream Theater's music. Derek Oliver saw this as an imperative step in their development, saying that it was the "right decision for them to take control of their material and recordings. Certainly I don't think there was anybody qualified at the label to offer them any advice or useful assistance."

The agreement of Elektra to simply allow Dream Theater to control their own destiny was also essential to their long-term development – a fact recognized by Rob Shore: "It probably lead to their longevity, as after *Falling Into Infinity*, they were pretty much left alone to do what they wanted. The record label certainly didn't put video money in, and it just became the type of thing where Dream Theater put out a record every couple of years, they made money on it, and nobody got in their way. The record label was more of an entity that got the record in the stores, did a little press, but anything beyond that was minimal – which may have served them both well."

The label were, however, happy to release the *Once In A LIVEtime* CD on October 27, 1998, that featured the band's performance from Paris and Rotterdam earlier in the year. A full-length home video entitled *5 Years In A LIVEtime* was also released, and took the format of a documentary detailing the band's activities following the end of the *Images And Words* Tour, as well as including promotional videos and live renditions of a number of tracks. Kevin Shirley recorded and mixed the live performances, and recalls it was a hectic schedule.

"This album tends to get knocked a little bit," he says. "Dream Theater have always been *very* tight on the budget. So I had to mix that in two days and do all the fixes. And believe me, on that album there were a lot of fixes. So that really was non-stop."

The cover was another Storm Thorgerson design and depicted an amphitheatre formed in the centre of a man's skull. Playing on the band name and the fact that it was a live album, the design was striking and bold, but Storm now admits that he was unhappy with the finished piece.

"I think I imagined that the inside of somebody's head was like a concert hall or amphitheatre," recalls Storm. "The amphitheatre is real and I think is in Arles, France. I had hoped that the amphitheatre might fit the shape of the head but I don't think it worked very well really. When you do these things, you hope to God that they work well, but they don't always. I think in hindsight the idea was fundamentally not very good. And I probably shouldn't have thought of doing it in the first place, or agreed to do it once the group had chosen it. But it sometimes happens. I think the band must have thought the same thing afterwards, because they never employed us again."

One noticeable aspect of both this sleeve, and Storm's previous effort on *Falling Into Infinity*, was the loss of the usual Dream Theater style of lettering. Replaced with stylized fonts, the move was unpopular with the fans and the old logo would return for all subsequent releases.

"Logos are usually ugly, so we don't like them very much," says Storm. "So we tend to either want to change them, use something else or use something more specific. But certainly that isn't a hard and fast rule. We did two different kinds of lettering and they obviously ended up not liking either of them."

"The *Falling Into Infinity* logo we used was blurred and softened around the edges, and then sharpened like it was through binoculars," adds Storm's colleague Peter Curzon. "The second one we did was a bit sci-fi looking, but I honestly can't remember why I did it that way."

The press reviews of the album were predictably mixed. *Kerrang!* took great delight in bashing the release, with Liam Sheils describing listening to the album as a "thoroughly unrewarding experience", adding, "Not that incredibly intricate music needs by definition to be soulless and tuneless drivel. When you add the intelligence of Rush's Neil Peart, the humour of Jethro Tull mainman Ian Anderson or the pop nous of Francis Dunnery, it can make for an exhilarating ride. Unfortunately Dream Theater have none of these. Just lots and lots of notes and a funny idea of how to spell the word 'Theater'."

But praise came from an unexpected source when mainstream magazine *Q* provided a relatively positive review, claiming: "The recording quality is suspiciously pristine, but the musicianship indisputably superb, especially when the band rock out on 'Take The Time' and 'Pull Me Under'. However, with the extended solos and the exclusion of the band's customary cover versions, *Once In A LIVEtime* is obviously targeting the already converted, who will undoubtedly wallow in it as a glorious celebration of Dream Theater's *raison d'etre*. Others will merely feel swamped."

Apart from the concerns over the record label, there was also another major issue that needed to be addressed – the keyboard position. Although Dream Theater had no gripes with Derek Sherinian's contributions or performances, they were becoming increasing perturbed about his showiness which seemed to be at odds with the rest of the band. In short, his appearance and mannerisms were becoming totally incongruous.

"The whole creative process with Derek was positive and he was an asset to us," explains Mike. "But differences between us and Derek were felt when we were on the *Falling Into Infinity* Tour. That was when the music wasn't at the forefront any more. When you are on tour it's all about the performance, and at that point Derek was really playing the role of the rock star. You know, dressing up like Bono meets Liberace, with platform shoes, lava lamps and fur carpeting all over the stage. He was really into the whole showman thing, almost to the point where it was out of place with the rest of us. Plus he was a single guy when all of us were married with children, and he was the one who was constantly trying to pick up chicks. The whole way he carried himself on stage, it came off as though the image was more important than the music, and that was never what Dream Theater was about."

That view is also echoed by Bill Barclay, who recalls that Derek was "A good player but he didn't really fit in with the temperament of the band. Dream Theater have a great sense of family about them. Not just within the band but with their wives and kids as well. They were one of the first bands I worked with who used to bring their wives and kids out on tour. A lot of people might think that would be a nightmare, but in fact to me it was never a problem. Derek was a young guy who thought he could pull all the chicks – which was fair enough. He was a young, single guy. But it didn't really fit in with what Dream Theater were all about."

That perceived eccentricity also extended to the fans. Many had resented the fact that Kevin Moore had left the band in the first place, and to see someone as revered as Moore replaced by the flash Sherinian had always been grating. And without the backing of a large proportion of the fans, he'd always been on distinctly shaky ground.

Typically though, John and Mike weren't about to make such a drastic alteration to the line-up without first having a replacement at the ready. Their choice was Jordan Rudess, who apart from a solitary live appearance with Dream Theater – in the aftermath of Kevin Moore's departure back in 1994 – had worked with the pair as part of the side-project band, Liquid Tension Experiment. That band also featured renowned bassist Tony Levin, with their eponymous, all-instrumental debut being written and recorded in a hectic fortnight in September 1997. The album was released in early 1998, and heralded a period when side-projects were an opportunity for the various band members to express themselves away from the confines of Dream Theater. Indeed, between 1996 and the end of 1999, James had released a solo album under the Mullmuzzler moniker, John Myung and Derek had collaborated on a Platypus album, with other members working on other projects including The Explorers Club and tribute albums to ELP and Rush. Later in 1998, Liquid Tension Experiment worked on a follow-up release – the unimaginatively titled 2 – and it was during this writing process that John and Mike casually sounded out Jordan about joining Dream Theater.

"One night, we kind of hypothetically asked him if he would join again if he had the opportunity," confesses Mike. "He said 'Absolutely'. So John and I kind of looked at each other and decided that it was time to make the change. It kind of sucked for Derek, as we had such a great musical relationship with him. Derek also unfortunately always lived in the shadow of Kevin and was always being compared to him while he was in Dream Theater. For some reason, people had such a soft spot for Kevin and held him in such high regard. He was like this enigmatic figure that Derek could never live up to. People always questioned whether Derek was the right keyboard player for the band. So John and I had this great musical experience with Jordan, and personally he was more like us – him being a family guy – that it just seemed like it was the right move. We felt horrible to do it to Derek, but we really had to do it for the sake of the band's survival."

Jordan Rudess: "Towards the end of the second Liquid Tension Experiment record, I was feeling a lot more connected with the guys and thought it was a pretty cool working environment. And I think the guys were feeling more comfortable writing music in our little group than they felt outside of it. They probably appreciated having someone that could play the game with them. I'm not saying that Derek necessarily couldn't, as he has a lot of good ideas, but I think that they felt a lot of camaraderie with me. Petrucci and I see eye-to-eye on a lot of musical and technical things, and it was really just a strong bond that you couldn't ignore. So a few days before we finished the whole Liquid Tension thing I remember seeing them huddled in a corner discussing something. And I was thinking 'I wonder if they're going to ask me about Dream Theater again?' So we sat down and had a chat, and Mike said, 'Hypothetically, if we asked you to join our group again, what would your feelings be?' So I thought about it and told them that I would really want to do it."

This just left the somewhat delicate task of informing Derek that he was out of the band. That predicament was compounded by the fact that they had arranged a short club tour – entitled "Home For The Holidays" – at the end of the year. Cancelling those shows wasn't an option, so they somewhat calculatingly decided to delay telling Derek of his destiny until after those gigs. It wasn't until early January 1999 that he was informed of his dismissal in a telephone conference – much to his disbelief.

"I really had no clue," reflects Derek. "We had played those holiday shows and they didn't give me any indication that I was on my way out. We actually sat at a dinner at TGI Friday's before playing the Birch Hill Night Club show [December 26, 1998, Old Bridge, New Jersey], discussing the concept album that we were to start writing in January. Even at that point, the guys knew that they were going to go with Jordan, as they'd done the Liquid Tension albums. So they were putting up this charade with me during that whole time, knowing that I was on my way out. In the end, it was a conference call with all of them on the line and they told me I was out. I was shocked and didn't see it coming. There was never a time when I was called to the carpet, or admonished for anything. I'm a pretty perceptive guy, so they were great actors during those shows. They just said that they had worked with Jordan and that they felt he was going to be more compatible with the band."

In hindsight though, Derek recognizes that his flamboyance and his single lifestyle were substantial factors in the band's decision to replace him.

"I'm sure there were a lot of things that bubbled up," he says. "Maybe my flamboyance on stage, or the fact that I was single and that they were married. I was on a different path to those guys. It's one thing getting fired and in your heart you know you fucked up and had it coming. But when I got fired, I knew it had nothing to do with my ability, talent or work ethic. It really came down to some personality issues, and other business issues as well where there was conflict. A lot of it had to do with when it started to get tense on that last tour. The band's touring costs almost doubled because we were taking out a second tour bus to accommodate the wives, *au pairs* and children. I remember we were even paying for dog kennels. Being a single guy, I felt uncomfortable with incurring that expense, and I expressed that quite vehemently at a business meeting in Milan with the band. So I think those guys probably sat and figured they didn't see me getting married any time soon, and so there was going to be a conflict. Plus more and more in the band, I was feeling suffocated as an artist by having to always be under John and Mike. Even though Dream Theater helped me develop as a player, there was still a curtain of restraint on the overall vision. So the moment I got out of the band, I immediately transformed into a solo artist and then I just went at it full force."

"But I will say now that if I were John or Mike, I would have made the same move," he continues. "It was the *smart* move. My position is this – it's *their* band and, it was *their* prerogative. They are entitled to create any environment in that workplace that they want to. And if it means getting in another guy who is married so that it is more cohesive, then that is the smart move. I respect that. And at that point, if you notice, Mike and John Petrucci totally took over the band. Instead of just saying 'We're a band and we're doing this' and taking control stealthily, once I was gone, it was totally blatant and everyone fell in line."

To the band's relief, despite Derek's shock at his sacking, they have remained on good terms. Mike in particular remembers being concerned that the keyboard player may have sued them.

"We were worried that he was going to hang up the phone and we'd be getting a call from his lawyer ten minutes later," he explains. "We thought he might take that real Gene Simmons approach, as Gene is one of Derek's music business heroes. We were really scared that Derek wasn't going to be civil about it. But to his credit he was a real humble gentleman. He said he felt sad but he respected our opinion and wishes, and also said he wanted to be as civil as possible. And God bless him for that, as I can't imagine what it would feel like to be fired from a band that you've just given four years of your life to."

John Petrucci: "It's always awkward to tell someone that they are not going to be in the band any more, especially as he didn't see it coming, and also because Derek is such a nice, cool guy. So it's not like we had a big blow-out or fight. So it was totally difficult to break that news. But at the same time, musically it was exciting for me because I had played with Jordan a couple of times, and got a taste of somebody that I felt a musical connection to. That gave what we were doing a purpose. If we were just telling Derek that he was out of the band and there was no real reason, then it would be weird. But as much as it was difficult and as much as I like Derek, I had the anticipation of playing with Jordan..."

TWELVE

FINALLY FREE

A *bona fide* virtuoso, Jordan Charles Rudess is one of the most affable people you're ever likely to meet. Unpretentious, generous and modest when describing his genuinely rare talent, he has let his unwavering passion for music steer his life. Jordan is the type of musician who you suspect would be content performing for pennies in a bar, restaurant or the street just as long as he can *play* his keyboard. Born on November 4, 1956, in New York City, Jordan's family lived in Queens before they moved to Great Neck, Long Island, in 1963. With his father working in the clothing industry and his mother giving up teaching to look after Jordan and his brothers, there had been a surprising shortage of musical talent in the Rudess family prior to his arrival.

"I'm kind of the freak, and the joke in my family is that maybe they picked up the wrong baby at the hospital," Rudess laughs. "I mean my mother is artistic, in the sense that she is sensitive to the arts and loves music, but she didn't play an instrument. We can't actually find any musicians in the family, and then I came along. So it's a real mystery."

With no musical instruments lurking around the Rudess family home for Jordan to tackle, his natural aptitude for the keyboard didn't manifest itself until he went to school, where he quickly homed in on a piano.

"I remember there was a piano in the second grade classroom and I used to play for the kids when they were singing their various songs," he explains. "One day, the second grade teacher just called up my mother and said 'Your kid is playing very nicely in the classroom. It's a pleasure to have him playing the piano'. My mother said that we didn't have a piano, so the teacher told her that she'd better get one! About a week later a white, Estey baby grand piano materialized and a local teacher was hired who'd come around to the house once a week. I began to do improvisation and I think that my mother kind of got the feeling that, since the teacher started to come for free and people started to react to my playing, maybe I had some talent. So she began to ask around to find out what the next more serious level would be. It just so happened that one of mother's good friends had a Hungarian woman, Magda Oscarwitz, living next door to her back in the old neighbourhood where we used to live. She was a pretty serious piano teacher, and her son was the pianist for Guy Lombardo's band. He had been going to The Juilliard School to be a concert pianist but somehow got off track. So when my mother took me to this woman's house, she decided that she was going to make sure that I was going to go to the Juilliard, stay there and go down a very classical route!"

Magda's determination to ensure that the young Rudess made the Juilliard grade extended as far as giving him the sporadic kick under the table when he missed notes, but despite such unorthodox teaching methods, by the age of nine he was enrolled in the Juilliard's preparatory programme. This involved attending the prestigious New York college for twice-weekly tuition, with home practice sessions lasting for up to six hours a day. Unsurprisingly, with such a crammed and frantic agenda, all other traditional school subjects soon began to be overlooked.

"I was floating along nicely until I reached the sixth grade and then it all started to fall apart," reflects Jordan. "I was never in school, because whenever I was, they used to send me little notes telling me to appear in the school auditorium to play for assemblies. So traditional academic life really went down the toilet and my musical life kept on a very steady and clear path. I ended up really excelling and getting all 'A' grades in music but not doing well in the others. At eleventh grade I was lucky, or unlucky enough, to be put in an experimental school called The Village School. It was a completely loose type of environment and meant that I never had to go to class or really report to anyone as they didn't even take attendance."

"I ended up studying during eleventh and twelfth grade playing piano and floating around," he continues. "The high school gave me a diploma and let me graduate, and I managed to get into the Juilliard School even though I didn't do the standard testing of the SATs which everybody needs to get into college. Juilliard made an exception for me because I was one of the top students there. So you had this kid who never went to regular school but who was let into the leading music school in the world, which really shows the funny balance of my life."

By the time he had entered his teenage years, Rudess was gradually seeking out alternative music away from the strict, classical regime at the Juilliard, and his interest in progressive rock began when a friend introduced him to the classic Emerson, Lake & Palmer album, *Tarkus*.

"I couldn't believe the power in the keyboard and it was a real awakening," he says now. "I thought it was amazing as I could really relate to the harmonies and rhythm that Keith Emerson was using. Then somebody also played me some very old Patrick Moraz stuff when he was with Refugee and I heard him do the Mini Moog lead with the pitch wheel. And that was really it – I needed to have one of those! The whole idea of changing pitch on a keyboard just blew my mind. I started to cut out pictures of Mini Moogs and put them all over my wall, and literally a whole side of my room was covered with these pictures until I finally convinced my father to buy me a Mini Moog, and that was kind of the beginning of the end!"

Continuing to investigate the progressive rock scene, Rudess rapidly enhanced his record collection with albums by such mandatory artists as Chick Corea, Genesis, Yes, Tangerine Dream, Gentle Giant and even Jimi Hendrix. However it wasn't long before his love for the genre caused a conflict between the progressive music he'd started composing and playing in his spare time, and the exacting, classical standards set by the college. Gradually it became apparent that something was about to give.

"There just wasn't enough room in my mind to really do the explorations that I needed to do and to remain focused in the Juilliard world," insists Rudess. "I would show up at my Juilliard lesson with one of the heavy, heavy teachers called Adele Marcus. I remember specifically coming in one day with the Chopin G Minor Ballad that I'd learned how to play. So I walked in, placed the music in front of me, sat down, played it, and then she came over and took the music away. So I told her that I needed the music, and she said 'You need to have it memorized!' I was like 'What? It's only been like one week!' It had been my first week of playing it but she was insistent. So I was just thinking I'm supposed to be doing that *and* listening to Hendrix? So the classical thing took a pretty fast downward spiral after that and I went for about a year and then I left."

Despite the preparation given to him by such a reputable college, Rudess was unwavering in his determination to widen his sound away from the traditional path. Fortunately he had also had the backing of his family who ensured that he didn't have to finance his growing musical aspirations by way of a day job.

"I've never had a day job in my life," he laughs. "I would have rather just starved and it really wasn't my scene. I was a spoilt kid in that I was just allowed to go down my route and do my music. But coming out of college was a very weird, spacey time for me. I wasn't ready to have a real career as a musician because I was still very much exploring. I was hanging out with people who were very much on the fringe. People like Saud Galiner, and my original theory teacher at Juilliard called Joseph Lyons. He was playing something at the time he called a Cromulizer which was a clear Plexiglas tube that had like elevator switches on it. We'd play the midnight shows on college radio stations and were just improvising and having a real kind of space out. I remember specifically going to one college radio station one night and we were all *extremely* high and were just playing. And it was around midnight and these phone calls would come in from people who were also obviously high, and were saying things like 'Hey man, thank you so much. This is unbelievable!'"

Seeking a change of scene, by the age of 22 Rudess had moved to Baltimore and joined a band called Apricot Brandy who made a healthy living performing at high school dances and proms. Naturally, playing Top 40 songs to engage the punters didn't always fit comfortably with Jordan's more experimental leanings, but with the band prepared to throw in the sporadic cover version to keep themselves entertained – such as "Karn Evil 9" by ELP – he was, for a while at least, content. Steadily though, his interest in the band began to diminish and with Rudess indulging in drugs and partying, the gig became more of a social event and less of the meaningful musical experience he was craving. It was at this point that Jordan received a timely phone call from two producers, Jerry Kastenetz and Jeff Katz who had first come to prominence after producing such "bubble gum" pop records as the toe-curling *Yummy, Yummy, Yummy* by Ohio Express and *Black Betty* by Ram Jam. The Kastenetz-Katz pairing were in the process of putting together a band, Speedway Boulevard, and remembered Rudess from a session five years earlier when he'd recorded a few of his compositions in their Long Island studio. The producers wanted Rudess to add his keyboard flourishes to a record which had already been slated for a release on the Epic label.

"I thought this was totally *it* and that I was going to be a rock star," he smiles. "Of course what happened was that the record came out and it pretty quickly faded away. There were a lot of people who hated Kastenetz and Katz because of the bubble gum stuff they had done, which didn't help. But musically it was very much an Eighties rock sound with a touch of a progressive element and a black singer."

Released in 1980, Speedway Boulevard's self-titled album made little impact and any hopes that the band would become a permanent and successful operation soon diminished, and Rudess departed. But within a few weeks an old friend, the Cromulizer-playing Joseph Lyons, got in contact with him with an appealing business proposition.

"Over the years he had talked about putting a computer company together and doing some interesting things with music and graphics," explains Rudess. "One day he actually called me up and said that he was finally going to do this, and the company was called Enhanced Technology. It turned out that my job was to go downstairs when potential investors would come to talk about investing in stock and I would play for people because they wanted to show how much we knew about music. So I'd do that, they'd think it was great, and I'd go back to my place and write some more tunes and practise. Then maybe another week later they'd ask me to go down there again if they had some people going in."

"So I was getting paid a decent salary and was considered to be the Musical Director of this company. But it wasn't the real thing for me, and I was basically just hired to appear every now and then to make them look good. Although it was a very interesting company the problem was that in those days, the computers were all eight-bit machines like Ataris or Commodores. They didn't sound or look good, so even though they had some great ideas, somebody looking at it would be like 'What the hell is this?'"

With his work at Enhanced Technology only providing him with an income but not satisfying his more creative desires, Rudess was struggling to find a direction. Fortunately, around this time he met his wife-to-be, Danielle, who he claims was instrumental in increasing his motivation and transforming his career.

"Danielle gave me some support so I could step out and enter the real world," he smiles. "I met her in the city and she basically said 'What are you doing? You've gotta get out of here and make a life as this isn't going anywhere.' I met her when I was 28 or 29. So we got together, moved up to Woodstock, New York, and I made a living playing piano for the restaurants and hotels. There wasn't really a whole lot going on but fortunately I got a call to do a gig with Vinnie Moore. That for me was the first step into the real world of the music business. I mean, I had been in Speedway Boulevard, but that was a long time ago and the dots never really connected. Vinnie was really popular at that time, being a neo-classical guitar player in the Yngwie Malmsteen school. I had done a convention for the computer company a couple of years before and I had walked around the convention with this little, portable Yamaha keyboard. I saw Vinnie playing at one of the booths and I just stopped and said 'Hey, can I jam with you?' He agreed, I plugged in my keyboard, we had a great jam, I shook his hand and left. Then two years later, I get this phone call from his manager to say that they'd been looking for me since then. So we connected and I played on his *Time Odyssey* album and we did a few shows."

Following this brief but productive stint with Vinnie Moore, Rudess was introduced to Jack Hotop, an influential sound programmer at leading keyboard manufacturer Korg. Suitably impressed with his ability as well as his naturally outgoing persona, Hotop offered Rudess a job at their Long Island office as a product specialist. Despite having qualms about whether he was suited to working in an environment he thought would be "too straight", he was persuaded by his wife Danielle that he could flourish in the role and that working for such a prominent employer would be both profile-enhancing and a shrewd career move.

"The job of product specialist was to show the guys in different music stores all across the country how to use the keyboards, and also to give clinics and do the trade shows," he explains. "So at these shows, people started to take notice of what I was doing and even people like *Keyboard Magazine* would write about me. At one show my wife Danielle was walking around when she saw Jan Hammer, and said to him 'Hey, you want to check out this wave station keyboard and maybe you can get one from Korg. Come with me!' So she took him into this room where I was playing and he heard me play and checked out the keyboard. About a month later I was working at the Korg building and a phone call came in to say that Jan Hammer wanted to get in touch with me. I found out he wanted me to help him by being a keyboardist in his band. He was going to do a tour with the drummer Tony Williams and Fernando Saunders the bass player. Korg actually gave me time to do this as I was going to be helping out one of the big artists. So it was a four-piece band, and we did some cool things, like playing The Bottom Line in New York and the Montreal Jazz Festival."

Resuming his responsibilities at Korg following the Jan Hammer tour, the opportunity arose in 1993 for Jordan to record his first formal album entitled *Listen*. Released on a small Arizona-based label, Invincible Records, it gave him the chance to purge some of the creative urges that had been building while he had been hurtling around the US playing somebody else's music. Although not receiving massive amounts of press coverage on its release, the record was a useful audio curriculum vitae for Jordan to demonstrate his ability to any prospective employers. But with the album not providing any sudden influx of money, Jordan began searching for a new direction and employer, and managed to use the network of industry contacts he'd amassed to secure a job with Korg's rivals, Kurzweil.

"They'd hired me to do a bunch of travelling and doing a similar thing I'd been doing for Korg," remembers Rudess. "But I was bored with all the travelling after a while and became what I called a music support manager. That basically entailed getting in touch with my friends in the industry and having them create all kinds of demos and sounds for the Kurzweil instrument. It was when I was with Kurzweil things started to happen."

Voted "Best New Talent" in a 1994 *Keyboard* magazine poll, Jordan's profile had risen to such a level that he started to attract the attention of Dream Theater and The Dixie Dregs, who were both searching for a keyboard player. As noted earlier, offers to join both these bands were frustratingly available to him at the same time, and Rudess decided in 1994 that the position with the Dregs was more suited to his lifestyle and critically wouldn't necessitate prolonged road trips. Rudess recalls that he first saw the Dregs a few months prior to him being offered the keyboard position.

"I remember sitting by the soundboard and thinking their drummer Rod Morgenstein was incredible, and I wished that he could have worked on my material," he grins. "But at that point it was a real pipe dream as I was just a guy in the audience. You know, wouldn't it be nice if that drummer drummed on my stuff! Anyway, a couple of months later I got a call from their manager asking me to come and audition for the Dregs. I sent them the *Listen* album, the guys liked it and so I did some gigs with them."

Rudess later joined forces with Morgenstein, releasing the *Rudess Morgenstein* album shortly afterwards, and being the opening act for Dream Theater on a number of tour legs.

"My connection with Dream Theater maintained itself over the years since my brief meeting with them at the Concrete Foundation gig. Mike called me for the Liquid Tension Experiment project and I was totally into it. The magic we felt in the studio working together was something everyone involved wanted to see continue on a full-time basis, so this experience brought me into the world of Dream Theater."

Within a couple of weeks of officially joining Dream Theater, Jordan found himself at Bear Tracks Studios working on what would eventually become the *Scenes From A Memory* album. To his surprise, his initial impression of the working environment – visually at least – was that it only varied slightly from what he had experienced during those Liquid Tension Experiment sessions.

"At first it seemed like the only difference between Dream Theater and Liquid Tension was that instead of a tall, bald bass player, there was an Asian guy with long hair," he chuckles. "That really was it, as James wasn't really there very much during the *Scenes From A Memory* writing sessions."

The failings of their last album had at least provided Dream Theater with a cast-iron argument to confront the record label. If, after the "commercial" approach on *Falling Into Infinity* there was no hit single or boost in sales, then from now on they were going to write whatever they wanted. The antithesis of an album as deliberately manufactured as *Falling...* could only be an expansive concept album, and the band had already told the label that this had to be their next step. The fact that the mere notion of a *concept* album in the late-Nineties was to many both unfathomable and unfashionable, only spurred them on. Yet, whilst this time around there had been no overt demands exerted by the label, there was a feeling within the band that this was a do-or-die release. If it became a success in terms of critical acclaim and sales, their case would be proven. But if it failed to surpass *Falling Into Infinity*, there was no predicting how the label might respond.

Determined to create the right atmosphere in which to gradually forge the album, the band decided to write and assemble the material in the studio. Consequently, Bear Tracks was booked for the best part of five months, with the band moving into the studio's on-site accommodation. Yet one of the more controversial and misunderstood aspects of their time spent writing was the establishing by Mike of an "inspiration corner." Trawling through his record collection, Mike had selected a number of classic concept albums which were brought into the studio to serve as reminders of the standard they were endeavouring to surpass. Consequently, The Who's *Tommy*, *The Lamb Lies Down On Broadway* by Genesis, *Amused To Death* by Roger Waters, Radiohead's OK *Computer*, The Beatles' *Sgt Pepper*, Marillion's *Misplaced Childhood*, Pink Floyd's *The Wall* and *The Final Cut* found their way to the studio's hi-fi. Intended merely as reference points to see how those bands had pieced the music together and developed storylines, such a move was seen by many as being contrived – a point put to the drummer by *Classic Rock*'s Dave Ling.

"That's a typical English journo question," retorted Mike. "Jeez. Anyone who tells you that they've made an album without any outside influences is lying out of their asshole. We've made a record that none of those bands would ever make – it's a Dream Theater record. We just wanted something that we could refer to, not to steal from."

John Petrucci also reveals that although the band have always set up an inspiration corner during the initial stages of each album's construction, he claims the media and fans often read too much into the significance.

"We've always worn our influences on our sleeves," contests John. "So that's just an insight into what was going on in the studio and it's always been like that. It's important to have influences to draw from to creatively do something new. I think the only problem with *certain* information is that it becomes convoluted. People like to over-analyze, over-speculate and a lot of the time things aren't really that complicated. Especially with the Internet – people over-analyze the motives. It's kinda like 'Isn't *The Wall* cool?' And someone will say 'Yes!' Or someone will say that they like *Operation: Mindcrime*. And that's really it. It's never as deep as people tend to speculate."

For the new boy, the concept of having such musical reference points lying around the studio was a novelty, and in some cases a musical education.

"That was a big Mike kind of thing. It was like 'We're going to do this album and here's the inspiration for it. If you don't like the albums, then that's too bad'," jokes Jordan. "I remember Queensrÿche was one of the things. I mean, I'd heard of them, but they didn't mean anything to me. There are certain things that do inspire me, but I'm less interested in tipping my hat to others, and more interested in possibly moving in a direction that others hadn't. So if in any way I can push the rest of the band to do original things then that's great. But for me it's kind of educational to be in Dream Theater in the sense that I learn about styles, such as finding out about Metallica, Iron Maiden and Queensrÿche and understanding their chord structures."

"Then of course I found out that entering the world of Dream Theater is like any organization that has been around for a long time in that they're well established in their ways. There was a lot for me to find out. I remember sitting with Mike and John Petrucci as we were mixing the Liquid Tension album and we were discussing my joining. Mike said 'I just want you to know that I'm a real control freak. I must have control or I just can't function!' So I was thinking 'OK – there's some honesty.' He described the kind of things he needs to have control over such as the set lists, album covers and other things. So they just wanted to make sure that I was going to be OK with the fact that it was going to be like that. Thinking back, that was probably a really good thing because it's a really intense part of our group. There was a new member coming into an established group, and they didn't want to change certain ways. They just wanted me to know that if I wanted to join, that was how it is. So I was like 'Err, I *guess* I still want to join the group!'"

With Jordan prepared to acknowledge the parameters set down by the band, the subsequent writing sessions were peaceful, with the bickering that had blighted the construction of earlier albums kept in check. Certainly the relationships between the members became more harmonious as a direct result of Jordan's recruitment.

"I think when Derek was in the band he was a really kind of interesting personality," surmises Jordan. "Joking around a lot, but also an intense character in his own right and I think his personality mixed with Mike. They would stir things up a lot. Mike would say something that would annoy Derek and then Derek would jump in, and the next thing you know there would be issues. There would be all these people stirring the soup. I'm a lot mellower about things and for the most part don't have a problem with the guys doing what they need to do. I think I'm more of a flowing energy which I think helps the guys. It helps them be who they are without interruption, and I think everyone feels comfortable with their role within the group. So those sessions were exciting and it was my period of just figuring out the group, and how I was going to relate to these guys."

Assimilating into the Dream Theater method of working was not going to occur immediately. Whereas with the Liquid Tension Experiment albums there were no musical boundaries, Dream Theater were more wary of veering too far away from their core sound. Consequently, a substantial proportion of ideas that Jordan had been armed with when he entered the studio were tactfully declined or deemed unbefitting of the Dream Theater way.

"I must have come in with fifty different things and said 'Here guys, listen to all this,'" smiles Jordan. "A lot were knocked down as inappropriate, or 'That's cool, put it in your solo album', or 'That would never make a Dream Theater album' or 'Yeah, I like that one'. So there was a lot of that and that was the only album that I came in with a lot of preconceived ideas for. For the later albums I was like 'You know what? I can't do that again. That doesn't feel very good.' But they knew what they perceived Dream Theater to be, so there was a definite filter on what came in. What ends up happening with me is that there's a portion of it that I guess does relate to Dream Theater, and a large portion of it that does not. So I can only try to keep submitting things that I think would be cool for us to do."

That's not of course to imply that Jordan's submissions were unwelcome – it was merely a case of tailoring his ideas to ensure they tallied with the Dream Theater way – as John Petrucci confirms: "That's what is great about Jordan – he just had a million ideas. You just play with the guy and he's like 'How about this, or this?' He's awesome and also seemed to fully understand where we were coming from. He would be able to contribute and create a synergy in the music that was being made. When you have that musical chemistry with people, it just gets better. It was wonderful."

That musical chemistry was also essential in reinvigorating the band's previously flagging spirits, and it can't be stressed enough that the Liquid Tension Experiment albums were critical in Dream Theater motivating themselves – something that John Petrucci noted in *Guitar World* magazine.

"When Dream Theater started out, we were incredibly enthusiastic and wanted to play as much as we could," he said. "Over the years, some of that spontaneous, play-as-much-as-you-can passion disappeared a bit. As soon as we started working on that first Liquid Tension Experiment album, I felt that spirit again and Mike and I brought it back to Dream Theater."

The band's decision to self-produce the album was vital, as it allowed them to take the necessary time to write and record concurrently while holed up at Bear Tracks.

"Mike called me one day and we had a conversation," relates John Petrucci. "He said that he didn't think we needed anybody to come in and tell us what to do. So we started talking and we had a very clear idea of what we wanted to do. It was a great moment. As much as I was open to different people, there's a point where you feel 'Wait a minute. I'm a grown man. I know how to do this – I've been in a studio before!' That was the beginning of Mike and I producing, as well as stepping up to the plate and taking the reins professionally. We wanted to do a concept album and write it in the studio – it wasn't like we were going to demo the stuff before. So we were thinking who would produce this while we were in the studio writing for months and then telling us what to do? That was really no place for a producer and really, who would do that? So we just wanted to have everything set up, walk in, write and maybe record something, maybe not. Work and hash out the story. And to this day, I can't think of a producer who would be in there and be able to do that with us. So it made most sense to self-produce. And our engineer, Doug Oberkircher, has been working with us forever, so it was a cool environment. It was just really comfortable."

Jordan: "A lot of people look at Dream Theater and say 'Oh, it's John Petrucci and Mike Portnoy's band'. They really see it as that and there are of course elements of truth in that in the sense that they take on a lot of the control of the band. I remember being in the car with Mike and he said 'You know what? I know we've all been working very hard and you've been writing all this music, but I just want you to know that I put so much time and energy through the years into this band that John and I want to produce it and I hope you don't have a problem with that.' So I said that I wasn't in any position to have a problem with anything at that point. I told him it was fine, and at the time Mike just wanted to have something in return for all the intense energy that he puts into this band. Which is understandable."

The resolution to work at Bear Tracks again was inextricably linked with John and Mike's wishes to self-produce the album, but it also offered numerous other benefits and comforts, as engineer Doug Oberkircher explains.

"I think they wanted to come to a familiar place where they had worked before as this was to be their production debut," says Doug. "They were comfortable with the studio but there were also many other reasons for returning to Bear Tracks. It's situated outside of New York City in a country setting and it backs up to a state forest. So when you open the back doors of the large recording room, you look right out into this forest. It's built in a turn-of-the-century stone barn and it's a magical place to be and record. The band at one point even thought of purchasing the studio and making it their own. The other nice feature about the location is that they could come up to Bear Tracks and be secluded, away from interruptions and distractions, yet close enough that they could commute if they desired. As Bear Tracks is a one-room facility, the band had the run of the place. They had an apartment to use with a huge lounge and kitchen, and of course the staff were available for whatever they needed."

In retrospect, the relationships between the band and all the producers who'd worked on their previous albums had never been harmonious. The causes of those clashes varied, but one recurring theme seemed to be that the band felt that there was nobody better qualified to dictate how their album should sound than themselves. And with their technical pedigree beyond reproach they had a point. All of which lends weight to the argument that Dream Theater are impossible for an outsider to produce.

"That's the way I always saw it," agrees Mike. "I always felt that there were too many chefs in the kitchen as it was. You already had at least four and sometimes five people interjecting opinions and we would sometimes spend days, weeks or even months banging out four bars of music and arguing over one note. We would finally resolve it within ourselves only to have some sixth guy – who had nothing to do with the writing of it – suddenly chuck it out the window. That rips your heart out. I always felt that bands like Bon Jovi maybe need that direction, and maybe a producer to shape them and turn them into a certain sound or style. But that was always the complete opposite to what Dream Theater was about. We were always about being different, following our instincts and not necessarily shaping ourselves towards the mainstream. So whenever a producer would come in and try to do that, it was always met with a lot of hesitation and resistance – especially by me."

One of those producers, David Prater, unexpectedly agrees with Mike's assertion, though any sense of acquiescence is quickly cancelled out by a stinging rebuke.

"He's one hundred per cent right," says Prater. "You know why? Anybody who makes any suggestion or assumes control in any way is, in their minds, *persona non-gratis* [*sic.*]. Look, if we were talking about Stravinsky, Holst or Elgar and one of them said that about producers in general, I would be a captive audience. We are talking about a very unsophisticated, sub-set of Long Island shredders. Dream Theater are now doing the only sensible thing that they have ever done. They're producing themselves. If you liked their last albums better than the ones I did, then you must agree with them. But the jury is still out as to whether or not they can even pull it off."

James however welcomed the producer's chair being occupied by his colleagues, declaring that "It's easier to communicate with Mike or John Petrucci. I think what they have done so far has worked exceptionally well. I'm sure that they would be the first to admit that it's not to say that there will *never* be another producer of Dream Theater. Who knows, it could happen at some point down the road. But at this point we know that it does work and we aren't seeing any problems because of it."

Doug Oberkircher: "I think the biggest reason that the production team has worked so well is that they were so frustrated with being produced by outsiders and having their vision for their music clouded by other people. So they knew the only way they could be happy was to produce themselves. As you know, Mike and John are the leaders of the band, and they are the decision-makers, the biggest voices musically in the band and they were basically producing themselves all along. They just needed a record company to give them the go-ahead to be the *only* producers. And Mike and John have learned to be diplomatic with each other. Over the years they have learnt to accept each others personalities, accept their differences of opinion and to work things out reasonably. They also share a common vision for the music and for the production values."

Adopting their usual practice of writing the music first and worrying about the lyrics later, the band had also decided that the album was to be a full-length follow-up to the epic track, "Metropolis – Part I", which had appeared on *Images And Words*. A tentative early version of "Part II" had already been written during Derek Sherinian's tenure with the band, although in an interview with *The Used Bin*, John

Petrucci later described it as "The most sloppy, horrible rendition of a complex song that you can think of." But it was nevertheless revisited to provide some of the motifs for the likes of "Overture 1928", "The Dance Of Eternity" and "One Last Time" on the final recording. In addition, scraps of songs that had been left over from as far back as the *Awake* sessions were also dusted off and utilized, as were some of the original themes from "Metropolis – Part I".

Ironically, when the band had written "Metropolis – Part I", they had no intention of even writing a follow-up, as Mike explained at the time.

"We sort of tagged the 'Part I' on the end to be clever," he said. "Then it ended up becoming one of the fans' favourites, so we were forever plagued with the question of 'Where's part two?' This time round we finally decided that it had to be on this record or else the fans would completely disown us. We went back to the version we wrote in 1996, picked out some bits we liked, wrote a whole new approach to it from scratch and expanded it into a full 77-minute album."

There were also carefully constructed lyrical references to the first track on the follow-up, although even Mike admitted that he had trouble comprehending the Petrucci-penned story of "Metropolis – Part I".

"I never understood what the fuck it was about," he confessed. "I used to look at those lyrics and say 'What the fuck is going on here? What does this mean?' And I don't even think John knew what it meant. I think it was a fictitious story but I don't think he had a definitive explanation for it. If you listen to the lyrics of 'Home' on the new record, there are a million references to 'Part I' and it finally makes sense of those lyrics. I wish I could take the credit for having this vision ten years ago and finally getting back to it. But the truth of the matter is that we actually had to make sense out of those old lyrics by shaping the new ones around them."

The somewhat complicated plot revolved around an elaborate reincarnation murder-mystery story. In extremely simplistic terms, the characters from "Metropolis – Part I" – the brothers Senator Edward Baynes (The Miracle) and Julian Baynes (The Sleeper) – make a reappearance in this follow-up. Central to the plot is the character of Nicholas, who after having recurring dreams of a past time visits a hypnotherapist. During the regression that follows, he discovers that he is the reincarnation of Victoria Page – a murdered girl who lived in the Twenties. Julian and Victoria were lovers before she had an affair with his brother Edward. This was later broken off by Victoria who wanted to go back to Julian.

As the story develops, it appears that (based on the testimony of the sole witness, Edward) Victoria was murdered by Julian, who subsequently turned the gun on himself. Case solved? Not quite. It turned out that Edward had killed the pair, and planted a fake suicide note on the body of his brother to implicate him in the murder. However, there was another sting in the tail. Back in the current time, Nicholas, upon discovering the truth, is killed by the hypnotherapist – who is the reincarnation of Edward.

The album's angle and firm plot had only become a reality once they had pieced together much of the musical backdrop, as John Petrucci recalls.

"It was basically while we were in the studio writing the music that I was researching the topic," says John. "Mike and I had talked about a couple of things, we had the initial idea and that got more focused on a story about a past life. So I began to read books about that subject, went to the library to research the time period to try and get some names and places that would set the scene. I picked up some hypnosis audio CDs and things like that to get the right kind of dialogue used in those types of sessions. And then it was a case of saying what the story was specifically outlined. I guess the music was already written at that stage. The story was outlined from beginning to end and then divvied up amongst the band members."

Mike Portnoy: "I remember John read a story about reincarnation and brought it in and showed it to us. From there we brainstormed a fictional story, and it was kind of a cross between that story he came across and the movie *Dead Again*. We used those as an inspiration to go to new places, and took the reincarnation idea and applied it to a murder mystery story."

Reincarnation was a topic that fascinated Petrucci, even if it wasn't something that formed one of his core religious beliefs, as he revealed in an interview with the *Theater Of Dreams* fanzine: "I'm Catholic and not Buddhist or anything like that," he said. "But the whole topic of reincarnation to me is incredibly interesting, and I think that's what sparked it for this record. Reincarnation, whenever you talk to anybody about it, is something you can easily get into a conversation about... A couple of the other guys were getting into it, so it gave us a lot to talk about. I don't know that much about it as far as one's soul transcending is concerned. I just kind of used artistic license to incorporate that element of it, but it's not my personal belief."

The recordings were completed in June 1999, and with James opting to record many of his vocal parts with legendary Rush producer Terry Brown, the only remaining issue was who was going to mix the album. Mike and John Petrucci had been struck by the abilities of David Bottrill following his work on both King Crimson's *Thrak* album and Tool's *Aenima*, and his services were duly employed. Mixed over a ten-day period at Electric Ladyland Studios in New York, the album was ostensibly finished and ready to deliver to Elektra. That was until John Petrucci paid a social visit to see Kevin Shirley.

"John came into the studio in the city to see me one day," says Shirley. "He said that they'd been mixing their album, that he was really happy with it and that he wanted me to take a listen. So I put it on and I played it. I told him it sounded OK, I turned around and he was as white as a sheet. He took the thing back and left. About two hours later he called me up and said, 'Hey Kev, sorry to bother you but what did you *really* think?' I told him it was great. He called me back the next day and I told him the same thing. Then he called me *again* one Sunday and said, 'I want you to break down and tell me what you really think.' So I just said 'John, it could sound better. It doesn't sound bad but it doesn't sound especially good.' He told me that it didn't sound 'anywhere near as good as one of your mixes.' So he then asked me to mix it – which I did in two days. They'd been ten to 14 days with Dave Bottrill and paid him a fortune, and then they get me to mix it in two days. And every so often I will get some snide comment from fans about my input, and if they only knew what these guys gave me to work with! The band have always pushed the envelope as far as budget goes, but I always try and make it work for them. I think it was a good thing they self-produced. They have specific ideas and it was good to see them come out with *Scenes From A Memory*."

The producer also reveals that he had been disappointed by the sacking of Derek Sherinian, and claims that he missed his contributions.

"I enjoyed Derek Sherinian's keyboard input, which I thought was way left of centre," he muses. "Not that I'm saying Jordan isn't a great player, but he is very much more of a foil for Petrucci really. Derek has those signature sounds going on and played separately from John, which I thought was good. I wasn't very happy when they decided to let Derek go. For him, it was all about being a rock star, whereas the other guys were family men. I didn't know why the two couldn't live side by side. But anyway, they moved on and then all of a sudden, we had keyboard and guitar histrionics at ten-thousand-miles-an-hour, endlessly, with never a millisecond between them. Maybe that's what the fans dig, but sometimes I get tired of it."

With only a hectic 48-hour slot available for Shirley to re-mix, it proved impossible for him to complete the entire album before the strict deadline. Consequently, four of the tracks ("Regression", "The Dance Of Eternity", "One Last Time", "Finally Free") were untouched by Shirley and remained in their original form on the finished product. But before the album's release, the band had made arrangements to perform a solitary gig at the Triport Festival in Inchon, Korea, on July 31, 1999. As the first major rock festival in Korea, the attendance proved to be massive, although the excitement was somewhat dampened by a typhoon that hit on the day of the gig. With dry ice being blown away in milliseconds and lighting rigs swaying precariously above them, Dream Theater still managed to deliver a lively set. But as if his live debut as an official member of the band wasn't pressured enough, Jordan's stress level was heightened by the wind.

"My music blew away," he laughs. "But I was somehow able to recover. That night was crazy and we didn't know if the gig was going to be on. The organizers were worried and saying things like 'All Americans go to stage right' as it was the only safe place!"

Playing for an hour, they resisted temptation to perform any material from the forthcoming *Scenes From A Memory* to ensure it was heard in context and entirety on its release. The next task was to ensure that the cover design was in keeping with the album's concept.

"The original idea, which was something that John Petrucci and I discussed early in the making of this record, was to make the album layout like a playbill," explained Mike in an interview with the *Theater Of Dreams* fanzine. "You know if you go to a Broadway show, you get a playbill that has a yellow square on top with black writing and it says 'Playbill'? There's usually a black striking image underneath it. Well we wanted to have the yellow box on top with 'Dream Theater' in black with just a single image that would have been representing reincarnation or murder. So that was our original approach and why we didn't even bother contacting Storm Thorgerson as we knew exactly what we wanted. We went back to the label and said 'Just make it' but they talked us out of going in that direction, and instead trying to get a more original piece of art."

"We had another artist to do the album cover and I just did not like at all what was delivered. The guy didn't take any of the concepts that we had put forward. Initially, we'd been given a portfolio of different artists that were available, so we went back to it and came across some stuff of Dave McKean's. There was this one image of this old man's face, made up of a million different old fashioned photos. I said 'This is fucking perfect. This is our album cover'. So I went back to the label to see if we could commission this photo. But it turned out that somebody had already licensed that photo for a comic book. It was *The Sandman* or something like that. But Dave said he was more than willing to create a new piece of art based on the same idea. So within a few days he had come up with this new artwork which ended up being the album cover."

"Yes, the band had seen a cover I did for *The Sandman* graphic novel *Brief Lives*," explains Dave McKean. "That was the image of a face made up of other faces, plus a bit of paint and photo texture. As the music was supposed to form a biographical story, the larger face could be made up of smaller snapshots from that person's life. I've done a few versions of this image now, including a cover for a Buffy The Vampire Slayer book. It's also cropped up in other images rather obviously copied by other people. But even though it wasn't the first, the Dream Theater cover is my favourite version."

Although the image may look pretty complicated, McKean explains that it was actually a fairly straightforward task to mix together all the various images.

"I had shot photos of a few people's faces for another project," he says. "There were also some photos supplied by the band and I remember using some photos from my own family albums. I did a painting in acrylic as a base, and collaged into it many photos. Some were re-shot to distort, flare – spotlights bounced off the surface at the right angle – or blue them. I am really satisfied with the way it turned out, and it's a permanent image in my portfolio and used for presentations during lectures that I do for art schools and events around the world."

Scenes From A Memory was unveiled on October 26, 1999, and remains to this day the band's most unyielding and resilient release. Given the subject matter and the fact that it contained a solid block of elegant, interwoven melodies that lasted over 77 minutes, it's a challenging but ultimately fulfilling listen. "Overture 1928" is the finest, compact instrumental piece the band have created; "Through Her Eyes" and "The Sprit Carries On" are exquisitely crafted softer moments, and the complexity of "Dance Of Eternity" is genuinely breathtaking. But it's the overall balance of the piece that's the most striking. Perfectly paced, the album has a natural flow that belies the manner of its drawn-out construction and proved the band were adept at mixing slower tracks with their more hard-edged tendencies. Ultimately *Scenes...* captured the essence of their sound and provided irrefutable evidence that, left to their own devices, Dream Theater could create something far more special than when attempting to write to order.

The specialist rock press also recognized the album's might. Writing for *Classic Rock*, Nick Shilton wrote: "Packed with memorable melodies and a few recurrent motifs the album covers numerous bases... and the overall quality of playing is magnificent. Ambitious and dramatic, at 77 minutes, *Scenes From A Memory* is dense and demanding. It's also likely to go down as one of the all-time great concept albums."

Metal Edge's Paul Gargano was similarly impressed, musing: "It kind of makes you wonder – with music this good and a storyline this compelling, can the bright lights of a Broadway rock opera be far off for Dream Theater? We can only hope, as *Scenes From A Memory* is the band's crowning achievement, a breathtaking release that legends are made of."

But there were those who relished the prospect of taking a swipe at the band for what they perceived as the release of an overblown and pompous album. Perhaps predictably, given their past form, *Kerrang!* were chomping at the bit, claiming in one of their features that Dream Theater releasing a concept album was a "real career killer."

"Absolutely not," retorted Mike in the same piece. "If you look at history, concept albums were usually the peak of a band's career. I consider *The Wall* to be Pink Floyd's pinnacle; *Misplaced Childhood* to be Marillion's greatest album; and *Tommy* and *Quadrophenia* to be The Who's. So by making a record like *Scenes...* there was no fear of it being commercial suicide. More than ever we said, 'Fuck radio! Fuck the record company! Fuck producers!' I know that a lot of people just want to listen to Korn-alikes, and that's something we have to live with. We simply won't change to suit their tastes. The reason we're as successful as we are is that we're doing our thing, not theirs."

For the band themselves, there was reason to feel somewhat self-satisfied. The album's creative and relatively commercial success (eventually selling more than 500,000 copies worldwide) had vindicated the decisions they had made at the end of 1998. John Petrucci also confesses to being relieved at the reaction to *Scenes...*

"We had taken a lot of chances at the time," he says. "There were a lot of people who didn't think it was a good idea to change keyboard player at that point in our career. And there were also people who thought it was a bad idea not to have a producer. I mean, making a concept album always made *me* nervous. My favourite concept albums are just so intense, and I recall thinking that it must have taken these guys years to write because the story was so cool. It was such an undertaking and I was worried whether it was going to be good enough, if the story was going to be cool enough, or if it was going to come out like some Spinal Tap rock opera! All those decisions were taking a chance. So having it become successful was like we had proved something."

"I'm glad that people accepted it and enjoyed it the way I hoped," agreed Mike. "I mean, I knew when we made this record that it was going to be something that the fans were going to love and that it would be the ultimate Dream Theater experience at *every* level – musically, lyrically, conceptually and production. So I knew we were making our masterpiece if there is such a thing. I just hoped it would be received that way, because I knew we were putting our heart and soul into it."

The tour opened in Hamburg, Germany, on November 8, 1999, and wound its way, through numerous legs, around Europe, North America and Asia for almost a year. The band had boldly taken the decision to perform the album in its entirety – a choice that was not without risk. Any casual or potential new fans in the audience would be perplexed and quite possibly turned off by the complexity of the piece. But the reality was that there was no other way to present it.

"I never actually thought twice about it," says Mike. "It really was the natural thing to do. When Pink Floyd did *Dark Side Of The Moon* and *The Wall*, they did them in their entirety. As did The Who with *Tommy*, Queensrÿche with *Operation: Mindcrime*, and Marillion with *Misplaced Childhood*. All of those great concept albums were performed in their entirety – at least on their first time out. So that was never in question in my mind. It just had to happen. And that was at a point in our career before we started to rotate set lists. In fact, it was probably as a result of that tour that I made up my mind to write different set lists every night, because playing the album every night for a hundred nights in a row started to become a little boring and tedious for us."

Spock's Beard provided the support for many of the gigs on the tour, and the bands developed a close and entertaining working relationship, as their then frontman, Neal Morse, recalls.

"That was a very exciting and funny time," he laughs. "One of the funniest things was that Mike would come out during our set and play 'June' with us, but he would be wearing a Kiss mask. And then after the song, he'd take the mask off and reveal his identity to the crowd. And I mean, he did this every night, never took a night off and I thought that was amazing. On the last night of the tour in Lisbon, he comes out and starts playing the drums as usual, but he was playing *really* badly, like a kid or something. I really didn't know what was going on. And then at the end of the song, the mask came off, and it was John Petrucci! It was *very* funny."

One notable gig – and for all the wrong reasons – occurred at the Palace Theater, Los Angeles on February 4, 2000. Dream Theater had run through most of *Scenes. . .* and were awaiting James LaBrie to return to the stage to sing, "The Spirit Carries On". But an insurmountable wall of police officers located at the side of the stage physically prevented him from retaking his place at the microphone. Seemingly, the local fire marshall (who was acting on an anonymous tip-off) had decided that the venue was overcrowded. The only solution in his eyes was to prematurely end the show by flooding the venue with police, pulling the plug on the band, and forcing (and in some cases manhandling) the audience outside.

"I came off the stage and I was talking to Chris Jericho, the WWE wrestler, who was there," recounts James. "So I'm getting ready to go back on and I saw all these police and fire marshals. This cop grabs me and said 'You're not going back on there, we're pulling the power.' I was like 'What? Fuck off! I'm the singer!' But he just said, 'Hey man, I'm telling you right now you aren't going *anywhere* on that stage again!' So I was there behind these cops, I couldn't go on the stage, the band were looking for me and Chris Jericho goes, 'Do you want any help?' I was thinking, 'I'd love it man, why don't you just kill these guys for me!' But I told him not to get involved!"

The exact reason for the closure of the gig has never been established, although James believes that "a lot of the people from upstairs had moved downstairs. So I guess it could have been interpreted as being ridiculously stuffed."

With James failing to arrive, Mike was forced to make an attempt to sing before realizing that he couldn't remember the words. Becoming conscious of the authorities' intention to prohibit the rest of the performance, the band made the decision to carry on regardless. Inevitably, the power to the main speakers was cut, leaving just the onstage monitors producing any sound. With that also failing to produce the intended result of stopping them playing – mainly because of the enthusiastic vocals being provided by the audience – the remaining speakers were also abruptly cut. The band were left with no other viable option other than to voluntarily leave the stage – although Mike still found the time to dash to the front of the stage, grab his crotch and direct a pelvic thrust in the direction of the authorities at the side. Predictably, the crowd failed to instantly leave the building – instead repeatedly chanting "bullshit" – and the riot police were called in to "encourage" the fans to vacate the hall.

"Mike was literally playing until they escorted him off the stage, but he was still trying to hit that last cymbal," laughs Chris Jericho. "It was unbelievable. We got outside and there were like 15 cop cars and fire engines sat there with their sirens blaring, and riot police everywhere. Honestly, you'd have thought that Charles Manson was holed up in there with a hostage or Osama Bin Laden was underneath the stage. It's just a good job it wasn't a Pantera or Metallica gig, because people would have been going crazy and there would have been a riot."

Predictably the band – and especially Mike – was furious. With the drummer enraged and having consumed a fair few beers and shots during and after the gig, he was quick to confront those responsible.

"He was really out of control, although he doesn't remember it," says manager Frank Solomon. "But it was a scene. I mean, there were more police, firemen and riot police than you could imagine in this place. I remember it vividly, and it was very early in my tenure and I was thinking 'Oh God. Don't tell me this is what it is going to be like *every* night.'"

On March 21, one of the more significant of the side-projects involving the members of Dream Theater was released – TransAtlantic's *SMPTe*. Written and recorded in the stupendously brief period of a mere week, it combined the talents of Flower Kings guitarist/vocalist Roine Stolt, Marillion bassist Pete Trewavas, Neal Morse (then with Spock's

Beard) on vocals/guitars/keyboards with Mike on drums. The album is a startling mix of progressive melodies that remains the decade's finest traditional prog album. *Classic Rock* described the album as an "absolute prog gem", and although the band would record a solid follow-up in the shape of 2001's *Bridge Across Forever* and two live albums, they could never surpass their debut.

Back with Mike's day job, the Dream Theater tour continued at an inexorable pace, and rolled into the Bronco Bowl in Dallas on August 24. One spectator was Dream Theater's past producer David Prater who was viewing the gig from the sound desk.

"At the time of the Bronco Bowl concert, I was living in Dallas, Texas. After I had greeted all the band members prior to the show, Mike suggested I go out front to view it from the house. He said there were several large video screens that really enhanced the concert experience. Well he was right, and it looked beautiful. I sat on a road case behind the console for almost the entire show during which time, and on several occasions, Dream Theater's sound man motioned for me to stand at the board and help him mix. I declined on each occasion. Finally, before the last song, he became really insistent and was like, 'Come on Prater! It's OK.' So finally I did it. All I can say is that you missed a very special evening. So I made some adjustments that I thought made a dramatic improvement on the band's overall sound. For once that night, I thought Dream Theater's mix sounded correct. Because LaBrie had earlier introduced me to the audience as being the producer for *Images And Words* and *A Change Of Seasons*, it's a fair bet to assume that some in the audience knew where I was sitting. I swear I could feel the audience responding differently from section to section by the way they registered their applause. The mix was so much more distinct. The song ended and the crowd voiced their approval in a strong ovation for an encore. Then to my surprise, the guitar arpeggio for 'A Change Of Seasons' began and I thought 'Oh fuck! I would love to mix this one!' I looked at their soundman and he nodded his approval as if to say, 'Fuck yeah! Keep on going, it sounds good!' They played the song in its entirety and it sounded superb."

Yet, given the animosity that existed between band and producer, was there not an overwhelming temptation on Prater's part to, well, mess with the sound and reap an audible and very public revenge on the band?

"It is impossible for me to sabotage the sound of anyone to satisfy my personal animus, anymore than a doctor would botch an open heart surgery," he explains. "When I was given control of the console, there was a discernible change from the way their mixer had been running it. The crowd picked up on something because, shortly after I did, they were on their feet for at least the next 45 minutes. I made it sound exactly how I would have made myself sound. So no, I didn't fuck with it."

Mike Portnoy: "Yeah, I find that incredibly comical. What really happened was that he was standing behind the console the entire time. He eventually weaselled his way behind the board and kind of started putting his hands on the board and making suggestions. Our sound man finally threw up his hands and was like, 'What the fuck? Get out of here!' And he let Prater stand over his shoulder for the last song or something. He's lucky our soundman didn't fucking wring his neck and kill him. He was acting like we actually wanted him there. No – he was just a spectator like everybody else, and was putting his hands in everybody else's business."

The producer takes issue with Mike's assertions and states that he "never stood over the soundman like Mike says and at no time was I a weasel as he mischaracterizes me. Afterwards when I saw the band, I answered questions at length from everyone except Mike about their rig, their sound and their performance, and there was no mention of me 'weaseling' my way on to the soundboard."

The last night of the American leg – at the Roseland Ballroom in New York on August 30, 2000 – had been earmarked months earlier as being the location for a special gig.

"We were in Japan in May 2000 when I came up with the idea for this show," explained Mike. "We always want to do at least *one* special show on each tour. So we'd done the Ronnie Scott's gig on the *Awake* Tour, and Rotterdam and Paris were special shows on the *Falling Into Infinity* Tour. I remember being on the bullet train in Japan bringing this up with the guys to do a show in New York as we'd never done a proper live recording in New York."

Declaring that this gig was to be the last time that *Scenes From A Memory* was to be presented in its entirety from start to finish, it was the perfect opportunity to record a live album and DVD. Once seeded, that idea was expanded to try and create what the band had wanted to be the "ultimate" Dream Theater show, with Mike adding, "Then there was the idea of doing a full production with maybe some actors and the choir, bringing Theresa Thomason out and Jay Beckenstein.,"

The inclusion of singer Theresa and a gospel choir would also enhance the live presentation, although the band's hectic touring schedule meant that they had virtually no preparation time in which to rehearse. There was also the added pressure of monitoring the setting up of the audio and visual equipment to ensure the evening passed smoothly, which led to a hectic afternoon.

"We only had a rehearsal that afternoon," laughed Mike. "Jordan had gone away and scored all the choir parts we'd done on the album, and sent them a tape so they were prepared. Then I was very caught up in the whole filming aspect and of what was going to tape, and we brought Kevin Shirley along to record the audio. And it ended up coming off great. I think it was the pinnacle of our career to have captured it. But it almost killed me!"

"It was a wild day," adds Jordan. "We had the whole gospel choir backstage and we were getting them all going. Mike was running around trying to get everybody co-ordinated, and even my wife was on hand helping. So everybody was doing something. Plus we had the actor there who was going to do the narrations. As you see on the DVD he was really hyper, and was about as far as you can get from a relaxing hypnotherapist."

The addition of an onstage actor playing the hypnotherapist succeeded in adding depth to the performance, but was more of a necessity than any serious attempt at a dramatic interpretation. Of course, the voice of the hypnotherapist on the album makes a number of appearances and was actually played by producer Terry Brown, who'd recorded James's vocal performance on the album. To ensure consistency, these spoken sections were replayed at the critical moments of the live performances on tour – seemingly without Brown's knowledge or consent. Consequently, his lawyer contacted the band after the producer had learned of the live renditions of the spoken samples. Mike was intensely unimpressed.

"Basically, halfway through the Metropolis 2000 Tour, we received word from his lawyer that he expected X amount of dollars from us for using his voice when we perform *Scenes...* live," wrote Mike on his website. "Now Terry knew damn well when he recorded his voice as the hypnotherapist during the *Scenes...* sessions, that it was a concept album that we would be performing every night on tour. Of course we would be using a sample of his voice in the performance, being that he opens the freaking CD and show! He also bitched about not being credited as the hypnotherapist on the CD sleeve – we purposely wanted it to be an unbilled cameo... We eventually had to pay Terry off to avoid a lawsuit and were forced to have somebody else come in for the Roseland show to play the hypnotherapist."

As always in these situations, there are two sides to the story. Sources close to Brown have revealed that the dispute stemmed from a genuine misunderstanding. Seemingly, when the producer recorded the spoken introduction, he was under the impression that this was merely a mock-up. Brown was perturbed to learn that that take had ultimately been used on the actual CD, as he was unhappy with the presentation. The replaying of his narration on the live tour was allegedly the final straw, and Brown took whatever steps he felt were necessary to prevent further airings. With both parties remaining at loggerheads, it ensured that Brown received a sarcastic credit of "No thanks" in the notes of the live DVD. All of which is a great shame, as it has prevented the two talented parties from working together ever since.

Given the special nature of the show, Mike had even extended an invitation to Kevin Moore in the hope that he might have agreed to make a guest appearance. The intention was for the reunited band to perform the previously un-played "Space Dye Vest" and another song (reputed to have been "Learning To Live") from his tenure with the band. But consistently avoiding any Dream Theater activities since his departure, Moore declined to travel from his then home in Costa Rica to New York, as he explained in an interview on the *Ytsejam.com* website.

"Well, the specifics of that I don't really know about, but he did ask me to play a show with them," said Moore. "I don't know, it just doesn't sound like fun to play a ten-year-old song to a bunch of people that already know it. For what? Just a cameo appearance? I don't even like it when I see other bands do it. From Costa Rica to play that one song. It just seems silly. I really don't have anything musical to offer. It's just gratuitous. There's nothing creative about it. There's nothing I'm going to learn. There's nothing I haven't experienced before. I've played that song millions of times for people. I'm not interested in just going up on stage and doing the reunion, just for old time's sake."

But despite his absence, the Roseland was still a monster, and apart from the full-length rendition of *Scenes From A Memory* also included a complete performance of "A Change Of Seasons", "Metropolis – Part I" and other songs from their back-catalogue that, even by Dream Theater standards, made this a protracted set. But despite the gig's success, the physical and mental exertions had taken their toll on Mike.

"I literally overdid it, and after the gig I almost went to the hospital," he said. "I was wrapped up in towels for hours and couldn't move. I had to get carried out of the venue. It was bad and as close to death as I have ever come. It was a combination of exhaustion, stress, overheating, not having eaten and de-hydration. Just the whole day was a lot of work – not to mention the four-hour performance!"

The exceptional performance that night brought praise from an unexpected source – *The New York Times*. In a glowing live review, Ann Powers wrote: "Dream Theater was best when it focused on virtuosity, the real point of progressive rock." *Metal Edge*'s Paul Gargano was equally buoyant declaring: "We experienced something timeless and special – a great band performing great music. Unfortunately, that's something that seems to happen less and less these days."

The band returned to Europe to complete the dates of the tour which finally ended on October 21, 2000, in London. That left Dream Theater with the small matter of contemplating how they intended to match, or even surpass, an album as complete as *Scenes From A Memory*.

THIRTEEN

INNER TURBULENCE

With the band returning home following another elongated series of tour legs, they were relishing the opportunity for a well-deserved period of rest and recuperation. But Mike faced a greater, ongoing challenge than merely recharging his energies in preparation for writing their next album. Over the preceding years, the drummer had realized that he was becoming increasingly dependent on alcohol to see him through a tour. Worse still, midway through those Spring 2000 European dates, cocaine had also become a presence behind his kit. Talk to anyone in or close to the band about those times – including Mike – and the phrase "out of control" will always be freely uttered about his conduct. Central to that developing problem was the fact that such an unhealthy concoction of alcohol, drugs and an obsessive-compulsive perfectionist was never going to end happily. The drummer was always someone who could explode if things didn't quite run to plan, and with a few Jägermeisters inside him, he'd vent his anger ever more frequently. But critically, he admitted to himself that he had a major problem and made a resolution to actively seek help.

"I think it was a culmination of just knowing that my drinking problem had become out of control," he says. "I could no longer control it as it was controlling me. For so many years, I kept it in check and I would *never* let my drinking and partying get in the way of my playing or my work with the band. I was never a day drinker, and would always wait until the end of the night, when all my work was done, before I started. I mean, for 15 years straight I drank and drugged every single day. But it was always *kind* of responsible and was always at the end of the night. The last few years of my drinking, it just started to creep into my day-to-day activities. As time went on, I would start to have my first couple of drinks before the encore. Jose [Baraquio – Mike's then drum technician] would hand me a couple of shots as I came offstage for the encore. Then Jose started giving me my drinks in the keyboard solo in the middle of the show. And then towards the end I was drinking earlier in the day while the opening band were on, and I would get onstage already half-crocked."

"Drinking was always my drug of choice, but of course I dabbled in everything else. I went through periods when I was a heavy pot smoker or popping a lot of pills. I was really into a lot of pills, and also occasional cocaine binges. Even towards the end, I remember on the Metropolis 2000 Tour, Jose was actually cutting me lines of cocaine on his tech box behind the kit. So in between songs, I would come back and have a couple of lines and a couple of shots. Instead of chugging Gatorade, I'd be chugging glasses of Jack Daniels. I am sure it was showing in my playing. Things had just gone too far when it got to that stage, and that was something I swore I'd never do. It wasn't something that a fan would notice, but the band did, and I would be coming off the stage shit-faced. It wasn't fun anymore. After 15 or 20 years of alcohol abuse, the fun wears off. I would find myself at the meet-and-greets after the show with a bottle of Jack Daniels, and being rude to fans and things like that. It came to a point where I knew that the jig was up and that I could no longer control it."

Sharing cramped conditions on the tour bus, and spending the majority of each day living in each other's pockets, the rest of the band had obviously noticed Mike's increasing dependence on alcohol. James in particular – given some of his vocal and performance problems – had been on the receiving end of Mike's substance-fuelled wrath on a number of occasions, but was unaware of the true extent of the problem.

"I really didn't know he was doing coke, as he really concealed it well," reveals James. "I knew he was drinking like a fish and that he was toasted every single day from it, but the booze *and* the coke? I mean holy smoke, what a combination. I could tell something was going on because Mike was just very difficult to be around at the time and I was avoiding him at all costs."

John Petrucci: "I didn't realize how much of a problem it was for him. Mike's always professional, so there was never anything like him not showing up for a gig, passing out or becoming belligerent on stage. He never did anything like that. I guess a lot of what he went through was more in private, so it wasn't as obvious as you think it might have been."

Tour manager Bill Barclay – who had experienced firsthand the effects drink had on Mike in Finland back in 1998 – was well aware of both the drinking and drugging.

"Yeah, but put it this way, I've seen a lot, lot worse," says Barclay who had previously toured with the likes of Mötley Crüe. "Mike wasn't hitting the drugs that hard and it wasn't that bad when it was around. Plus he was pretty discreet about it, but you just *know* don't you? I don't remember it really being the drugs – it was always the Jägermeister that affected him. But then again, who doesn't if they are drinking that shit? It's like bloody kerosene. So he used to get really vocal on booze and he was his own worst enemy, as I'm sure he'd tell you himself. The drink had a lot to do with the problems between Mike and John Petrucci, and the problems between James and Mike, and *whoever* and Mike. It was always the drink that came in between them. After a drink Mike would be a bit vocal and too personal with people, and that's going to piss you off after a while."

Mike consumed his last alcoholic drink on his 33rd birthday – April 20, 2000 – following the last gig of the tour at the Aula Magna in Lisbon, Portugal. Finally persuaded by his gradually sagging performances, he vowed to seek professional help once he returned home.

"The next night, I got on the plane to go home and I made up my mind that I needed to go for help," he sighs. "When I got home, I arranged two doctors' appointments. Both of them told me that if I didn't stop drinking, I wasn't going to make forty. That was a shock to my system, as I've got two young children that I want to be there for. It was just the thought of actually *becoming* a rock 'n' roll statistic like John Bonham or Keith Moon. As much as they are my heroes, I really didn't want to end up like them. So when two doctors in one day told me that, I went running for help. Thankfully I found the help of the Alcoholics Anonymous twelve-step programme that has kept me sober for six years and counting."

The temptation to drink would of course be greatest on the road, when the time would drag waiting for those few gratifying hours on stage. To try and avoid such temptations as the hotel bar, Mike would spend his time locked away in the confines of his room watching DVDs, planning set lists or the band's next project. But there was still the regular necessity for him to venture out to seek the support of local Alcoholics Anonymous meetings.

"I go to meetings almost every day actually," he reveals. "I have to find meetings on the road. My first couple of years it was really mandatory that I had to go every day. Now with a bit of a sober history, I am able to kind of let it go a couple of days and go once or twice a week if I can only handle that. But you know, that's one of the things on the road for the last five years that keeps me occupied on my down time. When I have a day off, I will be in my hotel room the entire time. The only time I'll leave is when I either go to a meeting or maybe go to a movie. But I try to make it a priority with my schedule, no matter where I am or what I'm doing."

Working in Mike's favour was the unwavering compassion and encouragement he received from his bandmates. The fact that there was nobody else within Dream Theater who took drinking, drugging or partying to the same level of overindulgence also made his task easier. They may have relished a few beers or glasses of wine, but it certainly wasn't something that had ever reached the stage of becoming a visible or daily necessity.

"Luckily, the rest of the guys in the band were never big drinkers so I would always be drinking with either the road crew or the opening band," explains Mike. "So when I finally got sober, the guys were so supportive that I was able to eliminate alcohol altogether from the dressing room, the riders, tour bus and from the backstage area.

Some of my first challenges were going to hotel rooms every night. I remember John Petrucci would even come by my room every time we checked into a hotel, empty my mini-bar into a bag and take it away with him. It was that kind of support that got me through that early sobriety."

John Petrucci: "Once you see that someone is overcoming something like that, and you obviously love the person having been friends for so long, you have to be supportive. There's no other way to be and what a great thing for him to overcome. I really can't imagine how difficult that must have been to have the strength to abstain from something that you seemingly don't have any control over. But now that he's not drinking, he's totally different. He is a way better man for it."

Rikk Feulner, the band's current tour manager, has also ensured on all subsequent tours that alcohol or other obvious temptations are kept well out of sight of the drummer. Those rules have also been extended to the road crew, and apply to any place Mike might find himself – such as the backstage area and the band's bus.

"We have it in our rider that there's to be no alcohol anywhere," he says. "A couple of the other band members drink wine and enjoy a good drink now and then, but they are respectful and they keep it away from Mike. They are respectful about it because they have seen what it's like at the other end, and him being out of control when he was drinking too much. I've been around enough people who've drunk and done drugs in their life to know that when they are doing that, they are very obsessed with it. All they think about is where they're going to get coke. I mean, I've worked with guys who've done crack. All they think about is how they are going to get crack, and how soon before they can start drinking. Mike has just turned his obsession into the band, and he doesn't think at all about drinking or partying. People like Mike are obsessive-compulsive which is why they become alcoholics. He's changed from thinking about drugs and alcohol all the time to thinking about the band and what they can do to make it better."

Having only recently joined the band, Jordan hadn't been around long enough to determine whether Mike's performances during those final gigs on the Metropolis 2000 Tour were afflicted by his alcohol intake. But he does admit to noticing a vast difference following the drummer's decision to stop drinking.

"I was new in the band and didn't really have much to compare it to," says Jordan. "So I couldn't really tell if his playing was sloppier than before, or if his personality was worse or better than before. But I can say that he has just become a nicer person to be around. He's still Mike, he's still intense and his core personality is the same, but his whole life has improved so much since those days. At the time I was just happy to be in the band. Now we have a smoother ride altogether. It's a very *boring* rock band really. The most interesting things about us are our chord progressions and our meter changes!"

With Mike starting to get to grips with his drinking, the next obstacle facing both him and the band was the making of their next album. *Scenes From A Memory* had marked a high point in terms of creativity, and consequently they faced the age-old problem of trying to find a way to top it. This was something that the band had plainly recognized, and were somewhat daunted by, before they re-entered the studio to work on a follow-up.

"I guess the key word is 'top'," said Mike at the time. "We just can't use or think of that word and we just have to make another record and hope it's really good. With *Scenes...* we did a concept album, we were self-producing and there were a lot of eggs we threw into the basket. I don't know if we *can* top that. It's going to be hard to follow that up as it was a really creative experience for us, but we just want to make something different. We've talked about some different things and some different directions. We know we won't do another concept album – that's for sure. We kind of took that as far as it could go with *Scenes...* and don't want to do the same thing."

Bear Tracks by now had become virtually a spiritual home for Dream Theater, as the pleasant atmosphere and tranquil location had proved conducive to both the writing and recording process. Following the maxim of not meddling with a winning formula, the band once again headed to the woods of upstate New York at the beginning of March 2001 to start work on the album that would later be christened *Six Degrees Of Inner Turbulence*. Apart from determining it wasn't going to fully revolve around another intertwining concept, the final musical direction was still undecided. One of the options considered was to create an album influenced by different styles of world music, and the band had even taken part in a number of master classes to guide them in that direction, as Jordan Rudess explains.

"I know a fellow who is an expert in all kinds of ethnic music, especially like Indian music, and he helped us a lot. We didn't have that many sessions, probably only three or four, and they were great. It was strictly done to inspire us and to give us fresh thoughts. I think it functioned very well and there are certainly a few skills that we used here and there that were influenced by those sessions."

"I remember we were in Europe and Jordan, John Petrucci and I were in a plane discussing plans to make the album some sort of world music album, but still keeping it Dream Theater," adds Mike. "What we were going to do was that each song would represent the style or flavour of a different country. We did take a couple of those master classes and learned some different, weird African rhythms and it was interesting. But you know what? The rhythms they were teaching us were things that we were already utilizing. The biggest irony was that Steve Vai's album came out and guess what the concept behind that album was? Every song was representing a writing style of a different country. We would have been totally pissed off if we had spent most of the year making this record and then the Vai record comes out and fucks up our entire plan. So it worked well that we ended up abandoning that idea."

Indeed, that direction was disregarded before the band even reached the studio, thanks to John Petrucci and Mike being enthralled at a Pantera gig at New York's Hammerstein Ballroom the weekend before the sessions began. The first track that was constructed (later entitled "The Glass Prison") proved to be broadly influenced by the Texan metallers.

"Obviously we had Pantera flowing through our blood come Monday when we entered the studio," said Mike at the time. "So the first thing we did was get going with all these riffs and 'The Glass Prison' became this total Pantera-meets-Megadeth, relentless ball of energy. Lyrically it was something I wrote which was personal to me for the past few years in dealing with addiction, recovery and twelve-step programmes. It's something I have been through the last few years, and it's dedicated to Bill W. who was the co-founder of Alcoholics Anonymous. So I wrote about the first three steps of the twelve steps of recovery."

The concept of the twelve steps was something that would be revisited on later releases, with at least one song on each subsequent album continuing that journey. By the middle of June the band had completed five of their intended six tracks before there was an enforced break. John Petrucci had agreed to become part of G3 – an instrumental tour that also featured fellow guitar wizards Steve Vai and Joe Satriani – and dates had been arranged between June 23 and July 22. With Mike Portnoy drumming for John's band (which also included the well-respected bassist Dave LaRue), there was no other option but to arrange a temporary pause.

"We actually used the tour as an excuse to finish the music before the tour, which would give us the time to write lyrics and then reconvene later to finish the album," says John. "I think we had a concept that we wanted to do and there was a deadline. So it put the pressure on. But I love that kind of pressure!"

On their return to the studio, there were only three scheduled weeks remaining to write and record the album's final track. It would have been logical for them to create a relatively short song in order to ease that perceived pressure. But in typical fashion, they managed to create an epic that lasted forty minutes, which not only ensured that those final days would be hectic as they hurtled towards the deadline, but that the album would have to be a double-disc release.

"Yeah, there wasn't that much time left," explains Jordan. "So that lit a fire under our butts and we got busy. What came out of that was the whole, second CD. I remember being in the studio with John Petrucci who had this idea of having these big epic themes. He was saying things to me like 'Play the saddest thing you've ever played to bring tears to my eyes' or 'Play something really happy.' I was having a bit of a party and we were improvising, running the tape and these ideas were coming out. So that made many of the themes, especially the introduction for the whole piece, and it was a wild improvization session with John as the director. We were getting some good ideas so it prompted some inspiration. The next thing you know, I'm orchestrating the entire beginning which was a challenge. All my keyboards were in the studio, leaning against the wall and loaded with all these orchestral sounds. So we were going for it and it was a whirlwind. Personally I like that second CD a lot more than the first, as I always go for the more melodic stuff, and probably the more keyboard side of what we do as well."

"We weren't even intending to write a forty-minute-plus song," smiles Mike. "I knew in my mind and even suggested it to the others that we make another 'Change Of Seasons' type song. I remember John Petrucci saying, 'OK. But let's not go past twenty minutes.' Next thing we knew, we started piecing the bits together and it was like, 'Holy shit! We're thirty minutes in!' And by the end of the process, it was like, 'Oh my God. We finished at forty fucking minutes!'"

With the bulk of the album recorded by the end of August 2001, the only remaining aspects to be polished off were some vocals and the album's mix. James flew into New York on September 10, 2001, in preparation for those sessions, but as the appalling events of September 11 unfolded, the obligation to complete the album became entirely insignificant.

"I was down there to finish the vocals for the title track. I was at the Paramount Hotel about three miles from the site," said James. "People ask me 'Did the ground shake where you were?' because you're talking about two towers, 110 storeys high. But I didn't feel it at all. The scariest thing was seeing that on the TV in my hotel room, watching it and knowing it was just a little way away. Then walking out of the hotel on to the street and seeing these *big* plumes of smoke. So I was pretty freaked out, and it took like two hours to get through on the phone to my family and everyone else."

As if the atrocities that struck New York and Washington that day weren't dreadful enough, the band would receive some unwanted publicity as a result of those attacks. September 11 was the date that Dream Theater's live triple-CD recording of their 2000 Roseland gig – entitled *Live Scenes From New York* – was scheduled to hit the shelves across

North America. In a barely plausible and horrendous coincidence, the centre portion of the album's cover featured the New York skyline in flames – with the twin towers of the World Trade Centre clearly silhouetted against the blaze. The design was an alteration to the flaming heart symbol that had appeared on the cover of both *Images And Words* and *Live At The Marquee*. The flaming heart had simply been replaced with a blazing apple to symbolize New York, with a superimposed image of the Manhattan skyline reinforcing the link with the concert's location.

"It was the most horrible coincidence I've ever seen," says Frank Solomon, who even now struggles to find appropriate words to convey his horror. "I mean, for it to be released on the same day? It was unbelievable. It hit me straight away. I just thought 'Oh my God. We've got an album coming out here today that has *this* on the cover.'"

James LaBrie: "I was more concerned with what was going on in the world and I thought our album was something completely insignificant at that point. But obviously we knew we had to deal with that bizarre coincidence. We discussed it immediately, got in contact with our management and label and said, 'It's gotta get pulled. We've got to show some sense of respect for what went down.'"

With the decision being made that something needed to be done to limit the damage, a statement was released by Mike Portnoy that read: "In regard to the live album's cover art, I can only say that it is a horrible coincidence that we obviously could have never foreseen. The timing of the release of the album happening on the very same day as this tragedy is merely an incredible coincidence. We are currently in discussions with the label as to whether or not we will recall the CDs and replace them with a different cover. Obviously, the recovery of everybody's personal lives here in New York is the first priority. Thank you to all concerned."

Various options had been discussed – such as issuing stickers to affix over the potentially offending part of the sleeve – but the band were adamant that the CDs should be recalled. The problem was that the album had already been distributed to retail outlets well in advance of the release, so an entire withdrawal proved unfeasible. Consequently, there are plenty of copies in circulation with the original art that have become rather an unsavoury collector's item. The illustration of the flaming apple on subsequent pressings was replaced with the Majesty logo, and the reissued album was released on October 16, 2001.

Ironically, the cover also meant that the band were the focus of the mainstream press – something that had happened only sporadically before and most memorably when they were caught up in the Kobe earthquake. Seemingly, Dream Theater could only attract attention for all the wrong reasons.

"It was seriously upsetting about the timing and it seems to be the only way Dream Theater seems to get any press," agrees Jordan. "I mean, it was even covered in *Rolling Stone*. They just don't seem to want to write about the music, they want to write about all these problems – in a typical fashion."

As life in New York gradually returned to at least a partial degree of normality, the band began mixing the album, with Kevin Shirley once again providing his services at The Hit Factory in midtown Manhattan. Following the time and financial constraints Shirley had endured on previous albums, for *Six Degrees* he insisted that a proper budget was arranged. But despite the relative comfort of those sessions, he did face the usual problem of dealing with Dream Theater's communal, and frankly amusing, perfectionist streak.

"We finished mixing the last track on *Six Degrees* at two in the morning, as it was a forty-minute song," he smiles. "I finished it and said, 'There you go', and all the guys were behind me and exhausted. Petrucci then said, 'I don't think the guitar is loud enough.' I said, 'John, you're kidding right?' and he said, 'No'. So I told him I thought that the song was finished. He said to me, 'It's not fucking finished until we say it is finished.' So I just told him that was fine and that I'd erase all the guitar in the whole, forty-minute piece. I said we can increase it half a decibel and cut it in and out. So we did that until three in morning with the guitar like half a decibel out. The next morning he calls me and says, 'Kev. Everything sounds great. I'm just not sure I can hear enough drums, bass, keyboards or vocals.' I *swear* this is the truth! So I told him I had something that could fix that, and went back and pulled out the old mix. He told me that one sounded great. But I love working with them. Their music is so different, and they are terrific to work with."

The artwork that decorated the cover and booklet took a vastly different approach to previous sleeves, and had a far more minimalist design. The white backdrop was decorated with a yellowing paper effect, a child's doodles, and scrawled handwriting which was far removed from the more embellished, progressive rock styling of earlier albums. The art was created by Dung Hoang, who had been approached by the Elektra Records in-house designers, and later Mike, who detailed the approach the band were seeking.

"I remember Mike had a certain look and feel that he wanted," recalls Hoang. "He wanted a stark, white look and something more artistic and painterly, and different to what they had done prior. So then I went off and they asked me to do whatever I wanted as long as it met that parameter. I do a lot of both digital and traditional work. So a lot of the textural work was done traditionally, using acrylics and oil where I built up the layers. Then I would take that and scan it into the computer and then layer that together. The advantage of that is I could move things around and change things in certain ways. So Mike would say things like, 'I like this, but can you move it' or 'Can you take this out?' So it's a lot easier for me to do. I mean, it's still a lot of work but pretty much anything can be changed."

With the album being Dream Theater's sixth, and given the album's title, the number six was obviously going to be referenced on the sleeve. But Hoang was determined to make these as subtle as possible to ensure they corresponded to the restrained feel of the piece.

"I had to kind of involve that element in there somewhere," he says. "And of course something that was required on every album was the Dream Theater logo – that symbol that they have – which in this work I made a part of the art so it didn't stand out. But one example is the anatomical hand inside the case. You have to look at it for a second before you realize what is different, there are six fingers, which reinforced the number six again and the idea of something not being normal. Even on the front cover, if you look right above the word 'Degrees' there are six in that mark rather than the traditional five that you'd see. Normally, you'd scrawl the four vertical marks and cross it with the fifth. But here there are six. So there are little discoveries like that for people to look through the booklet and find. The scribbles are of course lines taken from the lyrics. So from that idea we had the band members write a lot of notes and scribble, and provide them to me. Then I had to fit them in wherever it seemed appropriate on that particular page. I thought about using scribbles from my own kids or from kindergarten. I am always drawn towards kids' drawings. They have an interesting way of doing things."

In some respects, *Six Degrees Of Inner Turbulence* is reminiscent of the most controversial album in the Yes back-catalogue, *Tales From Topographic Oceans*, in that there are portions that, on a cursory listen, may appear an impenetrable tangle of time signatures and melodies. Yet paradoxically, that seemingly indecipherable heap of styles has also ensured the album's durability. Too often, rock albums that are instantly memorable rapidly transform into ultimately forgettable. *Six Degrees* holds an enduring appeal, but it has also been the subject of ferocious debate among fans as to which of the two discs – the darker, heavier first or the progressive opulence of the second – carries more impact.

"The Glass Prison" opens the album with a clattering mass of riffs and shredding that finds Dream Theater at their most grinding. Perfectly suiting the lyrics, dealing with Mike's battle against alcoholism, it sets the tone for the first half of the album. "Blind Faith" is more melody-driven, but is no less jolting with an accompanying LaBrie-penned lyric dealing with the overbearing power of religious leaders on their more blinkered believers. "The Great Debate" covered the pros and cons of genetic manipulation, which, in a peculiar twist, was originally called "Conflict At Ground Zero", but following the events of September 11, a name change was understandably required. "Disappear", and to a lesser extent "Misunderstood", showcased their mellower side. The lyrics for the latter were written by John Petrucci.

"Those lyrics were all based on a simple line that I heard somebody like Billy Joel say," recalls John. "He questioned how he could go from being in front of a million people to back in his hotel room all by himself. I thought that was pretty interesting and that I could write a whole song about that."

The second disc is, to all intents and purposes, a self-contained, mini-concept album. Running in at over forty solid minutes, it is broken down into eight distinct sections, and lyrically deals with six characters struggling with varying levels of mental illness. The instrumental orchestrations of "Overture" set the tone, with an almost classical swagger that wouldn't sound incongruous as a movie soundtrack. The classic prog rock leanings are augmented on the beguiling "About To Crash", with "Goodnight Kiss" also possessing some beautifully melodic moments. Throw on "Solitary Shell" to the uninitiated, and if they're of a certain age, you can virtually guarantee that they'll claim it sounds extremely similar to Peter Gabriel's "Solsbury Hill". Often referred to – even by the band – as John Petrucci's ode to that song, the similarities are impossible to ignore. But unwanted accusations of plagiarism aside, it is arguably the strongest part of the piece and was on the surface at least begging to be released as a single. But after the commercial failure of previous single releases, the band had taken the decision that trying to appeal to an uninterested MTV, radio and general public was futile.

"Songs like that *should* be hits and in a perfect world they would cross us over to new markets," claims Mike. "But we have a stigma that is attached to the name Dream Theater that has been ten of 15 years in the making. A lot of the press and media – whether on TV or radio – have a stereotype that's attached to our name. They're not even going to bother listening to the single we deliver because to them, we represent a certain style and audience, and they're just not interested in trying to look beyond that. So it's frustrating and we've given up on trying to cater for them. We just do what we do, and if ever we get radio or video play then great, it's a bonus. But we're never counting on it, and that was our philosophy all along actually. Plus now we have stopped doing videos. I'm not totally closed to doing videos and I'd be up for it in the future if there's going to be the support. But if nobody is going to bother playing it, we'd rather take that $100,000 and put it towards a concert video or DVD, and something that can actually mean something to the fans as opposed to a video for a song that's just going to sit on a shelf."

At least the press were appreciative in their evaluations of *Six Degrees*. *Classic Rock*'s Dave Ling wrote: "They occasionally reach levels of intensity that even Pantera would envy and a degree of complexity that Dimebag Darrell and company could never hope to approach. They're also capable of dropping to a whisper and allowing vocalist James LaBrie to impress with his usual authority. But it's the instrumental interplay between Rudess, Petrucci, Portnoy and six-string bassist Myung that should make other acts of their bent feel second-division by comparison... You really have to hear the music to appreciate its full magnitude."

There was also a pretty astonishing review in the mainstream *Entertainment Weekly* – a magazine not exactly renowned for lavishing praise on progressive metal acts – as they virtually heralded Dream Theater as rock's saviours. "Like the ceiling of the Sistine Chapel or that massive ball of twine in Kansas, some things are so humbling that their very existence leaves you gaping in open-mouthed, saucer-eyed awe," they wrote "It makes you wonder which act is gutsier: Eminem for slamming another teen pop-star or Dream Theater ignoring, and thereby dissing, every style of music that existed since 1976."

Securely entrenched in the incessant writing-recording-touring cycle, Dream Theater were soon back on the road again. In order to hone the material in a live setting, they performed a warm-up gig at B. B. King's in New York on January 19, 2002, before heading off to Europe for their opening date at the Manchester Apollo on January 25. That gig – along with performances in London and Copenhagen in the days immediately following – was unusual. With the album being released on January 29, the audiences had been unable to absorb the complexities of the music before witnessing a live rendition. Consequently, some of the audience – this writer included – were somewhat overwhelmed as the intricacies of "The Glass Prison" and "The Great Debate" were unveiled in all their bombastic glory. The gig at London's Hammersmith Apollo was reviewed by *Classic Rock*'s Dave Ling, who declared that the band's "popularity continues to grow at an astonishing pace, and it's easy to see why. There was even a touch of symbolism when Dream Theater segued seamlessly into the note-perfect instrumental conclusion of Rush's '2112'. 'Attention all planets of the solar federation,' boomed Petrucci gleefully. 'We have assumed control.' They certainly have."

One memorable gig, for a variety of reasons, occurred on June 18 at the Laviera Club in Madrid. At the show's finale, the band assumed their usual place at the edge of the stage to take the customary bow, with Mike throwing drumsticks into the audience. One stick was flung towards a girl in the front row, but it was caught in mid-air by one of the burly bouncers before it reached her. At which point, events took a downward turn and began to descend into chaos, as tour manager Rikk Feulner recalls.

"Mike was pointing at him and telling him to give the drumstick to the girl," says Rikk. "But the guy refused to give it to her, like he was going to keep it for himself or something. So Mike was yelling at this guy who was flipping Mike off. The security guy was being a jerk about the whole thing. So Mike just reached back and grabbed James's microphone stand and threw the whole thing at the security guard. That caused a *big* problem with all the security."

Realizing there was a problem brewing, Feulner rapidly ushered the band offstage and locked them in the dressing room, as a mob of unruly "security" bruisers wandered menacingly around the venue seeking vengeance.

"Basically, security wanted to kill Mike, the band and anybody else who was in their way," continues Feulner. "This guy's friends all joined forces and just wanted to beat up somebody. So then they were all waiting out by the back door, waiting for the band to leave to go to the bus. As they were on the street and weren't on the property of the building, the promoter couldn't do anything about it except call the police. But he couldn't really call the police unless they were actually doing something. And all they were doing was standing there. So it was a very awkward situation, and we had to work out how to do it without getting anybody beaten up."

"Obviously Mike may have been a little out of control and decided to do something that may not have been in our *best* interests," laughs Jordan at the memory. "He felt that was appropriate at the time and it ended in a pretty bad situation. But it was scary and really upsetting. I'd never known anything like that. And then of course you worry if you go back to that town if there is going to be a problem, if the guys remember."

The tension was temporarily broken by a surreal moment of humour. In a scene reminiscent of the moment in *Spinal Tap* when the fictional, comedy metal band performed at an Air Base, the wireless microphones continued to beam a signal back to the on-stage amps, as James explains.

"Needless to say that one of my wireless microphones which was on the stand was lost," he smiles. "But what was funny about that was that someone had got a hold of it, and as they were driving away in their car with my wireless microphone, we could hear them over the PA talking in Spanish! We couldn't believe that they had it. But it was scary because basically the security guys wanted to kill Mike. They all literally wanted to beat the shit right out of him, so it was pretty ugly. In a lot of clubs, security people go a little too far, get a sense of power and don't necessarily know how to use it properly and because of that incident, Mike was blowing up. And Mike isn't anything like the person he was back then. Then he was a very hot-headed individual, and that particular evening it could have got the best of him."

With a small regiment of angry bouncers standing guard outside the stage-door and blocking any direct exit from the venue to the tour bus, Feulner had to use all his experience and ingenuity to figure out a way to get the band safely away from the club.

"I got everyone's luggage and walked out the back door to put things on the bus, acting *really* nonchalant," says Feulner. "I just walked by them and didn't really acknowledge them. I got the band's stuff on to the bus, so then I just had to worry about the band. I ended up taking them back out on to the stage, down the front of the stage and out the front door. We walked around the side of the building and came down the blind side of the bus. The driver opened the door and we got on without anybody seeing us do it. As we were driving away, I was sitting up front with the bus driver and these huge security guys were wondering why the bus was leaving without the band! When we went back there on the next tour, needless to say I had numerous conversations with the promoter to make sure that they had different security!"

"Yeah, they had to pull me off the stage and get me out the front door to the bus because those fucking Spanish gorillas would have killed me," says Mike coolly. "I had another situation on the 1997 tour at the Chicago House Of Blues. The security guys were giving my wife a hard time. She obviously had a laminate and was trying to take a picture of us on stage from the soundboard. They came over, harassed her and took her camera. She showed her laminate, and they didn't give a shit. So we came offstage and I went at it with the two, three-hundred pound gorillas who could have squashed me with their pinky. But I guess when you're the rock star up there, that power feeds that controlling nature and that anger. As a result of that fight in Chicago, we never went to play the House Of Blues again. We get offers to play there every single tour, but we refuse because of that incident. But you know, nine out of the ten fights I have ever had with the band, crew members or anybody else had to do with me trying to do what is best for the band, fans, show or album."

In spite of Mike's avoidance of alcohol, that confrontation revealed that his temper could still get the better of him – although as Dream Theater's manager Frank Solomon explains, there has been a vast improvement.

"It still happens infrequently but it is always because Mike expects perfection," says Frank. "He demands it of himself and is attentive of every detail that he is responsible for, and he is responsible for so much. He expects others will be responsible too and also look for perfection. So when things start to run amok a little bit, that's when he has a tendency. And that is only because he wants the show to be incredible for the fans. That's what it's all about, every time – the fans."

That drive for flawlessness is something noted by Rikk Feulner who adds: "I've worked with a lot of bands that just don't care. The band are screwed up, the crew are screwed up and ultimately the show isn't good. The Dream Theater guys are perfectionists – every one of them. If they miss one note they are mad at themselves for the rest of the day. So, because they are perfectionists, they expect everybody else to be, too. And that includes all of their crew and everybody around them."

That unsavoury incident in Madrid was particularly unfortunate as it tarnished what had been an otherwise successful series of visits to Spain. On an earlier leg, the band performed a two-night stand in Barcelona [February 18 and 19], and Mike (who had for some time been the sole decision-maker when it came to set lists) had decided to incorporate a rendition of a classic album into the set. Indeed, this was the beginning of a tradition that exists to this day – if the band are in your city for two consecutive nights, you can expect to hear Dream Theater versions of a legendary rock album at the second gig. During this tour, this custom saw the band perform versions of Metallica's *Master Of Puppets* and Iron Maiden's *Number Of The Beast*.

That decision was generally welcomed by the rest of the band who relished the opportunity to break the monotony of a tour. Admittedly, the choice of album sometimes caused a certain amount of consternation – Jordan, for example, readily admits to never having owned or heard a Metallica album prior to rehearsing *Master Of Puppets* – but for the most part, the selections were embraced. But could the band perceive of any classic albums that they'd refuse to perform?

"Well I wouldn't want to do Tiny Tim if that was on Mike's list – which I doubt," said James. "First of all, I won't know until the time comes. I mean, if it happened to be a band that I just could not stand, then I would definitely voice it to Mike. Actually, he did want to do one tune in particular, and I'm not even going to tell you the artist because I don't want to get into that, [reputedly Ozzy Osbourne's 'Revelation Mother Earth'] and I just said 'Mike, I just can't stand that fucking song! I can't stand it! Do you really want to do it?' He went 'OK. Cool, let's do this other one.' So he's open-minded about it, and he's not going to make us do something where the other four guys are like 'This is going to bite'. We all have common interests in the band. Doing covers is fun but it's not something that I really linger on and go, 'Wow man, that was very cool – I'd love to do that again'. It's not top of my list as far as what I want to do. I get a hell of a lot more enjoyment out of doing originals than covers."

Surprisingly, not all the fans in attendance at the Barcelona gig were thrilled to see the band performing *Master Of Puppets*, and message boards were soon filled with disgruntled fans bemoaning the fact that part of the show had been dedicated to covering that album. The band were unimpressed with the venom and sheer nastiness of some of the criticism, prompting Mike to issue the following statement on his website.

"I cannot believe some of the crap I have been reading. Myself and some of the other band members are surprised and frankly disgusted at the immature and unappreciative behaviour of some fans who couldn't handle our choice of set list. Were the other two hours of Dream Theater material that night not enough? Or what about the three hours of different DT material played the previous night? Let me spell it out for you once and for all to avoid any future disappointment. If Dream Theater plays two nights in your city, and you cannot handle an 'experimental' set list or anything else out of the ordinary, do not come to the second show. Do yourselves and the band a favour and sell your tickets."

Those cover albums were also later released on CD via the band's own Ytsejam Records label. But what do the likes of Iron Maiden make of Dream Theater performing and recording versions of their albums?

"Well, it's nice when people do things like that but I wasn't actually sure why they did it," says Iron Maiden singer Bruce Dickinson. "Certainly in terms of why they felt the need to release it on a record. You know, thanks very much guys, but I was still left scratching my head. Partly out of sheer laziness, Maiden like to do other people's tracks as B-sides and extra tracks. We don't like to give away our vital essences as extra songs. So we've got away with knocking out some covers ourselves, but it's a big step to go from there to putting out someone else's whole record – I still can't quite fathom out their motivation on that one."

"Well the motivation for the concept of covering an entire album is simply to pay tribute to some of the bands and albums that shaped us, and perhaps introduce a new generation of Dream Theater fans to our roots," counters Mike. "The motivation for releasing these cover shows? Well, I wouldn't be doing my job if I didn't offer our fans around the world a chance to hear these unique shows."

A light-hearted moment occurred at the Stadthalle in Fürth, Germany, on October 30, as the World Tourbulence dates were drawing to a close. At the show's finale, James LaBrie was tackled football-style by John Myung, sending a shell-shocked singer and bassist to the floor. Totally out of character, it seems that the usually reserved Myung had been dared to do it.

"I think John Myung was in the production office," explains Rikk Feulner. "We were just bullshitting about nothing, and then he said that he was going to tackle James on stage tonight. We all said 'I'll put in $20!' We raised a couple of hundred dollars and nobody actually thought that he would do it. We were just fooling around. But he actually did it and we paid him. We were all in shock. In fact, those of us who knew about it were as shocked as James was. Who would have thought that quiet John Myung would tackle anybody?"

"The crew guys didn't believe he'd do it and money was put on it," smiles James. "They really didn't think he was going to do it. The last chord of the night was ringing out and I'm like saying goodnight to the crowd. Literally a split second before he hit me, I saw him coming at me. And we rolled around on stage and he was laughing. So I made a deal with him and wanted fifty per cent of his winnings for danger pay!"

But for James, there was seemingly more to be alarmed about than merely watching his back on stage for flying bassists. Throughout the tour, and to a lesser degree before it, James had been receiving an unparalleled level of condemnation for his live performances and onstage presentation. Although this hostility was mainly appearing in the odd concert review and comments posted on some of the harsher internet forums, the voracity of the denigration attained such a level that it was becoming impossible to ignore. Worryingly for James, some of the public thoughts of his detractors were matching the private feelings of his bandmates, who began to seriously consider whether the singer still had a place in Dream Theater.

"Basically, towards the end of the *Six Degrees* tour [World Tourbulence], several of us were really starting to question our future with James," confesses Mike. "There were aspects of both his singing and his presentation that we knew were probably holding us back. We've come to kind of accept that part of our inability to cross over to a more mainstream audience is probably James's voice. Back in 1991, he was the ultimate voice in terms of what we were looking for. But by 2002, when we had these discussions, maybe our taste had changed a little bit, and that style of singing wasn't necessarily what we considered to be our ultimate singer any more. And we were starting to be a little frustrated. We would look at all of our favourite singers and back in the Nineties they were people like Geoff Tate, Steve Perry and Bruce Dickinson. But come 2002, some of our favourite singers were people like Bono or Thom Yorke. You know, singers that were more musicians and songwriter types. Even like a Neal Morse or someone like that. So we were starting to question if maybe James was still the right singer for us."

Certainly, to replace a singer at that stage in their career would have been a hell of a gamble. There are countless examples of bands that have disintegrated after replacing their frontman, or those whose popularity has waned to such a degree they ended up playing clubs instead of arenas. But the result of this anxiety within Dream Theater led to extensive and covert discussions away from the singer's earshot, and the pros and cons of keeping or replacing him were dissected at length, as Mike explains.

"The cons were that we were a little frustrated that we had a singer that didn't write with us, and somebody who wasn't a songwriter, composer or a musician that played an instrument," clarifies Mike. "Then there was the style of voice and whether it sounded dated. Another con was that we were getting a lot of criticism for his stage presence and persona, the way he would run on and offstage and maybe talk down to an audience. Maybe he had gained some weight. So those were the questions that we were battling with. The pros are that we have a history with him, and we do get along with him personally. We do have a friendship and camaraderie, and a family feeling with him. He also happens to have a great voice. It's strong and he's got great range, it just may not be to everyone's taste, but the fact of the matter is that he has a great voice. And at the end of the day we came to the realization that he is the voice of Dream Theater, love him or hate him. He is the voice that everyone has known Dream Theater by, and the thought of us changing vocalists at this point in our career was scary. Maybe we could have opened up a whole new world by having a singer-songwriter like a Neal Morse or a Steve Hogarth. But then again, what if it didn't work and that was the death of the band? So we came to grips amongst ourselves that we need to try and make it work, and that James really is the voice of Dream Theater. It was probably more hazardous to replace him than it would be beneficial."

John Petrucci: "It's really difficult to picture. You've got somebody who has been the voice of Dream Theater for pretty much all our career. You don't take stuff like that lightly. When you have known people for as long as we have, you're a family, so you have to be compassionate and have understanding. The biggest thing for me was that it didn't seem like he was into it any more. It seemed like he wasn't enjoying it, he was sort of in a bad mood, wasn't there or involved. So it was a case of asking 'What's going on in your head?' But what a great thing. It's great to have people that are together and have that kind of concern. So we decided to have a conference call on the phone and any kind of meeting like that is difficult, but you've got to talk about that sort of stuff."

That perceived lack of input from the singer had also clearly begun to gradually irritate other members of the band. James frequently wasn't present during the writing sessions, and would only appear to work on his vocals relatively late in the process. With the band agreeing that the subject of James's future had to be broached, a meeting was arranged, and manager Frank Solomon was forewarned of the potentially volatile agenda.

"I just tried to tell everybody 'Look, you're going to do what you're going to do. But think about this,'" he recalls. "I said to them that it's not a small thing and it wasn't going to be a small discussion or easy. So just think about what it is you really want to say, how you want to say it, and what it is you want to accomplish. Don't just start making statements that you don't really mean. Because once you put something out there in a situation like this, you can't take it back. And let's work it out. We've possibly got a problem but let's figure it out sanely and quietly, and deal with it.'"

"So we had a big sit-down with him – which was almost like a shape-up or ship-out kind of meeting," remembers Mike. "We told him our concerns. I mean there are some things that he can't help, like the fact that he can't play an instrument, that he's not a songwriter, and that his range is what it is. Those are things that he can't help. So we decided to talk about the things that he *can* help, such as his presentation on stage. Another thing that bothered us was that he would always credit himself as a songwriter, and do interviews and talk about the songwriting process, when the reality was that he was never even there. It bothered us and there was resentment that he would kind of bullshit the fans like that. So one of the things we brought up was that 'We want you to be more honest with the fans, and don't take credit for things you don't do', and also, 'Why don't you join us in this writing process? Even if you can't contribute at least you are part of the band and you're there, and make us feel like a five-piece band and not a four-piece band.' So we kind of laid all this stuff out and gave him an ultimatum that we would rather not make the change, but unless we see changes, we are going to be put in a position where we may have to."

With the band venting their dissatisfaction, their next concern was how James would take that criticism. There was a real and pressing concern that he might become obstinate and protective of his role – a response that would have undoubtedly led to his dismissal.

"We didn't know how he would take it, whether he would be defensive and get up and say 'Fuck this, I am who I am, if you don't like it fuck you!'" recalls Mike. "But he had the opposite reaction, which was the one we had kind of hoped for. He listened to us with a very open mind and ear, and stepped up to the plate. He said that he valued this band, and didn't want to lose it."

Speaking to the band today, it's obvious that they had all been praying for that outcome. Sacking LaBrie would have been an unwanted and last desperate act should the singer fail to admit there were issues or stated an intention not to address them. With the advantage of hindsight, James openly admits that the criticisms he received that day had a certain amount of validity. Vitally, his response during that meeting was also measured, and he vowed to make the required improvements to ensure he retained his place in the band.

"Well I think if I had said to them 'Fuck you, I think what's going down here is fine,' then they would have said, 'That's not good enough and it's not going to work,'" says James. "To be honest, it was what I needed and I think I needed that shaking. I'd been in such a rut for so long. I almost needed a reality check and something to snap me out of that trance. To let me really review myself and reflect on everything that had happened up until that point. So it was like an awakening for me. They had a conversation with me where they were asking me, 'Are you into this any more?' They were concerned about my voice, saying that it was distracting, that my voice could be better and that I should do things to get my voice right back to the top of its game. And had I ever considered doing it, as they were feeling that they have been short-changed. So I said 'Guys, I hear you loud and clear, I understand your frustrations and I think it's at a point where I can make a change and I'm passionate about being in the band.'"

Of all the concerns the band raised, James is convinced that it was his vocal problems – specifically when performing live – that had gradually caused the widest rift between him and the rest of the band. Those frustrations had been acutely felt by Mike, whose never-ending quest for perfection had been thwarted by James's tendency to occasionally screech as he failed to hit the high notes. In turn, that led to a debilitating cycle where the drummer and singer were frequently at loggerheads which, on occasions, almost led to blows being traded between the pair.

"Mike knew I was having problems and he was frustrated that I was going out on stage and my voice wasn't at the top or wailing like when he was introduced to me," confirms James. "So I think there was a lot of frustration with Mike and a lot of disappointment, and I guess he didn't know what to do. I really respect him as he had the balls to confront me. In the past, if there were ever any major disagreements, it would usually be between Mike and me. We had years of friction where we just didn't want to be around one another and that was just the way it was. It was kind of strange because when I first came into the band, we were very close. We had a lot of fun. But over the years people change, and I think at the root of that was what I was going through vocally and the way he was interpreting that. He was disappointed and knew that although I was dealing with it, I wasn't overcoming it the way he had wished and there was a lot of friction because of it. No words had to be said but I was aware of it, and we were at opposite ends with one another."

"So there were some very hot moments and some confrontations which could have blown up and where Mike and I could have been throwing fists at one another. In fact there were a few times where it was as close as you could possibly get. But we didn't actually get there. And it was as simple as I didn't like being around him and he didn't like being around me. The fact we were in a band together makes it amazing that we actually lasted. So the relationship between Mike and me over the years has almost been love-hate, but I think it really benefited the band in the long run. I respect that of Mike, as he really speaks his heart and so do I. It has brought it to a point where Mike and I are now in a comfortable spot with each other."

Mike: "Yeah, James and I have almost come to blows on a couple of occasions. One time was literally seconds before hitting the stage in Budapest on the 2000 Tour. We were in the dressing room and I told James that I wanted Theresa to sing the bridge of 'The Spirit Carries On' at the Roseland gig. And he got really mad that I hadn't even discussed it with him first and that I had just gone ahead and arranged it with Theresa. We were literally pushing each other as the intro tape was rolling in Budapest. It's always stupid shit when you think back, but it was my control issues again, always trying to control the shows. And sometimes my controlling nature can probably rub people the wrong way. I just want the show to be *right*, and when it isn't, it freaks me out and causes a lot of tension. And then there was a night on the 2002 Tour in San Diego, which was the summer tour we did with Joe Satriani and Kings X. Each night on that tour, James was supposed to sing certain choruses of 'Pull Me Under', and other choruses he was to give the microphone to the audience. He kept being inconsistent with how he would do that. So there would be nights when he would hold the mic out to the audience and I would end up singing background vocals without him. I kept telling him a consistent way he could do this from night to night, and he kept messing it up. Basically, that night I just said something onstage on the microphone, it freaked him out, he threw his mic stand and walked off the stage. So we actually finished the show without him, and he wasn't even there to take the bow with us. We almost came to blows afterwards."

In order to get to that comfortable spot that James refers to, the turnaround in his routine and habits have been pretty remarkable. To address his sporadically wavering live vocals, he sought the help of a vocal coach – Victoria Thompson – who helped to hone and direct his sound. And looking back now, the difference in his live presentation has been pretty remarkable. Compare any live performance from recent tours to those around the late Nineties and it's more than apparent that James heeded the warning. Where previously his tone may have wavered, he now nails every note. In addition, for every album following *Six Degrees* he has also been in attendance during the writing process, contributing ideas and melody lines. A vigorous exercise regime has also ensured that he looks sprightly and trim.

"He really was awesome," says John Petrucci. "The man rose to the occasion! He's done a great thing and he reflected on the situation and what we had talked about, came back and faced it head on. He sounds better than ever and he is enjoying the process, and playing live and being together. And for recordings, he's just involved and present. So we have a stronger unit. Everybody in the band has a responsibility to have strength, and the stronger the people are in those areas the better we are. So whether it was making the change to have Jordan in the band, Mike making a change and fighting an addiction, or James making a change, they have all made us a stronger band."

"Well, I look back on it and think it was probably a good thing in James's life to have people come to him and kind of say 'Get it together,'" adds Jordan. "I felt really bad when that was all happening. I was newer in the band and I hadn't felt any tension with him, but I guess Mike and maybe some of the other guys did. It's tough, but in any intense workplace where you are doing something that really matters to a lot of people and there's pressure, you really have to be pulling your weight. You just do. The reality of it is that James stands in the front of the band and it is really important for him to look and sound good. If he wants us to look good, he really has to take care of himself and at this point in our lives he is a role model. He really knows how to travel, take care of himself, exercises, does his vocals and has a great voice teacher. I haven't spoken to him about that time period in a while, but I know that he is happy with where his life is now and what's going on. He really feels that he came to the table and did what he had to do. But it's scary you know? If a guy in the band is maybe slipping a bit, everybody is subject to comebacks from the other members if they're not pulling their weight or whatever. But I feel like the band in general is in a good place, and there's not a whole lot of that kind of thing going on."

Frank Solomon was comfortable by the manner in which the issues were addressed, and is convinced that the amiable approach taken ensured that the problems were overcome swiftly without any lasting damage to the band's morale.

"There are no hard feelings now and they handled it in a way that I personally was hoping that they would," says Frank. "Again, that's a credit to the band as they are mature and smart enough. There were issues that they had that festered and didn't arise over the blink of an eye. But the issues obviously weren't as big as everybody thought they were going to be, because they seemed to solve them fairly quickly. I think it was a question of everybody thinking they had a really big problem when in fact maybe they weren't so big after all, and they just needed to be aired out."

Indeed, the exposure of those issues and the subsequent improvements made by James has dissolved the tensions that had been building for years. Which, as it tuned out, were as much of a relief for the singer as his bandmates.

"All I know is that from five years old right until this moment I have been crazy about music," says James passionately. "All I ever wanted to do was sing and be a part of this vision. And this vision, fortunately, is a band called Dream Theater. Because of that, the band has become a lot stronger, as we are presenting ourselves in a better form. I'm onstage now singing with confidence. I feel a hundred per cent better about myself, and I feel I've brought my voice back to where it was at the beginning of the *Awake* Tour. And it has made the band a closer unit. We feel good around each other again, and there's a good vibe and a healthy environment."

"Basically James stepped up to the plate and really tried to improve all of the things that we and a lot of the fans had been complaining about," concludes Mike. "And I guess you can say we lived happily ever after – at least up to this point. And on later tours, the fans noticed. I think about other bands that have had a similar situation. There are four that come to mind that all tried to change their vocalist and ultimately came back to the formula that people wanted. Iron Maiden, when Bruce Dickinson left and they got Blaze Bayley in. It failed miserably and Bruce came back. Judas Priest did it when Rob Halford left and they got Ripper Owens. It didn't work and Rob came back. Van Halen got Gary Cherone, and that didn't work so they got Sammy [Hagar] *and* Dave [Lee Roth] back. Yes did the same with Trevor Horn, and after getting rid of Jon Anderson they had to get him back. It has been proved time and time again that when you have a line-up and especially a singer that people grew up listening to, that's it. That's the band that people want to hear. In all of those cases there will be people that don't like Yes because of Jon Anderson's voice or don't like Iron Maiden because of Bruce Dickinson, but it didn't matter. That was the sound that people wanted to hear. And it's the same with us. This is who we are. He is the right singer for Dream Theater. If we can never cross over to appeal to X amount of people because of our style of singer, then so be it. Take us or leave us…"

FOURTEEN

"BALLS 'N' CHUNK"

That essential bout of air-clearing behind them, Dream Theater had intended to take an extended break before they even had to contemplate heading back to the studio. And in an ideal world, that period of creative recharging would have lasted for anything up to a year. But their desire to recuperate had to be tempered by the harsh financial realities that face virtually every band. That's not to say that they were exactly struggling to make ends meet, but they certainly couldn't afford to head off on sabbatical and cause a lengthy interruption to their cash flow. Consequently, someone had to persuade them that a fairly swift return to the studio was essential. As always, that task fell to manager Frank Solomon.

"Yeah, that was me," he laughs. "I was like, 'Hey guys, we do need to make some payrolls here!' I mean, it would have been nice to take a ton of time off but there are unfortunate realities to life. As much as one might think that with increased crowd sizes and everything Dream Theater might be making more money every time they tour, the truth is they don't. The reason for that is that they throw the money back into the show. You know, they'll step up the quality and size of the video or whatever. They are always striving to give the fans more. A lot of times I catch flak from the fans – for example the cost of premium seating – but I'm telling you, they are not gouging. They are putting back for the fans continually as they just want a better show."

Renting a studio in Manhattan, the writing sessions for the album that would eventually become *Train Of Thought* began on March 10, 2003. But this time, their tendency to write for months on end was kept in check, and within the space of a mere three weeks the material had – with the exception of the lyrics – been completed. The brevity of those sessions was partly because the band had already decided on a firm direction before entering the studio. Indeed, it had been agreed that the album was to be unashamedly brutal, based on the notion of creating a "classic" heavy metal album.

"We started discussing the direction at the end of the 2002 Tour, when we were doing a third and final leg in Europe," said Mike at the time in *Metal Edge* magazine. "On that leg, we were covering the entire *Number Of The Beast* album by Iron Maiden, and earlier that year, we had done the entire *Master Of Puppets*. We were looking at those two albums and saying, 'We want to make an album like this, of our own. We want a classic metal album.' We started looking at those albums and looked at what made them classic, and every song was strong, and the album length was more concise. Every CD we've made – both studio and live since 1994 – has been past seventy minutes, so we knew this time around we wanted to make it a little easier to digest. We wanted to have around seven or eight songs around seven or eight minutes each. Once we started making the record, all that kind of expanded, but at least we had a destination we were shooting for. We also looked at all the tunes from our catalogue that always go over great live, and it's always the real heavy, grooving songs – 'Pull Me Under', 'Home', 'Glass Prison', 'The Mirror' – that are the most exciting, so we said, 'Let's just make an album where every song is like that.' That was the blueprint we outlined."

"If you listen to *Master Of Puppets* or *Number Of The Beast*, it sounds like guitar, bass, drums and vocals. Basically, it sounds like a live band, and it sounds great. That was our focus – to capture a live sound and to make it sound as good as possible. Our last two albums were written in the studio through headphones, and we did a lot of composing on tape. We wrote this album in a rehearsal studio with the amps on eleven, and wrote them as a live band before translating them to tape. I think these songs are going to be amazing live. It's funny, while writing this totally angry music, we're looking at each other going, 'Wait a second, we're forty-year-old men, and here we are, playing these aggressive riffs!' I guess you've got to grow old at some point, but it's important for us to never sound old."

But with the emphasis firmly on creating dark, grinding guitar riffs, Jordan was left wondering where his trademark keyboard tapestries could be woven into the overall sound. After all, the blueprint for this album didn't entail the use of many prolonged, traditional prog rock keyboard solos.

"No, it wasn't a keyboardist's kind of thing really, as it was more of a guitarist's world," he laughs. "It took me a while to get used to it because the amps were very loud and keyboard amps really don't make that kind of volume. It wouldn't have mattered if I had a hundred amplifiers; John Petrucci's one Mesa Boogie stack would have blown it out of the water! So it took me a little while to get used to what was going on, and it was a little bit of a shock to be thrust into the dream that the boys had for creating a metal album. It wasn't a personal dream, but it was their dream and I wanted to relate to it. When we first started, I wasn't really sure what to do or how to position myself. But that ended up being a lot of fun even for what it was. It was just like a garage band style, where we went in with amplifiers blaring into a rehearsal room. That just meant that I had to walk out of the room sometimes just to get a sonic break. Just to refresh myself and bring my composer mind back to the table. After a while it worked out well, and I was able to work in that environment."

Gradually easing his way into pretty unfamiliar musical territory, Jordan began developing an arsenal of heftier sounds for his keyboards which enabled him to mingle with the battery of guitars that were defining the album.

"It was easy for people to listen to that and wonder where the keyboards were," says Jordan. "But of course keyboards don't always make piano or string sounds. They can make any sound, and on that album it was up to me to decide what kind of sounds to make to blend in. So I ended up making a lot of sounds that were just really grungy and heavy, and when you listen to them it's hard to tell what it is. It could be a guitar or anything. Later on, when people saw us live and we played material from *Train Of Thought*, people realized that often the lead sound was mine. I guess the basics are that most people don't know who is playing the lead – whether it is guitar or keyboards. And that's OK with me in a way, but it's also a little bit sad for people not to understand what I did. The ego part of me wants to be recognized for what I play. But on the other hand I was really proud and continue to use some of those sounds in our work, and I've now got this collection of heavy stuff that goes so well with the guitar."

Mike Portnoy: "One of the biggest misunderstandings is that Jordan is not a part of the songs, or not part of the mixes. On most of these songs, he's doubling the guitar, just the same way two-guitar bands such as Metallica, Iron Maiden or whoever would. He took that approach to a lot of these songs. So a lot of parts where you think it's only guitar, it's actually guitar doubled with keyboards to help thicken it up, or add a different timbre to it. In those moments where it's really heavy, and you're not really able to distinguish a keyboard sound, he's doubling the guitars or thickening up the guitar parts."

Of course, the other visible difference during those writing sessions was the presence of James LaBrie. Following the shape-up-or-ship-out meeting a few months earlier, an integral part of solving the perceived problems was to involve the singer throughout the writing process and not merely fly him down from Toronto to staple his vocals on to the already completed music.

"That was one of the main points which were brought up at that talk, that I should be more involved," says James. "And I was like 'Fine. Then let me be. Have me come down from day one to day done during the writing and recording'. So that was one of the things that became a new situation with *Train Of Thought* and has continued since. Yes, after *Six Degrees* I was either going to get involved like that or I wasn't going to be a part of it anymore. Period. It was going to be 'see you later'. Don't ask me why it didn't happen sooner, it just happened to be the dynamics of the band. Some things take a while to come to where they are. I think they just finally got to a point of expressing that they wanted things to be a little different, and that sometimes people don't want to ruffle feathers and it takes a while to get to that point. To me it was a bit strange because it got to a point where I was thinking to myself that I should be more involved instead of just writing a lyric here or there, or suggesting a vocal melody here and there. So the fact that this is a new world for us has made the band much closer as musicians and people. To be honest it really has made the band that much better. There is no question that it brought the band much closer. It created a renewed sense of belonging and camaraderie. It's called growing pains."

One explanation for James not being present during the writing sessions for earlier albums dates back to his recruitment. At that stage in their career, Dream Theater were extremely wary of working with a singer who wanted to exert too much influence over the songwriting or direction of the band. Consequently, James met their requirements as – from the moment of their first meeting – he showed no inclination to try and change the band's approach. Was it not therefore harsh for the band to criticize him for a lack of involvement a few years down the line?

"Perhaps. We had become very used to writing instrumentally," muses Mike. "I don't know if his lack of involvement was because we forced him into that scenario, or if he just didn't really feel like he had anything to offer. Perhaps that writing formula which was already established before he joined did shut him out in a certain respect. And it was even the same with melodies – we would literally just hand him the melodies. But it had come to a head even before we had that conversation with him, as we had started putting on the album that the music was by the four musicians and not by Dream Theater. So we took that credit away from him. And also the lyrics and melodies for *Six Degrees* were written without James because we were tired of the charade, and basically John and I just handed him the melodies. After that, we decided to have him with us when we wrote the music regardless of what he contributed, and decided to work on melodies together. And even though the music on *Train Of Thought* was still only attributed to the four musicians, we may go back to saying music by Dream Theater because he's been here with us during the writing process, and has been a big contributor to the melodies. So I think it has been good."

The writing sessions were, however, rudely interrupted by a story that broke on April 1. Seemingly, a man in New York had been successfully passing himself off as Mike, gaining people's trust and then robbing their apartments. Although having only a passing resemblance to the drummer, he apparently knew enough details about Mike to be convincing. One person he contacted was Savatage guitarist Chris Caffery, who said of his encounter with the impostor: "He was very convincing but also very suspicious. I was with him as people 'recognized' him in bars and on the street. He had obviously been pulling this off for a while, and even went as far as to call drum companies and order stuff using Mike's name. I became sceptical when I listened to his attempt to play the drums."

Eventually captured, the news of his arrest soon reached the studio and as Mike recalls, he had to make an infuriating visit to a police station in Queens, New York.

"The day that the story broke happened to be April 1, 2003," he says. "So a lot of people thought that it was an April Fool's joke, but it just happened to come out on that day. I do remember that the day he was captured we were in the middle of writing 'Stream Of Consciousness'. We had such a great flow going, and then I got this phone call that they had captured the guy. They needed me to go into the police station, and I was so pissed as we were really in the flow of writing this instrumental. So we stopped rehearsal and all went in together as a band. We all got in John Myung's car and drove into Queens Police Station. I think he got maybe three years or something like that. It was bizarre."

A couple of days after that encounter at the police station, the band finished the writing sessions, and took a ten-day break before reconvening at Cove City Studios in Glen Cove, Long Island, to begin recording. Mike and John once again took charge of producing the album, with stalwart Doug Oberkircher engineering. In view of their history together, that combination had continued to work well and as Doug explains, their working relationship had never been better.

"Working with Mike and John has always been a great experience, they are professional and good natured people and of course masters of their trade," he says. "I've spent countless hours working with them individually and collectively and we have the utmost respect for each other. They use me because I make it so they don't have to worry about any of the technical aspects of the recording, they know I will take care of all that and make a great sounding recording. This allows them to concentrate on the music and the performance, and not on the other aspects of the recording, thus allowing them to be more creative. Since we have this long relationship of mutual respect, working with them as producers is just an extension of that relationship, and has been very rewarding. They are so happy to have successfully moved into the producer's chair and taken complete control of their music, and this translates into a relaxed and positive working environment."

Following a three-week stint at Cove City, the band transferred their equipment down the road to Pie Studios to begin overdubbing. With the music complete, an unexpected offer was made for them to embark on a co-headlining summer tour with Queensrÿche.

"We figured we should jump on it because it's something the fans have wanted for a long, long time," said Mike. "The timing worked out, because we'd been in the studio April, May, and June, and had done all of the music. It actually worked out good that we took a six-week break to do that tour, because we needed that period to write the lyrics."

There's an old adage that you should never work with or meet your heroes, as far too often you're left disillusioned when the imagined veneer fails to match your expectations. Queensrÿche, along with Metallica and Rush, had always been on Dream Theater's list of influences, bands that they would've dropped anything to tour with. The offer was therefore accepted, and the tour began in Houston on June 23 and trekked around North America before the final date on August 2 at the Paramount Theater in Seattle. Although the pairing of these two prog metal greats was a dream bill for many fans, backstage harmony was in short supply. Part of the problem was apparently caused by the arrangements as to who would headline each night. Technically, as the gigs were billed as co-headlining, the bands were to take it in turns to top the bill, with a jam featuring both acts closing the show. And although that went to plan, Dream Theater's tour manager for those dates, David "5-1" Norman, recalls it still caused a certain amount of backstage friction.

"There was a lot of animosity from the Queensrÿche camp as they thought they should be closing every night, although Dream Theater blew them off the stage nightly," he says. "And the jam at the end of the night was for the fans, not because they liked each other."

But whatever tension existed between the two bands remained private until early 2006. At the end of March, Queensrÿche singer Geoff Tate was appearing on New York rock DJ Eddie Trunk's show, along with Chris Jericho. During an off-air conversation, Tate allegedly made disparaging remarks about Mike Portnoy, and was completely unaware of the close friendship both Jericho and Trunk have with the drummer. This was soon followed by comments made by Tate in *Classic Rock* magazine when he claimed: "The truth is that I'd never even heard Dream Theater until they toured with us. People compare our bands all the time but I don't hear us in what they do. We're very different animals. We're about writing songs and they're about playing a lot of notes. What I believe music is about is anathema to them."

Mike was initially amused by those comments, and says: "Well that's because they can't play as many notes as us. We hear that all the time, and it doesn't surprise me coming from Geoff. Geoff doesn't really come from the world we come from. We realized that when we toured together, as he's a very different type of person. It doesn't surprise me when people criticize us for the amount of notes, the speed or the dexterity or the technical side. I could see where that would turn a lot of people off, maybe intimidate people or even make people jealous. It does surprise me when they criticize our songwriting ability. You would think after we spent two months on the road with Queensrÿche, when we play a song like 'The Spirit Carries On' or something like 'Solitary Shell' that that side of the band would be obvious. There are those songs in our catalogue where the songwriting was definitely the focus. And it's ironic to hear that coming from Geoff, who hasn't written a good song in about ten years!"

But after Tate's remarks became public knowledge, a war of words began on the various internet forums, prompting Mike to post a furious note that read: "For the record, Geoff Tate is a two-faced douchebag. Since he has begun doing *Operation: Mindcrime 2* press, he has been consistently bashing Dream Theater and even me personally in the press... But I'm tired of biting my tongue, when he obviously can't. When he was on Eddie Trunk's show Friday night, he was incredibly rude and insulting when talking about me off the air to Eddie and Chris Jericho. Eddie and Chris were fuming at him, and Chris immediately texted me from the studio saying he was ready to body slam him on the spot. His new name on this board should be Geoff Taint. Screw him – he's now on my shit-list."

That's not to say nothing positive came out of that 2003 tour. The issues that had exasperated Dream Theater at least provided a fertile ground for writing lyrics, with one track in particular, "As I Am", making numerous references to the behind-the-scenes difficulties.

"Those lyrics were directly inspired by some of the mumblings going on backstage on that tour with Queensrÿche," reveals Mike. "And especially their new guitar player Mike Stone. He would make comments like those [referring to Tate's *Classic Rock* interview]. He would be giving John Petrucci tips. This is coming from a hired gun who hasn't done anything in his career, and he's giving *John* tips? I find that to be the most insulting thing I've ever heard of. I wouldn't say it was insulting if it was somebody that was doing it nicely, but he was doing it very pompously. And it's like '*Hello?* You're telling John how to bend a note? Give me a break'."

In lyrics written by John Petrucci – such as, "*Lost in a sea of mediocrity / Slow down / You're thinking too much / Where is your soul? / You cannot touch the way I play / Or tell me what to say*" – the motives behind sentiments are clear when placed in the context of those irksome series of shows.

John Petrucci was, however, more diplomatic in a fanzine interview of the period: "Although that song is coming from my perspective, it really is the band speaking. In our whole career we have been known for doing our own style, not really going with the trend and a lot of times going against it. We sort of stick out, and I think that is what people appreciate who are into the band. There are so many people telling us, 'You should write shorter songs', or 'Nobody does this anymore', 'This is too Disney', 'This is too heavy', blah, blah, blah. We just do what we naturally creatively want to do. A lot of people accept that and some criticize. So that is basically what that song is saying. We are not going to change for people that try to mould us into a formula. We are just doing what we do, and hopefully people appreciate it. It's also for the fans that always stick by us, because it says: '*For those who understand, I extend my hand.*' So it's like paying homage to our fans as well."

Resisting the temptation to perform any of their fresh and incomplete material during that tour, the band were also deliberately trying to conceal the forthcoming album's direction. This decision was influenced by the endless and often misleading online debating by their fans that had occurred prior to both their previous releases.

"We are purposely keeping our ideas from the fans," said Mike. "In the age of the Internet, you have weeks on end of people taking the slightest piece of information, and dissecting it, and that leaves no room for the imagination once the record comes out. I don't want to give preconceived thoughts and put them into people's heads. I want them to listen to it with fresh ears and an open mind without someone else's opinion swaying them."

Returning home after those summer dates, Dream Theater returned to the studio to add vocals to the material. The idea was to finish the album quickly in order that it could be released before the end of 2003, as a tour had already been booked for early the following year. The experience of performing *Six Degrees Of Inner Turbulence* so soon after its release, to bemused audiences who hadn't had a chance to digest it, had spurred them to allow a decent gap between the new release and the start of the tour. The band also sought out the mixing expertise of Kevin Shirley, requesting he tweaked their sound to match the heaviness of the material, citing the likes of Mudvayne and Metallica as inspirations for the approach.

"John Petrucci came in when they were recording and said they wanted to sound more like Metallica," recalls Shirley. "So I took a different approach to mixing that album. In fact, it was pretty complicated to mix to get it to sound like it did, but I thought it came out great. I also think that Petrucci needed to get that done. Mike wants to keep the prog thing going, whereas John wants to keep the metal thing going."

The mixes were completed towards the end of September at The Hit Factory in New York, leaving the band the minor task of choosing a title for the release. In view of the forceful nature of the music, Mike felt that *Train Of Thought* was apt, saying: "It just seemed totally fitting, given the power and aggression of the music. It felt like a steamroller

– like a train just running you over – and that is what Dream Theater has always been about."

The album's cover was also strikingly shadowy in an attempt to match the bleak musical feel. With surreal black-and-white photos of eyes semi-submerged in the soil, a man with a tree growing where his head should be and other peculiar images, the visuals certainly were appropriate. The photographer/artist in question was Jerry Uelsmann.

"I pictured the sleeve for this record in black-and-white, with the aspect on the lack of colour because the musical direction was so dark," said Mike. "Then a fan actually e-mailed me this artist's website, I followed the link and I was like 'Holy shit, this is intense stuff!' It turns out that Jerry Uelsmann is an old guy who has been around since the Sixties. It had just the look that I had in mind for the album, and the tone was perfect. So I had the art directors at Elektra investigate the possibilities of working with him but he had retired and didn't produce any new work. But we were able to use his gallery work, and went through hundreds of photos and found some that tied in with the lyrics."

Train Of Thought was released on November 11, 2003, to a chorus of mixed reviews from the Dream Theater fan base. Many found the uncompromising heaviness of the album suffocating, and lamented the loss of the musical light and shade that had always balanced previous albums. And if truth be told, they had a point. Dream Theater had always provided a mix of melodic, progressive and metal influences in creating their sound, but on the surface at least, two key elements from that mix were missing. Consequently, only lovers of the more traditional and clattering virtues of metal were unwavering in their acclaim of *Train Of Thought*. But taken in the context of the band's desire to write and record a classic heavy metal album, they certainly came close. Whether it can be regarded as a classic Dream Theater album is more open to question.

The opening track "As I Am" introduces the direction with a barrage of feedback and jarring riffs, and perfectly sets the tone for the remainder of the album. The tempo is matched by "This Dying Soul", which lyrically (and to some degree musically) is a continuation of "The Glass Prison" from *Six Degrees*. Returning to the subject of alcohol abuse, it contains parts four and five of the twelve steps of the Alcoholics Anonymous recovery programme.

"Endless Sacrifice" is another extended track, to do with the subject of dealing with problems caused by prolonged periods of being on the road, with John Petrucci adding: "It's not something that was written about for the first time, as it's a common topic amongst anyone who travels or is away. Whether you're in a band or in the military, it is being away and longing for your spouse or children. On both sides there is a sacrifice. Your family makes a sacrifice so that you are able to do what you do. In my case it's being away on tour, and that's a very intense feeling."

The harshest lyric was penned by Mike on "Honor Thy Father", which he has regularly described as a "hate song directed towards my stepfather." Indeed, it's rumoured that Mike sent his stepfather a copy of the completed song, though whether it was listened to remains a mystery. One can only speculate on the reasons behind such lines as, "*You'll go to your grave a sad and lonely man*", and, "*You're the rotted root in the family tree*", but the fact that Mike was unceremoniously thrown out of the family home by his stepfather on his return from Berklee appears to have been the source of the problems. Although the pair have reconciled following the release of the album, Mike was scathing in an interview of the time.

"I want to make it clear that this isn't for my real father, Howard Portnoy, with whom I have an amazing relationship," said Mike. "He has been so close to me all my life and I love him dearly. My only concern was that people would misread the lyrics and think it was directed at him. That's why I put the lines: "*Don't cross the crooked step,*" and "*You pretended I was your own / And even believed that you loved me / But were always threatened by some invisible bloodline that only you could see.*" There are very few people that I'm angry with or hold a grudge against but he's one of the few. It was also very therapeutic to write those lyrics because I don't know if I'm ever going to meet him or deal with him again. It was my way of getting all the crap off my chest and to finally close this chapter of my life, whether he hears it or not. Knowing him and how selfish he is and unaware of anybody else in this family, he probably won't even know that this song is directed at him."

"Vacant" provides a fleeting interruption from the jarring guitar and keyboards, and is a relatively tender ballad, with the inclusion of a cello enhancing the sound before the instrumental "Stream Of Consciousness" jolts the album back on track. Arguably five minutes longer than necessary, it is a decent but ultimately one-dimensional piece that fails to match previous instrumental excursions such as "Ytse Jam" or "Overture 1928".

The album closes with "In The Name Of God", which deals with the thorny subject of religion and whether the various leaders of the faiths are guilty of encouraging or even promoting violence.

"I look at the cults that have popped up in the past years and there are a lot of extreme fundamentalist leaders that somehow convince people to follow them, and in the process they also convince them to do violent acts," said John Petrucci. "They say that it's in the name of God, and if you do this you'll be saved. It's a kind of backward way of thinking, twisting the fate of religion in order to achieve a violent end.

These people have done mass suicides, killed individuals and groups of people."

John Petrucci's lyrics had, on recent albums, also tended to venture into the political arena and away from some of the more sci-fi story-telling that were the subjects of his earlier efforts.

"Yeah, they have taken a political turn," he said. "The ironic thing is that when I was younger, I was really into U2. One of the things that used to turn me off them was when they were getting all political and it used to drive me crazy, but now I kind of get it. I see what they mean, and see how there are times when music is a place to bring up those types of things. Some of the things that I have talked about to do with religion and moral issues are a bit deep for a normal rock 'n' roll song, but then we're not a normal rock 'n' roll band, so I think it kind of fits."

Although Dream Theater's lyrics have dabbled in politics, the band are always extremely conscious of not overly inflicting their own views on the listener. The lyrics are merely food for thought, as James explained in an interview with *www.revaltionz.net*.

"Well, I don't think that we are standing up there with a certain flag or a certain political party saying this is what we support and this is what you should think," he said. "It's a lot less in the preaching sense. I think politically what we touch is our viewing of the situation, our interpretation of what's going on around us and it's not necessarily what we feel that everybody else should feel. It's just an interpretation of what we see going on around us in the world, and the world is in a very peculiar situation right now and has been for quite some time, terrorists and all. But when you really think about where this all stems from? It stems from religion and it stems from beliefs."

The lukewarm reception to *Train Of Thought* from many of the band's fans was something that they were anticipating, with Mike saying: "A lot of fans are going to be caught off guard by it, so I think it will take time for everyone to digest it. But as time goes on, people will begin to love it more and more. It's impossible to digest in one sit-ting. I've seen a lot of people saying, 'I've listened to it once. It is crap, and I can't listen to it again.' It's their loss."

"Music is very subjective, and you're not going to please everyone," added James. "Especially when you put out an album like this – you're bound to have a lot of controversy within the fan base. That first hit of the heaviness of it is what people are going to focus on. And then they're going to go: 'OK, this is very different from the band that I'm really into'. But it's a matter of coming to it, taking it for what it is rather than just saying, 'Uh oh, this isn't for me'."

Ironically, the press appraisal of the album was far more positive, and gathered virtually unanimously upbeat reviews. *Q* magazine wrote: "The Mars Volta are not the only geeks keeping progressive rock alive… These music college graduates love to show off with tricky time changes and fiddly-diddly solos, but they out-gun Metallica on 'As I Am', and on 'This Dying Soul' they sound like Tool jamming with Eddie Van Halen. And you don't hear that everyday."

Michael Deeds of *The Washington Post* was equally stirred, claiming: "Crushingly heavy and staggeringly complex, *Train Of Thought* will make headbangers lie down on the tracks and sacrifice themselves to the gods of metal. This is the Dream Theater we've dreamed of. This is the classic metal album that no classic metal band could ever pull off. Wear earplugs if you must, but the rest of us will go deaf in bliss." *Classic Rock*'s Malcolm Dome wrote: "Dream Theater have made a record that should finally flush away their 'stodgy' reputation. At a time when Queensrÿche seem to be floundering and Fates Warning have stagnated, Dream Theater must surely be the undisputed masters of heavy prog."

The first leg of the *Train Of Thought* Tour began in Manchester, England, on January 16, 2004, with stints in North America soon following. Reviews of the shows were in the main positive, with *Classic Rock*'s review of the London Hammersmith Apollo gig enthusing: "No band has the right to sound quite as seamlessly tight – a feat rendered all the more incredible considering they repeated only about half of the material played 24 hours earlier in Manchester." Even the often lukewarm *Kerrang!* raved: "Clearly Dream Theater have only gotten better at fusing their technical prowess with irrepressible catchiness. It almost excuses Mike Portnoy's massive three-bass-drum-and-giant-gong-kit from ridicule. Okay, maybe not. But judging from the fanatical cheers bouncing off the stage, no-one seemed to mind."

The band had something special lined up for their gig at The Pantages in Los Angeles on March 6. Ever since the release of *When Dream And Day Unite*, the band and fans had wanted to hear a re-recorded version which would eliminate some of the audio deficiencies of the original. Such a project would also allow James to put his vocals on the recording, but with the band having no rights to that recording following the split from Mechanic Records, it seemed an unlikely proposition. But Mike had realized that they could record a live version of that album, and he had set aside the date of the Los Angeles gig as the perfect opportunity – given that it was the 15th anniversary of the original release.

"I even said to the guys, and to our manager and booking agent 'I don't know where we're gonna be, but I'll tell you that on March 6, 2004, this is what we're doing!'" said Mike. "And we kept it completely under cover. We didn't want to announce it, we didn't want to promote it as we wanted it to be a complete surprise. I even mentioned to our manager and to our booking agent to try to put us some place cool on

March 6, and it worked out good that it happened to be in LA, and it happened to be in such a beautiful venue. It was totally great and it was exactly the special evening I hoped it would be. Doing *When Dream And Day Unite* has been something that the fans have been wanting for a decade now."

The event was enhanced by the appearance onstage of former members Charlie Dominici and Derek Sherinian – with the singer performing on both "To Live Forever" and "Metropolis" and Sherinian enjoying a keyboard dual with Jordan Rudess on the latter. Kevin Moore was also invited to perform, with the band even offering to meet his air fare from Istanbul, but he declined. Certainly Moore's reluctance to become involved in anything Dream Theater-related following his departure appears, to the outsider at least, both stubborn and odd.

"Well, Kevin's a bit odd," jokes Mike. "I think musically he doesn't want to be associated because he's in such a different place. If you listen to his new Chroma Key album there's nothing on there that has anything to do with playing progressive music. It's all soundscapes and soundtrack-type ambience. So musically he just wants to make his own statement in a whole different genre, and has no interest in playing keyboards in a progressive metal band. I did extend the invite for him to join us in LA for the 15th Anniversary *When Dream And Day Unite* gig, but in retrospect I can't picture him up there playing 'Metropolis' with us. I mean, I don't know if he could or whether his fingers can even move like they used to ten years ago. But I don't think he would even have any interest in it, being up on stage with us playing 'Metropolis' or 'Learning To Live'. That's just not where he's at. So I think that was the musical reason why he wants to be detached from us. And then there's the personal reason. I think he just wasn't interested in the fame and the glory. He had a taste of it when the *Images And Words* album broke, but that was enough for him to want to escape it. I just can't picture him wanting to go back in and be put back in the spotlight like he would be if he was ever to do anything with us again."

One unpleasant incident occurred in St Louis on March 17 during a gig at the Pageant Theater. As always, Mike was going through his routine at the end of the set by throwing drumsticks and drumheads into the crowd, as Rikk Feulner explains.

"Mike would always go out and throw them to the crowd at the end of a show," says Rikk. "If there was a balcony, he would go and throw one to the crowd and then one into the balcony, really trying to please everybody. Anyway the drumstick fell short of the balcony, a guy reached for it, came tumbling over and landed on someone. It was literally in slow motion and like something out of a movie. You saw the guy's arms and legs flailing away in the air. The person he fell on got hurt you know, because the guy was like 200 pounds and came crashing out of the air on to him which he wasn't expecting. The guy that fell didn't get hurt at all. I guess he was drunk and just ran out of the door. He was probably afraid he would get in trouble for hurting the guy he landed on. I mean he could probably have been arrested for assault."

"Of course, we got paramedics and tried to get the guy to hospital to get checked out, but he refused to go. So we brought him backstage and ice-packed his head and there was a nurse talking to him to make sure he didn't have concussion. And of course all the band members came out and said 'Hi' to him and made sure he was safe. The first thing I was thinking was, 'Oh God, we're going to get sued.' I wasn't even thinking that the guy was hurt, I was just thinking we were going to get sued. Which is really rotten, but unfortunately with the job I have, those are the type of things I have to think about."

Consequently, Mike has now stopped throwing either drum heads or sticks into the crowd. By April 2004, the tour had reached the Far East, passing through cities such as Nagoya and Osaka in Japan, before the undoubted highlight of the leg – a gig at The Nippon Budokan Hall in Tokyo. With such artists as Ozzy Osbourne, Cheap Trick and Bob Dylan all recording live albums at the prestigious venue, Dream Theater didn't pass up the opportunity to join that select list of acts, with the concert being filmed and recorded for a DVD and CD release. Typically, though, despite all their meticulous planning to ensure everything ran smoothly, Jordan realized seconds after setting foot on stage that there was a major problem with his keyboards.

"Yeah, that was really upsetting," sighs Jordan at the memory. "I walked out on stage and looked at my keyboards and went, 'Oh, my God!' My set is so programmed as I do things in a certain way. When I walk on stage, I expect to be able to step through the sounds. So I'll go from sound number one, and the last sound three hours later is like number 200. Playing on the one keyboard it basically cycles me and gives me cues. It'll say something like, 'Verse two times' or 'F♯ repeat three times'. So I go from these cues so I know where to put my hands on the keyboard, and I depend on them. So as I went on stage I saw a completely different set loaded in and for the first couple of minutes I wasn't actually playing anything – although of course I went back later and fixed it. But at the time, I just kept my hand on the keyboards pretending to play and then when the camera didn't seem to be on me I just hit the reload button on the machine. The problem was that it reloaded and about halfway through 'As I Am' the sounds came back in but then there were maybe four or five places during the night where I had a really fucked-up sound that wasn't right. And visually of course you can't tell there was ever a problem, which is the beauty of it. But it was upsetting for everybody and my tech at the time was really upset about that, but what can you do? Stuff happens and I was in shock."

As Jordan notes, it is virtually impossible to notice on footage of that night that he was suffering from such a catastrophic failure of his keyboard. Admittedly his eyes do have a look of mild terror when caught on camera during the opening bars, but apart from that, his miming worked. As Jordan explains, it certainly wasn't the first time that he had faced a critical onstage problem.

"I had this guy who was a crew member out of Texas and he was just with us for one tour," smiles Jordan. "We were about to play a big show in Italy and he came backstage to see me about ten minutes before the show and said, 'Jordan I'm having a bit of trouble getting one of your instruments to make a sound. I've been through your checklist but I just can't seem to get it to work'. So I just told him to get out there and make sure he went through the checklist again. Anyway, he came back again – by which time it's about five minutes before the show – and said 'I've been through it and it still won't make a sound. You're going to have to come out and check it out.' So this was *bad*. There were 12,000 people out there but I had no choice, and I had to go out before the show and do it. So I put a hat and hood on to try and disguise myself, walked out and went over to my keyboards. I could see the other guys at the side of the stage waiting to come on, and I looked down and realized the guy hadn't turned up the volume knob on one of my racks. So I just thought to myself, 'Oh my God, this guy is so fired!' He made me walk onstage in front of 12,000 people and he didn't check the volume knob!"

Following a handful of Italian dates in July, the band were offered the support slot on the North American tour of prog legends Yes. As Mike noted prior to the tour in an interview with the Man Room website, "We're excited about it. They are one of our all-time favourite bands and biggest influences. To us, it's an honour to be on the same stage as them. They are one of the few bands that we thought we could have a great touring package with. I think for the Yes fans, they're probably going to have heart attacks once we hit the stage. They won't know what hit them. So we're going to have to tone down our set a little bit to make sure we don't offend any of the older Yes fans."

In view of this, the set list was carefully selected by Mike to ensure its suitability. Therefore, the likes of "Solitary Shell", "The Spirit Carries On" and the progressive "Trial Of Tears" and "Stream Of Consciousness" were selected. The band also cheekily threw in an edited version of the underrated Yes piece "Machine Messiah".

"We're a very heavy band, but our catalogue of music is more varied than some critics might suggest, and Mike has put together a set list that Yes fans should enjoy," said Jordan. "That said, a couple of our harder-edged moments might terrify some of their fans. So apologies in advance – we can't help it!"

The reception from the Yes fans was in the main positive, although there were of course a few purists who were harder to please. But as James noted in an interview with *Hardradio.com*, that tour enhanced their reputation no end.

"A lot of these Yes fans were like, 'Oh my God, I'm going out to buy your stuff, I can't believe it'," he said. "We were thinking to ourselves, 'Wait a minute, you are into this kind of music?' But Yes are more of the light, classical approach progressively, whereas we're taking a much harder, edgier approach to the progressive elements. But it was incredible because we were out with a band that has been noted for its progressive brilliance, and here we were playing in front of people that were going, 'I've never heard you guys before.' In fact, a lot of them were saying, 'Oh, so you're just a new band and you came out a couple of years ago?' I kid you not." Equally important was the fact that Yes were also highly complimentary of the opening act, and on the final night of the tour (Monterrey, Mexico, September 22) their drummer Alan White joined Mike at the kit during "Machine Messiah".

James: "Jon Anderson also came in one night because he listened to most of the set. He said, 'Wow, I love you guys. It's really great to see a contemporary band like yourselves doing this kind of music, and doing it well.' That's a great compliment, coming from him."

In early October 2004, the band's *Live At Budokan* DVD (with a separate triple-CD release of the audio track) was released. Beautifully shot, the DVD captured the band as never before, and prompted positive press appraisals, with *Classic Rock*'s Jon Hotten noting: "It's immaculately performed with points docked merely for listing one section as an 'Instrumedley'. Just stop it!" Even the sometimes-cold *Kerrang!* ceded: "With jaw-dropping musicianship and vice-tight performances, Dream Theater could have recorded this in the studio… Will they ever hit a bum note? No."

The CD release was also welcomed by the critics, with *Record Collector* magazine's Tim Jones claiming that, "If you've got an ounce of musical nous, you can't fail to be impressed by the players' sheer virtuosity, stagecraft and showmanship. Stunning."

With that release and the Yes tour completed, the band managed to squeeze a couple of months' break into their schedule, before the studio beckoned once again.

FIFTEEN

FULL CIRCLE

Tucked away in Hell's Kitchen, New York City, the Hit Factory Studios were the location for both the writing and recording sessions of Dream Theater's eighth album, *Octavarium*, which began in November 2004. The studios had been in operation since 1975, with an extensive list of former occupants, all of whom had their gold and platinum records bedecking the walls in the reception and studio corridors. Michael Jackson, Bruce Springsteen, Madonna, Britney Spears, U2, Mariah Carey and John Lennon had all recorded here, and with the studios earmarked for closure, Dream Theater had the honour of being the last band to inhabit them before the doors permanently closed. For the most part, the band had been holed up in Studio Six, with such a range of keyboards, guitars and drums cramming every nook and cranny of the floor that it resembled the stockroom of an instrument store. Once again, the band had already decided on a concrete direction before they reconvened, and having previously recorded what they deemed to be a classic concept album in *Scenes From A Memory*, and definitive metal album in *Train Of Thought*, the band wanted to return to their roots in order to create what they hoped would be a "classic" Dream Theater album.

"Exactly – that was the idea," confirms Jordan. "It was a case of really going back to creating a real band effort, as well as drawing upon all our various stylistic influences. As usual, there were a lot of talks about the direction of the album and about what we wanted to create. I mean, I've yet to work with the guys when there aren't a lot of conceptual ideas floating around before the album is even composed. Partly, we wanted to rein in the style to make it less complex for people. Basically something that people could latch on to faster and, as a result, part of the album is like that. There are songs that are quicker to appreciate, but then there's also the title track, which I love the most, which takes a little time. So I think on this album we achieved a very nice balance. There are shorter songs that could be on the radio yet they still maintain a Dream Theater flair. It really was the perfect kind of Dream Theater offering."

That's not to say the band had made a calculated attempt to craft a more commercial album. They had merely sought to create tracks that covered a variety of approaches and songs of varying lengths. Consequently, shorter material such as "These Walls" or "I Walk Beside You" were probably the most accessible material they had written since the days of *Falling Into Infinity*, but the title track extended to a mighty

24 minutes and palpably dispelled any suggestions that the band were selling out.

"Most people think when they hear something like 'I Walk Beside You' that we are trying to write a single," says Mike. "But we write songs like that because we have that side to us. We love bands like U2 or Coldplay, as well as liking shorter songs. In fact, those shorter songs on *Octavarium* – 'I Walk Beside You', 'The Answer Lies Within' or 'These Walls' – were literally written as a challenge. We had been writing such long songs on *Train Of Thought* and *Six Degrees* and it had been a while since we had written shorter songs. Plus, *Train Of Thought* was so long and heavy. I mean, writing long songs is easy for us – it's the short ones that are difficult. But it wasn't like we were trying to reach for a radio hit as we knew that the label wouldn't have done crap with it anyway. If there was a hit single then great – it would just have been a bonus."

John Petrucci: "We wanted this album to be a collection of all the many different styles and sides to Dream Theater. We wanted to make sure there were progressive elements as well as some of the heavier influences from the previous album. I think in general the feeling was that we wanted the songs to be very strong. When we were writing, we actually stripped the sound down and sat there with piano, guitar and vocal to make sure that the melodies and structures were interesting to us and sounded original. So that was a real focus."

Jordan was also relishing the prospect of becoming more involved with the construction of *Octavarium*, with there being far more scope for his input when contrasted with the narrow, guitar-driven direction of its predecessor.

"It was more of a controlled scenario where we had headphones and more limited in-room volume," smiles Jordan. "Although with the drums in the room it's not exactly *quiet*, but it's definitely controlled. It was far more conducive to this kind of album and what we were trying to do. Plus now, I walk into the studio and just start writing fresh with the rest of the guys, which they like anyway. Mike especially likes the idea that we are all writing together. The reality is that ideas have to come from someone's head and the best thing is to have a little bit of space to do it. And even when we are writing together it's kind of like 'Hey guys, shut up for a second so I can develop this idea and then I'll show you what I'm thinking!'"

Another notable facet of those sessions was the relative absence of any nagging internal tension, with the band appearing to have reached a point in their career where they are comfortable with each other's foibles – a fact that is not lost on James LaBrie.

"The thing about this band is that we just get better because we've learnt how to work with one another, and can almost read each other's minds," says James. "We have a common goal and know how to get there quicker. It's just going to get better, even though most of us have been together for 15 years and some of us for 20 years. So I think that this is the healthiest we have ever been."

Jordan: "There are moments of tension here and there, but it has really been quite balanced. Since I joined the group it's been a very good ride and that's what enables us to keep going. Everybody gets along. I know as much as John and Mike enjoy working together, and have a lot in common, there has been tension between them that comes up now and then, but they work through it. So there's definitely that ability but I'm not highly strung like that. If something comes up, I'll work it out quickly and we'll move along."

For the band, there was the additional prospect of realizing one of their long-held ambitions – that of working with an orchestra. Of course, tracks such as "Overture" on *Six Degrees* had their orchestral moments, but those had been created through shred programming one of Jordan's keyboards. But for this album's title track, the equally complex "Sacrificed Sons", and "The Answer Lies Within", the band had arranged for a 16-piece orchestra to add lush passages in order to enhance and flesh out the sound. Consequently, on the afternoon of February 16, 2005, the Hit Factory's vast oak-panelled elevator was packed with classical musicians and their instruments, all making their way to Studio One on the building's top floor. Perched behind the mixing desk behind the mirrored glass that separated the control room from the studio floor, Mike, John, and the ever-present Doug Oberkircher were once again producing and directing activities. Probably the most impressive aspect of that session was the fact that the orchestra seemed to float in, set up and nail music they'd never seen or played before in a maximum of two takes. As conductor Jamshied Sharifi explains, that ability for the musicians to create rapid perfection was one of the criteria they had to meet to ensure their participation.

"They are all selected because of their sight-reading ability, and their job is to get into the new music as quickly as possible and to try and understand what the music is trying to say," explains Jamshied. "I guess I take it for granted as I live in New York City, and there are only a few places in the world that have that. It is one thing to be able to play your instrument but it is a whole other thing to be able to make music on a piece you'd never heard until that day. There are a group of people that we use, many of whom are from the Metropolitan orchestra in New York, but they tend to be the younger players and those who are a little more aware of pop music and non-classical music. So I have worked with them before, though the exact personnel changes with each session depends on availability. They are basically professional studio musicians, but they are pretty carefully picked to ensure they are flexible and good team players."

"One of the things that make a session work well is the source material itself. In other words, what is the music, who are the artists and what are we actually working on? When it's good, the players feel that quality, feel there is a reason to be there and they are that much more inspired. And talking to the players afterwards, they all had a great time on that session. They liked the music and loved the guys. They just thought it was a great project, and I can tell you that is not always the case. There have been plenty of sessions where it was like punching the clock. Let's just say that there is a lot of music out there that doesn't have as strong a reason to exist as Dream Theater's."

Jamshied had become involved after being contacted by orchestral contractor, Jill Dell Abate, whom the band had approached to enlist suitable players and ensure the smooth running of the session.

"I talked with John and he outlined what they were planning to do," says Jamshied. "So I then went to meet with John and Mike, and as I was talking to them I realized they looked somewhat familiar. So I was like 'Do we know each other from somewhere?' We compared dates and finally figured out that we had been at Berklee at the same time. I mean Berklee is a big enough school, so although we never crossed paths formally, we must have passed each other in the hall. Jordan and I knew each other from way back as we had both been involved with Kurzweil."

Although James missed out on watching the spectacle of the full orchestra and string quartet in full flow – he was ensconced in the confines of the vocal booth in the studio a few floors below – he was still enthusing about the album's direction. Critically, his passion for *Octavarium* was genuine and not just spouting the usual unjustified, this-is-our-greatest-album-ever hype that most rock stars bestow on an upcoming release.

"I'm really excited about this album as much as I was with *Scenes From A Memory*," he beamed. "When I listen to it from beginning to end, it's full of the things that have brought Dream Theater to what we are and how people interpret or misinterpret us. They think that we are all about the progressive and nothing else but there's much more to us than that alone. The album is very well arranged, written and structured. There is an incredible sound, feel and atmosphere to it. I truly think it's great."

James had a valid point. *Octavarium* was one of their most complete albums, and the balance of material mirrored that of *Images And Words*. The album opener "The Root Of All Evil'" contained parts six and seven of Mike's Alcoholics Anonymous saga, and was in many ways an archetypal Dream Theater track, tidily mixing heavy riffs with some progressive moments. Both "The Answer Lies Within" and "I Walk Beside You" were inherently catchy and perfectly suited to radio play – even if such a prospect was an extremely remote one.

Of all the tracks, the lyrics to "Never Enough" were the most contentious. Written by Mike, they were a direct attack on the small element within the band's fan base who – in spite of his extreme work ethic – still bleated that he could do more. With lines such as *"Neglect my wife and kids / All for you to be happy / And then you say how dare that / I didn't write you back,"* the target for his rancour was made abundantly clear.

"To me, one of the most frustrating things about the internet is all the whining, bitching, complaining and dissecting that our fans do over every single thing," said Mike in an interview in *Brave Words & Bloody Knuckles* magazine. I appreciate all their love and devotion... but it's very frustrating for me personally because I'm constantly tearing myself away from my family to give more and more to the fans. It's very discouraging when you see the fans complaining that they came to a show and didn't hear 'Pull Me Under'. Meanwhile, I've spent countless nights trying to write some special set lists for them, and the band has spent day after day rehearsing all this material in order to be able to deliver different three-hour sets from night to night. It's discouraging and makes me crazy sometimes."

"Sacrificed Sons" was also a tricky lyric, and dealt with the events of 9/11. The danger of such a topic is that it could become over-politicized, mawkish, insensitive or even sanctimonious. And although there are the odd awkward, lyrical moments, the band just about carry it off. But for many, the epic title track remains the album's centrepiece and highlight. Deliberately recreating the progressive rock sound of classic Genesis, Yes and even Pink Floyd, it's a complex but thrilling piece.

"We wanted to write an epic type of song that thematically developed where we could use an orchestra," explains John Petrucci. "So we had a concept of what was going on and where we wanted to take it. We wanted it to have a real prog treatment, and that changes the way you orchestrate it and the types of parts you come up with. But once those initial guidelines or seeds are planted, we sit down and write a million ideas, and we then try to sift through them and make sense of it to create something. The cool thing is that Jordan has all those major influences. He's into prog bands that nobody else has even heard of, and knows that stuff like the back of his hand. So he can pull out those concepts and ideas. It's not like he's imitating – it's just part of his style."

"I can only really talk about it from a musical point of view, as I didn't write any of the lyrics and I don't really listen to the words," adds Jordan. "But we were really trying to get the more classic prog feel to the track. We were looking for that ultimate Yes or Genesis influence, so I was digging back into my progressive roots and thinking about some of the things that got me going. It also came about in an interesting way. When we were writing some of the beginning parts, I remember we were in the studio and talking about what it was that made some of the old Genesis stuff so special. I was thinking early Genesis in that section, and that got created on my big modular synthesizer which was pretty fun. I had just got my modular synthesizer, and it's a big thing with all kind of knobs and stuff!"

"Anyway, we were saying that some of the chords were melodic but a little bit strange at the same time," continues Jordan. "I can remember that day in the studio when John Petrucci and I were really going for it and trying to get the *magic* chords. I'd come up with one, then he would come up with another, and it was going back and forth. And Mike would be saying, 'No, that's not special enough', so when we landed on it, we would all do a little dance! And I'd be writing it down, John would be memorizing it, and Mike would be thinking about the architecture of the whole song."

The finished piece certainly contained a vast array of melodies and a fair few blatant nods to some of the band's musical heroes. The introduction – played by Jordan on a lap steel guitar and his new continuum – bore more than a passing resemblance to Pink Floyd's "Shine On You Crazy Diamond", and if you listen carefully there's also a snatch of Queen's "Bohemian Rhapsody" as well as countless other less obvious references. Lyrically, the track also paid homage to the work of the prog rock greats, and there are so many subtle name-checks that a whole chapter of this book could be devoted to them. These ranged from the spoken sentence "Isn't this where we came in", that corresponds to the same words at the beginning and finale of Pink Floyd's *The Wall* through the use of various prog song titles – such as "Supper's Ready" by Genesis or the Floyd's "Careful With That Axe Eugene".

But there was also a bigger and less obvious plan that Mike had constructed, as he noted in an interview with *Musicplayers.com*: "Each song is written in ascending chromatic key. When the process started, I had an idea that I brought to the guys that this is our eighth studio album and I noted that we've put out five live albums in between. If you look at a keyboard octave, you have eight notes leading from A to A, and then the five black notes, the incidentals, in between. So I looked at our album structure kind of the same way."

This is our eighth studio album, an octave, we have five other live albums so here we are with 13 steps, you know, just like an octave. So I presented the idea of 'Let's write out the entire album based on the concept of a musical octave.'"

"So we started writing the songs and we specifically delegated songs for a different key. We started with 'Sacrificed Sons', which was in

E, then we started 'Never Enough' which was in D, then we started building up 'These Walls' in A. We then started delegating different songs to different keys, and then we put these little sound effects in the album to go in between. So when you go from an F to a G – which is 'The Root Of All Evil' to 'The Answer Lies Within' – there is a little sound effect that connects those two songs which is in the key of F♯. Basically, it was this grand concept that I brought to the band. Musically it's an octave, production-wise it's an octave in terms of those little sound effects, segues and lyrics. So a lot of the lyrics, like the title 'The Root Of All Evil', it's the root of the octave. 'Octavarium' is the octave of the octave."

The album also began with the final, dying notes from their previous album, *Train Of Thought*, which in turn had commenced with the final note from *Six Degrees*, which – you guessed it – started with the noise at the end of *Scenes From A Memory*.

"When we were making *Six Degrees* it was an idea I had because there was a Van Halen album, *Women And Children First* which ended with them starting a riff and then fading out," explained Mike. "I was always thinking, 'Wow, when the next album comes out, sure enough it's going to start with that ending riff'. But they never did it and they never took advantage of that. So I thought it was a cool idea to link together albums, and we started that with *Six Degrees*. I had the idea to start it out with the static from the end of *Scenes From A Memory* and then the beginning of *Train Of Thought* begins with the end of *Six Degrees*, and so on and so forth. I thought it was a cool idea but now I've dug a hole where we're expected to do it every time, so I solved that with *Octavarium* because the end of [the final track] "Octavarium" ends with the beginning of [the album] *Octavarium*. So now this album will be a cycle within itself, and we can walk away and have a fresh start with the next album."

On this and many prior releases, there had been an absence of lyrics penned by either Jordan or John Myung. In fact, the keyboardist has never written lyrics for the band and John Myung – whom many believe to have a knack for writing thoughtful lines – hadn't contributed since penning the words for "Fatal Tragedy" several years earlier. From the band's point of view, they were seemingly ready to accept Myung's input if he brought completed songs into the studio. However in the past, these have taken time to mould from the poem form (as John presented them) into a format that would match the song. As a consequence, his submissions dried up.

"But lyric writing is rewarding," says Myung. "It basically comes down to your daily life and my life has changed a lot. It is really hard to justify why you're not doing something because someone else is going through the exact same thing. But I do like writing lyrics. Maybe that is something I can get back into. I am open to it but that is not to say I'll do it. In a way I feel like there's still a lot more for me to do in that area."

Jordan also admits to a reticence to spending time writing lyrics saying, "On my first solo album *Listen*, I sang and wrote the lyrics on all the songs. So I do like to do that. On one hand I felt that my role in Dream Theater was large in that there is a lot to do in the keyboards. There are a lot of parts and sounds, and I felt comfortable with what I was doing. But on the other hand, I feel like the band is very established in certain ways and in order for me to write lyrics, I would almost have to step into the middle of something. If I presented lyrics, I feel like they would probably be analyzed to death before they would be accepted because they would be coming from a new place. There's a big part of me that feels very satisfied being in this group and doing what we do, but also having the ability to make my own albums. If I couldn't do my own solo albums, I would probably go insane. That's not to say that the group doesn't have my full energy and musical support. It's just there are a lot of things that I've done in my musical life, and things that I want to do that Dream Theater's not about."

Responsible for such classic Rush sleeves as *Moving Pictures* and *Hemispheres*, artist Hugh Syme provided the artwork for *Octavarium*. Depicting a huge Newton's cradle, complete with eight suspended balls and five birds to tie in with the album's overriding concept, Syme recalls that he and Mike bounced a number of ideas around before settling for the final design.

"I think the final concept had to do with our discussion to the effect that for everything you do in music you create either a cluster or triad," expands Hugh. "And then it became evident that for every action there is an opposite reaction. So I thought we could do something based on the Newton's cradle. We were looking for a reference point and something that could be used in multiples of eight, so it had to be a fairly long cradle. We played around with a lot of ideas for the cover that ended up inside the booklet. The maze was one, with the octagonal shape and the spider with eight legs, and then there was the octopus. It just became a reservoir of graphic elements to draw on, and we finally hit on the Newton's cradle which became the favourite idea. The other things just kind of fell into place where they seemed to be appropriate, and some of the images were more associated with the lyrics than others."

With everything in the sleeve seemingly having a link to the music, or a convoluted explanation, what was the significance of the girl on the rear sleeve who is bending over to avoid one of the swinging metallic spheres?

"I suppose it was just to make the inertia believable, and for there to be some kind of interaction," says Hugh. "It just makes it a little more urgent and maybe even a bit sexier. But it was more of the fact that it just gave some environment and energy that wouldn't otherwise have been there. Even though there's implied kinetic energy in the movement of the balls, this girl having to do this gesture to get out of the way just emphasized it. The landscape is a hybrid of two things. I actually have a studio in Indiana where I shoot skies because it is unfettered by anything to the horizon, so I shoot skies myself. There's also a hybrid of grass from Indiana and a background from the Lake District in England."

Finally hitting the shelves on June 7, 2005, *Octavarium* was met with a far more enthusiastic reaction from their fans than the rather muted response given to *Train Of Thought*, and the press were also appreciative. *Metal Hammer* writer Dave Ling noted: "They've been called a cross between Metallica and Seventies bands like Yes and Rush, but while 2003's dark and unnervingly claustrophobic *Train Of Thought* took them down the former path, their eighth studio release is lighter and more melodic. Fans can relax, however, as it retains their usual jaw-dropping levels of musicianship. . . 'The Root Of All Evil' and 'Panic Attack' are quintessential Dream Theater, the stopwatch obviously expiring during 'Sacrificed Sons' (10 minutes and 45 seconds) and the 24-minute title track – both of which feature an orchestra. Still setting standards to leave rivals gasping, this is a very special band." *Classic Rock* wrote "This is not an album that will suddenly wake up the wider world to Dream Theater... but followers will sink into its depths as blissfully as they would a hot tub filled with cheerleaders." *Kerrang!* were also unusually positive, claiming: "This is the sound of undisputed champions effortlessly asserting their supremacy."

Octavarium, which sold almost 27,000 copies in the USA in the first week of release, marked their final album on the Atlantic label, bringing to an end a contract that had extended over 14 years. Although for the most part the band had, in recent years at least, been left to their own devices in terms of musical direction, they felt that they weren't being given the promotional support or encouragement from the label moguls that they deserved. This point is emphasized by Frank Solomon when discussing their future options.

"More important than anything is that it's got to be a label that believes in us," says Frank. "It just can't be a case of 'Yeah, we'll take the album, give you X dollars and we know we'll get it back, you'll get this and be happy'. It's just not what it's about. They deserve more, and I don't mean money, but respect. I can't think of another band that has existed twenty years and is still on the upside. What band has been going for twenty years and continues to climb the mountain? There's nobody, and that's just an amazing tribute to them."

Within a few days of the album's release, Dream Theater were already on the road in Europe, criss-crossing the continent in order to promote it. Beginning on June 10, 2005, at the Sweden Rock Festival in Sölvesborg, a further 13 dates followed including an opening slot for Iron Maiden at the mammoth Parc De Princes stadium in Paris. The band then returned to the US to take part in a summer jaunt around North America as part of the so-called "Gigantour". Dream Theater co-headlined those dates with Megadeth – with Fear Factory, Nevermore, Dillinger Escape Plan, Symphony X, Dry Kill Logic and Bobaflex also making appearances through the extensive list of arena dates between July 21 and September 3. Although the atmosphere backstage was healthy and the gigs enjoyable, in financial terms they were far from a success. Only one date (Orlando, Florida) sold out, and a majority of the venues were only half full. Indeed, some of the gigs were barely attended, with the 19,000 capacity Sound Advice Amphitheatre in West Palm Beach, Florida, only attracting 3,500 fans. Seemingly, most Dream Theater fans were content to wait to see the band later in the year, without having to sit through acts they hadn't necessarily heard of, or had the desire to watch.

The main *Octavarium* Tour began at the end of September in Finland, and as had been the case with the *Train Of Thought* trek, the band had decided that the format would again be "An Evening With Dream Theater". Effectively, this meant that there would be no support act, and that the band would be on stage for the best part of three-hours with only a 15-minute interval for them to refresh themselves. When you add on the list of interviews the band undertook, the rehearsing of additional songs during soundcheck, and a meet-and-greet session with fans at the show's conclusion, it was hardly surprising that the band became physically and mentally drained. The set lists were also constantly rotated to ensure that there were few repetitions in their repertoire from the previous time that they had played a city.

"We're fried," said Mike. "I don't know if it's because we're getting older, if it's the material or length of the set. But I swear to God, every night when we end up on the tour bus, we look like we've been through a war. I think people look at what we do every night and think we're only doing three hours. But you have to remember that because of the rotating set lists we have to rehearse every day. We sometimes have to learn things for upcoming shows and may have been playing for an hour and a half at soundcheck. Then we have to put in at least an hour or so after the show with the meet-and-greets. So it's demanding, and we're putting in major hours for the fans. We could easily play the same set every night but we're out here to give the fans their money's worth."

Jordan: "Mike does it to himself. He's such a madman. He wants to play these long sets and then it's so tiring. I actually heard a hint the other day that maybe we would shorten things a little bit and I was like

'Thank you!' This man is finally coming to reason. I've always been of the thinking that it's too much for the audience as well – or maybe I'm just getting old. I don't know. I know there are fans out there that want more and more songs, but when you're presenting music at that kind of intensity and volume, I think it gets to be too much after a couple of hours."

The band continued their tradition of covering a classic album in its entirety whenever they perform a two-night stand in a city. This time, both Amsterdam [October 11] and London [October 25] bene-fited from a full rendition of Pink Floyd's *The Dark Side Of The Moon*. This had long been on Mike's list of albums he had always wanted the band to cover, describing it as "inevitable" that they would cover a Floyd album at some stage in their career.

"To be honest, my favourite Pink Floyd album is *The Wall*," revealed Mike prior to the London show. "In fact, *The Wall* is probably my favourite album of all time. So I thought about us doing that album for a while, and just listened to it for the first time in years. But it's such an exhausting experience and it would have been a major under-taking – not just for us but for the audience – to endure. So it became obvious that *Dark Side Of The Moon* was the right choice. But it's actu-ally amazing how many Dream Theater fans aren't Pink Floyd fanatics like we are. We kind of assumed that everybody grew up on Pink Floyd, but I guess our audience is a lot younger because we noticed in Amsterdam there were a lot of people who didn't know this album. So there were a lot of people who were almost bored! And inevitably, when picking an album you can't possibly please everybody. When we did Metallica or Iron Maiden the prog fans probably hated it. In doing an album like *Dark Side. . .*, the metal fans are probably going to be bored to tears."

The performance was visually enhanced after the band had man-aged to lay their hands on the original film clips that the Floyd had used as a backdrop when they performed the album during the Seventies. Additionally, long-term associate Theresa Thomason was flown over to both Amsterdam and London to add the vital female vocals to "The Great Gig In The Sky". Wisely, Dream Theater chose not to noticeably alter the arrangements of these seminal songs.

"Our version is pretty faithful to the original. The original is just so classic that you can't really fuck with it too much. It would be sacrile-gious to do a reggae version of 'Money'," joked Mike at the time. John Petrucci also relished the opportunity to perform the Floyd classic.

"I pretty much knew it, and the funny thing about that record is that there's not a ton of guitar as it's very loose," he recalled. There's a lot of repetition that goes on, but there are certainly a few classic guitar solos that are key. There are a lot of grooves and a vibe. It came out great, and the second show [London] was *way* better than the first. Sometimes you kind of capture the magic and it works. There were a lot of elements to that night. There was the whole video presentation plus we wanted to capture the Floyd thing. There are really successful cover bands out there like The Australian Pink Floyd and The Machine who do it really well, so we were challenged to rise to the occasion."

The London gig was reviewed by *Classic Rock* who wrote: "An album as subtle as *Dark Side*... may not have been the obvious pick for a band regularly accused of embellishing songs with 1,000-notes-a-minute histrionics, but guitarist John Petrucci delivered the solos in 'Time' and 'Breathe' with all the understated presence of the originals... Ultimately you genuinely run out of superlatives to bestow on a band as overwhelming as Dream Theater on this kind of form, and they remain prog metal's standard-bearers and standard-setters. God only knows how they can surpass performances as stunning as these. Worryingly for their contemporaries, you just know that by the next time they're here, they'll have found a way..."

Rock Sound magazine were also grudgingly impressed, with Will Stone claiming that "Whether you love or hate their glorious pretence, it can never be denied that what they offer live is nothing short of a highly intelligent and technical performance, developed by years of practice and hard work."

Early December saw the band heading for a rare visit to South America, taking in such cities as Buenos Aires in Argentina, Rio de Janeiro in Brazil and Caracas in Venezuela. There was also a gig at the Santiago Velodrome, Chile, which became the band's largest headlining gig to date, when they performed in front of 20,000 people. The two-night stands in Buenos Aires and São Paolo saw the band perform *Scenes From A Memory* in it's entirety – given that Dream Theater hadn't previously had the opportunity to perform their own "classic" album in South America.

The fact that Dream Theater were able to pull in their largest-ever audience some twenty years into their career is pretty staggering, and highlights their gradual worldwide increase in popularity. For a band who received the bare minimum in terms of record label support in recent years, that feat is made all the more impressive.

"Well, we had a quick surge with *Images And Words* that opened up the door and introduced a lot of people to us," explains Mike.

"Then once *Awake* came out, it was like a strainer. All the fans went through the filter and whoever was left was our real fan base. You had all these people who liked 'Pull Me Under' and by the time *Awake* came out a couple of years later, they had moved on to the next thing. But then there were the others who were left, and have been with us ever since and helped to develop us, spread the word from year to year and album to album. Plus the internet has helped. Ten years ago if you weren't being played on the radio, MTV or featured in the mainstream press, it would have been impossible to find out about a band like ours. Now that everybody's online you can download stuff and get the tour dates."

"The tour dates are actually essential to our growth, and our development has been a direct result of the touring we do. If you look at our album sales, they don't necessarily equate to our concert ticket figures. There are bands in America that are huge and are selling millions of records, but they can't draw a thousand people to a concert. Some of these nu-metal bands will sell millions of records but are still playing small clubs. Then you have a band like ours that may sell 100,000 or 200,000 albums in America, and we're playing theatres or nice-sized venues in the States. So we're kind of a strange case where the record sales and mainstream exposure don't necessarily equate to the band's developments. There are certain bands that are sold on mainstream sales and others that are sold on word-of-mouth and long-term development. And we're definitely in the latter category."

The world tour in support of *Octavarium* continued with an Asian leg that began on January 7, 2006. The cover album tradition was continued in Tokyo on January 13 and Osaka on January 15 when the band performed Deep Purple's *Live In Japan* in its entirety. After a fleeting break, Dream Theater headed off to play a solitary date in Colombia, before returning to North America to conclude the tour.

The band had already determined that a celebratory 20th-anniversary concert was to take place in New York, on April 1, 2006, and Dream Theater had arranged that gig at the prestigious Radio City Music Hall. Planning such a special evening so far in advance also allowed the band to make the necessary arrangements to record the concert for a DVD and CD release, as well as having a surprise lined up for those fans who had travelled from across the globe to attend. The first half of the show reprised many of the songs that had been aired during the earlier legs of the tour, with the ever-beguiling "Innocence Faded" making a welcome return to the set. But the real surprise was revealed following a short intermission, when the curtain was raised to reveal a thirty-piece orchestra stacked behind the band.

John Petrucci: "It was really Mike's idea. The gears in his brain are always running. We were sitting down and we were talking about the US tour. And he just said it all. He was like, 'Hey, guys? We'll end it in Radio City. We'll film it. It'll be our 20th anniversary and we'll play with an orchestra!' And I'm like, 'OK.' It was great! It sounded like a great idea at the time, and then a year later or whatever it was, it happened."

The idea of a rock band performing with an orchestra is generally about as appealing as watching an insipid unplugged set, and the concept became passé about a decade ago. This is especially true when you consider such hideous, watered-down examples as Metallica's orchestral dabbling on *S&M*, or the pitiful elevator music The Scorpions produced when working with the Berlin Philharmonic. But mercifully, the addition of an orchestral backing was unobtrusive and merely strengthened Jordan's already mighty keyboard presence. There are numerous songs in Dream Theater's back-catalogue that are perfectly suited to such a treatment. The second disc from *Six Degrees Of Inner Turbulence* was performed in its forty-minute entirety, with "Sacrificed Sons", "Octavarium" and "Metropolis – Part I" also sounding delicious when enhanced by a lilting string section. An unqualified success, the gig was far from cheap to arrange as manager Frank Solomon explains.

"It's cost a bundle and again it all comes down to them wanting to give a great show, as it's the 20th anniversary, and the fans deserve it," he says. "The band couldn't have done what they have without them. I sit here on the bean counter side of it thinking, 'Oh my God. This is going to be stressful, trying to pay for all this.' But it's gotta be done. It's amazing that the Radio City concert sold out just off the website. There was zero advertising for it, which was unbelievable."

Conducting the orchestra was Jamshied Sharifi, who had provided his services during the recording sessions for *Octavarium*. Jamshied had attempted to arrange for as many of the musicians who had worked on that earlier session to be present at the prestigious Radio City concert, in order to ensure a sense of familiarity as well as a certain amount of continuity.

"The orchestra part took some planning, and it was several months in advance to determine what the songs were and then have Jamshied work on pieces," said John Petrucci in an interview for *Ultimateguitar. com*. "The first thing is working with somebody who gets the music and understands what we're looking for, which Jamshied Sharifi does. We'll talk about what we're going for. Are we going for a grandiose, epic, movie-sounding thing or are we going for a more sensitive quartet type of thing. And then we talk about which part we wanted orchestrating and which sections of the music. He'll then take that home and work on it, and then try to do a mock-up with a synthesizer overdubbed over the actual tracks. So thanks to technology we were able to get MP3 files back and forth. We would just check our e-mails and send comments back and forth."

"I had the same concert master, which I totally insisted on, and told her that she *had* to do it," laughs Jamshied. "In fact, I think she actually got out of a Met performance to do it. So we had a lot of the same musicians. The Radio City orchestra was also larger than the record. The recording orchestra was 13 strings, two horns and one flute, and the

Radio City orchestra was thirty people. So we added another horn, two trumpets, trombone and clarinet, percussion and eight more strings."

With the event being filmed, the orchestra effectively had only one take to ensure that the material was presented in the right way. The pressure was also increased by the limited rehearsal time that they were able to squeeze into the schedule on the day prior to the concert.

"Yeah, we had a six-hour rehearsal with the orchestra," says Jamshied. "It sounds like a lot, but there were 90-minutes of music for us to prepare for, and I would have been much happier with 12 hours. We rehearsed at SIR Studios in Chelsea, and there are a number of rooms there, including one that was large enough to house the full band with their kit and the orchestra. So the band had a complete set-up there. It was a crazy schedule as Dream Theater had played in Boston the night before. So the tech crew started tearing down gear at eleven at night, drove it to New York, set it up and had to have it ready by one in the afternoon. So they were beat by the end of the Radio City concert. And actually, they even had the recording truck outside because they wanted to have a tech rehearsal to make sure all the microphones worked, and see what the sound leakage situation was going to be."

In spite of any in-studio tension caused by the limited rehearsal time and looming gig, the preparations were not without their moments of amusement, as Mike later recalled.

"One was in the middle of 'Metropolis'," he revealed in *Drummer* magazine. "We originally had the orchestra doubling the keyboard and guitar unison solo, doing all these crazy 32nd-note triplet patterns. I remember we stopped at one point halfway through the section, and all you heard was the entire orchestra laughing. To them it was comical to even try to attempt it. So we had to ditch that section. Another moment that comes to mind is that there was a cellist sitting in the front row, and every time I would slam a stick or bounce sticks off my snare drum, they occasionally will fly out of control, and once came really close to him. He got really freaked out and threatened to walk out."

Such distractions aside, the transforming of a Dream Theater song into one that was compatible with all the orchestral foibles was a delicate task that needed careful consideration and arranging. Consequently, Jamshied had been working away behind the scenes for weeks before the gig, ensuring that the approaches he had envisaged were compatible with the band's expectations.

"Well, 'Overture' was very similar to the recorded version," he recalls. "But on other songs there were opportunities to add certain parts. I felt, given that the orchestra was there, why not go for it? So it was quite a long process where I would take their original recordings, add orchestral parts, and then send the band an MP3 while they were on the road to see what they thought of the direction. I really didn't want to overstep the line as an arranger by adding too much new material and ending up with a song that was unrecognizable to the band or the fans. It's such carefully conceived and rich music, so I wanted to stay as true to that as I could. The writing process certainly felt good from my perspective, and Jordan and Mike were really enthusiastic on hearing the demos. But on the night itself, everything was great. What really took the musicians aback was when we first opened the curtain and we were playing 'Overture', there was an enthusiastic reaction. I think they expected that as they knew it was a surprise, but what really shocked them was every time we started playing another theme from *Six Degrees*, the audience would recognize it and go nuts. I don't think that they expected an audience at a rock show was going to be that tuned into the music. So that really gave everyone a wonderful jolt."

Despite the unquestionable creative success of the concert, there was a financial obstacle the band had to negotiate at the end of the show. Union regulations at New York venues are renowned as being probably the strictest in the world, and although the band tried their best to ensure the show ended at the 11.00pm curfew, they strayed over by three minutes and were instantly stung with a $30,000 fine.

"I was made aware during 'Octavarium' of how close it was getting and you'll see us running off for the encore and pretty quickly run back for 'Metropolis' to get going as quickly as possible," recalls Mike. "You also can see us running to move on and offstage super quickly for the bow, and I even forgot to take my inner ear monitors out. I had timed the set to fit the three-hour allotment perfectly, but a delay at the start of the show and a delay to begin the second set caused the three-minute overage. Although the union did in fact hit us with the $30,000 penalty, the promoter and the manager of Radio City were so cool to split the expense and cover it out of their profits so we wouldn't have to pay it ourselves. In addition to this penalty, you wouldn't believe the expenses the Radio City Music Hall union charged us. Let's just say, of the $600,000 budget for this DVD, almost a third of that money went to the local union to play this show. At all gigs, there are union and local crew fees. But to put that in perspective, at a typical show in USA, the fees for us at the end of the night may run between $5,000 and $10,000 dollars. At Radio City, it was in the vicinity of $200,000. So in the end, the DVD may have had to skip an audio commentary but at least the elevator operator or carpet sweeper at Radio City will be able to put their grandkids through college!"

As has been the case with notable and celebratory gigs in the past, Mike had also approached Kevin Moore with a view to asking the former keyboardist to perform a song or two with his former bandmates. True to form, Moore declined the offer.

"I remember I asked him out to do the *Score* show and the performance of *When Dream And Day Unite* in Los Angeles and he didn't do them," recalls Mike. "But thank God he didn't do them, because if he did, those shows would have been about *him*. And the *Score* show wasn't about *him*. It was about *us*. That night was about us celebrating doing it for twenty years and not celebrating the people who walked out and left us behind."

The concert may well have provided a fitting conclusion to the first twenty years of Dream Theater but there was still so much more for the band to achieve. As a band that could never be accused of resting on their laurels, there was an ever-expanding "to-do" list. And as the backstage party rumbled on into the early hours, the band were already plotting their next move.

SIXTEEN

FOCUS HERE, FOCUS THERE

So what happened next? Well, in the aftermath of that truly spectacular gig at the Radio City Music Hall, the band took their first true holiday in over a decade, spending the rest of the summer recuperating with their families from the toils of the best part of a year on the road. But all was far from quiet in the Dream Theater camp, and Mike slaved away for weeks producing and putting the finishing touches to *Score* – a live DVD and triple-CD release that captured that orchestra-backed New York performance.

"Throughout the months of putting together this DVD I was able to relive those moments over and over again," Mike revealed in an interview with *Drummer* magazine. "Even now, several months removed from it, I pop in the DVD and can still feel the magic in the air. I still feel the chills. We've played hundreds, maybe thousands of shows around the world throughout the years, and we've played to bigger audiences, but there was just something about that night that was incredibly special. A lot of times, when you film a live DVD, you wonder if everything is going to go smoothly, and this was one of those nights when it worked on every level."

And work it did. There was a period when the release of live footage usually meant a swiftly cobbled-together, frills-free video shot from the back of an arena with only the odd fleeting, grainy close-up. Mercifully, the advent of DVDs and rising expectations ensured that those times have passed. Always a band that relishes a challenge, with *Score* Dream Theater lovingly crafted an enthralling document of their 20th anniversary concert. The cinematic approach taken by Mike was spectacular, with imaginative and innovative camera angles and close-ups capturing every nuance of the performance. As live DVDs go, it's genuinely tough to recall a release that matches the attention to detail and sheer visual perfection of *Score*. Hitting the stores on August 29, 2006, the DVD was eagerly snapped up by the band's ever-expanding fan base, selling over 14,000 copies in the US during the first week of release – a feat that ensured it entered at Number One on the *Billboard* Top Music Video chart as well as later receiving a platinum sales award from the RIAA. The band's profile was further enhanced with an edited version of *Score* appearing on VH-1 *Classic*, and both John Petrucci and Mike were also interviewed by long-time fan and well-respected DJ Eddie Trunk for a piece on that channel's *Metal Mania* show.

With their seven-album recording contract with Atlantic expiring after the release of *Octavarium*, Dream Theater were faced with the prospect of having to locate a new suitor as well as write and record a new album. But rather than wait for a new contract to be agreed, they took the bold decision to finance the recording of the album themselves, and worry about reclaiming those costs and signing to a new label at a later date. Such a tactic also ensured that they guaranteed there would be no outside label interference or any misguided attempts to forcibly channel the direction of the new material. Not of course that Dream Theater would ever have signed to a label who might want to change their sound, but the last thing the band needed was the thought of A&R men hovering over their shoulders in the studio control room.

Returning to Avatar Studios in midtown New York on September 5, 2006 – where they had recorded *Falling Into Infinity* almost a decade earlier – the band followed their by now usual routine of concurrently writing and recording material. Working and lodging in the city from Monday through Friday every week, before heading home at weekends, the sessions lasted throughout the winter months, finally concluding in February 2007. Mike and John Petrucci again took care of the production, although one notable change was the absence of long-time engineer Doug Oberkircher. Paul Northfield – whose past credits include work with Rush, Porcupine Tree and Queensrÿche – replaced him in that role, and would also eventually co-produce the vocals and mix the album.

"It was really just time for fresh ears," explains Mike. "I guess it just felt like a new chapter for us, coming off the back of *Score*, having the summer off, and starting with a new label. So really it was just time for a change. Paul's obviously a very talented person and has great ears. He can come up with different sounds and recording techniques, and of course he's a veteran engineer having worked on so many albums. The relationship we had with him was very similar to the one we had with Doug. We were always open to any suggestions he may have, but ultimately we were producing the album, and so he never overstepped that boundary. We also got him to co-produce the vocals, so when it came time to do those, the floor became open for him to put in his two cents. We'd also been looking for an engineer who could also mix an album. It's always been weird in the past when we handed the tapes over to a mixer when they hadn't been there for all the months of tracking. They don't necessarily know everything that was tracked or where it is, or what our ideas were when we wrote the songs. But it all worked out great and we loved working with him."

Ironically, Northfield was one of the candidates on a lengthy list of producers who were considered by the band during the writing process for *Falling Into Infinity*, but he was eventually passed over in favour of Kevin Shirley. In hindsight though, he admits that he is glad that he managed to avoid the problems encountered by the band during that tumultuous period.

"Well, as I have said to the band, in retrospect I'm glad I didn't work on that record," says Northfield. "The strength of the band is their indulgence, and to artificially impose a more pop-formula structure on to a band like Dream Theater rarely works. I find it really rewarding working on records when you only have to please the people in the recording studio and you don't have to worry about any criteria as to whether an album will sell. The style of recording – by going into the studio without any songs and writing in the studio – was something that we used to do in the Seventies, but has been done very rarely since because of the cost. Sometimes it's totally prohibitive to do it that way but it was a conscious band decision, simply because they like the idea of being in New York as it is close to home. They would stay in New York for three or four days a week, and go home at the weekend and everything will be left set up, which is something that I admire them for."

Unusually though, the band hit the studio without the usual master plan in place which normally would dictate the album's emphasis and direction. *Octavarium* had been written specifically as a classic Dream Theater album, *Train Of Thought* was their attempt at creating a definitive metal album, and *Scenes From A Memory* was of course a finely honed concept album. With Mike's usual predisposition to determine the band's next move, it must have been an unusual feeling for him to wander into the studio without any firm musical blueprint under his arm.

"I think it was almost harder for him *not* to think of something," laughs Jordan. "That was part of the challenge for us, as both Mike and

John Petrucci just love to think of these great concepts for each album. So there was less planning than on previous albums, when I remember having more discussions about what we were going to do. This album was more a case of meeting in the studio and keeping it open. We just went in and shaped a plan there and then."

"Actually, I had inevitably started thinking about the new album and had a few ideas that came to me over the summer we had taken off," confesses Mike. "When we started the sessions in September, I had a couple of directions that I considered bringing up, but I purposely kept my mouth shut out of curiosity to see what would happen. So we started that way, and the first thing we wrote was a big 25-minute epic that eventually became 'In The Presence Of Enemies'. Once we were in the heat of that battle, I realized it was a real nice change of pace to just have a completely free palette to work with. So I never even brought the subject of my ideas up, just kept my mouth shut and went with the flow."

That said, Mike and John had stated that whatever form the finished album might take, they insisted that it must have "balls". The end-product may not have had the one-dimensional approach taken on *Train Of Thought*, but it does contain some of Dream Theater's heavier moments. And although Jordan was able to find plenty of room to ease his keyboard flourishes, there must have been moments when he wondered just how he might be able to fit in.

"Yeah, that was an interesting challenge for me," he smiles. "I have funny memories of those sessions when I started to feel a little weird because my involvement in the writing process at particular times wasn't what I wanted it to be. I would just let them hang out and do the seventh-string metal thing, and I'd just wait until it cleared and there was an opening. So I'd actually go in to my keyboards when they'd walked out to either listen back in the control room or get a little breath. I'd just turn on my sequencer and lay down something really wacky, like in the middle section of the track that became 'The Dark Eternal Night'. What's funny is that during those periods of time, I'd work really fast. I like to present riffs in a form that everybody can understand. If they walked in and I said 'How about this?', but played something using a piano sound, they might say it sounded like the Charlie Brown theme! So I'll take that little bit of extra time and quickly put things into my sequencer, orchestrate them and make a guitar, bass and drum version of something. Then when they come back in, I'll press go and say, 'Well what about this for the next part?' And often they'd think it was cool and I would be like 'But that's exactly the same riff I just played on the piano!'"

As an embedded and impartial observer of the writing process, Paul Northfield is perhaps best placed to provide an accurate guide as to how the band members relate to each other during weeks of musical creation. Certainly his impression of the complex relationships within Dream Theater is in line with what you might anticipate – with Mike and John Petrucci leading from the front and the other members all having their clearly defined roles and parameters – as well as a clear understanding as to what is expected of them.

"The vision of the band is obviously Mike and John's and they work closely together and bounce off each other," confirms Northfield. "Often Mike plays the role of movie director and is quite vocal when he decides which way to go. His relationship with John Petrucci gives them both a degree of security as they know each other really well, and crucially they know how to deal with each other's strong sensibilities about what they want. John Myung is quite solitary, just spending his time practising and working a lot on his own. He doesn't really get too involved in the writing. Once in a while they will be looking for something interesting and would turn to him to ask for some cool bass riffs. I remember a few times during the writing they would use something that was inspired by a riff of John Myung's. But for the most part he has got his agenda full just trying to perform the kind of things that John Petrucci and Mike want him to do. They often want him to perform things that are extraordinarily difficult on a bass. I mean it is one thing to have an intense guitar riff and then want to double it with a bass riff, but the bass is a different animal. So a lot of John Myung's time is spent trying to work out how to do it."

"Jordan is sort of like a hired gun," he continues. "He's a specialist who has got extraordinary ability and brings it to bear on the job in hand. Then when the job is done he can step back into his own world. He goes from being hugely influential with a dramatic orchestration, arrangement or the extraordinary riffs he does with John Petrucci, to then take a back seat and just let it be a three-piece, which isn't an easy thing for him to do. But at the same time, I think that he knew that was what it was likely to be like when he joined the band. So Jordan has to play different roles. I think it's his outside stuff that allows him to be able to settle into that, because otherwise you would have a lot more tension in a band like Dream Theater. Invariably when you get a lot of good musicians and people with strong ideas together, there tends to be a lot of conflict flying around. In this case there isn't really, because the roles are clearly defined and because they know each other, know what they are doing and why. They are all managing to find what they need within the band."

Throughout the period, Dream Theater were also continuing their hunt for a new home. The band had effectively been left to their own devices by Atlantic on their last few releases, with the label knowing they had a guaranteed number of album sales no matter how much (or little) backing they gave each release. Clearly the band had no intention of re-signing with Atlantic, and that was a decision that was reinforced by some of the business shenanigans that Dream Theater encountered as the contract ended.

"The big problem with *Octavarium*, and the reason Atlantic never supported it, was because when we delivered the album they knew it was our last record with them," says Mike. "We said we wanted to do a video for 'I Walk Beside You' and they kind of held us to ransom and said they weren't going to do anything for the album and support it unless we committed to them, and signed for another three albums. So we knew when we hit the road for *Octavarium* that we were on our own because there was no way in hell we were going to sign for them. They didn't want to go out of their way and market an album when they knew it was an album that was basically our swansong with them. Those fucking assholes basically put out the album, let us go and at that point we basically wanted nothing to do with them any more."

With no shortage of record labels wanting to sign the band, they were placed in the favourable position of simply matching their criteria to the offers that were on the table. Topping their list of demands was a label that would leave them alone to create the music they wanted, but who were willing and able to put a substantial marketing muscle behind their releases. There was also the issue of being able to forge a practical and productive working relationship with whichever label ultimately signed them. As fate would have it, in July 2006, Roadrunner Records had employed two faces from Dream Theater's past, with Derek Oliver (who had of course signed the band to Atco back in the early Nineties) and Dante Bonutto (Dream Theater's European A&R man during the same period) charged with signing established acts with a dedicated fan base to the label. After protracted negotiations, Dream Theater announced their decision to sign with Roadrunner on February 8, with an enthusiastic press release being issued by their new label.

"Dream Theater and Roadrunner Records have led parallel careers on the cutting edge of metal for many years," said Derek & Dante in the release. "We're thrilled to be working with a genuine market-leader, and when you add everything the guys bring to the table to the independent spirit and work ethic of the label, the results can only be exciting in the extreme!"

Mike Portnoy: "The whole thing with Atlantic had left a sour taste in our mouths and that's why, when we were looking at Sony or any of the other majors who were interested, we were gun shy to get back into that situation again. Roadrunner have all the muscle and marketing ability to match any of those labels, but with an independent spirit and

I think they really cherish us. They chose to sign us. It wasn't like they just adopted us like the people at Atlantic or Elektra."

Systematic Chaos was released on Roadrunner on June 4, 2007, and marked another change of bearing for this continually evolving band. Nodding more in the intense direction taken by *Train Of Thought* – rather than the more conceptually themed *Octavarium* – it is however still a varied and noticeably contemporary recording. Opening and closing the album, "In The Presence Of Enemies" was originally one 25-minute epic before it was decided to divide it into two parts. Of all the tracks on the album, it perhaps owes the most to the band's musical heritage and contains all the trademark riffs, melodies and complex interplay that have forged Dream Theater's reputation. The decision to split the track was made after it had been recorded and, according to Mike, there were a number of reasons behind that change of plan.

"Well, when we were thinking of the sequence of the album, it was really difficult to work out whether to put it on there first or last," he reveals. "I mean, you don't want to have a 25-minute song in the middle of an album. I thought that opening the album with it would have been too big a hurdle to climb to get to the rest of the album – so that eliminated the opening slot. And as for the closing slot, I really felt that we had just done that with *Octavarium* and I didn't want to repeat it. Actually John Petrucci suggested that we could cut it in half, just to be 'proggie'. At first I thought it was an interesting gimmick, but the more I thought about the sequence it began to make sense. Also the opening section of the song is such a good opener, and the ending is such a perfect closer, so that was also a dilemma. Splitting it solved that problem."

"One of my favourite records is Rush's *Hemispheres* which has a side-long suite written as a continuation of a storyline from a song on their previous record, *A Farewell To Kings*," explained John Petrucci in *Guitar Player* magazine. "I think the idea of having musical bookends to an album – a 'to be continued' storyline – is very much in keeping with our identity as a progressive band."

Petrucci was also responsible for that track's lyrics, and as with all his contributions on *Systematic Chaos*, they were firmly locked into a fantasy-fiction style and it tells the archetypal tale of the combat between good and evil, and the turmoil within the central character as he battles his dark side.

"All of my lyrics on this album are written from a fictional viewpoint and it's almost like fantasy writing," explained Petrucci. "And to me the dark angle is always the most interesting, more metal, and to me it fits better and is a lot easier to dive into that subject matter."

Addressing his obsessive-compulsive personality, the lyrics Mike penned for "Constant Motion" perfectly matched the track's winding and unremitting music. The song also became the album's first single, and although it wasn't released in the stores, it was downloaded free prior to the album's release by thousands of eager fans. Roadrunner also demonstrated their desire to fully back the band by producing a video for the track, which for Dream Theater was something of a novelty.

"Well, if I'm being honest, I'd wanted us to do videos for the last two albums," explains Mike. "Videos are being played again on metal stations so I felt that the timing was right. I had wanted to do one for 'As I Am' off *Train Of Thought* and one for 'I Walk Beside You' from *Octavarium*, but at that point, our old label wouldn't even do one for us. But the track itself is a metaphor for my brain and really is a look inside my head. When it was time to write lyrics for the song, it was just such a driving song that it felt like it would be a good basis for the lyrics. It really was the perfect metaphor for what is inside my brain 24 hours a day. The label picked that song as the first single as they wanted to come out of the box with something that was a little more heavy and progressive. Really it was just to establish the new album and get us out there."

The initial shoot for the video was, however, a disaster, with the captured footage not deemed to be of a high enough standard to even consider releasing it as James LaBrie explains:

"Well, first of all, everything was completely disorganised," he sighs. "The audio wasn't correct, and you might as well have had two little speakers attached to an iPod. Meanwhile, you're supposed to be pretending to be playing a really aggressive, metal song through these little speakers. So that delayed the process as they had to try and resolve it by bringing in new speakers. But by then you start losing momentum, the hours are clicking by and it just seemed like it was a case of them trying to wing it. And we were thinking 'Is this the best that they can offer us?' It just seemed that the whole thing was too much of an afterthought. We were all suspicious and we were thinking that there was no way that this thing was going to come out looking the way we need it to. I mean, you were already working with a band that is apprehensive and wary of that environment to begin with. And then we were confronted with something that looked completely confused and in complete turmoil. So in the end, we had to re-shoot it. It was apparent straight away that the second director who came in was extremely focused and had worked with a number of bands before, like Nickelback, and he had some good videos under his belt. So the second version did come out looking pretty cool."

That track featured Mike's vocals heavily , which have gradually become a prominent feature on recent releases. As always with Dream Theater, there were some fans who criticized what they alleged was an over-indulgence on his part. Yet the reality is that his distinctive vocals are now as much a part of Dream Theater music as Chris Squire's singing is with Yes. But despite developing into a core attribute of the band's sound, there were still those who somehow found it inappropriate.

"I think my vocal ration this album has increased maybe to accompany those heavier parts on a lot of the tracks," says Mike. "And as for it being appropriate or inappropriate? Well that's for the fans to judge. But for the heavy parts, it needed a heavier vocal, and we just didn't feel that James convincingly has that heavier, ballsier sound to his voice. So the vocals for 'Constant Motion' just fell into my lap, for me to be the token metal guy."

Also possessing its fair share of Portnoy vocals, and undoubtedly the most startling song on the album, "The Dark Eternal Night" represents Dream Theater at their most edgy. Incorporating some truly grinding, shattering riffs, the most shocking aspect is the use of gruff, distorted cookie-monster style vocals. And although they are not excessively used, for those who dislike this approach the track came as quite a shock.

"Oh my God! And for me it was a bit of a shock," laughs Jordan. "I was like, 'What is that? Why?' I think Mike got the opportunity on this album to kind of explore the metal side of what he likes, which is cool. You and I are probably in the same kind of place as far as those vocals go. I don't understand the whole movement. But really there's so little of that type of vocal on the album, that it's more a tip of the hat to that stuff."

"Yeah, it's more contemporary," adds Mike. "Not that we were trying to sell out to MTV or whatever, but if you listen to the bands that are out there today, that's the style and what everybody does. We are not trying to be something that we're not, but we do want kids to at least find us *listenable*. The verses and vocals are really heavy, but the middle section is up there with the middle section of 'Metropolis'. It's so incredibly over the top, and I think that song is like what Pantera would come up with if they tried to write a 'Metropolis'. But the riffs are no heavier or crazier than 'The Mirror' or 'The Glass Prison'. Maybe it's just the vocal approach. In fact when we first started working on the vocals, John had written the lyrics and presented them. But at that time they were really more sung and melodic, and I remember pulling him aside and saying that it just didn't sound fitting. You know, the whole song was so fucking brutal and I just felt that the vocals really needed to accompany that accordingly. So he actually went away, scratched all of his lyrics, all of his melodies, and re-wrote all the vocal part and it ended up what it became."

Although many of the lines were doubled with Mike's lower vocals, the approach was also challenging for James who had to adapt his natural style to fit the music. Indeed it could be strongly argued that simply because of the variety in his singing, his performance on *Systematic Chaos* is his most solid and impressive to date.

"On every album I'm trying to come out and use as much of my voice and all its different qualities as I can," affirms James. "That's what will keep the album dynamic and character-driven. It's really up to every vocalist not to become one-dimensional and to try and give each song its own signature, as otherwise it can become monotonous. But I'm sure there will be fans who are perplexed when listening to 'The Dark Eternal Night'. There's a lot of that kind of music around where it's very heavy and we've all appreciated bands like that – say a Pantera or more recently Lamb Of God. So it's going to be something that we have our own interpretation of. But on any given Dream Theater album you always have a split amongst the fans. There are people who appreciate it as a whole or those people who think it leans too much in one direction. But that's to be expected. I guess if we put out something and everything was appreciated, it would be a little scary."

Continuing the Alcoholics Anonymous, twelve-steps series of songs, "Repentance" follows on from where "The Root Of All Evil" on *Octavarium* left off. As parts eight and nine of the saga, it needs to be considered not only in the context of this album, but where it fits in with those tracks that have preceded and will ultimately follow it. Consequently, with "The Glass Prison", "This Dying Soul" and "The Root Of All Evil" all being hi-tempo songs and given the band's intention to one day perform all of these songs live as one continuous piece, "Repentance" is deliberately mellow. As Mike says, "We needed a breather in there somewhere". One feature of the track is the lengthy spoken sections which were narrated by a number of the band's industry friends. Mike put an invitation out to a long list of musicians, asking them to record their words and giving them a free rein to say whatever they wanted. The only stipulation being that they had to apologize for something that had affected their lives. So, Marillion's Steve Hogarth is narrating the lyrics to that band's song "The Only Unforgivable Thing" which dealt with Hogarth's marriage break-up, and Steven Wilson (of Porcupine Tree) publicly expressed regret for some negative comments that he had previously made in the music press about Dream Theater.

"It's kind of a weird story actually," revealed Wilson in an interview with *progarchives.com*. "Dream Theater were doing this new record, and they've got this track on there called 'Repentance'. It's all about regret for the things you've done that maybe hurt others, and the need to apologize for those things. And I thought about it for a minute and said 'Why don't I apologize for being negative in the press about Dream Theater?' I've been very honest about my musical likes and dislikes in the press. The thing is they are good friends of mine and they know I'm not really into their music. They don't mind it, but their fans get more irate about it as they're very passionate. It's a free country. I don't love Dream Theater as it's not my kind of music but they're great people and Jordan is one of my best friends. Anyway, I've heard the finished track, and it's amazing. I'm always happy to be proved wrong."

For the record, the other characters that appeared were Jon Anderson (Yes), Steve Vai, Joe Satriani, Mikael Åkerfeldt from Opeth, Corey Taylor (Stone Sour/Slipknot), Daniel Gildenlow, Neil Morse, David Ellefson from Megadeth and Chris Jericho.

"Yeah, I put the option out to a lot of people, although there were a few notable people who passed," explains Mike. "The three biggest that I was disappointed in who passed on this were Dave Mustaine [Megadeth], Geoff Tate [Queensrÿche] and Bruce Dickinson [Iron Maiden]. But I've got to say that I'm happy with the final list. Oh, and the only other person who passed at the last minute was James Hetfield [Metallica]. I wanted him to do the words at the end of the song that is based on the ninth-step promises. So there were four big passes but eleven big scores, and at the end of the day I'm a happy boy."

Another fresh approach was taken on "Prophets Of War", which possesses an almost disco feel before John Petrucci's guitar packs in a few meaty riffs and takes it to a whole new level. Lyrically, it also saw the band dealing with the prickly topic of politics – and more specifically the Iraq war – with James basing his words on a book written by Ambassador Joseph Wilson called *Politics Of Truth*.

"It's all about the way he was betrayed by the powers-that-be in the US government," explains James. "Really it's about their political agenda and ulterior motives, with the prophets being the leaders and their positions within government. And then there's the profits being the financial rewards of any given war to a select few. But it also goes further than that, and is not just being the brave men and women soldiers that have to go and fight these nonsensical wars. It's also about the idea that we are still trying to solve issues and differences by guns and warfare. It's absolutely ludicrous that we still can't get past using vicious acts. It has been proven several times throughout history that it might pacify the situation for a very brief moment, but it is through oppression, and sooner or later people rebel against that. So it's not just the initial people that get killed on the front lines in wars, but it is society as a whole that is also suffering. It's a very tumultuous and precarious world right now."

"The Ministry Of Lost Souls" is overflowing with lush orchestral arrangements and unsurpassed guitar licks, it contains all the colour and passion that the band are capable of producing on their slower tracks. It also expands to a hefty 15 minutes and manages to incorporate a breathtaking instrumental break mid-song before returning to the exquisite opening melody. With the lyrics again written by John Petrucci, it ventured into the realm of a far-from-cheery fantasy world.

"The musical style that we write is very dramatic," explained John. "So what I wanted to do was pull the listener in lyrically by telling a story in each song. It's about somebody who was saved by another person when they were drowning, but that person died in the process. So the person that was saved lives this life of being unable to live with themselves, they have all this regret and sorrow. They want to go to the other side to meet the other person, who eventually ends up pulling them through."

"Forsaken", and to a lesser degree a number of other tracks on the album, was singled out by some fans and the band's detractors as being the perfect example of Dream Theater contriving their material to sound like other bands. The introduction to "Prophets Of War" was also accused of having a Muse-like feel, and many of the vocals on "Constant Motion" have the air of Metallica at their finest. But it's "Forsaken" – with the gentle piano intro building to a powerfully orchestrated anthem that is strongly reminiscent of Evanescence – which has received the most stinging criticism. Jordan acknowledges the accusations.

"The band as a whole are definitely fans of certain groups, and we enjoy going in certain directions," he says. "Sometimes it's not about 'Oh we have to be the most original and Dream Theater must do something that no-one else has done'. In the case of 'Forsaken', we just wanted to write a really cool song in a particular vein. A song like that was very successful because it developed exactly like the vision that was laid out before we started writing it. You couldn't have planned it better. So people are going to say it sounds like this or that. And yes it does, in my opinion, you're right. It does. It's not a direct rip-off. We didn't sit there listening to anyone else's song and say 'Let's use those chords' or whatever. We just have a sound in mind, we start writing and that's what comes up."

"It's so interesting this whole process as we are five guys and everyone is in their own world," continues Jordan. "That's not to say that we are at odds with each other in any way, shape or form. But it's fair to say I walked in there having had a musical career before I joined the group, and I was a little bit established and older than the other guys. So I have certain values about what I do and that's fine. I keep those in a place, and they come out when they come out. But the other guys don't necessarily think in exactly the same way, and so they would be happy saying, 'OK, let's write a song and have it very Musey or Evanescencey, or this or that,' and they are content when it lands solidly on a sound that they like. But as a composer and from a very personal and independent point of view, in my own writing I am more interested in maybe an original, compositional voice. I don't think anyone is ever going to listen to one of my solo albums and say it sounds like, say, Evanescence. That's not my interest. But then I'm not a rock band on the commercial scene. Dream Theater, as much as we are progressive, we are a rock band in the commercial world, and it's a different set of parameters."

James LaBrie: "That's fine and valid. People are going to say that no matter what Dream Theater puts out. This song is too much in that direction, or that something is a blatant copy of another band. I think that is going to happen when they hear songs that remind them of a band that they're also close to. I mean they said that too on *Octavarium* when people were saying tracks sounded u2-ish. There always has been a certain level of mainstream presence with Dream Theater. But in the band, be it Muse or Evanescence, we appreciate what they have done musically. And if some of that tends to flow through us, all we can say is that we were being true to ourselves. If something does sound similar to this or that band then so be it. I know some people may say that it's contrived, too formulated or too close for comfort, but it's an opinion that I don't agree with."

Paul Northfield perhaps provides the most accurate assessment of such criticism, noting that it is the band's overall love of music rather than any cynical attempt to achieve commercial success that is behind other musical influences creeping into their sound.

"They just love playing and are serious music fans, and when they like something, they don't mind letting it show," he explains. "I admire them for that. There aren't many bands that have been in the music industry for a long time that remain serious music fans. These guys are, and they don't care if other people's music comes into what they are doing as long as they feel good about what they are doing. For the most part they think structurally when writing. They use other songs they like as structural inspiration. They would say, 'Lets do one in this style'. One of their strengths and challenges for them is whenever they use another band's music as a reference. You know, 'How about we do a track like Tool or King Crimson?' Their ability with their instruments is such that they can just go wham, and instantly do something that sounds so much like those groups that it's like, 'Whoahh!' So they tend to spend most of their time using those as inspirations, but then spend a lot of time trying a unique twist on a certain style of arrangement or approach. But hopefully people will appreciate the end result, see the influences are there but at the same time realize there is a core Dream Theaterness amongst it all."

And let's be honest, for every section that might fleetingly show the contemporary nuances of Muse, there are other less fashionable bands such as Gentle Giant, Frank Zappa or King Crimson that have also played a major part in influencing Dream Theater's distinctive sound. It would be spurious to suggest that the band is somehow trying to emulate Gentle Giant's wacky approach in order to try and achieve greater commercial success.

Perhaps the overriding feeling *Systematic Chaos* generates is a sense of heaviness – both lyrically and musically – that runs throughout each of the album's tracks. With Roadrunner being a label that is synonymous with artists that would fit firmly into the metal genre, accusations were rife that this Dream Theater album was an attempt to fit into that roster.

"I know people are saying that this is our Roadrunner album, but one thing that really has to be pointed out is that when we made this album, we didn't know what label was going to be releasing it," counters Mike. "We went into the studio, did the album as free agents and didn't start meeting with the labels until halfway through the process. And for that matter Roadrunner didn't hear a single note until the record was done and we had signed with them. So if anyone ever says that we have made this record for Roadrunner, it's not the case at all."

"Let's face it, we have been recording albums that way since *Scenes From A Memory* when the label didn't hear a note before we delivered the final album," adds James forcibly. "So when people say that this is our Roadrunner album I really don't agree. Would that have been the case if we had done *Train Of Thought* for this label? I mean *Train Of Thought* is a much more bombastic, in-your-face album that you would expect from some of the artists that are on the Roadrunner label. OK, this album is aggressive and heavy, but there's a balance there and diversity in styles."

That opinion is shared by Jordan who although acknowledging the forcefulness of many of the tracks, denies that this was deliberate. He also makes the valid contention that the heavy metal side of Dream Theater is something that has always been present in their music.

"We never once got together and said, 'OK, we're going to drop what we're doing musically and go in this direction because this is our new label and we have to be a metal band,'" adds Jordan. "That has *nothing* to do with the reality of this group as we do pretty much exactly what we want to do. And again the vision came into reality when we all got together and started to work, the guys were saying let's make this really heavy and dark and keep that theme throughout. So any happy riffs basically got tossed out of the window. I think that a major point in the success of this band is the ability to stay focused on a path. I have to credit John Petrucci and Mike at being really good at knowing what is within the Dream Theater window of parameters, which is what people will accept."

"There was an awareness that this was a cool rock label and that we have to make sure that we are in the realm of cool, and deliver something to the heavier side of Dream Theater," continues Jordan. "For us to go a little bit deeper in that direction makes sense because it's part of our style and of all the things we do. You know, as John and Mike would say, to 'Give it some balls'. I really think the strongest interest is the amount of people who are into the metal side of what we do. And now we have this record company that is totally in that world, I think it makes a lot of sense to ride with that a little. So to a very small extent things are pushing in that direction. But it is definitely a side of Dream Theater that has always been there."

The more cynical observers suggested that the band's image had also undergone a radical overhaul in order to try and fit in with their new, younger label-mates. James LaBrie's altered appearance was perhaps the most noticeable, with a trim beard suddenly emerging. So was this an attempt to look, well, fashionable?

"No. It's because I'm a huge *Pirates Of The Caribbean* fan. Jack Sparrow at your service," he laughs. "You can't just stay looking the same. You get bored with yourself. I remember a conversation I had in passing with Mike where he said 'You know, you should bring back the facial hair you had in 2000'. And I had actually been thinking about it and that little push was enough. I thought why not? It's easy to grow. So it's just a change. John Petrucci is growing his hair long again, John Myung's hair has pretty much remained the same as it has always been, and Jordan has got the Tony Levin look going on – so it's all cool."

Indeed, John Petrucci also began sporting a bushy beard to match his growing hair – a look that initially even alarmed his bandmates.

"I think we are pretty fashion conscious, especially our guitar player who is notorious for having a completely different image every time I see him," recalled Jordan in an interview with *dprp.net*. "The other day I saw him at the airport and I swear to God, as he walked up to me, he could have been either a woodchopper after an extended stay in the woods or from the band Pantera. He had his hair pulled back and had this really bushy face of hair. I thought 'Oh my God!' But he is into it and it's great. We are in the arts, we're entertainers and we're having fun."

As for the album's title, Mike revealed in an interview with *terror-verlag.de* that they hadn't christened the recording until well into the mixing process.

"We sat down with all the lyrics, read through them together and wrote down any words or phrases that jumped out at us," he said. "And the word 'chaos' was in one of the songs, and it was like, 'Oh man, that's a fucking cool word'. And then we started thinking about how everything about this band musically is controlled chaos. The music at times – our instrumental stuff – could be totally out there, crazy and chaotic, but at the same time it's completely controlled and meticulous. So we looked for a word that was the opposite of chaos and came up with the word 'systematic'. And that sums up our music in a lot of ways. So it felt like it was the right title, it sounded good and had a good ring to it."

Press reviews of the album were consistently positive, and it achieved top ratings in some of the world's most influential rock magazines. Writing for *Kerrang!*, whose support for Dream Theater has at best been patchy, Raiziq Raul radiated enthusiasm claiming *Systematic Chaos* was "An awe-inspiring musical journey... Cast any prog aspirations aside right this moment because regardless of your musical background, preference or prejudice, *Systematic Chaos* is guaranteed to find a way to blow your world apart." *Classic Rock*'s Jon Hotten was similarly impressed, stating that Dream Theater "Perform with the inner conviction necessary to take the listener along. On occasion it's like hearing Metallica embark on a grandiose cinematic folly, at others there are hints of Queensrÿche and Pink Floyd. And if you happen upon a section you don't like, well, don't worry: there will be something entirely different along in a minute."

Renowned journalist Dave Ling was also supportive, writing in *Metal Hammer* that the album was "Built upon Pantera-like slabs of riffery and nimbly-executed tempo changes... *Systematic Chaos* crosses the brooding heaviness of 2003's *Train Of Thought* with their *Octavarium* disc; *Systematic Chaos* is guaranteed to send those suffering Attention Deficit Disorder into a schizoid rage. By the same token, it's thoroughly recommended to those that demand depth, thought and skill in their listening pleasure."

Of course such high praise in the metal press could come at a price. With the band now apparently being suddenly "cool" again, releasing a contemporary-sounding album, and a hoard of new younger fans appearing at gigs, could there be a danger that their long-standing fan base may feel alienated and drift away?

"No I don't think so," argues James. "I think for us to try and stay true to the classic era of prog rock or rock would further alienate us because it would become – for the lack of better words – archaic or antiquated. And I think that would chase away a lot of the younger fans. When we look out into our crowd these days, we're seeing people aged anywhere from 16 to 65. So the demographics are quite wide. I think that's because of the way we have written our music in the past. We have our heavier elements, progressive, rock, jazz and fusion. So there's a quagmire of musical styles going on at any given moment. I don't think we are ever influenced about if we go too far in one musical direction, whether it will hinder our progress. We can't think like that. If we did it really would be constricting us."

Mike Portnoy: "The most important thing is maintaining our fan base, keeping them happy and giving them what they expect from Dream Theater. But our ultimate goal is continuing to grow which means making new fans. And as long as it is done on our terms and we aren't blatantly selling out, then I don't think there is anything wrong with that. We just want to grow, blossom and further our career. It's going to be nice to have a label that, on the surface at least, will actually give a shit about us. The people at Roadrunner have got a great roster of bands that really do eclectic stuff. Everything from Opeth, through Stone Sour, Nickelback and Slipknot. These are all bands that do their thing, have their own identity and Roadrunner doesn't seem to try and change that. It looks like that is going to be the same with us. They are going to let us do what we do but at the same time give us the promotion and marketing. We've always said that it's amazing what we have done on our own. Just imagine what we could do with a little support from a label. We're not looking for them to turn us into Metallica or Guns 'n' Roses, but just give us the attention that you would give any of your other bands and I'm sure that there will be that many more people who will discover us."

Certainly, Roadrunner kept their word, and the promotional support given to *Systematic Chaos* had not been seen for a Dream Theater album since the heady days of *Awake*. With high-profile interviews in metal and musician magazines, the aforementioned free download of "Constant Motion", a substantial advertising campaign, and a 5.1 surround-sound version of the album coupled with a 90-minute documentary on a limited edition two-disc release, it was an encouraging start.

"We haven't had this much attention before, certainly in the time I have been with the band, and in fact, I'm a little bit scared," jokes Jordan. "I hope we don't over-saturate and the fans don't get turned off. But it's exciting as we've always wondered what our band could do if we had somebody behind us, as we've become so incredibly self-sufficient until now. So who knows what could happen? Maybe word will spread about what we do. I know our management are saying that they have never seen anything like this before. There's just such strong report from the record label. Everyone just feels that this is a great opportunity. The other reality of the band is that we have within it this brilliant guy, who makes the set lists every night, has a total awareness of what's going on, can really dial-in on to what we need to do in each environment that we're in. Mike is amazing at that. So I think we'd have to work really hard to go wrong."

"Yeah, and up until now, Dream Theater have had great success but what we have achieved has been self-propelled," interjects James. "It's been coming from our hard work plus creative and artistic decisions on how to self-promote ourselves. Yet as much success we have had, it still has that certain feeling of being underground. I think there's a lot for us to achieve. I think with Roadrunner we can make more people aware of us than was possible in the past. So there's a lot of road for us to go down. This really is a new chapter and the sky is the limit. Each time we go out we play bigger venues and the album sales are consistent. So we are very fortunate, and we hope to increase on both of those."

One irony was that a mere matter of days after signing to Roadrunner, an announcement was made that their new label had been bought for a reputed $74 million by Warner. Given the band had spent eight years trying to escape from the conglomerate that was Warner/Atlantic/Elektra, that news was understandably viewed as a troubling development. Fortunately though, so far Roadrunner have been left to run their own affairs without any dabbling from their Warner bosses. But at least it also gives both the band and Roadrunner the opportunity to prove a point, as noted by Roadrunner product manager Vinne Hartong in an interview with *Billboard.com*.

"It's cool to take this band that has been shown no label love in like ten years and finally give them what they deserve," said Hartong. "We have a point to prove. I'd love to prove to Atlantic, 'If you guys had just done an ounce of work, this is what you could have had.'"

That dedication to the band also extended to ensuring that the 2007 summer tour was prominently plugged in the press, as Dream Theater headed into Europe in early June to make festival appearances and the odd headlining gig. Those dates began at the "Gods Of Metal" festival in Milan, and true to the band's desire to be predictably unpredictable in their set list selection (and to celebrate the album's 15th anniversary) they performed "*Images And Words*" in its entirety. It was a set they would repeat on a number of occasions during the leg, including a gig at Newcastle City Hall on June 9. That concert was ostensibly billed as a warm-up show for one of their most critical career performances, the following day's appearance at the Download Festival in Leicestershire, England. Although not making it on to the main stage but to a second, tent-based stage, they still managed to take the festival by storm. Indeed their popularity was such that even though there were in excess of 7,000 fans levered into that enormous tent, there was another solid ring of a few thousand more left outside, straining to catch every nuance of the performance. That European leg concluded on July 1 at the Rockwave Festival in Athens, and the band headed home for a fortnight's break before resuming their tour in the US and worldwide.

One milestone gig of that second European leg occurred on October 13, when the band finally made the step up from theatres to arenas in the UK with a gig at Wembley Arena. In what might prove to be a watershed appearance, the band performed in front of over 9,000 fans and only time will tell as to whether this is a permanent step up for future tours. The press was unanimously positive in their reviews. Writing for *Kerrang!*, Ryan Bird declared: "It's the type of lengthy set that can often wear thin, no matter how good the band might actually be. Tonight however, no amount of time seems like enough, because Dream Theater are about as perfect as you can get without going under the surgeon's knife. Timeless, magnificent and utterly mind-blowing, Dream Theater remain a truly amazing force – the experience of a lifetime."

Classic Rock's Dave Ling went one step further with a bold prediction for the band's future. "During the encore, guitarist John Petrucci and Portnoy tease the arena with a snippet of the Rush standard 'Xanadu'. In doing so, the point they make is crystal clear. Neither Rush nor Iron Maiden will be around forever. With this Wembley spectacle and the summer's triumph headlining the second stage at Download, they leave us in no doubt of their position as hairy heirs to the throne of both."

Critically though, the band's appearance at a venue as notable as Wembley Arena had also attracted the attention of the mainstream national press, with even the reputable Times newspaper sending a correspondent to review the gig.

"As a line of worker ants scuttled along a network of industrial tubing and other cosmic cartoons played out on the screen behind them, Dream Theater wove a web of intricate sonic thunder that not only tested the limits of rock's compositional boundaries but also delighted their fans," wrote David Sinclair. "It was a display of daunting complexity that also proved surprisingly entertaining."

Indeed the Chaos in Motion Tour included a number of other Dream Theater firsts as they headed for both China and Australia to make emphatic debut appearances. Online Chinese news agency Xinhuanet reported on the band's Beijing show on January 23, declaring that "Dream Theater packed their longstanding classics as well as new hits from their latest album *Systematic Chaos* into a dense two-hour show. Several leading Chinese rock musicians including Cui Juan were among the audience. Local critics were quoted in media reports using words like "astonishing", "comprehensive", "infectious" and "perfect". In spite of such plaudits, the band were far from impressed with the Chinese infrastructure as Mike recalls.

"The truth is that it was our least favourite show on the tour," he says. "It was a very difficult gig and we were flabbergasted at how the country wasn't together, especially since they were hosting the Olympics a few months later. It was just a really difficult gig and they just didn't have it together in terms of preparation and accommodation. This is horrible to say, but a lot of places we go on tour, particularly if we have a bad gig or venue, we will blacklist the venue. After the China gig, I called our manager and said that not only are we blacklisting this venue, we're blacklisting the entire country. We don't want to go back to China."

One intriguing feature of the tour was the appearance of Jordan Rudess's Zen Riffer – effectively a keytar that allowed him to leave the somewhat restraining surrounds of his keyboard racks and to play at the front of the stage and exchange riffs with John Petrucci at close quarters.

"Oh that was so much fun," smiles Jordan. "I had a couple of custom instruments made for me and it was really cool. It really was a trip for me to be able to kind of step away from my position on stage, come up front and rock out in that way. It was definitely very liberating and I can't wait to do it again."

The record label continued to show their support for the band with the release "Forsaken". Although not available at retail stores, a digital download was released on March 31, 2008, and the single was backed by another video. For once, Mike relinquished control of the creative process, allowing John Petrucci to take on the project. In view of the otherworldly content of the song's lyrics, John took the decision to use an animated approach, and engaged the services of the Japanese anime studio Gonzo. Their director Yasufumi Soejima headed the project team and the finished piece gained the hoped-for airplay on MTV.

The band also released their first 'best of' album, in the form of the self-deprecatingly titled *Greatest Hit (... And 21 Other Pretty Cool Songs)*, which drew material from their time with the Warner label. The album cover art was designed by Hugh Syme, and depicted a red armchair which sporting a large white stain which had been created by a passing seagull. A closer look at the title also revealed the word 'shit' had been marked out in red text as part of the title. Selecting tracks from their years with Warner, the double-disc set was intended to be a starting point for new listeners. However, bearing in mind the loyalty of Dream Theater fans, the band ensured that there were enough rare versions and single edits of songs to keep even the most ardent fan satisfied. Kevin Shirley was also involved and he remixed the three tracks taken from the *Images And Words* album – "Pull Me Under", ""Take The Time" and "Another Day" – which made the compilation.

"The album title and artwork is all very tongue-in-cheek, kind of making a mockery of the whole idea of a Greatest Hit package," revealed Mike in *Metal Edge*. "They're just commercials to lure somebody in, to hopefully go deeper and look at the bigger picture, which would be the catalogue of our albums. Inevitably when your contract ends with a record company, they're going to take advantage of the back catalogue. Frankly that's fine with me, because I was able to have total control over it. If an album like this is going to exist, then I'm glad I was able to be hands-on with it. The track listing I picked was really to serve as a nice introduction for somebody that doesn't know who Dream Theater are, but there was also a big emphasis on making it interesting for the existing fans as well."

Another of the band's ambition was also realized in the spring of 2008, with the launch of the inaugural Progressive Nation 2008 Tour. The brainchild of Mike Portnoy, this festival was designed to celebrate the diversity of progressive rock and metal, with Opeth, Between The Buried And Me, and Three joining Dream Theater in a tour that began in Mexico City on April 29 with gigs across North America before a finale on June 4 in San Juan, Puerto Rico.

"With all the U.S. touring festivals out there each summer, I felt it was time for us metalheads that still appreciated some 'real musicianship' to unite and bring an annual tour to all of the like-minded fans," declared Mike. "The inaugural run of the Progressive Nation 2008 Tour will feature three other bands whose 'prog tendencies' are all very different from each other and show just how diverse progressive music can be. And myself, as the music fan I've always been and always will be, gets to play ringmaster and dream bill matchmaker each and every year with Prog Nation, bringing the best in quality, kick-ass bands together to buck the system and do shit our way. Progressive Nation is musicians and music lovers with open minds and ears playing music for other musicians and music lovers with open minds and ears. One nation under prog!"

"What we do is so different from everything else out there that's popular, all the trends and the fads," confirmed Mike in an interview with *terrorverlag.de*. "We are so blatantly uncool. You know, when you open up a magazine you'll see Mastodon or whoever. All these bands, they kind of all look the same. They're all tattooed and wearing the same outfits. And we totally don't fit in. So in one sense it sets us apart from everybody, made us who we are and made us a completely individual sounding and looking entity. And that's why we've succeeded all this time. Here we are, 22 years later, and our fans are still standing behind us and helping this band grow and blossom. And that's because we just do it our way and don't pay attention to the fads, trends and how we're supposed to sound. We do it our way and the fans seem to support it."

The emergence of such a triumphant, progressive rock tour was also evidence that Dream Theater, by sticking to their beliefs, ideals and streak of originality have managed to become a major musical force. The mere notion of a prog rock package tour a few years ago would have been unthinkable, and it's testament to Dream Theater's persistence that they have, against all the odds, succeeded on their own terms.

With the tour drawing to a close, Mike began his so-called break by beginning work on a live DVD. Billed as the ultimate tour souvenir and released on September 30, 2008, *Chaos In Motion* was a double-disc collection of live footage, behind-the-scenes documentaries and promo videos. Taking more of a relaxed approach rather than the slick, multi-camera production approach used on the likes of *Score* or *Live At Budokan*, there were those fans who were unhappy with such rough and ready footage.

"Well, I was definitely very upfront before it was even released," countered Mike in the *Voices* fanzine. "I tried to make the fans aware so that their expectations weren't raised to the quality level of *Score*. But I'm proud of it and I think it's a great tour souvenir. There's a great range of songs and once again I made sure that the song list was something new from the previous DVDs. There's also a tremendous amount of behind the scenes footage, so there's really a lot for the fans to get into. The only complaint I can see that's a legitimate one is that it is a lot rawer. When we did *Budokan* and *Score*, and even *Live Scenes From New York* to a certain degree, we had a good budget to prepare the pre-production and do a proper high quality shoot. This time around, when you are covering the entire tour, you can't set up a half a million dollar shoot at every single show. The purpose of this DVD was to capture life on the road for a year and a half, and I had to basically work with much rawer footage."

For all those minor criticisms, the live footage still captures the essence of the band in the environment in which they are at their most content, and it is engaging viewing. With Dream Theater getting into the habit of releasing a live DVD following the end of each tour, there was of course a danger that they might saturate their own market and become almost predictable. It was therefore a wise decision to avoid the typical, single concert recording and venture into creating a document of songs performed at various venues around the globe. With the ninety -minute documentary adding to the value of the package, it was a release that was savoured by Dream Theater fans and achieved the aim of being an honest and scintillating souvenir. The DVD also sold enough copies in the first week of release to attain a position of Number 2 in the US music DVD chart. There was also a limited edition which included a 3 CD set of the live tracks. There was even talk at the label of releasing the CD's on their own as Mike recalls.

"Yeah, the label wanted to do that," he says. "I urged and begged them not to because it is a much rawer collection. When you are watching a DVD you can see that is the approach and feel. Yet when you are listening to a CD, and especially if it's going to be an official live album like *Score*, I want it to be up to the level of what is expected. Ten years down the road, when you are looking at your CD collection, you are not going to remember it as 'Oh this one was supposed to be a rawer take'. To me it was very important not to offer it as a live album because it didn't feel like a live album. This was more of a collection."

With *Systematic Chaos* finally and justifiably projecting the band on to a new and wider world stage, Dream Theater were on the cusp of achieving all they had aimed for over the last two decades. Their next move would undoubtedly be a crucial one, and as they now were firmly ensconced in the seemingly never-ending studio-album-tour cycle, there were already thoughts as to where they might go from here.

SEVENTEEN

THE BEST OF TIMES

Echoing the writing of *Systematic Chaos*, Dream Theater had taken a few months off to convalesce from the lengthy exertions of the world tour before they again headed to Avatar Studios in Manhattan on October 7, 2008, to begin writing their next album. As with its predecessor, the band had opted to live and work in the city during the week before heading off to their respective family homes at the weekend. It's a system that offers them the prospect of being able to concentrate solely on the music whilst not being too far from their families and is clearly one that they have become comfortable with, as Mike explains.

"We've kind of tried all different ways," he says. "When we did *Awake*, we went to Los Angeles and were completely away from home and didn't see our families for months. So that was a little too confined. There were other times, like when we recorded at Bear Tracks Studios, when Jordan and myself would commute. For me, that was hard to stay focused because you are juggling home life and music every day. So this is the perfect medium where we are actually able to be away from the rest of the world all week long and just stay in the city Monday through Friday, and then go home on the weekend to be with our families. It's hard because we all live in different places now. We've got James in Canada, two guys in New York, and two guys in Pennsylvania. New York City is the best middle ground and the best place to make a record. You have everything at your fingertips. So it's actually the best of both worlds. We've been doing this for the last two or three albums now and it's definitely the best way for us."

"Yeah, exactly," interjects John Petrucci. "I don't live too far from the city but I'm still about a ninety-minute drive, or on a bad traffic day it could be two and a half hours. So yes, it's commutable and a lot of people do commute from Long Island to New York. However, with the hours that we work, it doesn't make sense to be driving home at one in the morning, getting home, and then having to get up early to go back. It's not very conducive to creativity. So we stay in the city, and it enables you to really focus on being creative. You can be intense, not scattered, and you can really concentrate on what's going on. So it's very cool in that sense. And I'm close enough to home so that if there are things I need to be home for, I'm able to do. So if I need to commute one day or get home for an event or something at school for the kids, we've been able to work all of that out. So there's definitely that convenience factor."

With Dream Theater also taking complete control of Avatar for both the writing and the recording process, it's not an especially economic way to record an album. But apart from the convenience factor, engineer Paul Northfield offers another advantage to such an unusual working practice.

"It's a very specific and expensive way to make records especially these days when you have so many other alternatives," he asserts. "I know from a lot of other bands that I've worked with that they like to work on neutral territory. So even though they have their own studios, it's always an idea to be on neutral territory so that no one feels that they were put upon. Also for Dream Theater, the process of recording is part of their life and isn't a question of being expedient. The cheapest, most expedient, way to do a record is to write in a rehearsal place, put together all of your songs and then go into the studio. But for Dream Theater, as they're spending so much of their time on the road, they need to take the opportunity when they are recording to use it as a way of living close to home. New York is, of course, the closest centre to where they live and is equidistant between Mike and John's house. So that really drives the whole thing."

Prior to the sessions even beginning, there had been intense speculation as to how Dream Theater would respond to the success that the contemporary sounding *Systematic Chaos* had brought them. With fresh, younger fans being attracted by some of the heavier riffs and growling vocals, there might have been a temptation to carry on in the same musical vein merely to maintain this new and enlarged fan base. There was even a suggestion that the band might consider partially eliminating the more progressive side to their music, preferring to permanently move in a heavier direction.

"Well, that's a valid concern," admits Mike. "But we're never going to make a record that's just trying to get younger fans. We certainly love the prog side and it's a huge part of this band but it's not the only part. The metal side is a big part of us and we aren't just trying to attract 16-year-olds with that. It's just something that has always been a part of us. Ultimately, I think that metal side of us is what has made us a little bit bigger than a lot of the prog bands. You know, I'll go to NearFest and I'll see all these bizarre prog bands from Norway or Canada. They will typically sell about a thousand copies of their albums and play shows to only a hundred people a night. Then I look at what Dream Theater has become, how we're playing to thousands of people a night and selling hundreds of thousands of albums. I wondered what was setting us apart from them, and I realized that it's the combination of all the prog and metal elements. But it's the metal side to Dream Theater that has made us bigger and more mainstream. And we're not trying to capitalize on that, it really is just a natural part of our sound that has helped broaden our appeal."

John Petrucci also claims that the band have never considered such a clinical moulding of their sound simply to appeal to a wider, metal-orientated market. However he does confess that some of the more overtly classic-sounding progressive rock doesn't have the same resonance with him as it once did.

"That's just a matter of taste to be honest with you," says John. "I think it would be dangerous to think that way because it's kind of not what started our whole philosophy. We need to have the freedom to go in any direction but at the same time it's definitely a matter of taste. Some of it just hits me like 'I just don't like that style any more'. But there's never a feeling of 'We can't do that because it will turn away metal kids'. Definitely not. That would be very dangerous thinking and close-minded and that's not what we're about. Our basic sound – and I've said this for years and years – is a mixture of prog rock and metal. I think if you lose that, you just turn into any other band. Obviously there are tons more bands that are like that now and have that mixture, but even now, I still hear the separation. When we are mixing an album, I'll reference a lot of music just to make sure that our music is compatible with the latest mixes in terms of sonic range or whatever. And as heavy or riffy as we get, or if it sounds like this band or that, we definitely still have our own thing. There are definitely curveballs in there that we are throwing out and there's a sound. I don't know if it's because it's a mixture of the keyboards and orchestration, or the vocal style. But there is definitely still something that's uniquely related to Dream Theater as a sound. And I think that we are always conscious to keep that. The last thing that I would want to do is to sound like every other band. That would suck. I'd hate that. You'd just blend in and you wouldn't have a legacy. I'm really not about that. Our direction and sound has changed over the years to be more current in the way that metal is now and metal probably is a bigger part of our sound now. But to me that's fine, as it is part of our evolution. I love what Roadrunner did and I think it is incredibly encouraging to meet kids who are 14 and just getting turned on to the band."

Shortly before entering the studio, Mike had also alarmed a number of fans when he described Dream Theater as a band who were entering a "maintenance phase" of their career. Such an expression brought to mind the countless number of bands who have been more than satisfied to rest on their laurels and keep producing albums with near identical musical direction. With a band as free spirited and innovative as Dream Theater, such a prospect startled a large proportion of their fan base.

"Yeah, I really hope that comment wasn't misinterpreted," considers Mike. "I don't ever want to be seen as an AC/DC or Iron Maiden, where we are going to be content to have our style and make the same record over and over. When I said maintenance, I meant that we want to maintain what we have but continue to build on it. And that's not only musically and creatively but also in terms of our audience. We don't want to lose our audience and dwindle down. We want to maintain them and continue to build on it. Plus we also want to maintain the sound and style that has made us what we are and build on that as well. But I don't ever think we are going to stray. It's funny because when you look at bands that have strayed from their sound, like Metallica or Queensrÿche in the Nineties, they have all realized what has hurt them and are all coming back to what made them popular to begin with. The Metallica album, *Death Magnetic*, is the album they should have made after *And Justice For All* and it only took them twenty years to get back to it! So I don't ever want us to stray."

The start of the writing sessions for the album also mirrored its predecessor as there was no central master plan in place before the band began the process of putting together ideas. The absence of any openly declared or predetermined musical direction was something that Jordan believes has arisen due to the band having more confidence in allowing the music to grow more organically.

"In the earlier days when I started, at some point I would expect to go in and there would be a master plan," explains Jordan. "You know, was it going to be a concept album? Or was there going to be a move in one single direction? But these days it hasn't really been like that. It was fine. I think what is happening in some ways is that everybody is getting more easy-going and less controlling about that kind of stuff. Or realizing that their energy is better spent in other ways. Mike, who is certainly a person who is capable of taking effective control, is realizing that if he just walks in and we just start writing music, the chances are that it's going to go really well. So that's kind of the way that this album happened. We went in there, kept writing and it kind of shapes up as we go along."

Although there may not have been any master plan that the album would be a bold step in any specific musical direction or possess a defining central concept, the band had decided that they wanted to bring back something which had made their earlier albums so distinctively Dream Theater – the mixing up of styles within a track.

"After every album, we will reflect on what we're going to do next," discloses John Petrucci. "You know, working out what we did right on the last album, or what we did wrong. If there's any criticism that I can give myself and the band with an album like *Systematic Chaos*, sometimes a song would stay too long in one direction as opposed to mixing it up during the song, which is what we honed in on more on the earlier albums. So a song like 'Constant Motion' is exciting but it kind of just stays in the metal style. That would be my only criticism in that maybe it could have been a bit more interesting and original if we mix it up a bit. As we were kind of developing our sound, probably from *Train Of Thought* onwards, one of the things that we realized was that we had moved away from the mixing up of styles and textures. Not within the album as we were doing that, but within a song. A lot of our favourite songs from past albums did that and we decided to revisit it. We wanted to use what we've learned over the past several albums in terms of style, power and production, but marry it with the philosophy that we were conceived with of mixing things up a little bit and throwing in curveballs within a song."

"Yeah exactly," agrees Mike. "If you look at *Systematic Chaos* or *Octavarium* you could say well, this is the heavy song, this is the prog song or this is the mellow song. We realized that in the older days, on *Images And Words* or even *When Dream And Day Unite*, it was all just jumbled together and every song had all of those elements. So that was one aspect that we wanted to make sure was incorporated. The other was that we wanted to have a little bit more of a non-traditional arrangement rather than the verse, chorus, verse, chorus, instrumental section, chorus and then out. We wanted to do songs where it was like verse, chorus and then veer off to almost a whole new song. And then do a verse, chorus, verse, chorus within that song and then veer off into another direction. So that was another aspect of our earlier writing that we wanted to tap into a bit more."

Mike had also secretly hoped that the writing would also steer the band towards creating an album packed with lengthy tracks. Although he never expressed that desire openly to his bandmates, the music they created in those early writing sessions naturally moved in that direction.

"Yeah, I felt it was the right time for Dream Theater to have an album almost like Rush's *Hemispheres* or Yes's *Close To The Edge*," he says. "In those albums, you had just three or four songs that were all long epics but with them being twenty or thirty years old, they were only forty -minute albums. I hoped we would do our version of that and just have five or six epic songs totalling seventy minutes. So really trying that kind of idea but obviously done on a more contemporary level. This was something that I felt we have never really done. If you look at the favourite song lists of fans that are polled or compiled, it's always stuff like 'A Change Of Seasons', 'Learning To Live', 'Octavarium', 'Six Degrees Of Inner Turbulence' or 'In The Presence Of Enemies'. It's always the epics. Usually, we would only have one or two on an album but I thought it would be cool to have an album with four epics and maybe two shorter songs. I wasn't going to force it and I was hoping it would naturally go that way, and that was ultimately what it ended up being."

Indeed the writing sessions rapidly produced masses of material which would form the foundations of the album. The band had swiftly settled into their routine, almost treating it like a day job as they stayed and worked in the city.

"We'll stay in the same hotel a few blocks away from Avatar Studios," explains Mike. "Usually we will get to the studio about two in the afternoon, have some lunch, and then start getting behind our instruments about three or four. We would then work through until midnight or so. So that was the general routine. Normally what happens is that within the first couple of days in the studio we will start playing and a million ideas will come out."

Paul Northfield was again engineering the album, and a substantial part of his role during those early writing sessions was to ensure that all the musical ideas, jams and spontaneous inspiration that the band created is recorded and catalogued at a moment's notice.

"Mike tends to keep a log of everything that they do, so I have to be set up to record anything at any moment," explains Paul. "So from day one, I need to be in a mode where I can instantly start recording. They all have their own headphone system so they can hear each other, and Mike has a constant feed going to a CD burner that would record everything that they are doing in the studio. It's like a stereo and a talkback microphone so he can speak onto it and make notes. And that gives him a note pad so that every idea that went on in the studio is logged. Then, if they have a strong idea, I can record something on a multitrack which can be edited together so they can listen to it as one piece when they go home at night."

"Well there are a couple of different ways that we work," adds John Petrucci. "Sometimes it's like when we did the Liquid Tension Experiment albums, in that a lot of it is born out of improvisation. We set everything up and basically get all our live gear together and set it up in a circle. Everything is set up to be recorded and is mic'd up with headphones. We do a lot of improvisation and during that, things will start to come out and riffs will develop. Anything we start to latch on to or develop, we write down and basically keep an inventory. And some of those riffs and ideas don't end up being used, but others end up sparking a direction. Once we get a direction we start to arrange the song. You know, 'This would be a great intro' or 'This would be a cool verse' or whatever. And then it becomes just a little bit more methodical. So it would be less improvised and more crafted. Other times, people bring things in. If I have an idea at home, I'll record it and bring it in for the guys. Or Jordan will have ideas, put them into a sequencer, play them for us, and we'll use those. But it's definitely very collective once we are all together."

Paul Northfield: "They basically just hack around with ideas and often in Jordan's case, inspiration would come from sounds, as he is invariably digging through new sound libraries. But at the start of the day they would stand around for a bit and sometimes nothing might come for a bit. Other times it will go fast and furious for a bit and then it would flow. They are so spontaneous in terms of their ability to take an idea and then reinterpret it and do it in different ways and styles. Sometimes it's a conceptual thing. Like trying to, regardless of what melody or riff you might have in your head, to decide stylistically what they are looking to achieve. So that might be deciding whether they wanted to do something harmonic and easy on the ear, or if they wanted something aggressive or challenging. That's different from other bands where someone writing a traditional song would sit down and have a chord progression and work something out on the guitar and then the lyrics and melody. It's a completely different process with these guys. They're looking into unusual grooves under that kind of thing. At that point in making the record, they are in their own world and it's almost like they have their own language in terms of the way they communicate ideas and the references they use. They have all this terminology that they would use from a writing point of view. Some of it is self-referential when they are referring to other albums they've done in the past and sometimes it would be other bands that are doing a particular style of thing. So, as an outsider, you're thinking 'What the hell are they talking about?'"

"But the album was perhaps more spontaneous than the last record," he continues.

"They went from being not sure as to what they were going to write to suddenly things flowing and writing a lot in a short space of time. And that was without spending too much time pondering what they were going to write. They were quite excited at the time as the music just started to flow very quickly which was great."

One notable change from the recording of the album was the

absence of James for a large proportion of the writing sessions. Ever since the crisis that almost led to James leaving the band following the tour to support *Six Degrees Of Inner Turbulence*, James had been present for all the writing and recording sessions. However, in a return to the situation that existed in the Nineties, James was rarely seen at Avatar.

"We were in the studio for 22 weeks, and James was with us for one week during the writing and the two weeks that he recorded his vocals," confirms Mike. "So basically he wasn't really with us for this record. I think that we have come to accept that this is the chemistry and this is the way it works. The last couple of albums he did come out and hang around in the studio, but that was just to be part of the spirit. He really didn't add anything to the chemistry and he never really contributed to the musical writing. This time around, we started the first few weeks without him. He was originally going to join us, but the chemistry was good and it was working so we all kind of felt that it would be throwing an extra body into the room. The reality is that we write the music without him, so we felt it would be better to continue that way. The less people in the studio the better. We try to keep as few people around as possible because otherwise the studio can get very busy and distracting."

"It was kind of funny how this worked out," recalls James. "I went down there initially to have a meeting and get some things on the table as to what we wanted to do and what we wanted to see happen in the future. I then went away and said to the guys 'OK, I'll be coming back down soon and I'll see you then.' The guys had all their gear set up so they started to work on some ideas. The next thing I knew, I got an e-mail from Mike saying, 'Oh my God, we've written the first song!' And things kind of seemed to keep going in that direction. So I can say that I completely stayed away from everything. I really did. I just sat back and went, 'You know what, I'll come down when needed as you guys are basically writing the same way that you've always written. You're sitting in a room and bouncing ideas around.' On the previous albums, I was able to make my suggestions right in the moment when something was going down. I might say, 'You know what guys, I'm not feeling that. That's not right.' Or 'That's really cool what's going on there.' This time around, what would happen is that they would send me the demos of the songs, or as far as they had got with it, and if there was something I wanted to comment on I would e-mail them. So they would take my suggestion and if they wanted to do something with it, then fine. Or if there was something that they didn't want to change it would always be explained to me."

"At this point in the game, and this is me being totally honest, it comes down to me realizing that I can contribute to melodies, and I can contribute lyrics but I'm not going to be busting down a door to do so. I think when you get older, you're not so driven through pride or ego, and you start to think to yourself what is it that we are trying to accomplish here? And if the end result still comes out sounding great, then so be it. I think with John and Mike, they realize that I could contribute to the melodies and lyrics. In fact there was a communication breakdown because I guess the way it was first talked about was going to be, 'ok, you guys go for it. Write the melodies, write the lyrics, and you just do it. I'm going to sit back here and I'll see you when I come down to sing.' But then John Petrucci contacted me and said to me, 'Are you writing lyrics for this particular song?' And I was like 'What? What are you talking about?' So there was a bit of a communication breakdown there but needless to say it worked out in the end. I mean granted, there is a lot of controversy out there about why didn't James contribute this or that. Well it's not that James isn't willing to but it just comes down to how the process unfolded and what was communicated throughout the band. At the end of the day, if it's going to be then it will be. I'm fine with that because I'm not a man in his twenties any more saying 'Wait a minute, you have to have me in there otherwise this is bullshit.'"

Although James takes a pragmatic approach when viewing his place and role within the band, he clearly retains a desire to be involved at a deeper level on future albums as he explains: "I did have a conversation with John and Mike and said, 'ok, this is how this one unfolded, but with the next album guys? No way'," he says firmly. "I don't want to be sitting back and not wanting to contribute the melody and lyrics for the songs. This was how this album unfolded, and that's cool, but on the next one I don't want to see this go down. And it wasn't said in an aggressive manner. It wasn't a case of, you know, screw you and all that kind of stuff. It was just mentioned so that it is known that 'Hey you know what guys? I'm passionate about melodies too. I'm passionate about lyrics as well.' And that, quite simply, has to be considered. Period."

Yet as Paul Northfield surmises, although James's participation was limited, the band were ever mindful of his abilities when writing the album and he feels that despite the singer's absence from the sessions, the excellence of the end product speaks for itself.

"The band were pretty clear on where they were going direction wise and they were very conscious of trying to write stuff that was in a comfortable range for James," he recalls. "So he wasn't down as much during the process of making this record. It's always a tough thing for him when he comes in and is handed the melodies. He would of course get demos sent to him in advance so he could spend time with it, listen to it and think about his presentation. Mike and John are very specific in terms of what they are looking for in the melodies and the phrasings. But I do think that not withstanding that, they've made an album where he is sounding very good on it. The record has got a good flow to it and it came together very well indeed."

The speed of the writing process was also not lost on Jordan. Whereas in the past, the band may have argued for hours over chord changes, he cites Dream Theater's ability to go into the studio and get the job done as one of their major assets.

"One of the things that I think makes Dream Theater work is that we are able to go into a studio, get these ideas down and commit to our musical ideas," he says. "So after two or three days, we have a piece of music, put our stamp of approval on it, and go 'ok. That's it.' It happens really fast. And then it takes more days to lay down the parts. You have to do the final drums, the final bass, the final guitar, keys and vocal. It's kind of like the writing of the music was the easy part and then you've got to write the lyrics!"

Writing lyrics has always been a bit of an afterthought for Dream Theater – a task that was shared out amongst the band once the music was finalized. Previous albums had seen the lyric writing duties falling to Mike, John Petrucci, James and John Myung. For this recording though, only John Petrucci and Mike were involved. As already mentioned, James didn't make any contributions and John Myung also passed on the opportunity. Despite some perceptions that Myung's undoubted lyric writing ability was being blocked within the band, Mike claims that the bassist is still always welcome to make submissions.

"You know what? Let me get something straight," he said in an interview with the New Voice fanzine. "I have been encouraging him to write lyrics for every album. So I wish people would stop blaming everybody else for John Myung's actions or lack or actions. John is a big boy and is responsible for what he wants to do. Yes, John Petrucci and I produce the records but we encourage everybody in this band to be all that they can be. Whether or not they step up to the plate is their own decision."

For some bands, those tasked with penning lyrics might carry around a scrapbook full of notes, poems and ideas which they would utilize during the formation of a song. But for Dream Theater, the words come in a blitz of creativity at the conclusion of the writing sessions. Both John Petrucci and Mike have very different methods of writing, with Mike preferring to write alone in the sanctity of his hotel room late at night and John choosing to treat the task almost like a day job.

"The lyrics are their own thing," explains Jordan. "For instance, when I was doing my keyboard parts, John Petrucci had set up his office in the other room in the studio. He has his dictionaries, thesaurus, computer, pens and pencils, and special lighting in there and was working on his lyrics. So that's another adventure."

"It really is a job in itself," adds John. "I set up an office, with the music and a whole bunch of pads, reference materials and things around me. Computers do make it easy now as there is so much reference material out there. But to stare at blank page and come up with something could be a challenge. I think that is why for me, once I have the topic, I am able just to write pages and pages of notes on that topic. And once you've done that it becomes a lot easier. It's really just getting past that first barrier."

Mike: "You know what? For this album I ended up using my Blackberry because I had it with me at all times. So a lot of the ideas for lyrics on this album would come to me when I was food shopping, or sitting at home watching a movie and something would spark an idea. And as my Blackberry is always on my hip, I would just pull it out, jot it down and compile it that way. I find that most of my lyric writing through all these years is always a very late night thing. I'll be lying in bed and trying to go to sleep at four in the morning, my wheels are still spinning and I end up having to get up and jot it all down. But both of my sets of lyrics on the album are based out of personal experiences, and they were both very therapeutic to write. You had one of the songs ['The Shattered Fortress'] closing off the 12-step saga and the other one was really, really emotional to write a song for my Dad ['The Best Of Times']. In both cases they were things that were right out of my life and those emotions are with you all the time. So it's not like I have to sit down and read a book for inspiration or create a fantasy world. I'm just writing about things that are part of me."

One of the criticisms levelled at *Systematic Chaos* was that lyrically – certainly in terms of those written by John Petrucci – there was a tendency to dwell on supernatural tales. Although there was unquestionably a proportion of the Dream Theater fan base that lapped up songs about dark masters and vampires, there were those who found those lyrics incongruous and impossible to relate to. Perhaps recognizing that fact, John deliberately veered away from fantasy worlds as a subject matter.

"Yeah, this album is all reality for me," explains John. "I thought I'd try something different, went in the exact opposite direction and I wrote about real experiences. I was talking to my wife before I started writing the lyrics, and she was saying that I have so many interesting stories that I'm always telling. She was saying 'Why don't you think of some of those events as you have such colourful stories.' And it seemed so obvious but I guess I've never really done that. I've written songs that are fantasy-based, and even early on in our career, I'd done that with songs like 'Metropolis' or 'The Killing Hand'. But at the same time, I've also written songs that are reality-based about my own experiences. So those are songs like 'Take Away My Pain' or 'Another Day'. But I realized that I've never written stories about things that actually happened to me. You know, about situations that I went through that were unusual or bizarre, or interesting. Whenever I wrote about reality it would always be more emotional. It would be about a loss, a feeling, a philosophy or generalization about something. So this album, I wrote about experiences and I started to think back 'What are some interesting stories that I've told my friends'. You know, like 'Guys, you'll never believe what happened to me!' So I started to realize that these were really cool stories. And when you do that you are able to really write from your heart and you're not making it up. You are just reflecting back and thinking about what happened. All these people that seem like really weird characters are actually real people. And when you hear the lyrics you will be like 'What the hell happened here?' Who the hell are these people?'"

Released on June 23, 2009, *Black Clouds & Silver Linings* was perhaps Dream Theater's most consistent and striking album in at least a decade. It was also possibly their most critical from a purely commercial perspective since *Awake*. With the success of *Systematic Chaos* putting the band on a higher stage, both those fans who have admired the band for decades and those relative newcomers who had been turned on to the band by that album had colossal expectations for the follow-up. Somehow, Dream Theater managed to surpass even their own notably high standards and produce an album that was their finest since *Scenes From A Memory* and arguably their strongest to date. Where *Systematic Chaos* may have faltered due to a lack of musical complexity and having the aura of a transitional album, *Black Clouds & Silver Linings* recreated the spirit of such gems as "Metropolis" and "A Change Of Seasons". That's not to say that the band were harking back to former glories though. The songs may be epics in terms of their progressive nature and length, but they are infused with a contemporary edge that sounds so fresh and advanced. And whilst there might be criticism in some quarters for the use of growling backing vocals, they are used sparingly and never sound contrived or incongruous. This is an album that in years to come will stand like a beacon in Dream Theater's back-catalogue. The album title was also a perfect match for the lyrics and the music, and came to Mike when he was driving into the city on a particularly cloudy and gloomy day.

"I thought that summed up where we were at, as both musically and lyrically there's some heavy stuff on this album," he explained. "And there's that expression that every cloud has a silver lining and I think that's true. Everything you look at you can be either optimistic or pessimistic. Lyrically the album is dealing with very heavy, dark subjects.

You know, death, recovery from addiction, near fatal accidents and near death experiences. In all the cases the lyrics are dealing with these topics but with a really optimistic outlook. Any of the lyrics on the album can be looked at with a positive spin. So that's the silver lining. Musically it applies as well, as there are some moments that are very dark and heavy but at the same time it has that progressive, melodic dynamic edge that is part of the Dream Theater balance. So I think it was the perfect title to sum up this album."

Opening the album with a clap of thunder, a creepy piano introduction and some dark and imposing riffs, it's easy to see why "A Nightmare To Remember" had a working title in the studio of "Halloween". The track also neatly defines the direction of the album, lasting 16 minutes, containing some blistering melodies, impeccable musicianship and crammed with time signature changes.

"Yeah and I think that direction is there for everyone to hear immediately," says James LaBrie. "The song is just so driving and you feel like you're being pushed along this extremely potent musical path. I know it's 16 minutes long, but honestly it doesn't feel like that, because it really is so exciting."

Lyrically, the song relates to a serious car accident that John Petrucci and his family were involved in when he was a child travelling home from his cousin's wedding reception.

"It was at night and I believe it was a drunk driver that hit us," he explains. "I was pretty young and I still remember the crash, the mayhem and what happened. It was a while back so there were no seatbelts or anything. My father went through the windshield. My brother went flying up, as he was just a baby and my mother was holding him on her lap. Then I remember being in the hospital and having a light shined into my eyes. I was pretty young and had glass in my eye and I still have a little scar there. So I was really just recounting that story. I couldn't have been more than eight or nine and it was a scary thing to go through. Anytime you are telling a story, you try to add in things to make it more dramatic. So the whole hospital section, I tried to make it like they had me drugged up on morphine and stuff but I was just a little kid."

The track also featured some of the highly divisive, growling backing vocals delivered by Mike, which triggered a barrage of criticism in various reviews and on internet discussion forums. Ironically, that section of the track had been toned down by the band and Mike's original thought of singing these in full Opeth, cookie monster-style was eventually rejected, as he explained in a riposte to the critics.

"I knew my vocals in 'A Nightmare To Remember' would surely spark some controversy and it looks like I was right," he wrote on his website. "I felt the original melody that John Petrucci had to this section didn't work with the music. This section of the song has a really heavy, driving Judas Priest/King Diamond vibe musically and JP had a melody that was more melodic. I felt James's high voice really softened up the music to this very important dramatic section of the song. I really kept hearing a Mikael Åkerfeldt-type, Opeth death growl. Like 'em or hate 'em, the section was really calling for it to my ears. The thought crossed my mind to ask Mikael himself to do it, but then I figured I'd end up having to do it live every night on tour, so it might as well be me on the CD. In the end, JP and I discussed it and he just couldn't hang with the cookie as he thought it was just too radical for DT fans to swallow. So I agreed to try adding James doing a bit of a 'counterpoint' to my cookie monster version to possibly help soften the blow. But I didn't dig this approach as James's clean vocals were still softening up the music to me and the counterpoint approach made it all too confusing and distracted from the drive of the music. So John and I went back to the idea of keeping my vocals for the section to keep it heavy and driving, but getting rid of the Opeth cookie monster approach and going for a more Robb Flynn/Machine Head approach instead (kind of like my 'Constant Motion' voice and in the end, that is what we went with)."

"I did indeed know that no matter what, we wouldn't please everybody with the idea, but I really felt a 'heavy' approach was needed to keep the heaviness of the section. This is really aimed to clear up my side of the street amongst the bashers. I must say the amount of hatred and negativity towards me on other Dream Theater 'fan' sites is truly incredible (you know who you are) and my skin is not as thick as you may think! It baffles me that as the member of DT (or any band for that matter) that must be one of the most fan-driven musicians in the industry, I am so slammed by our 'fans' while other artists (who will go unnamed) that couldn't care less for our fans are put on a pedestal. Sorry, I am still human and can read these forums and it indeed hurts sometimes."

The debate over the "cookie monster" style vocals is certainly intriguing and highly contentious. On one hand, it can be argued that their use keeps the metal side of Dream Theater's music contemporary when you consider their prolific use by other bands. The flipside is that in years to come, that vocal style will drift out of fashion leaving the tracks sounding dated and tied to an era. Take for example the use of electronic drums on metal albums recorded in the Eighties – they might once have been fresh, but ironically they now sound far more dated than records released 15 years earlier. Used sparingly and appropriately though – as they have been on both *Systematic Chaos* and *Black Clouds & Silver Linings* – the vocal style does add another dimension to Dream Theater's music. The only concern is that any future over-reliance would unquestionably cause further splits in the fan base and could damage what the band have worked so hard to achieve.

Of all the tracks on the album, it's perhaps the faultless "The Count Of Tuscany" that will in time be revered in the same way as "A Change Of Seasons". Indeed, apart from the song's length (it clocks in at over 19 minutes), both tracks also share a common heritage. With a vast array of time signature changes, intermingling melodies, bombastic heavy riffs and appreciative nods in the direction of Yes and Pink Floyd, "The Count Of Tuscany" contains all the facets of a Dream Theater track that the band's fans adore and their detractors openly despise. One abiding question is how the band can construct a song as perfect and expansive as this and still leave it sounding cohesive?

"Well, we'll use the riff inventory that we have," explains Mike. "Then as we start assembling songs, we will say 'ok let's go to that F-sharp or that G-minor progression. Basically in the case of 'The Count Of Tuscany', it was a combination of some different ideas which had been waiting in the wings from the four of us collaborating and jamming. Then once you start plugging in those ideas, once you start focusing, it naturally takes you to new places. So really you just start building it, and it's just like painting a picture. You put something down, and that will inspire something else and you just keep adding to it."

"In that song, there's so much going on stylistically, but it's all for the right reasons," notes James. "It's all in the style that has made Dream Theater music so exciting. I really do think that it represents a resurgence of some of the music in Dream Theater's past that really has excited people."

Another Petrucci-penned lyric, the song relates the bizarre events that occurred during a day off on the Italian leg of a world tour. Despite being slightly tongue-in-cheek, the lyrics were heavily slated in some areas of the press and on numerous internet forums.

"Yeah, I've been reading some of the reviews of the album and that is the most criticised lyric with people saying that it is cheesy and blah blah blah. But to me it is just funny," smiles John at the memory. "I guess it does come across as a little bit creepy or funny but it really was so much fun to write. It's an experience I had with Mark Snyder and John Myung. We played a couple of shows in Italy at one point and Mark came out to see us. He's in the wine business so he imports wine and has his own winery in Brooklyn. Anyway, he wanted to check out this winery in Tuscany as he was looking into maybe importing their wine. It was a day off, and Mark asked if we wanted to go for a little trip. So myself, Mark, John Myung and Mike's drum tech at the time, Eric, agreed to go. Mark explained that this count guy was going to meet us at the hotel. So he meets us, we get into this little crappy car and we drive to this castle. On the way, I guess we were in Florence, he was showing us where his family grew up in the city there and pointing out the buildings. And he was telling us, 'You know the story in the movie Hannibal? You know when Hannibal Lecter is in Florence and he was the curator of the library? That character was based on my brother.' So he was showing us the house where that library was and it was really interesting and pretty wild. We were driving forever and of course had the Hannibal thing in the back of our minds!"

"We then pulled up at this vineyard and it was unbelievable," continues John. "It was breathtaking and was a combination of an old castle with servants' quarters and vines with a more modern distillery section. We went in there and met his brother and he was a total character right off the bat. He was smoking a pipe and speaking with an English accent, even though he was Italian, and he was telling us story after story about the wars and the land. So we did everything from look at the grapes on the vine to going down into the cellars to taste the wine right from the barrels. It was really interesting but there were just so many bizarre things that kept on happening. We had this Hannibal thing in the back of our heads and any time something freaky happened we would just look at each other and be like 'Well, it's been nice knowing you!' They were like 'Do you want to go and see our chapel?' So we go to this little chapel and there was this mummified saint in there behind the glass. I don't know if you have ever heard of that? It's so freaking weird. It was like a mummy which was the size of a child and it looked like it was dressed in royal robes with a crown and a black face. It was very weird and creepy. Then we went into the cellar, down the winding stairs in the dark and you don't know what's going to be in the next room. It was like 'Go into the corner of that room and stick you head in that barrel!' Then there was one room that had these massive floor-to-ceiling barrels. He was explaining how during the war, the soldiers would come in and hide in the barrels, but that they never escaped. It was like 'Are they still in the barrel?!' It was an unbelievable once-in-a-lifetime experience. So it was just a bizarre story, and it was kind of creepy and funny. You can take it tongue-in-cheek, but it really happened."

Written by Mike about his late father, Howard, who passed away on January 4, 2009, after a lengthy battle with cancer, "The Best Of Times", must have been an exceptionally challenging song for the drummer to write. With a beautiful piano introduction followed by a few Rush-like riffs and melodies, it could – given the subject matter – have been a distressing or even maudlin listen. Yet it is a deeply moving tribute and a song that somehow manages to remain ultimately uplifting.

"That to me kind of sums up the whole of *Black Clouds & Silver Linings*," agrees Mike. "It is full of heavy, dark experiences but taking the optimistic aspect of those, trying to make the most of it and turn it around. This is a perfect example. I didn't want to write a gloomy, sad, depressing song for my Dad. I wanted to write something that focused more on the 41 great years we had together, and it was only the last six months that were very, very difficult and sad."

Listening to the track, it's hard to comprehend that the music was written long before Mike had decided to select that musical piece to add lyrics to. The music and the lyrics seamlessly fit together and are a perfect match.

"That was the second song we wrote musically," recalls Mike. "I remember I had an instrumental tracking demo of it. We had just finished and I was flying out to see my Dad as I was going out to see him in California every couple of weeks or so because he was sick. I remember listening to it on the plane and in the rental car, and I just thought that the mood and themes of the music were so sad. I thought 'You know what? I've just got to write about my Dad and what is going on.' It was bringing me to tears musically without any words even attached to it at that point. It was just such a moving song musically that I knew it would be the perfect one to write about what I was going through. I ended up writing the lyrics and finishing them before my Dad passed away. It was the greatest gift. I actually did a demo of the song with me singing and I was able to play it for my Dad. We were sitting at his bedside and we listened to it holding hands, and we cried the whole time. It was an incredibly moving and powerful experience that I'll never forget. For me to have been able to have shared that song with him before he died meant the world to me and him. It was amazing. I played the demo of me singing it at his funeral as well and everyone was sat there crying. It was really heavy."

With the song being so personal and with Mike having already added rough vocals to the track, was it a worry having to contemplate James singing the song and adding his own vocal nuances to the track?

"Yeah that was a concern of mine after writing those lyrics, singing the demo and playing it for my Dad," confesses Mike. "Especially after playing it at the funeral, I was thinking it could be really strange to hear somebody else singing the words. So that was a part of me that was torn, but I knew that I didn't want to be singing lead vocal on a Dream Theater album in that capacity. It is one thing to be singing a quick verse here or a metal thing there, but something like this was so filled with emotion and such a powerful message that I knew it had to be delivered with the strength of James's voice. But I was a little concerned as to how it would go over. But ultimately, once he started to sing it in the studio, he totally nailed it and pulled it off. Realistically he has been doing that for many years now. He has been singing our lyrics and trying to put himself into it and convey our messages and our words, and deliver them the best he can. So I think he did a great job with it."

"Well, with the lyrics, whether it was Mike or John who'd written it, I will always sit down and read them, and try and work out what they are saying to me," adds James. "Then when it gets close to actually singing, I'll start thinking about how I want to express it. You know, in terms of texture and the tonality that I want to use. Then I'll sit down with the guy who wrote the lyrics and ask them to give me a literal interpretation. Really, just so I can really become what the lyrics are trying to convey. And that's basically how I approach each and every song."

One song that James would have been instantly familiar with was "The Shattered Fortress". The track was the final piece in the Alcoholics Anonymous, twelve-step suite that Mike had commenced writing back in 2002 with "The Glass Prison" on the *Six Degrees Of Inner Turbulence* album. Effectively the suite is a concept album that has been spread over five albums, and consequently "The Shattered Fortress" reprised many of the musical and lyrical themes that had evolved on those earlier pieces. So how did the band approach the writing of this final, musically stunning song?

"We would really just think about it when we started writing each album," explains Mike. "I had a lyrical vision that spanned over the course of the five albums, but musically we just approached it freshly each time. We would look back at where the previous chapters had gone musically and pick out parts that we wanted to incorporate. In the case of 'Repentance' on *Systematic Chaos*, we knew we wanted to have something very mellow and hypnotic. With 'The Shattered Fortress', we knew it was the final chapter so we actually sat down and listened to all four of the previous tracks. We then made notes on the progressions of the parts, and the melodies that we liked and wanted to reprise. As this was the grand finale, I knew it would really be made up of all the musical and lyrical references from the past, and bring them all together to wrap it up, like any good concept album would. I look at these five tracks as basically a concept album that just happens to be spread across five releases. Ultimately it was composed in the way it would be if you were writing a concept album or a big epic piece."

With Mike having faced the trial of producing lyrics for the suite on every album, it was a relief to have finally completed it. Although the finished piece is strong musically and lyrically, the obligation of having to write another piece every time the band entered the studio had clearly started to become a chore.

"I feel I kind of dug myself into a hole with it," says Mike. "It was a nice idea seven years ago. I didn't realize that it would take so long to complete but I guess I should have. After a while it became like an obligation hanging over my head, like a homework assignment. So it's nice to finally be finished with that vision."

"Wither" is a welcome break from the album's intensity and is a concise ballad that's harmonious and intensely hummable. Lyrically it deals with the creative process, and with such lines as "Find the words and let it out / Staring down nothing comes to mind / But I feel I'm getting nowhere and I'll never see the end" John Petrucci eloquently describes his frustrations.

"It was the first song I was writing lyrics for and I actually wrote a full set of lyrics but I ended up scrapping them which happens sometimes," says John. "I started to think about creative people, whether you are a lyricist, songwriter or an artist, and how there's that point when you are starting at that blank canvas. There's that point where it's like, 'What do I do?' So it's kind of about the spark of that creative process. But it's not just limited to writer's block and it's a bit broader than that. The reason I used the word 'wither' is because sometimes with inspiration you can try too hard. It's the same thing with music, too. If you try too hard, you almost put up obstacles and, not wishing to sound too existential, but if you just let it flow through you, you take your boundaries off and it kind of comes out. You can't really explain where it's coming from, it's just inspiration. So the sound of the word 'wither' does sound kind of wimpy, you know? Why would you wither when you're a big strong person? But it's not in that sense as it's more in the sense of just letting yourself go and getting out of your own way. Letting your ego float away and just allow the creativity to flow through."

The track was also credited solely to John, as he had constructed the basics of the song before presenting it to the rest of the band in the studio.

"John came in one day and played it on the piano," recalled Mike in an interview with Scott Hansen. "Although he doesn't really know how to play the piano, he is able to play block chords. So he sat down and showed it to Jordan and sang the melody. We were like 'Yeah, that's really nice, let's turn this into a song.' It was such a simple song that was there no reason for us to Dream Theater-ize it. It was really something he had and we brought it to life."

"A Rite Of Passage" was chosen as the album's lead-off single, and with an amalgam of catchy riffs, frenzied instrumental sections and an infectious chorus, it was a natural choice. Reminiscent of "Pull Me Under" in terms of its approach, the song manages to combine the essence of Dream Theater's style with an immense sound that is verging on the commercial. And, much like that solitary hit from 1992, "A Rite Of Passage" runs in at over eight minutes and consequently needed to be ruthlessly edited to reduce it to an acceptable and practical length for both radio and video. Amusingly, even after chopping long sections from the track, the edited version still ran in at over five minutes.

"Sometimes, as much as you can reduce things, you can lose the really good stuff," considers Paul Northfield. "So it's not easy sometimes to shut things down. 'A Rite Of Passage' is an eight-minute song which is an intricate, powerful, and sophisticated performance track. So that obviously required chopping down because they can't do much with it at eight minutes. They really wanted something that was a really good track the people could make use of. And of course if you make them too long, that limits how people are going to be able to use it or play it. But I do think they managed to chop it down in a reasonable way, without losing too much, and it is still a great track."

"Lyrically that's about freemasonry," says John Petrucci. "It's one of those topics that I find very interesting and very elusive. When you ask someone what freemasonry is, a lot of people don't know. You watch documentaries on the History Channel or whatever, and it's all shrouded in conspiracy and how all these presidents and leaders were freemasons and how the city of Washington, D.C., is laid out according to Masonic systems, and all this crap. I started reading about all the other secret societies like The Rose And Cross, and the others associated with colleges such as the Skull And Bones. I make a reference to a book that was written by an ex-freemason called The New World Order that was trying to tie it in with satanic rituals but it ended up being a bunch of bullshit."

James LaBrie: "Basically, if you think about what you read about the Masons, it's usually people who are in powerful positions. It's really people who want to be free thinkers. They don't want to be told what is acceptable, what the boundaries are and not afraid to cross the line. I think it was really for them to be able to express themselves, be able to have that freedom of thought and also by a very indirect way to bring those ideas into the real world. And let's face it, there are people who think they are a cult which they were not. I think there are a lot of misconceptions and misinterpretations as to what they were. They were tradesmen and it was to ensure that any kind of soliciting or contractual situations would come through them. There is a lot out there about the whole Masons thing. Basically, 'A Rite Of Passage' is all about this."

Unlike the disastrous first shoot for "Constant Motion", the video for "A Rite Of Passage" went smoothly with the band and label being satisfied with the finished visual projection. The project was aided by the presence of a strong-minded director in Ramon Boutviseth who had both the technical ability and necessary visualization to present both the music and the band in the best possible light.

"Well the director was very focused and had a specific vision as to how he wanted the song to be interpreted," recalls James. "I am sure that he and Mike would have talked about that as well as John Petrucci.

But the guy came in and it was really well organized, and very professional. He has some very good ideas and I personally think that it's definitely going to be our best presentation video wise. Which let's face it, I don't think promo videos are really our forte to be honest with you. I think with Dream Theater, the perfect format for us is a full-length DVD which shows us in our more natural environment on stage. It's funny, because I've always said that videos are very contrived. I think when you're watching them being filmed it's pretty cheesy. There are lots of things in the video that you're going, 'Oh my God, this is so phoney'. I mean, you are just trying to create something that is so unnatural. But at the same time, you're trying to achieve something that looks like it is natural and that it was done in real time. But other than that, I think it is going to be a fabulous video."

James certainly has a legitimate point. The video is pretty slick and centres on the band running through the track in a studio environment. With a dark backdrop, smoke, wind machines and even snow floating around, it is visually striking. Quite what the significance is of a number of extras dressed as monks in bright red habits, or the mysterious figures warming their hands on a glowing cube, isn't clear, but as Mike explains they left the creative decisions to the director.

"Yeah, we gave the director a lot of creative licence and the next thing we knew our gear was getting covered in fake snow," he laughs. "But I don't know what the concept really is. Having said that, I don't know what the concept of any video is. I see videos all the time and I have no idea what the hell they are about! It was just us playing. In fact we were playing and all of a sudden it started snowing on the set. You know, this was fake snow – we were indoors. So they had all this fake snow with fake wind and then there were flashing things in the background. So I've no idea as to what was going on, but it looked as cool as hell. I don't think we've ever done a great music video. I think this is our eighth or ninth video and I've never been happy with any of them. But I have a good feeling about this one."

Given his involvement in directing previous videos, as well as consistently taking an overview of how the band are presented, was it tough for Mike to surrender the control over this video shoot?

"Yeah, well I am alright with relinquishing the role for music videos as that is not my forte. I'm not a big music video fan. So when it came to directing our music videos, I just don't care. I have no problem relinquishing the power in that department!"

The album cover was once again designed by Hugh Syme who has established himself as the band's permanent choice as artist. Harking back to the days of Awake and *Images And Words*, the cover featured a batch of lyrical references, as well as playing on the optimistic message in the album's title.

"Well yes, it takes all the different elements from the various songs," says Mike. "There was no deep thinking there and we always want to work with Hugh. We have worked together really well over the last few albums. He's a great guy and an amazing artist. So the art just kind of went in that old-school direction. It certainly wasn't an intentional decision to make an album cover that maybe looks like *Images And Words* or *Awake*. It just kind of naturally happened that way."

In order to try and address the problem of fans downloading the album illegally for free, Roadrunner were keen to release *Black Clouds & Silver Linings* in a variety of formats that would appeal to fans. So apart from the standard edition, there was a three-disc version that included an instrumental version of the album, as well as a bonus disc of Dream Theater performing cover versions. And with a double LP record, and a special edition that included isolated stem tracks of individual instruments to allow budding producers to make their own versions of the album, there were plenty of incentives to buy the album in one format or another.

"The only good thing that's coming out of the downloading craze is that record companies, in a desperate scrambling attempt to hold on for dear life, are putting out all these special edition box sets and deluxe editions," explained Mike in a radio interview with Eddie Trunk. "So really, this has been a good thing for the fans as now they are able to get all this extra stuff. It's good because it's enticing the fans, even if they have downloaded the album illegally in advance, there is still something to bring them into the stores when the album is released and gives them something to look forward to that they can't download illegally."

Those cover songs were stylistically wide-ranging and were also a way of Dream Theater acknowledging those bands who had been important influences on their music. Ranging from Rainbow to Zebra, King Crimson to Queen and the Dixie Dregs to Iron Maiden, the band provided a refreshing and often unique take on some classic tracks.

"Dream Theater have always done covers but it was always live," said Mike. "I've also done some covers in the studio with other projects like Transatlantic, Neal Morse and OSI but I have never with Dream Theater. So I thought it would make a good bonus disc. I chose a couple of metal bands, a couple of classic rock bands and a couple of prog bands. In some cases they are bands that aren't even very well known or famous and I thought it might introduce our fans to some good new music. The first track is 'Stargazer' by Rainbow which I think is perfectly suited to Dream Theater. Another one of my favourite Rainbow songs is 'The Gates Of Babylon', which Dream Theater used to cover 23 years ago in our early days. But I thought 'Stargazer' would be a good one because I knew James would sing the hell out of it as the vocals in that song are incredible, and there's a great guitar solo. The second track is three Queen songs which are pretty obscure. They are from the *Sheer Heart Attack* album. I've always wanted to cover them and this seemed like the perfect opportunity. When you're covering Queen you want to be able to have the production as it would be very hard to play these songs live. So doing them in the studio was a great opportunity to really nail the Queen style. James did the lead Freddie Mercury vocal but all the other vocals are me. I just went nuts one day in the studio and did all the Roger Taylor and Brian May harmonies and just stacked them and it was a lot of fun!"

The band's take on Queen didn't go unnoticed. Their legendary guitarist Brian May was suitably impressed, writing on his website that "Dream Theater seem to be amazing. It's beautifully done, with great vocals, great musicianship and a great production. And cop that solo in 'Tenement Funster'. Ouch! I love it and it's a great compliment to us. It's great to hear someone do our stuff, fathom all our conjuring tricks and then add some great new ones of their own." Queen drummer Roger Taylor also described the track as "The best Queen cover job ever."

The cover of "Odyssey" by the Dixie Dregs is also inspired, with Mike explaining that "The Dregs are surely one of our biggest instrumental influences and we were honoured to have them as our opening act in 2000 in America. Musically they are real heroes and I always thought that this was probably their greatest musical masterpiece and is truly an odyssey."

The most obscure selection was the Zebra track "Take Your Fingers From My Hair" which first appeared on their 1983, self-titled album. With an acoustic melody gradually building to a straight-ahead rock crescendo, the song provided a perfect opportunity for Dream Theater to put their own inimitable stamp on this little-known track.

"Zebra were an Eighties band who were local heroes where we grew up in Long Island," revealed Mike. "They are a band from New Orleans but they really made their career playing clubs on Long Island. They put out a debut album that was a classic and every song on that album is amazing. One of our biggest shows in our early days was opening for Zebra. Now they are kind of a forgotten-about band but they're still playing the clubs and are still together thirty years later. So this was our way of paying tribute to a great forgotten band and debut album."

Acknowledging the genuine excellence of *Black Clouds & Silver Linings*, the specialist music press were noticeably eager to praise it. Writing for *Classic Rock Present Prog*, Razif Rauf stated that "Both 'The Best Of Times' and 'The Count Of Tuscany' showcase just what Dream Theater do so brilliantly. These songs will remain in set lists and 'best of' collections for years to come. Despite one or two nagging gripes, there's no doubt that Dream Theater have created yet another challenging and rewarding listen with some dazzling arrangements. Even if you're already a fan, prepare to be amazed." Metal Hammer's Dave Ling was similarly stunned, rating the album at a 9/10 and adding: "Dream Theater have crafted an album that matches and occasionally surpasses past achievements."

Even *Kerrang!* – who have in the past been highly critical of the band but seem to adore them now their popularity has risen – glowed in a five-star review that the album was "written from some deeply personal perspectives, the usual flood of time changes and virtuoso musicianship are imbued with more outright emotion than Dream Theater have mastered since their 1992 breakthrough album *Images And Words*. Giddy with its own stuffy sense of seriousness *Black Clouds & Silver Linings* may be, but when the book of prog metal is written, Dream Theater will be its cover stars." *Classic Rock* also lavished praise on the album, with Dom Lawson declaring the album to be "as brave as inventive as anything in their prodigious catalogue, this album hums urgency, desire and self-belief, as the band strike a sublime balance between self-indulgence and self-discipline. If you crave a musical journey with a few more twists, turns and hairpin bends, Dream Theater remain masters of the form."

Reflecting such praise as well as the unremitting loyalty of the Dream Theater fans, the album made a startling impact on the album charts around the globe. Although entering at the coveted Number One spot in the pan-European combined chart, the most impressive result was that *Black Clouds & Silver Linings* flew straight into the US Top 10 at Number Six. As their highest ever chart debut (the previous high was the entry of *Systematic Chaos* at Number 19) it also outstripped *Awake* in terms of sales.

"It's truly amazing and especially in 2009," beams Mike. "It's incredible for us to have our most successful first week and to sell more records in the first week than we did 16 years ago right off the heel of *Images And Words*. And that was when people were buying records. It just goes to show that our audience defies everything that is calculable in this industry. So it's a great middle finger to our previous record company and shows them what they could have had. The strange thing about it is that it is our most daring album to date. You know, with just six songs and with four of them which are longer than 12 minutes? That makes it even more satisfying. It wasn't like we had put out this sell-out record. Plus, the record leaked five weeks in advance of the release date which we thought would be incredibly damaging. So it just goes to show that everything about Dream Theater is unpredictable – even to us."

The tour was also lengthy and included a career-highlight performance in front of 93,000 metal heads at Donington Park, Castle Donington, on June 14, 2009.

"Oh my God, that was amazing," smiles John Petrucci. "It was certainly the biggest crowd we ever played to and rumour has it that there were 93,000 people here. It seemed like people were into it. We're a funny band really in that we don't fit in to a lot of situations, you know? You had Whitesnake, Journey, Def Leppard and Tesla on the bill, so you wonder how our music fits into that. We are progressive and more metal, so you're not sure how the music is going over. But the beauty of playing a festival like that is that you are playing to different people. So maybe there was somebody there who has never heard of us and might check out our albums. It was fun hanging out with some of the other guitar players like Neal Schon and I even met Brian May. He watched our entire show from the side of the stage. It's funny as when I met him, it was like I was meeting an old friend. He was saying how he loved our version of the Queen songs we recorded for the last album, how he liked my solo, and he was just so nice. You're talking about a guy who is a legend, was in one of the biggest bands in the world, and he was just so down to earth and sweet. He was giving us compliments saying that he was embarrassed to not have been into Dream Theater before. There aren't too many people in the world that have that status and make you feel that humble."

Indeed, May was so enthralled with their performance that he posted on his website that Dream Theater were: "A revelation. The whole band are virtuosos and I'm kind of ashamed that I never discovered them before. Their set was completely without any hint of 'playing to the gallery'. They took their time mapping out their songs, which I can only say succulently drip with the best kind of complexity. It was wonderful playing and I will be back for more. So will about 80,000 *Classic Rock* fans who gave them a great reception in the old 'Monsters of Rock' fields."

"It really was one of those career highlights," adds Mike. "I guess that has to register as probably one of the biggest shows we have ever played. It was just a beautiful day, and was a perfect afternoon. It felt very satisfying and gratifying to be at this point in our career and still have moments like that to look forward to and come our way. It was amazing and I think we really made our mark on the stage that day."

EIGHTEEN

THE SHATTERED FORTRESS

It was on the afternoon of Monday August 30, 2010 – a particularly scorching and humid day even by New York standards – that the members and management of Dream Theater had arranged to meet and cement their future plans. The venue was the Affinia Manhattan, an imposing brownstone hotel on 7th Avenue, and their manager had reserved a plush suite for the band to leisurely discuss the fine details of recording a follow-up to their most successful album to date. With Mike Portnoy's tenure in Avenged Sevenfold scheduled to come to an end in December (he'd stepped in to help that band record and tour their new album following the death of their drummer James 'The Rev' Sullivan), their agenda seemed clear. Now, it was simply a case of discussing where, when and how those long-planned writing sessions would take place. Yet. the drummer was to reveal to his unsuspecting bandmates that he wanted to mothball the band – a decision that would ultimately lead to him leaving Dream Theater just over a week later. What's more startling was that nobody in the Dream Theater organization had any inkling of the bombshell that Mike was about to drop.

"As the meeting started, Mike said, 'Wait a minute guys, I've got to tell you some stuff'," recalls Jordan. "He basically said to us that he felt he really wanted us to take a hiatus and was looking for ways to do it. I think our jaws hit the floor and you could feel the energy in the room just sink, because we were all a little bit in shock. I mean, I guess he had this amazing job with Avenged Sevenfold, and in the back of my mind before the meeting I was thinking 'Oh, maybe he'll come in and he'll tell us that he is leaving and joining Avenged Sevenfold or whatever', but I didn't think that was possible for a second. But then he came in and was basically saying: 'I feel more happy when I'm away from you guys now.' The rest of us just felt like, 'You know what? We've *had* a really cool break here and we're just looking forward to making music.' I think, with his usual kind of conceptual world vision, he had this glorious rock 'n' roll vision of having this amazing reunion with us down the road but we just didn't want to go there. We weren't ready to let go of what we'd been working on for these years."

"Yeah, basically we went into a meeting expecting to talk about details of the studio and when and where, and it took a *whole* different turn," adds John Petrucci. "We were supposed to go into the studio in January, and we'd actually extended our break a bit so that Mike could finish out the rest of the year with Avenged Sevenfold. Then he brought it up that he wanted to take a hiatus. There wasn't anything that led up to it in our minds and it kind of shocked us you know? We weren't expecting that at all. We've known each other for a long time, but from my perspective you could take those same elements [Mike did], the fact that we'd been a band for 25 years at that point, that it was something that we had built up and that we love. It's part of our identity and our family, and our career and our business and we love it. We had no intention or reason to stop it, see it end or take a break."

Throughout rock history, musicians have quit bands, but usually such dramas can be predicted. There may have been long-standing tensions, jealousies, fights, back-stabbing or even the catch-all-evil of "musical differences". But Mike's declaration of a wish to take a long-term break was unforeseeable. One of the most surprising facets of his announcement to the band that day was that there were no warning signs that he was contemplating making such a dramatic decision. Indeed, the only hint of the turmoil that was unleashed in that meeting was something noticed by James during the band's US tour supporting Iron Maiden, when he detected that the drummer was displaying signs of becoming detached and unusually distant. Although at the time he had dismissed his concerns as simple paranoia, with the hindsight provided by the events in New York that day, the singer now accepts that these were a portent of what was to come.

"I really didn't see anything until probably during the latter part of that tour, when I just kind of noticed that he was a little more withdrawn and slightly moody here and there," he recalls. "I just thought that usually somebody is withdrawn or a little irritable when something is bothering them. You know, you can think many things. You can wonder if it's something personal that's going on or if it is band related. I had a conversation with Mike then and I just said, 'I know that you're going to do this Avenged Sevenfold thing and it's going to be exciting. I don't know if I'm getting paranoid here but I would hope that this doesn't jeopardize who and what we are as Dream Theater.' At the time, I could even see him being a little uncomfortable with that conversation, as if he were saying: 'Look I can't be completely honest with you here, I can't really give you an answer because I don't know what I'm thinking.' Of course, the hammer fell when we met in New York and he basically said, 'Guys can I take the floor because I think what I have to say is really going to alter where we go with this.' Well absolutely. It altered everything."

So where did it all go wrong? Seemingly, from Portnoy's standpoint, the bond between him and the rest of the band had started to deteriorate to such an extent that he viewed an instantaneous band vacation as essential if Dream Theater were to survive at all. Questions were naturally asked as to whether he perhaps considered that the music had become stale, but this is something he vehemently denied, claiming that he merely needed a break from the various personalities and day-to-day rigmarole of the band.

"Honestly, it had nothing to do with the music itself or the musical chemistry within the band," he says. "I was always very inspired when writing and recording together and I'm as proud of our last few albums as anything else in the catalogue. It really was more of the behind the scenes, personal relationships within the band. Yes, on the surface it may seem that life was great and full steam ahead for Dream Theater. Things like playing Download and Wembley, the Iron Maiden tour in the US and a Top 10 entry on *Billboard* were all nice feathers in the cap but beneath the surface, there was a lot of friction and burn-out. I think Dream Theater really needed a bit of a break to rejuvenate our relationships."

Mike's only proposed solution was for the band to go on an indefinite hiatus, believing that a break would help to rekindle his enthusiasm for both Dream Theater and his relationship with the other members. What seems to have especially unnerved the band was that the drummer had been vague as to how long this projected gap would last.

"Yeah, the timing was definitely very strange from my perspective and it didn't make any sense," says John Petrucci. "We are in this position because of something we have built up very steadily and where we have the support of very loyal fans on a worldwide basis. I felt that the point we were at was better than at any time in the past. With our *Black Clouds & Silver Linings* record doing so well and debuting higher than any of our other ones, and just having played with Iron Maiden, it just seemed like we were at a very successful point in our career. It didn't make sense to me. It was very weird."

"Yeah, he was saying a few years, three years, five years or whatever," said Jordan at the time. "I really believe that's what might've been best for *him* but of course there's the reality that there are four other guys who also happen to have Dream Theater as their lives. I think a lot of the problem was with us personally but to me the vibe within Dream Theater was fine. And I've really got no problem with him doing what he was doing with Avenged Sevenfold. I think it's pretty cool going out and playing with a really successful rock group. I just have a little bit of a problem with him thinking that he could control Dream Theater."

Mike himself recalls being somewhat disappointed that the band hadn't welcomed his proposal for a temporary split, saying: "Well, I knew my proposal would be met with some shock and hesitation, but I honestly hoped the guys would see my need for a break or a hiatus and respect it. It's not the most insane request in the history of rock and *many* bands have done it, only to return bigger and stronger than before. Soundgarden, Rage Against The Machine, Jane's Addiction, Faith No More, Alice In Chains, Megadeth, or Phish. Even Rush, Genesis and Pink Floyd have all taken extended breaks in order to keep the band together."

Following Portnoy's declaration of intent, he departed from the meeting, leaving behind four stunned musicians to contemplate the various options that were open to them. That sense of disbelief and the realization of how this could affect their career was enhanced by a very visual reminder lurking outside the hotel window.

"Here's the crazy thing," laughs LaBrie. "Our manager was staying overnight, so he had rented a large suite with a big living room and all that. It had a balcony that went off and we were about 27 floors up. You could walk out on to this balcony and you're looking right up 7th Avenue, and right across from there was Madison Square Gardens. We were like 'We just played *there* with Maiden and everyone in the industry and our camp is saying that with the next world tour, we could play there and do really well.' We were all just looking at it going 'This is bizarre. What? Here's where we should have been standing saying "Hey guys. After the next album, *that's* where we're going."' And instead it was 'What the hell just happened?'"

Although the remaining members of the band hadn't discussed it in any detail, as they left the hotel that night there was an unspoken and underlying determination that there would be no sabbatical for Dream Theater. There was also a tangible resilience and defiance that as far as they were concerned, Dream Theater contained five musicians who had worked tirelessly to nurture and enhance the band's stature for years. The departure of one of them was regrettable but not something that they hadn't overcome in the past. Dream Theater clearly wasn't something they were going to give up lightly.

"We love what we do and didn't want to wait around as things became unstable," says John Myung. "What was initially a four-month break suddenly turned into a hiatus, then changed to a year and four months, which then could have turned into anyone's guess."

Within a matter of hours, the band had decided that their preferred solution was to persuade Mike that there were ways around the problem. A phone conference had been arranged between the entire band and their management for the following week, which gave everyone the chance to fully comprehend the situation and examine the possibilities. Critically though, Dream Theater had also decided that if Mike couldn't be persuaded back, they needed to concoct a plan for finding a replacement.

"The four of us were in contact throughout most of the next day," says James. "We were just saying what we needed to do, this is what we need to consider and let's start to orchestrate things. It wasn't something that any one of us wanted to sit around on, feeling sorry for ourselves or thinking that this was something that was insurmountable. I think we all knew deep down inside, and we had touched very briefly on it even with Mike present, that more than likely this was something that we weren't comfortable with and that ultimately we're all going to come to the conclusion that we needed to move on."

By the time of that phone conference on September 8, 2010, the band reiterated in an exchange with Mike their desire for him to join them in the studio but also explained their intention to continue, with or without him. Although not put quite so aggressively or in those terms, effectively they were issuing him with an ultimatum and calling his bluff.

"We just told him again that we really wanted to move forward with our plan, as intended, with him in Dream Theater, as it should be, you know?" says Petrucci. "You can't twist someone's arm or change their mind, but being understanding of what he was going through and accepting, we said: 'Listen our door is open. You're our drummer, we're here and we want to move forward.' So that message once again was very clear, but he said that he wasn't ready to go back in."

One suggestion put forward by Mike was for him to continue with the band for sporadic live shows during 2011, although this would have entailed the band delaying the recording of a new album until 2012 at the earliest. There was also a proposal that they could enlist a session man to record the album and tour with the band, with Portnoy returning in a couple of years. Although appreciating the gesture, Jordan Rudess reveals that these offers wouldn't have solved the problems.

"Yeah he did, he said he'd work double time and we'd do some gigs," Jordan says. "But you know what? I don't think anybody else in our band wanted to play second fiddle to anybody, ever. He would be out there doing a great exciting rock 'n' roll thing, and what? We're going to sit there playing gigs if we can squeeze them in at the moments where he might have a spare 24 hours or something? No. That didn't really interest us. Mike also said: 'Well maybe just go and get a substitute guy or something for the year, who can play the album and do the tour'. That was something that I thought of myself that maybe might work. But after I'd thought about it, it didn't fly very far before we thought that it wasn't cool. We would have a half-assed Dream Theater that is going to go out and nobody is going to take seriously because it's like some temporary thing with everybody waiting for Mike to come back into his role. That's not what we wanted to do."

With Portnoy still reluctant to return to the recording studio and insisting on taking a break, the course was inevitably set for him to exit the band. The drummer was also at pains to point out that the blame didn't lay with Avenged Sevenfold, and that the troubles were evident well before he recorded and toured with them. It was also plain that he was wounded at having to leave Dream Theater, but that such hurt doesn't prevent him from rationalizing the situation.

"I'd be lying if I didn't say that I'm devastated they chose to continue without me rather than take a break," he added in an interview with *Classic Rock Presents Prog*. "After giving my heart and soul, blood, sweat and tears to them and the band for 25 years, I hoped they'd value me and our relationship enough to respect my need for us to take a little break. The big irony here is that I wanted a break to help mend and strengthen our relations and ultimately bring us closer together. But I could not honestly return to the band to make an album in January without feeling resentment and being uncomfortable that I was forced into doing something I wasn't ready to do. At the moment, I am very happy playing with Avenged Sevenfold and I don't want to stop doing something I am happy doing to go and do something I'm not very happy doing. I cannot do something with my life and career because I 'have' to, I need to 'want' to do it."

With all options being dismissed, and realizing that the band resolutely intended to continue, Portnoy believed there was no other option but for him to depart, thus allowing both parties to move forward. It was simply an impasse that could never be resolved, although that didn't make it any less emotional when the moment of resignation came.

"It was an *extremely* emotional moment and the whole thing to me was very heartbreaking and very sad," says Petrucci with a sigh. "You know, you walk around afterwards going 'Is this really happening?' But I think the whole beauty of Dream Theater is the collective nature and that everybody has their talents. I think we've always been about more than just one individual and that's part of our strength. So we moved forward, as was our right."

Within a matter of hours, Mike had posted a resignation statement on his website which detailed the reasons behind his decision. For Dream Theater fans, this was the first inkling that everything was not as settled within the band as they had come to believe. Writing that "the DT machine was starting to burn me out and I really needed a break from the band in order to save my relationship with the other members and keep my DT spirit hungry and inspired", he declared that he "had decided to leave Dream Theater". As with all band splits, fans have a tendency take sides and there were those who questioned why the band were unable to take the time out that Mike had hoped for. Superficially, at least, that would not seem to be too unreasonable. However, that romantic vision ignores the reality of the situation. With Mike playing with Avenged Sevenfold – a relationship that at the time of the split he had perhaps hoped would continue on a more permanent footing – his proposed sabbatical would leave Dream Theater twiddling their fingers until a time when the drummer deemed it right to return. From the band's perspective, that was never going to happen. They had already had a decent break away and were suitably refreshed and reinvigorated for the next stage in Dream Theater's career. In an interview with *Musicradar.com*, John Petrucci revealed that he had concerns that Mike's work with Avenged Sevenfold could have set a dangerous precedent.

"I remember he told me he was going to play on their album, which was OK by me," he recalled. "I thought, 'Oh, that's cool.' But then he told me he was going to go on tour with them, and I remember telling him, 'I don't think that's such a good idea, Mike.' We had some pretty intense conversations about it. But you know, I can't control what Mike does or what anybody wants to do. Going on the Avenged tour was his decision, but I made it very clear how I felt about it. Doing projects? That's fine. We all do outside things. But playing in somebody else's band and to that degree? That's different. I thought it was treading dangerous waters, for sure."

With Mike's departure a reality, the band wanted to move quickly in order to find a suitable replacement and continue the momentum that they had built up over the preceding years. There was a perceptible determination to locate a drummer who could match the high standard set by Mike and perhaps more importantly find someone who blended in well with the band on a personal level. The band drew up a shortlist of around ten potential candidates, with the band's manager then contacting the drummers in order to determine if they were interested or available to audition. With a couple passing on the opportunity, the remainder were invited to attend the audition process in New York at the beginning of October, 2010. The full list comprised Aquiles Priester (Angra, Hangar), Peter Wildoer (Darcane, James LaBrie solo albums), Marco Minnemann (Paul Gilbert, Kreator), Virgil Donati (Planet X), Derek Roddy (Hate Eternal), Mike Mangini (Annihilator, James LaBrie solo albums, Steve Vai / Extreme) and Thomas Lang (Glenn Hughes band, Robert Fripp). With those selected being e-mailed or telephoned by Dream Theater's manager, the band had to be clear in their own minds exactly what the criteria would be in order that they could select the one drummer who was the closest match for their needs.

"That's right, and that process was like a casting call for a play or something where there are just so many variables," explains Jordan. "When you're casting for a play you need someone to fit *exactly* into a role. It's not just that they're a great actor or actress but they need to be a certain type. For Dream Theater, it's very particular. First of all, it's a very specific type of drummer. He has to be able to be very technical, has to be able to play metal, has to be able to play a little jazzy if it's called for, the straight-ahead rock and the heavy, he has to be able to play in different time signatures. Beyond that, we were at a point where we were bringing in a new person to a band that has been established for so many years and we needed to make sure that person was someone that we could really, really get along with. We were very concerned with the personality of the person. You know, we went through a whole thing with a person who basically left because he said he didn't like us any more. Well let me rephrase that. He was burnt out on us. So we needed to find someone who was very compatible with us."

The auditions began in sound stage 2 at s.i.r. Studios on 10th Avenue in New York and were centred on three distinct phases. Firstly, the band ran through renditions of some of their back-catalogue, performing tracks that were representative of Dream Theater's varied styles – "A Nightmare To Remember", "The Spirit Carries On" and "The Dance Of Eternity". They then jammed with a few new musical ideas before sitting down and having an informal chat to try and ascertain how each drummer's personality might blend with the band. The entire process was also documented on film and later released online to generate interest in the announcement of Mike's ultimate replacement.

With the sheer quality of the drummers who auditioned, deciding who would become their bandmate was an understandably difficult decision. However it was narrowed down to two drummers – Marco Minnemann and Mike Mangini – and after careful consideration it was Mangini who was offered the role. Footage from that aforementioned documentary revealed an emotional Mangini accepting the telephone call in which the band informed him of their decision. From an outsider's perspective, Mangini appeared to be a perfect fit. Apart from his world class ability as a drummer, his background also matched the Dream Theater mould. He was a Professor at Berklee – where the band had formed many years earlier – and coming from the East Coast of the USA he shared a similar mindset. Add into that an easy-going and humorous personality, it was obvious why he was offered the job.

"Absolutely, it totally fits and I feel like he's one of us," concurs John Petrucci. "There's a certain kind of person. We're all East Coast guys of a certain attitude and temperament and he just fits right in. There's the Berklee connection, he knows the metal thing, he has the chops and plays with great feel and sensitivity when it's needed. He's into the craft of his instrument, still practises and is into getting better. He just fits right in and he's a guy that you feel you've known for so long."

"It's the fact that he's such a terrific player, a really nice guy and also that he really wanted this position," interjects Jordan. "He felt like it was something very synchronous in his life to be offered this and that was one of the factors that made a difference to us. I mean we had some really incredible drummers come down who were just mind-blowing, so on drumming alone it was hard to totally make a decision. But I guess like any job, if you come in with an attitude of 'This is for me. Everything I have done has led up to this. I want this, I can do this', it has a strong effect. This is the most important thing that we do in our lives professionally and the commitment really matters a lot to us. So somebody offering that very clearly from moment one of this whole thing just made a big difference in our decision. There's also a similarity in the type of musician that he is. He's super dedicated and he practises a lot. His main concern is how he plays the drums and we can really relate to that. We were at a time where this was obviously a really rough situation and we wanted someone to come in that we could just feel happy about and Mangini's a funny, upbeat and energetic character. So that helped us to make this transition."

Born in Newton, Massachusetts, on April 18, 1963, Mike Mangini began learning drums at an early age and by the time he reached High School, he was already accustomed to performing with a variety of school bands before he headed to college to study software engineering. Quitting the course part way through, he began working in the defence industry, on software for the Patriot Missile system.

"I actually left college to play in a band and I only spent a year and a half studying accounting and computer software," he recalls. "I started off in that job as an engineer's aid because I did not have my software engineers degree. I eventually worked my way up to be a programmer on the training software for the troops using the Patriot Missile. I still didn't have a degree but I was going to school at night, was playing in a band called Rick Berlin: The Movie, and had some drum students as well. When I got the promotion, I knew that something wasn't quite right for me. I went to my office every day and I stared at those piles of computer programs and that voice in my head said 'You need to leave now.' So I did. I started a teaching business that actually supported me. It felt right."

Over time, Mangini continued that teaching as well as developing a worldwide reputation as one of the finest session drummers, leading to countless appearances on a wide variety of albums. This in turn led to him becoming a member of Canadian metal band Annihilator in 1993, before joining Extreme the following year and working with Steve Vai from 1996.

"I learned a great deal from each situation," he explains. "I had a lot of maturing to do on two different levels. I had maturing to do as a player because I practised so much alone that it's a different protocol when you're working with people. From a behavioural standpoint, I also had to figure out how to sleep three feet from somebody, be a person who didn't upset anybody and was able to work with people. I have positive experiences from all of the tours that I did. With Annihilator, it was the first time that I had ever travelled with a band. I will never forget the first show that I did, which was at the Underworld in London. I had the most fun of anybody on that entire side of the planet. It was the power of the heavy metal, the power of guitar, bass and double bass drum in perfect unison that was heavenly."

The challenges posed by joining Extreme were numerous, not least the fact that he was joining a hugely successful band and replacing founding member Paul Geary. Additionally, with Extreme's guitarist Nuno Bettencourt effectively leading the band and renowned for his high standards, Mangini had to devise a way to blend in.

"With Extreme, it was my first opportunity to consistently play for a lot of people on a mass level and have a fan base that was really, really rabid," laughs Mangini. "I learned their songs that I wasn't on, note for note, and then I went ahead and did my thing to them without changing the main beats. I also learned a little bit about getting into Nuno's way of drumming which I needed to adjust to. Nuno wrote the music and many drum parts. That gave me the chance to get into someone else's head as to what they wanted to hear the drums do. Off tour, I spent the most time with Gary and shared a lot of fun following sports and carrying an athlete's attitude to the stage, trying to be the best we could all the time. After Extreme, I began working with Steve Vai. His music contained really dense material that I think I really needed to play in order to use a lot of the rhythmic chops I had developed. There was so much to think about during our live show. I had external time sources like an ADAT click track and samplers in my ear and I used a metronome. So for me to run that spaceship as a kind of mission control at my fingertips was a huge responsibility. Truly loving being around Steve, Mike Keneally and Philip Bynoe just made it a great place for me. Their musical talents and sense of humour simply made me happy when we hung out. On the *Fire Garden* Tour, we hung out every single night after the show and just laughed our heads off at certain TV shows and told stories. It was liberating. With all of these bands I had a lot to learn. The only band that I contributed compositionally to was Extreme and little by little, I started to write music on keyboards and build up a database of songs and song ideas. Most were not written around the drums. Being on that side of the equation sure changed my perspective on drum parts. Vai suggested that I follow up on my writing and recording and eventually put my own album or band together."

Mangini later went on to work with James LaBrie on his Mullmuzzler and solo albums, and continued his session work before becoming a professor at Berklee College in Boston. It was in early September

2010 when he received a call from Dream Theater's manager Frank Solomon enquiring if he would be interested in auditioning for the role of drummer. Delighted to be given the opportunity, Mangini set about meticulously preparing to ensure that no matter what happened he would have devised a plan.

"You know, I wasn't nervous at all and that was because I thought about the process of auditioning as my primary focus," he remembers. "I actually made quite a long list of 'What ifs'. 'What if there aren't enough such and such stands', 'What if I don't warm up', 'What if I'm sick'. I'm used to doing this all the way back to junior high school and it has yielded a spotless audition history numbering about 44. I believe that's because I've trained my mind to define what an audition is, and to understand how to think the right things at the right times after preparing as meticulously as I can. In addition to my wanting to audition, I wasn't nervous because my mind was thinking 'OK. We're going to start with this tune and this is the sound I'm going to hear in my head. I'm going to look over at John Petrucci because he's starting the tune and I'm then going to make eye contact with Jordan because he then comes in with a piano line'. Those were my thoughts. Rather than just sitting there letting my mind control me, I controlled it and prevented it from sabotaging me with worrisome things. I'm pretty trained with this. I knew not to think about the meaning of it while I was there because frankly it's too late at audition time to change who and what I am as a player. You know? It's too late to all of a sudden be able to play something that I never learned or physically cannot execute. So it's almost like I programmed an operating system in my mind to make me think the right thing at the right time. I had no time to be nervous. I felt like the person on the bench of a soccer game, just going up to the coach and saying, 'I want to go in now and I am going to put the ball into that net.' That's what I felt like. In fact, I was at peace the night before to the point that I kept my Sunday night routine, even though I was in New York City. I went out alone to watch *Sunday Night Football* on TV. I got chicken wings, beer and I politely cursed the Jets as usual like a good Boston guy should. I had a blast."

Leaving the audition and heading home to Boston, Mangini felt that he'd done enough to at least be one of the top candidates, but with the band's deliberations taking almost a fortnight he became increasingly nervous that perhaps he hadn't made the grade.

"It was an extremely painful, difficult and stressful time," he reflects. "I can tell you that it meant so much to me that I was getting sick waiting. I was getting stress sick and I just wasn't well. I would visit the church across the street and pray quite often. I was just sitting there thinking: 'Come on, come on, come on guys'. It was rough. I don't want to say that waiting on the DT news was on a par with waiting on news when someone close to me is sick, but to me, it was like that as it was a life-changing decision, not just a job change. It was an extension of me fulfilling who I want to be when I'm alive. We're all given gifts. It would be a crime not to do the most we can with them if we have the opportunities to. It's a big deal."

When the call finally came, Mangini's reaction was captured on film for the aforementioned documentary and, understandably, an overwhelmed Mangini was in tears. Undoubtedly, a large part of that was sheer relief but it was coupled with a feeling that for all the enjoyment he found teaching and working as a session man, he might finally have found a musical home.

"I've always worn my emotions on my sleeve and I'm not shy about saying it because it really does bring that much joy to me," he laughs. "That's just how it is. It's wild and it's really on two levels for me. It's about these human beings, this organization, this band, this music. On an inner level, it's my life, my struggles, my aspirations, my not being able to know what it was that I was going to end up doing. So it's amazing to me. You know, whatever it is that drives you in particular to be happy, you have feelings about it and you visualize it and think about it. You have thoughts about it and you know, some people find this place in their lives early on and others don't. I really didn't until now, because so many things that I love are part of my new life and that's just the truth. I loved all the bands I was in as well as teaching. In 2000, I was brought to Berklee by the Percussion Department Chair, Dean Anderson, to teach while maintaining a high profile in the drum community to inspire the students. Doing that helped me to be a better and more inspirational teacher, while also connecting students to gigs. Also, I was happy he wanted me to be a part of the faculty that he put together as they are all amazing players. Ultimately, I had to make sure that the course material got taught and the students were happy. I did. I was able to balance my teaching responsibilities and my professional career with autonomy."

Although enjoying working at Berklee, Mangini reveals that the demands of his "day job" began to impinge on his time away from the College, limiting his opportunities to accept session work.

"As time went by, there was an increase in office space issues, and all the required administrative and student counselling types of tasks and meetings piled on to our department, calls for work that I wanted and *needed* to do and could not accept, the traffic, the parking, it all really got to me. With all the required time I had to be at the school, I couldn't do what I was brought there to do any more with autonomy. Although I was grateful for the security of the job and I liked my co-workers, I heard that voice in my mind telling me to move on if I could. I acted. By 2010, I did two band tours and three clinic tours taking as much high profile work as I could while making more connections. The price was high as I had to do it all summer long and not see my family or help out at home. Now, from the time I get up in the morning to the time when I go to bed at night, what I'm doing is the pinnacle vocation for me. That's because of the people, the time I have to be with my family, practice and travel is built in as part of my job. I'm finally able to develop more practice systems that were burning inside of me to finish up. I can still teach via Skype when I have the time to and because I love to do it. It made me so happy to know this that I cried from joy when receiving *that* phone call, especially in realizing that I could live a life of constant musical progression with LaBrie, Myung, Petrucci and Rudess in a life and in a working situation that supported my family and me. Why not show how happy I was?"

As highlighted by the other members of the band, part of Mangini's appeal was his easy-going, humorous personality. Couple that with the similarities in their background, mindset and tastes, and it's even more obvious why he was selected. Plus, given the trauma of Mike Portnoy's departure, the last thing the band needed would be to recruit somebody whose drumming was impeccable but whose personality was abrasive. It's something not lost on Mangini.

"Yes, but I have to tell you though that the music does come first with these guys," he muses. "All these things that we're discussing make that clear. However, had I not gone in and utterly lived, ate, slept and drank those drum parts and that music, I would not be the guy for it. What makes the relationship so pleasant for me is the level of respect that's in the room that seems to be mutual. From a technician, to a manager to a band member, it is absolutely incredible to see. The amount of respect that I have for each of these people is so huge. Things that might have gotten under my skin in the past, about equipment or music, tempo or whatever it is, just don't happen with this group of people. Everything is very natural. The amount of occurrences, if I wanted to make a list of things that make us compatible, would be pretty extraordinary. It's bizarre. We have similar tastes in so many things. Even with the food and the riders, and the kinds of things that everybody eats, I can sit there and go 'yeah, yep, that's good with me'. It's like 'yes, yes, yes, yes' and it makes things easier when you think alike."

For Mangini, the waiting was equally painful as he was unable to reveal to friends or even family that he was Dream Theater's new drummer. He had, however, resigned his post at Berklee College and even though many had guessed the real reason behind that departure, he wasn't able to reveal it to his immediate family until April 18, with the official announcement made on April 29, 2011.

"Yeah, I didn't tell my family until April 18 which is my birthday," he reflects. "Can you imagine that? I mean, they were hurt that I didn't share any news with them but what am I supposed to do? Any leaks that would've occurred were at least not going to put someone on the spot so that they have to either lie that they know it was me, or feel like they betrayed me by spilling the beans. Burdening anyone with this news was a lose-lose scenario and I couldn't do that to my family, friends, students and co-workers, especially with the Internet the way it is. The band wanted to offer fans a unique gift and look at this. People who might hear of the band because of this and can have a fish-eye lens look into the world of 'Wow. How does somebody do this? What is it that happens behind the scenes?' So in order to give the documentary the impact that it really deserves, the word couldn't be out there. As much as anybody said that they knew it was me or thought it was, I really don't know how that was possible. I mean there are people in the organization, like the crew, and even they didn't know it was me."

Naturally questions arose as to how Mangini would manage in terms of potentially negative fan reactions to him replacing one of Dream Theater's founder members. Yet, as even Mike Portnoy has said, this was a wonderful opportunity for Mangini which he could never realistically accept if he was overly concerned about negative comments from the band's fans. With Mangini's personality undoubtedly being laid-back and endearing, it's not something that excessively worries him.

"I don't have to fake anything with regard to what I am about to say," he muses. "I completely respect Mike [Portnoy] on both a professional and personal level. I respect the environment that is Dream Theater on both a personal and professional level. Here's how I feel about it. I respect every fan's right to adore Mike and his playing. If he wasn't so great, then he wouldn't be so popular. I'm not going to try and win over anybody. Of course, I want people to appreciate and like what I do, because I'm pouring my heart into it but at the same time, this helps me not be a jealous person. I understand people. I think I know how they work, so I have that kind of opinion. For a fan, I don't propose to tell them what they should like or not like. Of course I hope that they like what I do. As Mike's replacement, I feel wonderful and I feel like I am going to go into that soccer game knowing I won't be perfect, but really and truly thinking that I'm not going to miss the penalty shot. I'm not going to miss and that's just the end of the story."

Yet the drama hasn't subsided with Mangini's appointment. Although Mike Portnoy was technically only "filling in" with Avenged Sevenfold until the end of 2010, it's widely believed that he had hoped that he would continue to play with them for a longer period. This theory gained credence when Avenged Sevenfold's guitarist Zacky Vengence revealed the background to their relationship in an interview with San Francisco radio station *The Bone*.

"He'd been talking about quitting Dream Theater, that he wasn't necessarily happy, and he was excited to be playing with us," said Vengence. "We were playing huge shows and stuff and I think he got caught up in the moment and got excited. We begged him to consider what he did, because we were in no position to find a permanent replacement, because in all honesty you can't replace Jimmy [Sullivan], who was first and foremost our best friend besides being an amazing drummer. So it just wasn't the right time and the place. And he told us, 'Hey, I've got good news and bad news. I quit Dream Theater.' We were like, 'Oh, no. Well, if you're happy, then that's good.' And he was saying 'Now I can be with you guys'. And we were like, 'That's not necessarily what we decided upon. And you should take your time and reconsider.' And he was like, 'Well, I put out my press release.' We were like, 'Dude, that's not how we do business. You should have talked to us before.' Then it was back and forth, and we were out of it and had nothing to do with it. We were just trying to get back on our feet, so when all that was going down it was causing us a lot of heartache to be honest, to see our name in this kind of drama-filled love triangle. He helped us out at an extremely vulnerable time and for that we will always be extremely appreciative, but we were so unstable at that point that any unneeded attention for us was just very harmful. Obviously it didn't work out and I think it's for the best for him and for us."

It's then perceived by many that once he had realised that he wasn't going to be joining Avenged Sevenfold on a permanent basis, Portnoy attempted a last ditch reconciliation with Dream Theater, something which he confirmed in a post on his website in December 2010.

"Just for the record, this is indeed true," he wrote. "Fairly recently, I reached out to the guys to try and make amends and offered to reconcile for the sake of having peace back in our lives (plus I know how much it meant to a lot of the fans). I figured it was still possible to try and save us because they hadn't made any announcements yet. Or begun any public activity with another drummer. But sadly, they declined my offer."

"When he left the band, we tried everything but he made it clear that he did not want to go forward," sighs Petrucci. "So after that, we said 'OK. Well this sucks', we rolled up our sleeves and said we need to find a new drummer, we need to sort of re-group, we need to discuss how we're going to do things and we moved forward in doing that. We had done the auditions, we had chosen Mike Mangini, he had left his professorship at Berklee, we had begun writing the record, we re-organised our internal affairs and were set to go back into the studio and everything else was in full motion. So a couple of months later, Mike coming back and saying that he wanted to come back in, unfortunately we had already moved forward so much that it was too late. I think that if there was *any* feeling when he left that it was something he wasn't sure or clear about, maybe it could have been different, but he was like 'I can't do this, I have to leave.'"

"You know, Mike Mangini resigned from Berklee and we were in motion with him," explained Jordan in an interview with *Music Radar*. "We were invested in Mike Mangini and our future. Everything was going full steam. So Mike Portnoy came to us and asked to rejoin saying, 'Hey, guys I've reconsidered, I've made a mistake.' It was like, 'Oh my God, you can't do this to us. You can't pull the rug out from under us like this.' It was hard. We went through this whole drama, and we finally found this new guy whom we were happy with. At a certain point, you just throw up your hands and go, 'This can't be happening!'"

With such a tumultuous few months behind them, a settled line-up and a desire to prove to the world that they could remain a musical force, it was time for them to decamp to the studio and start doing what they wanted most – making music…

NINETEEN

NEW REALITIES

Assembling back at the familiar surroundings of Cove City Studios in Glen Cove, Long Island, on Monday January 3, 2011, Dream Theater began work on writing and recording what would be one of their most pivotal albums. Their mood was optimistic – especially given their induction into the Long Island Music Hall Of Fame six weeks earlier. Although they had seemingly overcome the obvious quandary of replacing their founding drummer, there were still countless legal and business issues that needed to be resolved. Yet, as James explains, the band managed to avoid becoming too stressed with such potentially distracting external matters.

"To be honest with you, once the hammer did fall, we knew we were swimming into uncharted waters," he reflects calmly. "The legal situation was definitely going on when we were in the studio and that can sometimes be a distraction, but you've got to put everything in perspective. That's something that you can't ignore and we knew it was going to come with the territory. We all also realised that this was going to be an exceptionally important album for us, that it was going to be scrutinized and that there would be scepticism that would surround its whole unveiling. So yes, we were aware of what was expected of us.

For the most part, it was a matter of just making sure that it would be a classic Dream Theater album. So be honest with you, I don't think it was what most people would interpret as being a stressful period. It was just us accepting our situation and that we had to move forward and handle it with grace."

As James astutely points out, the album was going to be a critical one. Release an album that fans perceived as sub-standard, and the natural if ill-conceived assumption would be that Mike Portnoy's departure had somehow stunted their creative ability. If they moved too far away from their blueprint, or stacked the album with "filler", they would immediately be castigated for letting Mike Portnoy leave in the way he did and for rebuffing his attempt to rejoin the band a few weeks later. There was also a need for the band to record an archetypal Dream Theater album – one that didn't veer wildly away from what was expected – in order to reassure their fans that it was business as usual.

"Whenever you write a new album, it's an opportunity to start again," agrees John Petrucci. "You can reinvent yourself if you want, reunite with what made you special in the past or even do something completely different. You have this clean slate. The biggest thing with writing that album was that we knew that without having Mike Portnoy there, it was going to be different. So we just wanted to make sure that we focused on all of the elements that make Dream Theater special. Also, with the craft of songwriting, we wanted to make sure that everything was as good as it could be. We just really focused and spent a lot of time questioning ourselves. 'Is that riff as good as it can be? Could that be developed better? How can we turn this around?' So that was the focus. 'Let's just really take our time and make this something that we were incredibly proud of.'"

"Obviously we will have people who love Mike Portnoy, who won't be able to accept the change, won't be able to just listen to the music and will probably still be bitter," admitted Jordan at the time. "I guess that's just one of the things that we'll have to accept. That's just real life. Mangini could be God's gift to drumming and it wouldn't matter. People will still be upset or they will miss Mike, which is understandable. I mean with his personality and ability he was such a big part of our situation and yeah, I'm going to miss him, too. But musically speaking, we're all happy, the music lives on and I'm very pleased with how the album turned out."

It was with that focus in mind that the band decided against involving Mike Mangini in the initial writing process. Perhaps wary of breaking the writing relationships that had served them so well over the previous 27 years or even putting pressure on Mangini, they decided to write without a drummer in the room. Instead, the demos were written with John Petrucci using a drum machine to sketch out the rough patterns, which were later passed to Mangini to interpret in his own style. Mangini explains that he was more than happy with that arrangement.

"I had many discussions with John Petrucci before they went in to write about philosophies, thoughts and all kinds of things to do with the creation of the album," he recalls. "We were both on the same page when John informed me that I would not be a part of the writing process. I'd had a little bit of anxiety prior to that discussion because I really wished in my heart that they would just go and do it themselves. That was for two reasons. One reason is that, and again this comes down to respect, is that as a fan I was actually dying to see what they had come up with without a drummer. Just with a guitar, bass and keyboards and a melody. And on another level, the other part of it for me was that I really didn't want to be in the position of being tested in that kind of environment. I wanted to try and live with as much of the music as I could privately, so that I wasn't afraid to test things. What really mattered to me was that they were happy. They got to write together for the first time and they knew that I supported it. I meant it from the bottom of my heart. I said 'I really want you guys to be happy. Go in a room and have a ball.' And because they knew that they had my 100-per cent support, it just made for a very special set of compositions that to this day are blowing my mind."

"The reason that we wrote the album without Mike Mangini was that we wanted to make sure that we were focused as core composers," relates John Petrucci. "I guess we weren't sure how it was going to go with a new person, a new personality and influence. So we thought that we would kind of bring it back to basics. It really reminded me of earlier times when we would just write in our hotel rooms, homes or basement where John [Myung] and I, or Jordan and myself, would write together. We did that for about two months and actually fully demoed the album. I started to get better and better at the drum programming, so much so that it was starting to get funny. I'd be sending stuff to Mangini and I was like 'Is that something that a drummer would actually play?' And he'd come back to me and say 'Well I can play it!' So it was interesting. We did that for two months and at that point Mike was itching to get in, so it was like 'OK. Pack up your drums and get in here'. Sometimes he just played it as I had programmed, but the idea was to give him some sort of template as to what we were feeling when we wrote it. So of course, he added his own ideas and interpretation. It actually turned out great and he was incredible to work with. He was just unbelievable and I've never worked with somebody like that before. He could play anything and never makes a mistake, it was just ridiculous."

As has happened before with Dream Theater, when original vocalist Charlie Dominici was replaced by James LaBrie in 1991, or when new keyboard players come into the band in the form of Derek Sherinian and then Jordan Rudess, a fresh face has always revived the internal dynamic and added an edge to their music – something that John Petrucci is well aware of.

"It's funny and I was thinking about some of our albums and when you reach a turning point and something changes," he considers. "Maybe there's a new member who comes in, you get a bit of a perspective change and there's a little bit of a shift. It freshens things. You might not even know that it's happening but you start to think a little bit differently. It's not like you're just coming back to work. There's a different sort of energy that's in the room."

With Mike Portnoy's departure, the reconvening members of Dream Theater discovered that the in-studio dynamic had considerably changed. According to the band, his departure actually led to a more relaxed atmosphere in which they were able to explore musical ideas and themes at their own pace without feeling rushed.

"Mike and John Petrucci would, in the past, be the ones who would say 'That'll fly', 'I like that' or 'No, I don't like that'," muses Jordan. "But the reality is that the composers hadn't really changed as it's really about John Petrucci and I, with some help from the others, writing the music. When it comes to putting down the notes, the chords and what's really going to happen on the instruments, that part hadn't changed. So I feel that the core compositional team of Dream Theater is the same. You know, a lot of people don't really understand that, I guess because of the past and the way things were positioned but that's just reality. We didn't have any drums or have a drummer in the room when we were writing. So for one thing, it was a whole lot quieter and honestly for me as a composer, having time and space really helps a lot. I mean it's kind of fun to write when there's a drummer in the room as they can certainly add something to the writing, but I prefer to write in a peaceful place. There was an atmosphere of patience surrounding the writing of that album. We would give each other the time and the space to fully go through whatever we wanted to pursue and that was pretty cool. In the past we maybe wouldn't take the amount of time to see through an idea."

"You could see that the atmosphere was much calmer, more relaxed and far more interactive," agrees James. "I think because of that, it really allowed for everyone to really assert themselves in any situation throughout the entire process. The fact is the main composers all along have always been John Petrucci and Jordan Rudess. They've always been steering the ship in terms of ideas and riffs and where you can go within any given section."

Certainly, much of that ship-steering would be led by John Petrucci, as he became even more involved in the organizing of the recording sessions, especially given his role of producer.

"My role as producer was to determine the creative as well as sonic direction for the album, to assemble the right team that would best be able to make it all come to fruition, and to foster a positive working environment in the studio so that every musician was able to put forth their greatest performances to date," recalls Petrucci. "I knew that working with engineer Paul Northfield was the best to ensure that vision was realized from the start of the sessions. Also, returning to Cove City Studios on Long Island would be the perfect place for everyone to reach their creative potential. From inception, I heard this album a bit different than our other releases. I imagined what it would sound like to have intense progressive music mixed in a very contemporary, hi-fidelity and polished way. Andy Wallace was the only man for the job in my opinion and I was thrilled that not only did he share my vision but that he was very excited about being a part of this album. Watching him do his magic and put his final touches on the songs in the mix studio in New York City was something I'll always treasure. I also felt that it was very important for James to shine on this record and knew that the best way of achieving that was to bring in Rich Chycki (Rush) to record the vocals. Rich is James's long-time friend whom he has worked with many times in the past and whom he felt very comfortable with. After the lyrics were written, the vocals were recorded up in Canada and as songs were completed, Rich would send the files to me at Cove for approval. Most of the time, they just needed a few tweaks or edits. The system worked out great. Towards the end of the sessions I flew up to Rich's studio to work on a couple of songs with James. Namely "Build Me Up, Break Me Down" and "Beneath The Surface". Of course there are always countless details involved in producing an album, but seeing your hard work pay off as it all comes together while having the trust of the band to make it happen is 100 per cent worth the time and effort."

Unquestionably there will have been those who might have imagined that life for Dream Theater without Mike Portnoy may have been daunting, yet it would appear that the band had, by necessity, become closer and banished some of those issues that their former drummer had cited in his resignation statement. There's therefore a massive irony in the fact that by leaving, the problems that Mike Portnoy had cited in his resignation stated were addressed and overcome. Undoubtedly, his departure caused the band to reassess themselves on both musical and personal levels before recording an album as fresh as *A Dramatic Turn Of Events*. It's certainly a theory that was not lost on LaBrie.

"Oh yes, it's *really* ironic and I'll tell you I'm one to believe that the universe has a way of orchestrating things to happen for a reason," he said vehemently at the time. "Ultimately I think that the universe wants to give us back positive energy and vibes and that's exactly what's happened here. A lot of people are saying that you can really feel and see the spirit on stage every night now and they really feel that positive energy, fun and enjoyment. I think that has been missing for quite some time as far as I'm concerned, though we did a good job of camouflaging it."

Such a surprising admission would imply that the camaraderie that existed in Dream Theater in their early days had been deteriorating for some time, with sheer professionalism getting them through the job in hand. So can LaBrie pinpoint a time when the excitement of being on tour had started to perceptibly fade?

"Oh my God, I don't know," muses James, before tailing off into thought, as if unsure as to whether honesty is the wisest option. "Well, OK, personally, I think that it had been a little challenging in certain aspects within the band, probably off and on, since 1999. I might even dare to say maybe even more. I think that you just keep finding ways to keep everything in check or, worse, you start to accept it. You start to think that maybe this is the only way that it can exist and it's not until you're flipped upside down, and somebody gives you a fresh perspective, you can even see it in that light. I think that if anything, what happened to us in that year proved to be a good thing. The bottom line is that we really do love what we're doing and I think that only enhanced an appreciation for what we are fortunate enough to be doing in our lives. It's something that we have embraced whole-heartedly. We were very determined to show every sceptic out there that we were still the band that people fell in love with."

With *A Dramatic Turn Of Events* – released on September 12, 2011, in Europe and a day later in the US – the band released an accomplished album that achieved their stated aims of recording a "classic" Dream Theater album which would dispel any concerns that their fans may have had. With an album title that only hinted at the unbridled chaos that had engulfed their world over the previous year, they returned with a renewed vigour. The careful craftsmanship and time taken in writing the album provided a fresh edge to the music that was at times spiritually reminiscent of such standout albums as *Images And Words* or *Scenes From A Memory*. Progressive metal as a genre has a sliding scale between the two poles, and the material veered more towards the prog, which many would say was no bad thing. The growling vocals have mercifully vanished to be replaced with typically complex musicality and countless melodies. Critically, the album was not immediately gratifying, and required several listens in order to fully grasp exactly what the band had achieved. This was the sound of a band having fun, playing to their strengths and infusing their work with an energetic new edge without at any point resorting to prog metal cliché. It's also easy to fall into the trap of viewing the lyrical content of the album as perhaps hinting at the turmoil of the previous year, and "This Is The Life" falls into that category. With lines such as "Some of us choose to live gracefully/ Some can get caught in the maze and lose their way home/ This is the life we belong to" reading almost like a revised mission statement, it remains one of the most wonderfully tranquil pieces of music the band have ever created.

In an interview with *MusicRadar.com*, John Petrucci revealed that he had fully demoed the song early in the writing process before bringing it to the band, adding that the title of the song came about one day when he was "driving in the city. We were stopped at a light behind this pickup truck, and on the truck was a bumper sticker in Spanish that I interpreted as 'This is the life.' At the same time, I was playing the song for my Mom. Right then, I looked at her and said, 'That's the title of the song!'"

"Beneath The Surface" is a similarly striking mellow track and was the last song that John Petrucci wrote for the album.

"We'd tracked all of the drums on the other cuts, and we were working on keyboards when I realised that the record needed something," says John Petrucci. "Everything else was very intense, so a cooldown felt right. With the exception of 'This Is The Life', I was writing about very heavy topics such as political unrest in America, uprisings in the Middle East, ancient Persian armies and shamans. For the closing song, a lighter, more poignant lyrical message was in order, something that would reach deep into your soul in a very honest way. I have to give my wife Rena credit for encouraging that I go in that direction. She has always been able to offer me creative perspective and as a long time Dream Theater fan, knew that such a poignant song would be welcomed amongst the more intense and musically adventurous pieces already on the album. It can be difficult at times, when opening up emotionally in a lyric, to trust that your audience might respond on such a raw level. Yet 'Beneath The Surface' turned out to be a favourite amongst many fans, so I'm so glad that she inspired me to complete the song and include it on the record."

Harking back to some of the themes in *Scenes From A Memory*, "Outcry" contained the type of musical dexterity that drove "The Dance Of Eternity" over a decade earlier, but was combined with a prominent vocal melody. "Far From Heaven" was a lilting, heartfelt piano-led track that provided a continued balance to the album. Perhaps the most audible contrast with previous albums (and no doubt for the Dream Theater hardcore) the most widely anticipated song was

"Breaking All Illusions" which contained John Myung's first foray into lyric writing for many a year. Ultimately, *A Dramatic Turn Of Events* was a breathtaking album – it was just such a crying shame that it took such cataclysmic change within the band for them to create it. What was especially noticeable was the balance of the album. In past years, the band had received some criticism for perhaps leaning too heavily on the metal aspects of the sound at the direct expense of some of their softer, more progressively tinted moments. According to James, this was something that they were keen to address.

"Yeah absolutely and you know the situation is that you have five people within the band and for the most part you're agreed upon your direction," he says. "I've always referred to a rock 'n' roll band as a dysfunctional democracy. So I think that at times you're always going to have disagreements and it's a matter of how long you fight it until you realize that it's just not worth it and you need to go with the flow. I think that on some of our other albums – even though I'm proud of every one of them – I probably felt the heavy element was overtaking the more progressive element. Not that those weren't existing but they were almost taking a bit of a back seat. The beauty of that album was that everything was in its place, everything was necessary where it was, and wasn't just something thrown in to make it exciting, bizarre or absurd. I think that one of the great things is that the communication within the band became much more transparent. The other beautiful thing about it was that John Petrucci did a phenomenal job producing this album. He was focused, extremely dedicated and really took it to another level."

The press reviews were similarly glowing. Writing for *Metal Hammer* magazine, Dave Ling declared: "This album, which takes a small step back from metal to re- emphasize the band's prog rock credentials, is fantastically overblown but it also delivers strong commercial hooks in the shapes of 'Lost Not Forgotten' and 'Build Me Up, Break Me Down'. There's a reason Dream Theater are the world's biggest prog-metal band: they're the genre's leading exponents. That statement holds true even now."

Classic Rock Presents Prog writer Grant Moon explained that "The band step up as if they've got something to prove. There's rarely been such an appropriate album title, yet *A Dramatic Turn Of Events* sounds strong and assured. Facing down recent adversity, Dream Theater continue to reach their own lofty standards and purvey high-end progressive metal. It's a genre they still define."

For all the obvious connotations of the album title, John Petrucci revealed in an interview with the *Voices UK* fanzine that it had nothing to do with Mike Portnoy's resignation.

"I would just like to take a moment to say that the title had nothing to do with our situation, nor were any of the songs about it either," he claims. "We wouldn't do that. It would be really cheesy and disrespectful. I came up with the title when I was looking for something that would generalize all the songs' subject matter. Most had something to do with dramatic events that happened either historically or recently. For example, the song 'Outcry' was about the uprising in North Africa and the Middle East. Some of the songs were about dramatic, spiritual events or situations that people have experienced. We were looking and looking for a title, and at one point we had over a hundred possible titles. I saw this one – it just popped. One of the first things I thought was 'Are people going to think that it has to do with our situation?' But it was like 'Ah, screw it!' So I showed it to the guys and Hugh Syme who said, "I love that title! It's so Pink Floyd! That's awesome!" At that point, he'd already done the artwork, so it all totally worked."

The tour that followed the release took them through the summer festival circuit of 2011 before a full world tour catapulted them around the globe until well into the summer of 2012. Naturally, all attention was on Mike Mangini to see exactly how he interacted with the band in a live setting. And with a drummer of his credentials, there would never be any real musical concerns but the band would perhaps be wary that there may have been heckling from the crowd. Yet Mangini was universally welcomed, and his introduction in the form of an expanded drum solo enabled the Dream Theater fans to appreciate his mesmerizing talent. The fan acceptance of the new line-up wasn't lost on John Petrucci.

"We couldn't be more grateful, you know. I really feel a sense of pride," he said in an interview for the *Voices* fanzine. "I feel really proud of the band for making the record that we did and I feel proud of our fans for being so cool about it, and accepting. For example, when we introduce Mike and they all cheer. I feel like everyone's all on our team. Like it's 'You guys go!' There's a feeling of belief and support in us and that welcoming feeling is contagious. Because initially, the whole thing, with Mike leaving, it was like hell. So for us to go from that point to this, it's really very satisfying."

James also reveals that the offstage atmosphere has also changed, claiming that "It's a little less guarded for sure. It's all good. Without getting into details about all that, the camaraderie is fully intact and we're just really enjoying where we are at this point and we're all extremely proud of *A Dramatic Turn Of Events*."

The band were also shocked to be nominated for a GRAMMY award for best hard rock/ metal performance for the track "On The Backs Of Angels". Given that Dream Theater tend to veer away from radio-friendly tracks and the fact that they're still hardly household names, such a recognition of their music was especially gratifying.

"It still makes me smile every time I think about it and the reality of receiving such an honour still hasn't set in," revealed John Petrucci in an interview for the GRAMMY website. "Being in a band who writes twenty-minute long, prog rock epics about topics that aren't exactly radio-friendly, I never would have thought that we'd ever be nominated, and the thrill still hasn't worn off. I was on a plane to California the evening the nominees were announced and as a Recording Academy member and music fan I was bummed that I was missing the telecast, as I always look forward to seeing who receives the year's honours. I was at baggage claim when I got the call from our manager and all I wanted to do was scream out and dance in celebration. Sharing the news with my wife and kids, bandmates, family, and friends was an incredible moment and one I'll always remember."

"I was sitting in a Japanese restaurant in San Diego when my cell phone rang," revealed Jordan in the same interview. "It was John Petrucci and he said, 'Jordan, we got a GRAMMY nomination.' Receiving a GRAMMY nod is not an everyday experience and it kind of blew me away. John was very excited as well. Leading up to this point had already been an amazing whirlwind year for us with our new drummer Mike Mangini, our new album, *A Dramatic Turn Of Events*, and some very strong shows to support it. Receiving this nomination for the song "On The Backs Of Angels" has been so rewarding for us on many levels, as musicians who have all spent countless hours focusing on each of our instruments, as well as band members who have worked together for years, both in the studio and on the road. Although I am always grateful to have a life filled with music, as well as the rare ability to be able to earn a living doing it, this GRAMMY nomination just gives me and my band a real world pride and connection that is deep and meaningful."

The band attended the ceremony on February 12, 2012, and although they didn't win the award (the Foo Fighters track "White Limo" received the plaudit), the exposure and mainstream recognition was clearly appreciated.

So is there a happy ending for Dream Theater? They've attained their current level of success based solely on their own self-belief and determination, with little support from the men in suits over recent years. Given the right promotion, backing and the freedom to create their own distinctive music without label interference, there would seem to be no limit to what they can achieve.

"It's an amazing story," says Frank Solomon. "Without any record label help for the seven years before Roadrunner came along, it's been an incredible job. We've come so far and we've got so much further to go. And I know we'll get there."

Certainly, the potential is huge. Each album that Dream Theater release continues to match or surpass the popularity of its predecessor, and their live following has expanded to such a level that they're justifiably moving from performing in theatres into arenas. And for a band who are almost 25 years old, that's no mean feat.

"I do get people coming up to me and saying things like, 'I thought you would've been on the downslide'," laughs James. "Which is kind of like, 'Well thanks a lot! I really appreciate your optimism!' But I think that it's very apparent when we're on stage, and we're looking out, that the demographic of our fans is ridiculous. It's anywhere from a 14-year-old up to a 65-year-old. But when I think about that, it's not unlike when I go to see a Rush, Pink Floyd or Roger Waters concert. Those guys are attracting a very young crowd as well as the diehard fans from the 1970s. But that's what this music really invokes in people, in that once you become a fan, you stay a fan. You're not moving on a couple of years later and that's one the most amazing things. Plus it helps that everything we put out is on our own terms, and it is music that we can be proud of until the day we die. And that really pays off, because you do have longevity, and a career that wasn't something that was over in the blink of an eye. So I think we are very fortunate, and we will continue to appreciate what we have."

"In some ways it feels very surreal that we're still together and playing songs that we wrote at Berklee," adds John Petrucci. "It's incredible, and we are all very blessed and fortunate to have such a long career – not only where we started in America but all over the world. We've obviously been a band for a long time and we're not the new young guys. So I think we have to really maintain credibility, viability and relevance. It's essential that you have new generations of people being turned on to the music. I think it's an awesome thing and I love it. I love that when we play there are a lot of young kids and young fans because it keeps our whole thing alive. It means that you're not one of those bands where people say things like 'Oh you remember those guys?' So I think it's really cool. It just shows that if you work hard and you're diligent, you'll get there."

Steve Sinclair, who has been credited as being the man who "discovered" Dream Theater is equally satisfied with their achievements to date.

"I am indeed very proud of discovering, signing and recording Dream Theater, and I'm surprised that over twenty years later they are bigger than they have ever been," he says. "This is the ultimate artist development story and I am so glad to have been a part of it. I wish all who were involved continuing success and prosperity. A great karmic equation has unfolded, the band ascending and the industry which stood in their way descending. It's a nice finale to a great story."

Yet there is still so much for Dream Theater to achieve, and there is no sign yet that the band have hit a creative peak. And you can be sure that they have all carefully considered what they as a band can still achieve and how they might progress from here.

Their journey to this point has been an eventful one. From taking the bold step to drop out of college to an uncertain future, their ever-present battles with their record labels, through losing two keyboardists, a string of singers, the loss of Mike Portnoy, surviving internal personality clashes and management tribulations, until the period of recent stability and artistic success, it has been a hell of a ride. The one thing you can guarantee is that now they finally seem to have halted some of those instabilities, Dream Theater will carry on creating their own idiosyncratic brand of music for their ever-growing fan base as long as they maintain the motivation to continue. These last 25-odd years may simply have been the precursor to another few decades of continued growth. Any sense of inner turmoil has also vanished over recent years, and the likelihood of any of the members making a bolt for the exit is remote. Of course things can change, but for the foreseeable future, it's inevitable that their following will continue to grow as their career takes another upward swing. And let's be honest here, after over twenty years of hard graft and toiling against mainstream indifference, no one can begrudge them that. But for now, the last word goes to James LaBrie, who neatly summarizes the band's perspective of the story thus far, and what might lie ahead.

"We've been very fortunate to be able to be doing this for over twenty years and we're still thoroughly enjoying it," he explains. "We've had a very big transitional period... but I think if anything, it has given the band a resurgence of energy and spirit. I think that we've really upped our game because of it. It's a whole new beginning for us and a whole new chapter. Everything is really just in a good spot for Dream Theater right now. We're all feeling this great camaraderie and positive energy and we're going to be riding that for as long as we possibly can."

RICH WILSON

Rich Wilson has been writing about rock music for longer than he cares to remember. A graduate of Bradford University, Rich has been a regular contributor to *Classic Rock*, *Prog Magazine*, *Rock Hard*, *Metal Hammer* and *Record Collector* over the last fifteen years.

Rich lives on the outskirts of Manchester, England with his wife and Labrador. He is renowned for his love of dodgy 1970s prog rock bands, and his collection of even more dubious 1980s heavy metal albums. *Lifting Shadows* is his first book. Rich is currently completing work on his second band biography, which is due early 2014.

Also available from Rocket 88

**BARRETT: THE DEFINITIVE
VISUAL COMPANION TO THE
LIFE OF SYD BARRETT**
Russell Beecher and Will Shutes

"Beautifully packaged, eruditely
written and full of insight
(but, inevitably, tinged with
sadness), Barrett feels like
the ultimate work of art."
MOJO

ISBN (Classic Edition)
978-1-906615-10-9
ISBN (Signature Edition)
978-1-906615-11-6

FAIRPORT BY FAIRPORT
Fairport Convention with Nigel Schofield
ISBN (hardback) 978-1-906615-48-2

SPIRIT OF TALK TALK
*James Marsh, Chris Roberts
and Toby Benjamin*
ISBN (hardback) 978-1-906615-39-0

MUSIC & CULTURE

THE CLASH
The Clash
ISBN (ePub & Kindle)
978-1-906615-09-3

ESSENTIAL NEIL YOUNG
Steve Grant
ISBN (ePub) 978-1-906615-50-5
ISBN (Kindle) 978-1-906615-49-9

I WAS A TEENAGE SEX PISTOL
Glen Matlock with Peter Silverton
ISBN (hardback) 978-1-906615-35-2
ISBN (paperback) 978-1-906615-36-9
ISBN (ePub) 978-1-906615-38-3
ISBN (Kindle) 978-1-906615-37-6

IN THE SIXTIES
Barry Miles
ISBN (hardback) 978-1-906615-76-5
ISBN (paperback) 978-1-906615-77-2
ISBN (ePub) 978-1-906615-78-9
ISBN (Kindle) 978-1-906615-79-6

**PINK MOON – A STORY
ABOUT NICK DRAKE**
Gorm Henrik Rasmussen
ISBN (hardback) 978-1-906615-28-4
ISBN (paperback) 978-1-906615-29-1
ISBN (ePub) 978-1-906615-24-6
ISBN (Kindle) 978-1-906615-23-9

rocket88books.com

CPSIA information can be obtained
at www.ICGtesting.com
Printed in the USA
BVHW081452211218
536176BV00026B/1302/P

9 781906 615581